Eccentric Britain

A PRACTICAL GUIDE TO A CURIOUS COUNTRY

Bradt Travel Guides, UK

The Globe Pequot Press Inc, USA

Third edition published May 2011
First published 2000
Bradt Travel Guides Ltd
IDC House, The Vale, Chalfont St Peter, Bucks SL9 9RZ, England
www.bradtguides.com
Published in the USA by The Globe Pequot Press Inc,
PO Box 480, Guilford, Connecticut 06437-0480

ISBN: 978 1 84162 375 7

British Library Cataloguing in Publication Data
A catalogue record for this book is available from the British Library

Photographs Alamy: Jon Arnold Images Ltd (JAIL/A), Keith Nuttall (KN/A); Chris
Conder, with courtesy of http://wrayvillage.co.uk (CC); D Legakis/Athena Picture
Agency (DL/APA); David Lowman (DL); Dreamstime.com: Gail Johnson (GJ/D),
Paul Edwards (PE/D), Scotturner (S/D), Tomd (T/D), Yulia Belousova (YB/D);
Drew Gardner, www.drewgardner.co.uk (DG); Glyn Williams, www.welldressing.
com (GW); Jonathan Farber, Farber.co.uk (JF); Lyndon Yorke (LY); Mark Scase
(MS); Martin Gallagher, on behalf of The Loony Dook South Queensferry (MG);
Paul Biggins (PB); Peter Gettins Photography (PGP); Photolibrary: Adam Woolfitt
(AW/P), Andy Williams/The Travel Library (AW/TTL/P), Britain on View (BV/P),
Cotswolds Photo Library (CPL/P), E&E Image Library (E&EIL/P), Jean-Marc
Teychenne (JMT/P), Kathy de Witt (KW/P), Maggie Murray (MM/P), Pamla Toler
(PT/P), Splashdown Direct (SD/P), Sunniva Harte/P (SH/P)

Maps Chris Lane (Artinfusion Ltd) (based on source material from Awa Graphics)
Cover artwork Neil Gower (www.neilgower.com)
Illustrations Rowan Barnes-Murphy (www.rowanbarnes-murphy.com)

Typeset from the author's disc by D & N Publishing, Baydon, Wiltshire
Production managed by Jellyfish Print Solutions; printed in India

Staffordshire Library and Information Service

Please return or renew or by the last date shown

CODS B

If not required by other readers, this item may be renewed
in person, by post or telephone, online or by email.
To renew, either the book or ticket are required

24 Hour Renewal Line
0845 33 00 740

Staffordshire
County Council

CONTENTS

Travel Information

PRACTICAL DETAILS of getting to a specific festival or place mentioned in the text, together with relevant phone numbers, including tourist information, are given at the end of each chapter, or with museums at first mention. Note, where one mode of travel is impractical (car in central London, or train/bus/walk to some distant small monument), it is ignored. Certain things are fascinating ideas but not something you'd need to visit: hence no travel info. We also consider our readers also know vaguely where Central London or Oxford are without explanation! Postcodes are often given because some people rely on them for satnavs. Use at your own risk, because with some things on windswept beaches or mountains they are an educated guess – eg: a nearby pub. If you're the type who drives right past the 200ft monument you're looking for and into the lake because the pratnav told you ... don't blame me. And some things are *meant* to be nigh-impossible to find, like the Pub With No Name.
   Symbols are as follows:

☀ Tourist Information	☎ Telephone	🚆 Rail
	🖼 Website	🚌 Bus
⊖ Tube	🚗 Road	⛴ Ferry

ACKNOWLEDGEMENTS

With thanks to all those whom I have interviewed or contacted for help with my assurance that the term eccentric in my mind carries no necessarily pejorative judgement (as in barmy, folly) but almost always a compliment (as in exceptional, fascinating, intriguing); to those surprisingly helpful local officials, information officers, heritage bodies, etc, who have explained the inexplicable with great patience; to my publishers and their hard-working editors, including Antonia Cunningham and Elspeth Beidas, illustrator Rowan Barnes-Murphy, map maker Chris Lane, designer Shane O'Dwyer, etc, who immediately and enthusiastically saw the potential of a rather unorthodox book; to Jill Donachy and Richard Mcdonald who provided heaps of information; to my family for enduring countless diversions to check on this or that monument or obelisk while supposedly on holiday; and to the Devon author who always intended to write a book perhaps like this but never quite got round to it. I hope this book measures up.

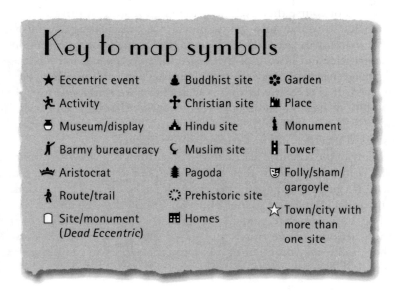

Key to map symbols

★ Eccentric event	▲ Buddhist site	❀ Garden
🕴 Activity	✝ Christian site	🏛 Place
♨ Museum/display	☘ Hindu site	⚱ Monument
🕴 Barmy bureaucracy	☾ Muslim site	☗ Tower
⌒ Aristocrat	♠ Pagoda	☻ Folly/sham/gargoyle
🚶 Route/trail	⁙ Prehistoric site	
☐ Site/monument (*Dead Eccentric*)	▦ Homes	☆ Town/city with more than one site

PREFACE

This book started with my job as a sub-editor at the *Daily Mail*, London, where I work on other people's reports from around the world. From time to time, I would be allowed to slip a paragraph into odd corners of features pages about things that struck me as curious – why vicars preach on horseback to a mounted congregation, the strange castellated house above a railway tunnel, the bizarre cheese-rolling, black-pudding-throwing, coal-carrying, gate-smashing contests – in short, the eccentricities of Britain, past and present.

It caught people's imagination and letters started to pour in offering information, or asking for more, and asking if there was a book of such anecdotes.

There wasn't. There were old books about past eccentrics, but none with a comprehensive guide to present-day oddities in terms of bizarre buildings, unbelievable customs, strange rituals, daft sports, etc, that you can visit, witness or endure. Tourist guides sometimes touch on strange festivals, but offer no background or depth in this fascinating field, and of course they exclude Britain's great store of private or past eccentrics. Thus they miss out on much that is fascinating or amusing.

So, many years later, here is the complete guide to both the ongoing eccentricities and history of Britain's oddest eccentrics, and reportage of strange private goings-on and interviews with the peculiar people involved. It is eccentric in that it is neither pure travelogue nor pure description, tackling subjects in themes rather than as a geographical tour. Thus you will find, for example, all Britain's weird pyramids discussed together, not in separate county chapters.

Many of the eccentric places, things or customs described do not need to be visited to appreciate their peculiarities; but to make the book more useful as a guide to some of the places which can be visited, I have included maps and a calendar of strange events in Britain throughout the year.

Did I say complete guide? Of course it is not. There will be some deadly serious strange rituals and follies that need to be added, and others, sadly, may drop out of use. Drop me a line so I can update the book. It'll keep me out of my boss's hair.

INTRODUCTION

WHAT IS A GENUINE ECCENTRIC?

To the world-weary traveller, the global village means a McDonald's sameness being inflicted everywhere, the jumbo jet wheel smoothing out the bumps in cultures, making everything universally bland. Today, someone wearing branded American cowboy denims, Korean plastic trainers and an Italian T-shirt could equally be in Düsseldorf, Detroit or Danang. And yet the British eccentric has proved peculiarly resistant to this process, thank God.

True eccentrics don't think of themselves as such. They know they are reasonable and it is the rest of the world which is bizarre. A genuine eccentric does not consciously adopt an odd style or mode of behaviour for effect. Students doing a sponsored pogo-stick over the Andes wouldn't qualify, and neither do young fogies, punks, Goths, or others adopting what is merely a different kind of uniform. True eccentrics think it is not at all remarkable to take a plastic lobster for a walk on a string, as one Edinburgh lady does – Oscar Wilde, after all, once did the same with a friend and a real lobster in the Strand. Years later, the eccentric millionaire Sir 'Union' Jack Hayward (who saved Lundy Island and the SS Great Britain for the nation) took a goat as his guest to a cocktail party.

But what about today's Britain? Is it hard to find the genuine eccentric? Made-for-media figures with eccentric dress, gait, speech or hairdo may not be genuinely eccentric – some sort of vague wackiness is *de rigueur* nowadays to keep the jaded, TV-soaked public tuned in. Equally, entrants for Mr Loonyverse, members of the Eccentrics' Club, or guests at the Odd Ball, will probably not be the instinctive eccentric. A true eccentric thinks himself entirely normal and wouldn't dream of joining such a group, although one such group, the Idiots' Club, which used to meet at the French House in Soho's Dean Street, was laudable if only because its founder, calling himself Baron Peter de Massenbach, greeted potential members with 'An idiot, I presume'.

The same caveat applies to defining the quintessentially eccentric building, the folly. A rich person such as Lord McAlpine putting up a self-declared folly in recent years is amusing, but not quite pukkah. The truly eccentric landowner must think the structure eminently sensible and useful; it is for others to judge it, preferably universally, a patently useless folly. If it performs a real function, it's not one hundred per cent a folly.

Of course, being rich helps ensure that there will be lasting testimony to your eccentricities – in the form of follies, or whatever – but less concrete manifestations of oddness such as giving your children peculiar names are open to us all. Thus a celebrity consort of pop stars, the late Paula Yates, may have named her children Fifi Trixibelle, Peaches Honeyblossom, and Pixie, plus, best of the lot, Heavenly Hiraani Tiger Lily; but, to take one example of so many, less well-known Gloucester butterfly buff Matthew Oates and his equally entomologically minded wife Sally named their children Euphrosyne, Lucina, Camilla and Arion (Latin names for their favourite pearl-bordered fritillary, Duke of Burgundy, white admiral and large blue butterflies respectively).

Eccentricity was exported the world over during Britain's imperial heyday. In many a scorching tropical outpost, only 'Mad dogs and Englishmen went out in the midday sun', as Noel Coward wrote. The image of Englishmen – dressed in full uniform for dinner in the steaming African jungle – lives on in films of the era. The British went 'troppo' in a big way, as their brains cooked in the heat, with a liberal intake of sundowners and Singapore slings, and the Empire reeked with eccentricity.

In fact the odder you were, the further you were likely to go – in seniority and geographically – because you had less chance of making headway at home in Britain.

There was Our Man in Calcutta, **Sir Richard Strachey**, who lived out his retirement in English suburbia respecting only Indian time. Or the Calcutta judge, ATT Peterson, who built mad Mogul towers in deepest Hampshire retirement (see page 276). Or the general who addressed his troops in Burma stark naked. He may have approached that fine line between delightfully dotty and frankly funny-farm barking, of course, and many a colonial crossed it.

It was also in Burma that the Roedean-educated **Ursula Graham Bower**, born in 1914, became the 'Queen of the Nagas', a tribe of headhunters whom she fearlessly led into battle to decapitate the invading Japanese during World War II. She had gone to the area in 1937 to study the tribes – which under previous British influence had almost entirely dropped their interesting habit of presenting a human head to females with whom they wished to mate – when the Japanese invaded. She organised a fearsome army of headhunting Nagas, using looted Japanese arms as well as spears. Their dominance of the mountain passes helped keep the Japanese out of India – a turning point in that war's history. In fact, the Japanese made a point of keeping as clear as possible of the areas she ruled, while she ensured Allied airmen could escape back to India – except on the odd occasion when her men decapitated them by mistake.

British eccentricity in the form of mad inventors and single-minded obsessives was the spring that nourished the industrial revolution.

It isn't, of course, politically correct to believe there are differences in national character. But while the Japanese and Germans are excellent – yes, often better – engineers and manufacturers, where did the ideas of radar, jet engines, television, hovercraft, radio and steam trains come from, to name a brilliant few? To put it another way, name 20 great comedians, for humour is surely another creative facet of the same flawed gem. Take off-the-wall ideas such as the *Carry On* films, Monty Python, Basil Fawlty, Mr Bean (even the inventions of Edward Lear and Lewis Carroll, to go further back).

If the mention of Lear's *Book of Nonsense* isn't enough to convince you of the direct link between eccentricity and humour, you should have heard **Professor Stanley Unwin's** weird monologues in the 1960s. He spoke in a strange Unwinese that was apparently gibberish, but despite his altering words such as terrible to terribold, for example, you could just about follow what he was saying. Here he is advising someone who has eaten too much Christmas dinner:

'If you've done an overstuffy in the tumloader, finisht the job with a ladleho of brandy butter, then pukeit all the way to the toileybox.'

Not everybody found it funny, but it was eccentric. Unwin died in 2002.

Talking of Mr Bean, there's a total eccentric in south Wales called Barry Kirk – or **Captain Beany** from the planet Beanus, as he also likes to be known – who is rather keen on beans. Captain Beany, who spends his leisure time dressed as a baked bean, was fined £140 by Port Talbot magistrates after driving for eight months with a Heinz baked bean label on his windscreen instead of a tax disc. 'It looked rather nice. No one noticed the difference for ages,' he was reported as saying. When dressing as Captain Beany he wears a red cape and tights and paints his bald head bean colour. His obsession with the flatulence-generating tomato-sauce-covered navy bean started when he had to sit in a bath of them for charity. Since then he's eaten them every day.

Another relevant facet of the British psyche is a kind of bloody-minded, stubborn resistance to change. For example, in the 1960s it was decided that on **Britain's railways** the small branch lines would have to go, and steam engines too, with the entire stock being sent to scrapyards by 1968. So what's happened almost 40 years later? On any summer weekend you can find 100 privately run branch lines with the lovingly restored steam monsters of yesteryear, rescued from scrapyards, South African mines, Greek factories, Javanese sugar plantations or wherever, chuffing along over tracks rebuilt by an army of 100,000 unpaid enthusiasts. Barmy, but splendid.

Nowhere is this more the case than in **local government**. Why, half a century after the county of Middlesex was abolished, are there still new 'Welcome to Middlesex' signs, a Middlesex Hospital, University, and Cricket Club? And why do more than a million people still put Middlesex at the end of their addresses? It's the kind of stubbornness that forced the government to reinstate tiny counties, such as Rutland, after two decades when people refused to admit they had been abolished. It makes no sense, unless you're British.

On **Foula**, a remote island west of mainland Shetland, they still celebrate Christmas on 6 January because they don't approve of the calendar change made in the 18th century, which cut out about 11 days (so, in fact, they agree with the Russian Orthodox lot). The last time I spoke to anyone from there I was told there were 13 households, a school with two pupils and one teacher and at their 6 January Christmas everyone visits everyone else and gives them all presents. 'Some new folk, incomers, go away for the New Christmas [that'd be our 25 December] and then come back for the real one. But after a few years here they get the idea.' And at least they've got New Year to look forward to on 13 January. So you could have two Christmases and two New Years in three weeks, thus ensuring a fuller, fouler Foula hangover.

In fact the people of Foula knew full-well when the rest of Britain was going bonkers for the Band Aid charity's somewhat patronising song *Do They Know It's Christmas* that as the African nation concerned was more Christian than Britain and observed the same calendar as Foula, the answer was 'Yes' and 'But it isn't yet.' Not that the aid wasn't needed, of course.

And the same issue gives the reason why **Britain's tax year** runs to such an eccentric date, 5 April. The tax man couldn't be bothered to cope with an incomplete year when the 11 days were nicked to fit in with Europe (and some people rioted to get the 11 days back, or at any rate not to pay rent for them) so the tax year ran on from the usual quarter day, 25 March, and we've been stuck trying to catch up ever since. I believe the taxman wants to make a mammoth effort to catch up one year but never quite does.

There are eccentrics at all levels of British society. We even have a suitably eccentric king to come – **Prince Charles**, for all his other problems, at least talks to plants, meditates in the Kalahari desert, does Goon impersonations, dabbles in alternative medicine and wears Arab dress in Gloucestershire. Good for him.

Politically, what other country would field **Monster Raving Loony Party** candidates (founding father Screaming Lord Sutch, slogan 'Vote Loony, you know it makes sense') at most elections? Three Raving Loony councillors were even elected, although in 1997 one defected to the Tories, whatever that said about his insanity. Even the choice of England's patron saint is downright eccentric – on 23 April, the English celebrate St George, an obscure Palestinian, famed for slaying somewhere else an animal that didn't exist.

Britain also retains the myriad odd, very peculiar **ceremonies and customs** which visitors can still watch with disbelief and which this book sets out to detail. Some are beyond rational explanation and almost all are carried out with the utmost seriousness.

Most official British customs are nonsensical to the outsider, and even sometimes to the insider. For example, outside radio broadcast vans go to great trouble every 11 November to broadcast two minutes' silence (not last year's silence, mind, which they could easily repeat). We have a monarchy that has built the highest order of knights in Britain's chivalry on a humble undergarment – the **Order of the Garter**. Then there are about 900 plays every winter, 100 of them professional, where the principal boy must be played by a girl, the leading lady must be a man and not one of the stories must ever be at all original. I refer, of course, to the great British pantomime.

So the suggestion that the British reputation for eccentricity is waning might be premature, if hard to define. Perhaps outsiders can identify it best. When the somewhat manic explorer **John 'Blashers' Blashford-Snell** (see page 81) of the Royal Engineers struggled ashore with his ragged party after descending the White Nile, an American onlooker was heard to intone to her husband: 'Gee, these guys must be crazy.' He responded: 'Hush, dear, they're only British.'

For the true barmy Brit, it's all understood – and understated. In 1997 **Miss Debi Reader** from Manchester was attempting to beat Briton Ffyona Campbell's record set nine years earlier for walking across Australia, baking empty deserts and all, in 95 days. Just two days before she finished, Miss Reader was astonished to hear that another walker, Craig Brown, had, at that moment, beaten her to it. Her response was quoted as: 'My first reaction was astonishment that anyone else would be stupid enough to attempt it. But then we realised he was British, so it made more sense.' Or is it less...?

Since then an intrepid Londoner called **Jim Shekdar** has rowed a boat to Australia from the USA, an almost unbelievable feat that took months and involved fighting with sharks, a typhoon and nearly being run down by a tanker. Well, he didn't row *all* the way. As he approached Oz through heavy surf he was tossed out and swam ashore after his craft. He told onlookers: 'I always knew that bloody boat wanted to get there first.' Asked why he did it, he said with classic understatement: 'I needed to lose a bit of weight.'

In 2004 I looked around to see if Brits were still doing

daft things. I noticed in just one week three extreme activities: one Sean Morley was kayaking around Britain. As he had included the Channel Islands and the remote Scottish ones, this was taking him six months.

Then there was **Bob Brown**, a teacher from Cornwall who won an utterly amazing running race across the whole of the United States. It had taken more than two months at a rate of two marathons a day, although this epic had earned little media interest, presumably because most of the other entrants had dropped out, died or gone even more bonkers. Whatever the cause, few of them made it to Central Park, New York.

Then there was my favourite of that week's crop of eccentrics, a certain **Edward Genochio**, 27, from Newtown, Devon, who was reported to be cycling around the world but had come a cropper in Ulan Bator, Mongolia. The item flashed up on a TV screen with 'Mongolia.... Breaking News' (which is not something you see every day in Britain).

After cycling 16,000km since leaving his home near Exeter five months previously, he had pitched his tent as usual, and locked up his bike. But he hadn't allowed for the Mongolian horde (well, one of them) and their age-old habit of rustling horses, goats, possibly women and certainly bicycles by lassoing them. He was quoted as saying:

'Before going to sleep on Saturday night I had locked my bicycle to my tent. The next thing I knew, I was woken up by the sounds of galloping hooves and ripping canvas.

'This being Mongolia, rather than cutting the lock, the thief had tied the bike to his horse with a rope before charging off and tearing my tent in two.

'For five months I have lived my whole life on my bicycle and in my tent. Suddenly to lose them both leaves me feeling completely hollowed out.

'Locals I have spoken to say they totally understand the feeling – it's the equivalent of a Mongolian nomad losing his yurt and his horse.

'I am desperately hoping that a cycle manufacturer will take pity on me and ship out a bicycle.'

A new bike was indeed dispatched by a sympathiser who recognised a true eccentric Brit when he saw one. Mongol hordes or not, Mr Genochio jumped back in the saddle for the next 3,000km to Shanghai.

Last word to Salvador Dali. He said that the British would never take to surrealism because they wake up to it every day. Spot on, old melted clock chum.

Part One

ECCENTRIC THINGS WE DO

ATLANTIC
OCEAN

Orkney
Islands

Isle of Lewis

Thurso

Isle of
Skye

Inverness

Inner
Hebrides

SCOTLAND

Aberdeen

Old Christmas,
Foula

Up Helly
Aa

Shetland Is

Island of
Mull

Burning the Clavie,
Burghead

Fireball Ceremony,
Stonehaven

Islay

Flambeaux Procession,
Comrie

Kate Kennedy's
Procession,
St Andrews

THE ECCENTRIC YEAR

Arran

Burry Man Festival
& Loonydook,
South Queenferry

Glasgow

Swamp Soccer,
Edinburgh

Herring Queen, Eyemouth

Whuppity Scourie,
Lanark

Tweedmouth Feast,
Berwick-upon-Tweed

Ne'erday Bonfire,
Biggar

Selkirk
Common Riding

Shrovetide Football, Alnwick

ATLANTIC
OCEAN

NORTH
SEA

Alternative Scottish Games,
Castle Douglas

Carlisle

Hoppings,
Newcastle upon Tyne

Horse Fair,
Appleby

Allendale
Guizers

World Egg Jarping Championships,
Peterlee

Isle of
Man

Gurning,
Egremont

Festival
of Fools,
Muncaster

Burning of
t'Owd Bartle,
West Witton

Middlesbrough

ENGLAND

Viking Longboat
Races, Peel

Scarecrow
Festival,
Wray

Bed Race,
Knaresborough

Giant Yorkshire-pudding
Boat Race, Brawby

Tin Bath Championships

Tram Sunday, Fleetwood

York

Shrovetide Skipping, Scarborough

IRISH
SEA

Pace-egging

Bradford Leeds

Kingston-upon-Hull

NORTH
SEA

Bacup Nutters Dance

Rhubarb Festival, Wakefield

Black-pudding-throwing, Ramsbottom

World Coal-carrying Championship

Anglesey

Liverpool

Manchester

Haxey Hood & Sway

Holyhead

Garland Day, Castleton

Sheffield

Toe Wrestling, Wetton

Well Dressing, Tissington

N

Royal Shrovetide Football, Ashbourne

Derby

Goose Fair,
Nottingham

World Snail-racing
Championships,
Congham

0   80 km
0   50 miles

Horn Dance, Abbotts Bromley

Straw Bear,
Whittlesey

Herring Day,
Great
Yarmouth

Well Dressing, Newborough

Conker Championships, Oundle

Norwich

Olympian Games, Much Wenlock

Wolverhampton

Cheese Rolling, Stilton

Cardigan
Bay

Santa Run, Newtown

Birmingham

Man v Horse Marathon &
Bog Snorkelling, Llanwrtyd Wells

Arbor Day,
Aston

Hare Pie Scramble,
Hallaton

Cambridge

Race of Bogmen,
Great Finborough

Coracle Racing, Cilgerran

Olney Pancake Race

Fishguard

Ipswich

WALES

Shin-kicking,
Chipping Camden

May Day Frolics
& St Giles Fair,
Oxford

Mud Race, Maldon

Beca Mountain Race

Onion Fair, Newent

Walrus Dip,
Pembrey

Swansea

Cheese
Rolling,
Brockworth

Pooh Sticks,
Little Wittenham

Garter Ceremony,
Windsor

Plank-walking Championship,
Queensborough

CARDIFF

Wife-carrying, Dorking

LONDON

Oyster
Ceremony,
Whitstable

Bristol
Channel

Illuminated
Carnivals,
Weston-Super-Mare
and West Country

World Marbles Championships,
Tinsley Green

Robertsbridge
Bonfire

Hunting the Earl of Rone,
Combe Martin

Lawnmower Grand Prix, Wisborough Green

Battle
Bonfire

Day of Syn & RHD
Railway, New Romney

Barnstaple Fair

Nettle-eating,
Marshwood

Chilli Fiesta, West Dean

Soapbox Races, Goodwood

Dover

Turning the Devil's Boulder

Exeter

Blazing Barrels, Bath Race, Poole

Portsmouth

Blessing the Sea, Hastings

ATLANTIC
OCEAN

Padstow 'Obby 'Oss

Ottery St Mary

Garlic Festival

Birdman
Bognor

Lewes
Bonfire Societies &
Pea-throwing Championships

Hurling the Silver Ball,
St Columb Major

Orange Races,
Totnes

I of Wight

Knill Ceremony &
Hurling the Silver Ball,
St Ives

Penzance

Blessing the Lifeboat, Brixham

Furry Dance, Helston

Worm-charming,
Blackawton

Tom Bawcock's Eve, Mousehole

ENGLISH CHANNEL

World Pilot Gig Championship, Scilly Isles

THE ECCENTRIC YEAR

Week by week, the strangest customs of Britain unfold, few of them behind locked doors. This is your guide, the most comprehensive yet produced, to when and where to find the bizarre and inexplicable – to where the unexpected can be expected. As events and venues can change over the years, you should check with information centres in the towns concerned before making long journeys. Travel information is at the end of the chapter. Partake at your own risk!

WAYFARER'S DOLE Hospital of St Cross, Winchester, Hampshire (see page 126).
YELLING OF NEWS By Town Crier, 11.00, Coppergate, York.
ONE O'CLOCK GUN Edinburgh Castle.
WAKEMAN'S CURFEW 21.00, for at least the last thousand years: City Hornblower in Ripon, Yorkshire, wearing his tricorn hat, blows the Wakeman's curfew horn at each corner of the Market Place obelisk.
BLOWING OF THE FOREST HORN Bainbridge, North Yorkshire, to help people on foot up on the moors in the dark (winter only).
CEREMONY OF THE QUEEN'S (OR KING'S) KEYS 21.53, Tower of London (see page 125; Travel: page 130).

Daily Events

JANUARY

ANNUAL BATH RACE In Poole, Dorset, dozens of contestants race alongside the Quay in baths. Paddling is allowed, but judges pull the plug on anything too fast, such as a proper double-ended paddle, a sail or an outboard motor. An organiser told me: 'Sometimes people strap several baths together. There was a brilliant one last year with nine baths and a crew of 20 making a human-powered paddle steamer. Well, it would have been brilliant if it hadn't broken apart and submerged halfway through.' It takes 10–15 minutes for about two dozen shivering contestants to traverse the chilly waters, if they make it. Tap dancing not recommended. It's in aid of a hospital charity. After that, it's back to the Blue Boar pub for a restorative dram or three. *New Year's Day, usually 12.30*; Travel: page 64.

LOONYDOOK A few brave, not to mention loony, souls jump into the ff-freezing ff-Firth of ff-Forth at South Queensferry, near Edinburgh, at the boat house steps at noon, assuming the sea hasn't frozen solid. Said to cure any hangover. Usually some 50 madmen and a few women take part, waving a Scottish standard, and if you find, when you are knee-deep, that getting further into the icy water is a little difficult, do not worry about whether the hundreds of spectators on shore might jeer or laugh, or whether the other swimmers splash you or push you over. Of *course* they will. *New Year's Day.*

MAPPLETON BRIDGE JUMP Throw yourself off a high bridge in this village near Ashbourne, Derbyshire, into a freezing river, then race across a field, having ridden some rapids in a tiny boat before the bridge jump. Instant cure for a New Year's Eve hangover, I'd say. You get hot soup at the pub at the end. Ice and lemming, Sir? Or go and watch the mad beggars. The prize is the Brass Monkey Trophy. This is named (and used in phrases such as 'brass monkeys weather') because being a cannon-ball holder in the Navy, and contracting at a different rate to iron cannonballs, you could freeze your balls off ... *New Year's Day*; Travel: page 68.

NEW YEAR'S DIP In the near-freezing North Sea, Whitley Bay, Tyne & Wear. Often includes over-70s in age, never in temperature. *New Year's Day.*

UPPIES AND DOONIES Kirkwall, Orkney Islands. A massive 200-a-side communal scrum lasting four hours (see box, page 11). Also 25 December. *New Year's Day.*

MALDON MUDATHON 200yd dash in often icy conditions through waist-deep oozing mud, Blackwater River, Maldon, Essex. Sometimes as early as 26 December. Sometimes the stick-in-the-muds don't even bother till early January (it's them tides). Ever wondered how our ancestors felt emerging from the primordial slime? This is your chance to find out. When you consider that organisers warn that you have to gaffer tape your shoes to your legs, you begin to understand how awful it is. And how funny for everyone on shore. As usual, an idea in a pub (the Queen's Head) is to blame for starting it all, and charities benefit. *1-ish January*; see page 68.

FOULA CHRISTMAS DAY On Foula, west of mainland Shetland (see page xii), Christmas day is celebrated on *6 January*; New Year's Day follows a week later on *13 January.*

HAXEY HOOD GAME Ancient, colourful village scrum, Haxey, Lincolnshire, recalling a 700-year-old act of chivalry (see box, page 6). *6 January*; Travel: page 67.

STRAW BEAR FESTIVAL In Whittlesey, Cambridgeshire, a gruesome figure of a straw bear, followed by sword dancers, cavorts through the streets, ending with burning the bear on the Saturday night. Friday and

5

The chivalrous origins of hoods and boggans

IN PROHIBITION-ERA CHICAGO, the term 'hood' referred to gangs of ruffians who played by their own rules and chased a moll's skirt now and then. In Haxey, Lincolnshire, each 6 January (or 5th if the 6th is a Sunday) the term hood refers to a gang of ruffians who play by their own rules and chase an item of lady's clothing – a hood, to be precise.

There the similarity falls down, as do many of the participants in this, another example of ancient inter-village scrummaging.

It's all due to Lady de Mowbray who, riding near Haxey some 700 years ago, lost her hood to a mischievous gust of wind. Thirteen gallant farm workers took part in a muddy race across the ploughed fields to regain the item, the one who caught it being too shy to bring it back and another returning it with exaggerated courtesy. This so amused her ladyship that she donated a piece of land so the drama could be re-enacted annually.

The land – Hoodlands – is 13 half-acres in memory of the 13 farm workers, the characters of those who returned the hood perhaps being recalled by the Fool and the Lord. There are also 13 colourfully dressed Boggans who assemble with the throng at the old village cross near Haxey Church at 3pm on this, the old calendar's Christmas Day.

The Fool makes a speech urging playing by the unspoken rules but is smoked from his position by a pile of burning straw. (Once in living memory the Fool had to be extinguished.) The Lord, or King Boggan, with his wand of 13 willows leads the crowd to the 13 half-acres where 13 sacking hoods are thrown in the air so people can attempt to get them past the Boggans.

Then the real game begins with the Sway Hood, made of rope bound with leather. This is a mass inter-village game with the goals being the pubs in either Westwoodside or Haxey. As in the similar Shrove Tuesday games at Ashbourne, Derbyshire (see page 10) and elsewhere, the Haxey Sway has been known to flatten fences and stone walls, rampage through homes and splinter trees, but unlike the hoods of Chicago, those left on the ground can stand up and cheerfully join in again. Usually.

Saturday before Plough Monday (first Monday after Twelfth Night, 12 days after Christmas). *Early January*; Travel: page 70.

INDOOR WINDSURFING CHAMPIONSHIPS Part of the London Boat Show at ExCel, London's Docklands. Pleasantly bonkers – the whole point of windsurfing is the outdoors and nature, but then, why not? Huge fans (of the electric variety) enable contestants to perform just feet away from their huge fans (of the human variety). Next challenge: underwater hang-gliding and cloud-top croquet. *Early January*.

BURNING THE CLAVIE A flaming whisky barrel is rolled through the streets in Burghead, Morayshire (see box, page 58). *11 January*; Travel: page 65.

HUNTING THE MALLARD CEREMONY Bizarre official hunt across the rooftops, singing the ancient Mallard song and carrying lanterns, at All Souls College, Oxford, where a great mallard duck was found hiding when the college was being built in 1437. The whole building is searched from roofs to cellars. The hunt takes place all night, once every 100 years (2001, 2101, etc). *14 January*.

WASSAILING THE APPLE TREE The traditional singing to apple trees, putting cider-soaked toast in branches and firing shotguns in the air over them are all practised to ensure a good crop. The date is the old Twelfth Night, 17 January. At the Butcher's Arms, Carhampton, Somerset, at the Victoria & Albert Inn, Stoke Gabriel near Totnes, Devon (usually on the nearest Saturday and involving a Mummers play), and at the Somerset Rural Life Museum at Glastonbury. There are versions in many southern counties. *17 January or nearest Saturday*; Travel: page 70.

PLOUGH STOTS Colourfully dressed bands of young people, carrying steel swords and a plough, dance around Goathland, near Whitby, Yorkshire, backed by teams of musicians with fiddles and some kind of squeezebox. The sword dances involve holding the tips of the neighbour's sword and also interlocking the swords to make a hexagon, which is lowered over the head of one of the crowd. This 'Lock' is reduced in size while the dance goes on around the 'victim' and then the swords are dramatically withdrawn with a flourish leaving the 'victim' feeling lucky still to have a head. A stot is a northern word for a bullock but here refers to the young men drawing a plough. This traditionally takes place on the Saturday following Plough Sunday, the first Sunday after Epiphany (6 January). This usually works out at the *second or third Saturday in January*.

UP HELLY AA A Viking boat is paraded and burnt in Lerwick, Shetland, at 7.30pm (see box, page 59). *Last Tuesday in January*; Travel: page 70.

FEBRUARY

ANNUAL CLOWN SERVICE If you have enormous shoes, a red nose and rainbow-coloured trousers that are 20 sizes too big, you'll fit in well at the Annual Clown Service in memory of Joseph Grimaldi (the original and greatest) at Holy Trinity, Beechwood Road, Dalston, East London, E8. A glance through the congregation shows shocks of blue hair, ludicrous clothes and outrageous make-up, tiny hats perched on bald heads and subversiveness like trying to parade a toilet brush on a stick through the church instead of a cross. The outfits and make-up are known as full motley and slap, apparently. The collected clowns pray forgiveness for sins such as failing to see a joke, mourn clowns who have died since the last service and make irreverent farting, hooting and tooting noises. Station: Dalston Kingsland. *First Sunday in February*; Travel: page 66.

HURLING THE SILVER BALL St Ives, Cornwall, 10.30. An ancient mass rugby game (see box, page 10). *Monday nearest 3 February; but not 3 February.*

SHROVE TUESDAY

Shrove Tuesday's date is variable.

See box opposite for details of extraordinary events all round Britain.

SHROVE TUESDAY, any schoolchild will tell you, is Pancake Day. True, you can witness many traditional pancake races in many a village, such as that run at **Olney**, Buckinghamshire, since 1445, allegedly the mother of all pancake races, commemorating an absent-minded woman who ran late to church upon hearing the bell, without putting her pan down. The service would have been a shriving, or blessing to help the faithful through the Lenten fast until Easter: hence Shrove Tuesday. Rich foods would have been used up, hence the pancakes and the name used elsewhere, Mardi Gras, meaning Fat Tuesday. And if you weren't given the full shriving, at execution for example, you received 'short shrift'.

Tossing pancakes? You haven't seen the hurling

The **Olney Pancake Race** (Travel: page 68) starts at the marketplace and ends at the church, where the winner gets a prayer book and a kiss from a verger. In **Toddington**, Bedfordshire, children climb Conger Hill and lie with their ears to the ground to listen for the witch frying her pancakes as the clock strikes noon (the midday bell itself is a recurrent feature of ancient Shrove Tuesday customs). An equally ancient pancake race runs at **Winster**, Derbyshire, but don't eat any titbits that fall from the pans. These are special racing pancakes made for toughness. **Yarmouth**, Isle of Wight, also holds a race in the town's square.

(CONTINUED OVERLEAF)

9

Tossing pancakes? You haven't seen the hurling

However, more weird and wonderful things happen on Shrove Tuesday than the odd bit of egg on face. Much seems to involve screaming scrums of muddy men instead of women in aprons.

At **Ashbourne** in Derbyshire, for instance, there's the **Royal Shrovetide football game** (Travel: page 69) between the Up'ards and Down'ards, defined as people living on opposite sides of Henmore Brook, along whose course the riotous game, starting with the ball being 'turned up' at 2pm on Shrove Tuesday (and again on Ash Wednesday), runs back and forth until well into the evening.

The ball for each day is beautifully made from leather stuffed with cork and painted with scenes relevant to that year's 'turner-up'. Those won become prized family heirlooms. The goals are three miles apart at Sturston and Clifton and the shops are boarded up against damage as 'the hug', as it is called locally, heaves back and forth. Trees are split, fences flattened, and washing poles uprooted. No-one knows what started it all.

In **Atherstone**, near Nuneaton, Warwickshire, another great scrummage of a Shrovetide football game starts with the ball being thrown from the upstairs of Barclays Bank at 3pm, and the main road is closed for the game. No-one knows exactly why, but here the ball can be water-filled, and the winner is the person holding the ball at 5pm.

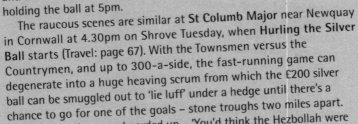

The raucous scenes are similar at **St Columb Major** near Newquay in Cornwall at 4.30pm on Shrove Tuesday, when **Hurling the Silver Ball** starts (Travel: page 67). With the Townsmen versus the Countrymen, and up to 300-a-side, the fast-running game can degenerate into a huge heaving scrum from which the £200 silver ball can be smuggled out to 'lie luff' under a hedge until there's a chance to go for one of the goals – stone troughs two miles apart.

Again the shops are boarded up – 'You'd think the Hezbollah were coming through,' said enthusiast Ivan Rabey – and as the pitch covers

Tossing pancakes? You haven't seen the hurling

the parish, the game makes *Guinness World Records* for having the largest playing area. The game was already old by the reign of Queen Elizabeth I. Its origins? 'No-one knows', said Rabey. Similarly huge scrummages take place on massive pitches at **Sedgefield** near Darlington at 1pm, and at **Alnwick** in Northumberland where the Duke of Northumberland's piper leads the ball on to the pitch, usually at 2.30pm. The goals are a quarter-mile apart and each team is 150 strong.

A similar mass football game to the Ashbourne one takes place at **Workington**, Cumbria, on Good Friday, and also shortly after Easter – usually the next Saturday and one other day. **Hailing the Ball** involves a specially made coloured ball being thrown up at the Cloffocks car park and two huge teams, the **Uppies and Downies**, heaving up and down to get the ball their side of the River Derwent. At **Jedburgh**, Borders, its Uppies and Doonies is held a couple of weeks earlier, but it's all basically the same game, as is the Orkney Islands' version at **Kirkwall** on Christmas Day and New Year's Day.

Near **St Ives**, Cornwall, another **Hurling the Silver Ball** (Travel: page 67) takes place on the Monday nearest 3 February, but not on 3 February. It is thrown by the mayor some time after 9.30am and passed, not hurled, from person to person over the whole town; whoever is holding it at noon wins a crown coin. At one time, the sides were selected as simply anyone called John, William or Thomas against the rest of the world.

Very different is the ritual at **Corfe Castle**, Dorset, where at noon on Shrove Tuesday those who have completed quarrying apprenticeships must carry a quart of beer, a penny loaf and the equivalent of 6 shillings and 8 pence to the town hall for the solemn conclave of the Ancient Order of Purbeck Marblers and Stonecutters. They then kick a football all round the town and carry a pound of pepper – why pepper, no-one really knows – down to Ower Quay in Poole Harbour to mark their right to carry stone there.

A more elegant form of exercise is undertaken at **Scarborough**, Yorkshire, where, when the Pancake Bell is rung at noon, the town takes to the South Foreshore for skipping in great lines with long ropes, plus a few pancake races. The bell is a remnant of that once-common old shriving bell. But why skipping? A tourism official said: 'Well, it's been going on for at least 200 years, and it helps get an appetite up for pancakes, but the truth is, no-one knows.'

MOONRAKING FESTIVAL A giant paper moon is floated on a canal, raked out by a team of women in memory of a smuggling legend (see page 233), then carried round the village by a procession of 'gnomes' bearing hundreds of homemade lamps. Canal End, Slaithwaite, near Huddersfield, West Yorkshire, around 6.30pm. *Saturday of second weekend of half-term. Odd numbered years only.*

WAKEFIELD RHUBARB FESTIVAL This celebrates the product of the 'rhubarb triangle', Yorkshire-forced rhubarb, which enjoys the same coveted legal status as champagne or Parma ham. Visit the forcing sheds where rhubarb is harvested by candlelight. Rhubarb wine, rhubarb recipes, Battle of Stamford Bridge re-enacted with rhubarb (actually that last one is just rhubarb). *Late Friday and Saturday in February*; Travel: page 70.

MARCH

WHUPPITY SCOURIE Odd race round church, Lanark (see page 180). *1 March.*

WIFE-CARRYING RACES, DORKING, SURREY About 250 metres, and up and down a bit. The wife must wear a helmet, lest she gets dropped. The idea comes from Finland – one Finn leads to another – where it originated in carrying off women from the next village. The most ergonomic position is with the wife's legs around the man's neck and her face looking at his bum, so she's upside down. Winner gets the wife's weight in beer. *First Sunday*; Travel: page 70.

KIPLINGCOTES DERBY Near Market Weighton, Humberside. Britain's oldest and oddest race. *Third Thursday*; Travel: page 84.

DRUIDS MEET In Tower Hill, London, to celebrate spring equinox. *21 March.*

Tichborne Dole Tichborne, Alresford, Hampshire, about 2pm (see page 126). *25 March.*

Pooh Sticks World Championships At Day's Lock, Little Wittenham, near Didcot, Oxfordshire, usually at noon. If you haven't read *Winnie the Pooh*, the sport consists of more than one person simultaneously dropping sticks into a river on the upstream side of a bridge, then racing or strolling (depending on the rate of flow of said watercourse) to the other side of the bridge to see whose stick comes out first. Throwing the sticks is not allowed, nor are carbon-fibre computer-designed racing sticks. They must be natural sticks and they must be dropped. Willow is best. The event, which attracts up to 2,000 serious contestants, benefits the Royal National Lifeboat Institution, which may be a good thing given the possible effects of the deluge of sticks from this event on the next event, further downriver. *A late Saturday;* Travel: page 69.

The Oxford and Cambridge Boat Race Odd in that it isn't in Oxford or Cambridge; up to a quarter of a million people turn out to watch even though most of them know absolutely nothing about rowing, are not supporters or graduates of either Oxford or Cambridge, and will be able to see only a small part of it. Around another nine million watch on TV. But in eccentric England things have become much-loved traditions for much less reason. It takes place on the Thames in London, from Putney Bridge (Tube) to Mortlake (rail from Waterloo). More info: www. theboatrace.org. *Last Saturday in March or first in April.*

APRIL

All Fools' Day *1 April;* see box, page 14.

Changing of the Quill This is a learned address made to the portrait statue gracing the tomb of the 16th-century historian John Stow. After the address, given by an historian, the Lord Mayor of London changes the quill in his hand for a new one. Church of St Andrew Undershaft, London EC3. Every third year (2011, 2014, etc). *5 April or near.*

Kate Kennedy Procession Pageant of Scottish worthies, banned as profane for half a century, St Andrews, Fife. Date can vary. *10 April.*

OCT NOV DEC

THE BEST APRIL FOOL ever perpetrated was 1 April 1698 and made a laughing stock of the gentry of London, great numbers of whom turned up in their carriages and finery at the Tower of London to 'see the lions being washed' as instructed on their gilt-edged invitation cards. A menagerie of animals were kept here at the time, before being transferred to London Zoo in 1831.

This day, in the North of England originally called April Noddy Day, is the traditional time for sending apprentices to fetch things such as a tin of striped paint, a soft-pointed chisel, a box of straight hooks or a new bubble for the spirit level.

Village signs are waggishly amended. (Four Marks in Hampshire gained the official-looking addition 'Out Of Ten' on 1 April a couple of years ago.)

All such foolery is strictly supposed to end by noon. Hence the rhyme: 'April Fool's gone and past; You're the biggest fool at last', or in the North of England: 'April Noddy's past and gone, You're the Fool and I am none.'

All Fools' Day

The concept is ancient, going back to the medieval Feast of Fools and the Roman feast of Saturnalia.

In Scotland it is traditionally Huntigowk Day for sending people on a gowk's errand (a gowk is a cuckoo or fool) whereby someone is sent from house to house, everyone being in on the joke except the victim.

Memorable April Fool jokes included Richard Dimbleby's *Panorama* programme on the spaghetti harvest in 1957, including shots of rows of spaghetti trees, and the declaration of independence of Hay-on-Wye in the 1970s. Whitehall declined to send in the Army after it heard that the town was issuing edible banknotes printed on rice-paper.

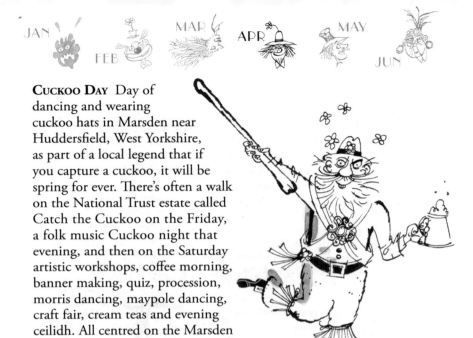

CUCKOO DAY Day of dancing and wearing cuckoo hats in Marsden near Huddersfield, West Yorkshire, as part of a local legend that if you capture a cuckoo, it will be spring for ever. There's often a walk on the National Trust estate called Catch the Cuckoo on the Friday, a folk music Cuckoo night that evening, and then on the Saturday artistic workshops, coffee morning, banner making, quiz, procession, morris dancing, maypole dancing, craft fair, cream teas and evening ceilidh. All centred on the Marsden Mechanics Hall. *Late Saturday.*

EASTER

Date fixed by Golden Numbers – dead complicated, ask the Pope for explanation. Always after 20 March. Covers a period from Maundy Thursday to Easter Monday and, related to the feast, Ascension Day, which occurs 40 days after Easter Sunday.

MAUNDY THURSDAY

LADY MARVYN DOLE Ufton Nervet near Reading, Berkshire. Bread and possibly cloth handed out through Manor House window to the 'poor' (see page 127).

ROYAL MAUNDY MONEY DISTRIBUTION This takes place in Westminster Abbey in even-numbered years and other great cathedrals in odd years. The monarch gives specially minted coins to as many old people as years of their reign, travelling by royal train to further cities. The Queen's Nosegay Maker has to attend (just this once a year) with a secret blend of flowers, for the monarch originally had to wash the feet of the poor.

GOOD FRIDAY

HOT CROSS BUN CEREMONY Widow's Son pub, Devons Road, Bow, London E3, noon. A sailor or Wren adds a bun to the somewhat stale collection going back at least 150 years, to the time when a widow whose only son was at sea, put out a hot cross bun on Good Friday expecting his return for Easter. He never came back but each year she laid out another, refusing to take any away.

Eccentric Easter

ARE BRITISH ECCENTRICS losing their marbles when faced with increasing Euro-conformity? Not if Easter events anyone can witness are anything to go by.

The **World Marbles Championship** on Good Friday is held on special pitches at the Greyhound pub, Tinsley Green, near Crawley, West Sussex (Travel: page 71). It's a knockout tournament for individuals and teams that goes nearly all day. Its origins are said to date from when two local lads competed for the hand of a rare beauty in 1600.

On Easter Saturday or sometimes Monday the town band of Bacup, north of Rochdale, Lancashire, strikes up for the **Bacup Nutters Dance** (Travel: page 64). The Morris-like team sport blackened faces, black uniforms and white breeches, with wooden clogs. The 'nuts' are wooden discs on their hands, waists and knees, with which they set up a rhythmic clatter. The dance dates from at least 1857, and possibly from an earlier Cornish miners' parody of Moorish (hence 'morris') pirates. The team is officially called the Britannia Coconut Dancers.

Easter Day (Sunday, or sometimes Monday) includes the **World Egg Jarping Championships**, which takes place at Peterlee, County Durham. It's a bit like conkers, but played with hard-boiled eggs. No strings – you hold them in your hand and crash them against the opponent, pointed end first. Losers must eat their eggs; the winner is the last intact egg. We shell overcome, as it were.

The **World Coal-carrying Championship** (Travel: page 70) sees the nation's coalmen converge on Ossett, West Yorkshire, on Easter

PACE-EGGING A puzzling name for an ancient custom that involves marking Easter in the Upper Calder Valley, Yorkshire, by a troupe of colourful actors touring towns and villages such as Midgley, Mytholmroyd, Hebden Bridge, Luddenden, Heptonstall and Todmorden with a good-versus-evil mumming play. When you recall the French for Easter is paques (and the Easter flower is the Pax Flower), the name might make sense. Sort of.

Monday (or the following Monday) for a back-breaking event. One hundredweight of coal (51kg) must be carried uphill from the Royal Oak pub in Owl Lane to the maypole in the High Street, a distance of five-sixths of a mile (1.3km). The winner gets a gold medal, and there's also a trophy for the first in the ladies' race carrying 28lb (13kg) of coal over 100 yards (91m), which usually takes place about noon, followed by the men's event. (More on page 84.)

Easter Monday sees an outbreak of football rowdiness which one Leicestershire village is rather proud of. **The Hare Pie Scramble and Bottle Kicking** (Travel: page 67) at Hallaton has its origins in the gift of a piece of land to the rector of Hallaton in 1770, on the condition that he provided two hare pies, two dozen penny loaves and a quantity of ale to be scrambled for by the poor.

Hare pie is still produced at the church gate at 1.30pm and pieces are hurled to the good-natured mob who then make a procession led by a hare on a pole – it used to be a dead one but is now a bronze sculpture – up the hill to a spot where the 'bottles' are blessed, before the start of a rugby-like mass football game between Hallaton and nearby Medbourne. The aim is to get the bottles (three small iron-hooped wooden barrels) across the goals – streams a mile apart – and there is no limit to the numbers on each side.

One recent rector of Hallaton said: 'People take the tradition seriously – there's a village saying – "No pie, no parson". There was a time when the steelworkers and railwaymen from the nearby towns used to come and perhaps too much was drunk, so a few heads got cracked, but now the drinking is more moderate and the game played in a better spirit.'

World Marbles Championship Tinsley Green, Crawley, Sussex. See box, on page 16; Travel: page 71.

Easter Saturday

Bacup Nutters Dance Bacup, Rochdale, Lancashire. See box, page 16.

Easter Sunday

Baron Berners's Folly Faringdon, Oxfordshire. Open, see page 219.

World Egg Jarping Championships Peterlee Cricket Club, County Durham (see page 16). *Sometimes Monday.*

Easter Monday

Biddenden Dole Medieval Siamese twins remembered in strange food hand-out, Kent (see page 127).

Clog Cobbing World Championships Men and women compete to throw a clog down a path beside the Roebuck Inn, Burnley East, Waterfoot, near Rawtenstall, Lancashire. You have to throw the clog backwards over your shoulder. Travel: page 66.

Egg Rolling Painted eggs rolled down slope and eaten. Avenham Park, Preston, Lancashire and Shotover Country Park, Oxford.

Hare Pie Scramble and Bottle Kicking Hallaton, Leicestershire, see page 17; Travel: page 67.

Race of the Bogmen and Egg Throwing Outside the Chestnut Horse, Great Finborough, Suffolk. Originally a race to win contract to plough fields, now for fun.

World Coal-carrying Championship Ossett, West Yorkshire. See page 16; Travel: page 70.

Tuttiman Collect Tax Curious customs unfold at Hungerford, Berkshire; see page 122. *Hocktide: Monday and Tuesday of second week after Easter.*

(DG)

❝Eccentricity has abounded when and where strength of character has abounded; and the amount of eccentricity in a society has generally been proportional to the amount of genius, mental vigour, and moral courage it contained.**❞**

John Stuart Mill, *On Liberty*, 1859

Island of Lewis

1

Stornoway

same scale

Orkney Is

Ring of Brogar
Stone Circle

Pentland Fir

Thurso

**Octagona
House**
John o'Groat

Wick

Cape
Wrath

Tongue

**Wolf Monument,
Sutherland**

North Minch

A T L A N T I C

O C E A N

Ullapool

Dornoch

Moray Firth

Gairloch

Cromarty

6

8

Nairn

Elgin

Inverness

Stones of Clava

Portree

Strathcarron

S k y e

Kyle of Lochalsh

Grantown on Spey

Ballater

Mallaig

7

Kingussie

**Neptune's Staircase,
Fortwilliam**

Tobermory

Pitlochry

**Meikleour
Hedge**

Logierait Mortsafes

**Tealing
Dovecote**

M u l l

Oban

Perth

5

Firth of Lorn

Crianlarich

Crieff

Inveraray

Dunblane

A T L A N T I C

O C E A N J u r a

Lochgilphead

9

10

Glenrothes

M90

Dunfermline

Greenock

Dumbarton

**Falkirk
Wheel**

4

M9

EDINBURGH

Glasgow

Rosslyn Chapel

Largs

Paisley

Renfrew

M8

Motherwell

Whuppity

Hamilton Mausoleum

Ne'erday Bonfire, Biggar

Scourie

Kirkwall

Old Christmas,
Foula

★ Scalloway ②

same scale

Shetland Is

Fraserburgh

○ Keith

Aberdeen

③

NORTH SEA

Brechin ○
○ Montrose
○ Forfar

North Lodge and
Fraser Mausoleum, Arbroath

○ Dundee

Kate Kennedy Procession,
★ St Andrews

Fife Ness

☆ₑ EDINBURGH
Perfect Pyramid, Castle,
Pets' Cemetery, Deacon Brodie's Tavern,
Swamp Soccer and Elephant's Toenail Museum

Forth
North Berwick

Phantasie Doocote ★ Herring Queen Festival,
Eyemouth
★ Tweedmouth Feast

Ben's 10

① Callanish Standing Stones, Lewis
Better than Stonehenge: spooky, ancient
no car parking charge, no gift shop,
no explanation (see page 266)

② Up Helly Aa, Shetland
This was Viking territory not so long ago,
and it still feels like it in Europe's largest
fire festival (Late January, see page 59)

③ Fireball Ceremony, Stonehaven
Truly spectacular, vaguely heathen
brightness in winter's gloom (New Year,
see page 58)

④ Burry Man, South Queensferry
A startling, alien apparition in what is
anyway an amazing place (August,
see page 38)

⑤ Flambeaux Procession, Comrie
This friendly little town has another of
Scotland's great fire festivals (New Year,
see page 58)

⑥ Burning the Clavie, Burghhead
Fire barrels, drama and a wee dram on
the old New Year (January, see page 59)

⑦ Concrete Bob's Viaduct, Glenfinnan
Superb setting, dead horse, Bonnie Prince
Charlie, Harry Potter and steam
(see page 238)

⑧ Sueno's Stone, Forres, near Inverness
Remarkable, mysterious carvings – also see
the Stones of Clava nearby (see page 266)

⑨ Wallace Monument, Stirling
A spectacular, well-sited romantic rocket of
a tower, and a tribute to Scotland's hero
(see page 275)

⑩ The Pineapple, Dunmore
Britain's best architectural joke bore fruit
here. Uniquely nuts (see page 281)

N

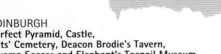

0 ▬▬▬▬ 80km
0 ▬▬▬▬ 50 miles

Greenock
Dumbarton
Falkirk Wheel
EDINBURGH
Glasgow
Renfrew
Livingston
Paisley
M8
①
Largs
Motherwell
Hamilton Mausoleum
②
★ **Ne'erday Bonfire, Biggar**
Kilmarnock
Campbeltown
A r r a n
Firth of Clyde
Ayr
Sanquhar
Moffat
Rathlin I
Mull of Kintyre
Girvan
Drumlanrig Castle
Twelve Apostles
★ **Samye Ling Buddhist Monastery, Eskadalemuir**
Johnnie Turner's Grave & Sculptures
Dumfries Milestone
Laggangairn Standing Stones
★ **Alternative Scottish Games, Castle Douglas**
North Channel
Stranraer
Sweetheart Abbey
Kirkcudbright
Annan
A T L A N T I C
O C E A N
Wren's Egg
Whithorn
Solway Firth
Mull of Galloway
Pencil Museum
Whitehaven
Castlerigg
0   80km
0   50 miles
St Bee's Head
Wainwright's Ashes, Haystacks
Point of Ayre
★ **Gurning Championships, Egremont**
N
Ramsey
Viking Longboat Races, Peel
★
ISLE OF MAN
★ **Festival of Fools, Muncaster**
Tynwald Ceremony, St John's
★
Douglas
Stan Laurel Museum
Calf of Man
★
Tin Bath Championships, Castletown
Lille Cottage & Gleaston Mill
Tram Sunday, Fleetwood

Ben's **10**

① **Rosslyn Chapel, near Edinburgh**
Far spookier and more brilliant than *The Da Vinci Code* conveyed (see page 293)

② **Whuppity Scoorie, Lanark**
A rather sweet custom that is probably older than we know (March, see page 180)

③ **Selkirk Common Riding**
The best of these Wild West-style mass ride-outs (June, see page 27)

④ **Transporter Bridge, Middlesbrough**
The barmiest bridge in Britain, a contraption like a pair of mating pterodactyls (see page 237)

⑤ **World Coal-carrying Championships, Ossett**
Of all the daft things dreamed up in a pub, this is one of the best, 'appen (see page 16)

⑥ **Haxey Hood and Sway**
A truly ancient, spectacular, chivalrous, humorous and bizarre mass scrummage (January, see page 6)

⑦ **Plague Sunday Service, Eyam**
Moving event to mark a stricken village's heroism (August, see page 180)

⑧ **Wentworth Woodhouse Follies**
Some very odd structures near a very odd stately home (see page 274)

⑨ **Black-Pudding-Throwing World Championships**
Brilliantly bonkers, but then clog-cobbing is just down the road (September, see page 44)

⑩ **Long Meg and her Daughters**
A great yarn about standing stones, and not far from two more spooky sets (see page 267)

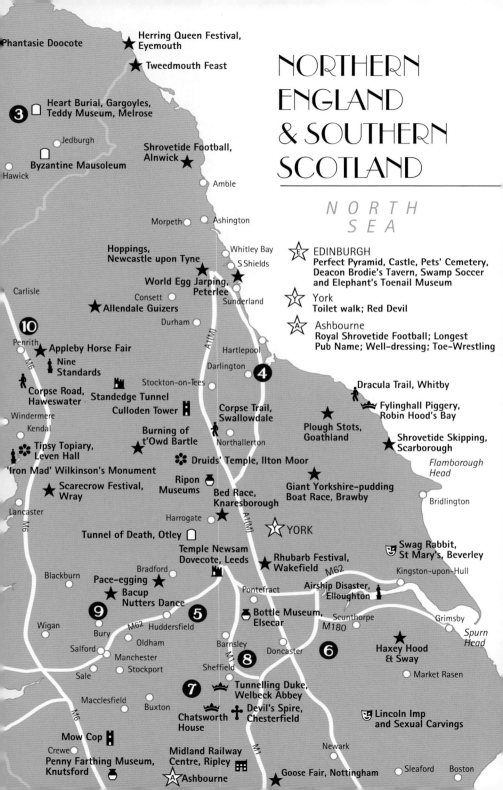

Phantasie Doocote

Herring Queen Festival, Eyemouth

Tweedmouth Feast

3 Heart Burial, Gargoyles, Teddy Museum, Melrose

Jedburgh

Byzantine Mausoleum

Hawick

Shrovetide Football, Alnwick

Amble

Morpeth   Ashington

NORTHERN ENGLAND & SOUTHERN SCOTLAND

NORTH SEA

Whitley Bay

Hoppings, Newcastle upon Tyne

S Shields

Carlisle

World Egg Jarping, Peterlee

Consett

Allendale Guizers

Sunderland

Durham

10 Penrith

Appleby Horse Fair

Nine Standards

Corpse Road, Haweswater

Windermere

Kendal

Standedge Tunnel
Culloden Tower

Stockton-on-Tees

Hartlepool

Darlington

4

Corpse Trail, Swallowdale

Dracula Trail, Whitby

Fylinghall Piggery, Robin Hood's Bay

Plough Stots, Goathland

Shrovetide Skipping, Scarborough

Flamborough Head

Burning of t'Owd Bartle

Northallerton

Tipsy Topiary, Leven Hall

'Iron Mad' Wilkinson's Monument

Druids' Temple, Ilton Moor

Ripon Museums

Scarecrow Festival, Wray

Bed Race, Knaresborough

Giant Yorkshire-pudding Boat Race, Brawby

Bridlington

Lancaster

Harrogate

Tunnel of Death, Otley

YORK

Temple Newsam Dovecote, Leeds

Rhubarb Festival, Wakefield

Swag Rabbit, St Mary's, Beverley

Kingston-upon-Hull

Blackburn

Bradford

Pace-egging

Bacup Nutters Dance

Pontefract

Airship Disaster, Elloughton

9

Wigan

Bury

M62   Huddersfield

5

Bottle Museum, Elsecar

Scunthorpe

M180

Grimsby

Spurn Head

Salford

Oldham

Barnsley

Doncaster

6

Haxey Hood & Sway

Manchester

Stockport

Sheffield

8

Market Rasen

Sale

Macclesfield

Buxton

7

Chatsworth House

Tunnelling Duke, Welbeck Abbey

Devil's Spire, Chesterfield

Lincoln Imp and Sexual Carvings

Mow Cop

Crewe

Penny Farthing Museum, Knutsford

Midland Railway Centre, Ripley

Ashbourne

Newark

Goose Fair, Nottingham

Sleaford

Boston

EDINBURGH
Perfect Pyramid, Castle, Pets' Cemetery, Deacon Brodie's Tavern, Swamp Soccer and Elephant's Toenail Museum

YORK
Toilet walk; Red Devil

Ashbourne
Royal Shrovetide Football; Longest Pub Name; Well-dressing; Toe-Wrestling

Ben's 10

1 Triangular Lodge, Rushton
This is a mathematical puzzle and religious code in stone – a total treasure (see page 285)

2 Tomb Doggerel, Ely
So corny, so tragic and such a wonderful church (see page 165)

3 Dunmow Flitch, Essex
Brilliant fun, and centuries old. A medieval panel game, in which you can bring home the bacon (leap years, see page 118)

4 Bonomi Pyramid, Blickling
We have more pyramids than the Egyptians, and this is the best. Plus a haunted stately home (see page 155)

5 World Snail-racing Championships, Congham
Ready, steady, slow! The creatures avoid a French cooking pot yet again (July, see page 35)

6 World Conker Championships, Ashton, Northants
Eccentric to other nations, at any rate (October, see page 48)

7 Fantasy Village, Thorpeness
The east coast's answer to Portmeirion in Wales, check out the House in the Clouds (see page 248)

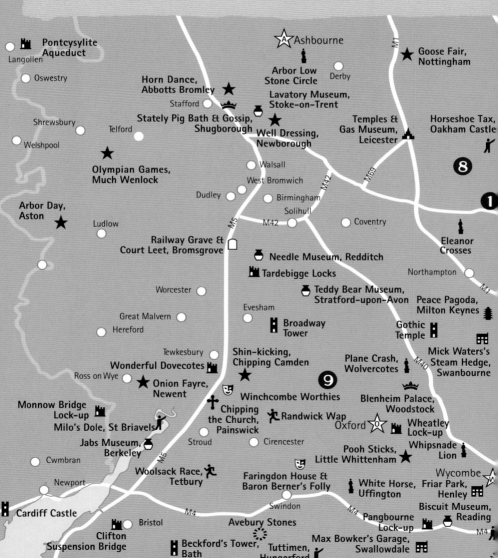

Pontcysylite Aqueduct
Langollen
Oswestry
Horn Dance, Abbotts Bromley
Stafford
Stately Pig Bath & Gossip, Shugborough
Shrewsbury
Telford
Welshpool
Olympian Games, Much Wenlock
Arbor Day, Aston
Ludlow
Railway Grave & Court Leet, Bromsgrove
Dudley
Worcester
Great Malvern
Hereford
Tewkesbury
Wonderful Dovecotes
Ross on Wye
Onion Fayre, Newent
Monnow Bridge Lock-up
Milo's Dole, St Briavels
Jabs Museum, Berkeley
Cwmbran
Woolsack Race, Tetbury
Newport
Cardiff Castle
Clifton Suspension Bridge
Bristol
Beckford's Tower, Bath

Ashbourne
Arbor Low Stone Circle
Derby
Lavatory Museum, Stoke-on-Trent
Well Dressing, Newborough
Walsall
West Bromwich
Birmingham
Solihull
Coventry
M42
M5
M42
Needle Museum, Redditch
Tardebigge Locks
Evesham
Teddy Bear Museum, Stratford-upon-Avon
Broadway Tower
Shin-kicking, Chipping Camden
Winchcombe Worthies
Chipping the Church, Painswick
Randwick Wap
Plane Crash, Wolvercotes
Stroud
Cirencester
Oxford
Faringdon House & Baron Berner's Folly
Swindon
Avebury Stones
Tuttimen, Hungerford
Max Bowker's Garage, Swallowdale

Goose Fair, Nottingham
Temples & Gas Museum, Leicester
Horseshoe Tax, Oakham Castle
8
Eleanor Crosses
Northampton
Peace Pagoda, Milton Keynes
Gothic Temple
Mick Waters's Steam Hedge, Swanbourne
Blenheim Palace, Woodstock
Wheatley Lock-up
Pooh Sticks, Little Whittenham
Whipsnade Lion
White Horse, Uffington
Friar Park, Henley
Wycombe
Biscuit Museum, Reading
Pangbourne Lock-up
M40
M1
M4
9
M5
M69
M42
M40

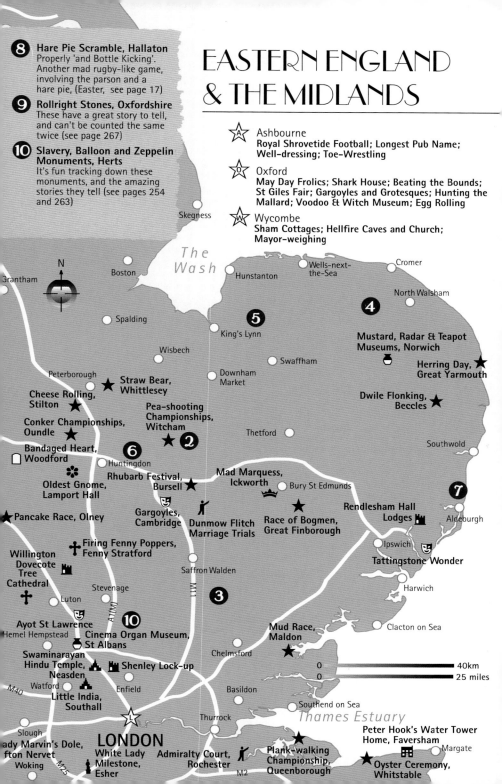

8 Hare Pie Scramble, Hallaton
Properly 'and Bottle Kicking'.
Another mad rugby-like game,
involving the parson and a
hare pie, (Easter, see page 17)

9 Rollright Stones, Oxfordshire
These have a great story to tell,
and can't be counted the same
twice (see page 267)

10 Slavery, Balloon and Zeppelin Monuments, Herts
It's fun tracking down these
monuments, and the amazing
stories they tell (see pages 254
and 263)

EASTERN ENGLAND & THE MIDLANDS

A Ashbourne
Royal Shrovetide Football; Longest Pub Name;
Well-dressing; Toe-Wrestling

O Oxford
May Day Frolics; Shark House; Beating the Bounds;
St Giles Fair; Gargoyles and Grotesques; Hunting the
Mallard; Voodoo & Witch Museum; Egg Rolling

W Wycombe
Sham Cottages; Hellfire Caves and Church;
Mayor-weighing

The Wash

N

Skegness

Grantham

Boston

Hunstanton

Wells-next-the-Sea

Cromer

North Walsham

Spalding

King's Lynn

5

Swaffham

4

Mustard, Radar & Teapot Museums, Norwich

Herring Day, Great Yarmouth

Wisbech

Downham Market

Peterborough

Straw Bear, Whittlesey

Dwile Flonking, Beccles

Cheese Rolling, Stilton

Pea-shooting Championships, Witcham

Thetford

Southwold

Conker Championships, Oundle

Bandaged Heart, Woodford

6

Huntingdon

2

Mad Marquess, Ickworth

Bury St Edmunds

7

Oldest Gnome, Lamport Hall

Rhubarb Festival, Bursell

Rendlesham Hall Lodges

Aldeburgh

Pancake Race, Olney

Gargoyles, Cambridge

Dunmow Flitch Marriage Trials

Race of Bogmen, Great Finborough

Ipswich

Firing Fenny Poppers, Fenny Stratford

Tattingstone Wonder

Willington Dovecote
Tree Cathedral

Saffron Walden

Harwich

Stevenage

M11

3

Luton

Ayot St Lawrence

Clacton on Sea

Hemel Hempstead

Cinema Organ Museum, St Albans

10

Mud Race, Maldon

Swaminarayan Hindu Temple, Neasden

Shenley Lock-up

Chelmsford

0 40km
0 25 miles

Watford

Little India, Southall

Enfield

Basildon

M40

Southend on Sea

Thames Estuary

Slough

Thurrock

Peter Hook's Water Tower Home, Faversham

LONDON

Lady Marvin's Dole, fton Nervet

White Lady Milestone, Esher

Admiralty Court, Rochester

Plank-walking Championship, Queenborough

Margate

Woking

M25

M2

Oyster Ceremony, Whitstable

Ben's 10

1 Captain Skinner's Obelisk, Holyhead
A great spot for a great sea-farer's yarn, on magical Anglesey (see page 257)

2 Marquess's Leg, Llanfair PG and Plas Newydd
Of the three monuments to this leg shot off at Waterloo, this is the best (see page 156)

3 Fantasy Village, Portmeirion
Star of the Prisoner, this is deeply odd even in West Wales (see page 147)

4 Bog Snorkelling, Powys
My-oh-Mire! Forget Soho, if you want deep filth, this is it (August, see page 42)

5 Santa Run, Newtown, mid-Wales
Thousands of Santas turn the town into a sea of red and white a few weeks before Christmas (see page 55)

6 Gloucester Cheese-rolling, Brockworth
Deeply dangerous, bloody-mindedly traditional, and utterly pointless. Therefore a Good Thing. (May, see page 22)

7 Lavatory Museum, Stoke-on-Trent
Lifts the lid on the pottery that freed the world of pongs. A lot to go on (see page 105)

8 Cardiff Castle
'It may not be very Welsh, nor even mediaeval, but my goodness it's wonderful,' said John Betjeman (see page 278)

9 Transporter Bridge, Newport
A distant cousin of the Middlesbrough crazy contraption, this once made sense (see page 237)

10 Ugly House, Capel Curig
Worthy of a visit on the way to see the Marquess's leg for its great story (see page 202)

IRISH SEA

Anglesey

Caernarvon

Gerlert's Tomb, Beddgelert

Lleyn Peninsula

Pwllheli

Portmadoc

Cardigan Bay

Aberystwyth

N

Cardigan

Fishguard

Coracle Racing and Beca Mountain Race, Cilgerran

St David's Head

St Non's Well

Carmarthen

Nelson's Tower, Llanarthney

0 — 40km
0 — 25 miles

Milford Haven

Walrus Dip, Pembrey

Pembroke

Tenby

Swansea

Ashbourne
Royal Shrovetide Football; Longest Pub Name; Well-dressing; Toe-Wrestling

WALES & THE MARCHES

BRISTOL CHANNEL

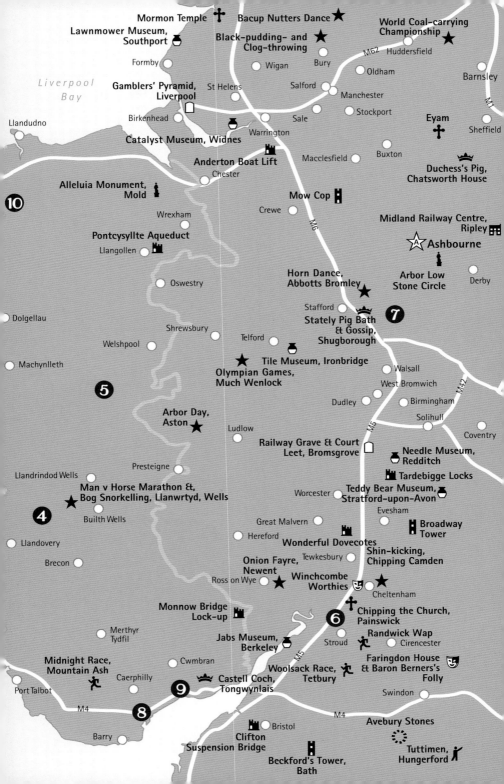

Mormon Temple

Bacup Nutters Dance

Lawnmower Museum, Southport

World Coal-carrying Championship

Black-pudding- and Clog-throwing

Liverpool Bay

Formby

Wigan

Bury

Huddersfield

M62

Oldham

Barnsley

Gamblers' Pyramid, Liverpool

St Helens

Salford

Manchester

M1

Llandudno

Birkenhead

Sale

Stockport

Sheffield

Eyam

Catalyst Museum, Widnes

Warrington

Macclesfield

Buxton

Duchess's Pig, Chatsworth House

Anderton Boat Lift

Chester

Crewe

⓵⓪

Alleluia Monument, Mold

Mow Cop

Midland Railway Centre, Ripley

Wrexham

A Ashbourne

Pontcysyllte Aqueduct

Llangollen

Horn Dance, Abbotts Bromley

Arbor Low Stone Circle

Derby

Oswestry

Stafford

⓻

Dolgellau

Stately Pig Bath & Gossip, Shugborough

Shrewsbury

Telford

Welshpool

Tile Museum, Ironbridge

Walsall

Machynlleth

Olympian Games, Much Wenlock

West Bromwich

⓹

Dudley

Birmingham

Solihull

Arbor Day, Aston

Ludlow

Coventry

Railway Grave & Court Leet, Bromsgrove

Needle Museum, Redditch

Presteigne

Tardebigge Locks

Llandrindod Wells

Teddy Bear Museum, Stratford-upon-Avon

Man v Horse Marathon & Bog Snorkelling, Llanwrtyd, Wells

Worcester

Evesham

⓸

Broadway Tower

Builth Wells

Great Malvern

Llandovery

Hereford

Wonderful Dovecotes

Shin-kicking, Chipping Camden

Brecon

Onion Fayre, Newent

Tewkesbury

Winchcombe Worthies

Ross on Wye

Cheltenham

Monnow Bridge Lock-up

Chipping the Church, Painswick

Merthyr Tydfil

⓺

Randwick Wap

Midnight Race, Mountain Ash

Cwmbran

Jabs Museum, Berkeley

Stroud

Cirencester

Faringdon House & Baron Berners's Folly

Caerphilly

Castell Coch, Tongwynlais

Woolsack Race, Tetbury

Port Talbot

⓽

Swindon

M4

⓼

M4

Avebury Stones

Barry

Bristol

Clifton Suspension Bridge

Tuttimen, Hungerford

Beckford's Tower, Bath

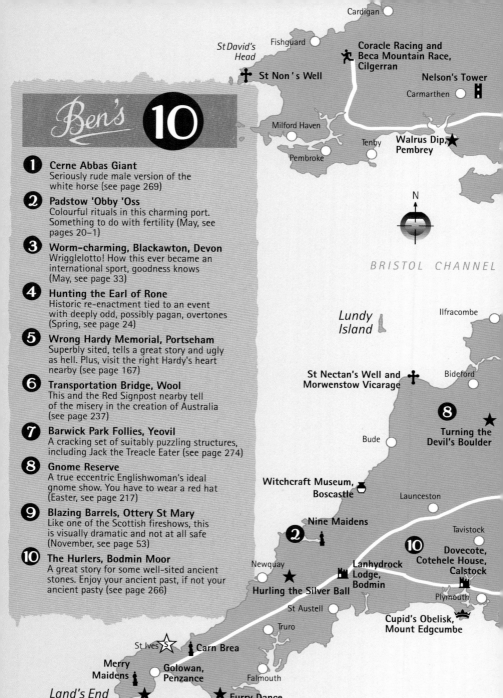

Ben's 10

1 Cerne Abbas Giant
Seriously rude male version of the white horse (see page 269)

2 Padstow 'Obby 'Oss
Colourful rituals in this charming port. Something to do with fertility (May, see pages 20–1)

3 Worm-charming, Blackawton, Devon
Wrigglelotto! How this ever became an international sport, goodness knows (May, see page 33)

4 Hunting the Earl of Rone
Historic re-enactment tied to an event with deeply odd, possibly pagan, overtones (Spring, see page 24)

5 Wrong Hardy Memorial, Portseham
Superbly sited, tells a great story and ugly as hell. Plus, visit the right Hardy's heart nearby (see page 167)

6 Transportation Bridge, Wool
This and the Red Signpost nearby tell of the misery in the creation of Australia (see page 237)

7 Barwick Park Follies, Yeovil
A cracking set of suitably puzzling structures, including Jack the Treacle Eater (see page 274)

8 Gnome Reserve
A true eccentric Englishwoman's ideal gnome show. You have to wear a red hat (Easter, see page 217)

9 Blazing Barrels, Ottery St Mary
Like one of the Scottish fireshows, this is visually dramatic and not at all safe (November, see page 53)

10 The Hurlers, Bodmin Moor
A great story for some well-sited ancient stones. Enjoy your ancient past, if not your ancient pasty (see page 266)

Cardigan

St David's Head

Fishguard

St Non's Well

Coracle Racing and Beca Mountain Race, Cilgerran

Nelson's Tower

Carmarthen

Milford Haven

Tenby

Walrus Dip, Pembrey

Pembroke

N

BRISTOL CHANNEL

Lundy Island

Ilfracombe

St Nectan's Well and Morwenstow Vicarage

Bideford

Turning the Devil's Boulder

Bude

Witchcraft Museum, Boscastle

Launceston

Tavistock

Nine Maidens

Dovecote, Cotehele House, Calstock

Newquay

Lanhydrock Lodge, Bodmin

Plymouth

Hurling the Silver Ball

St Austell

Cupid's Obelisk, Mount Edgcumbe

Truro

St Ives

Carn Brea

Merry Maidens

Golowan, Penzance

Falmouth

Land's End

Tom Bawcock's Eve, Mousehole

Furry Dance, Helston

Lizard Point

ST IVES
Knill Ceremony; Hurling the Silver Ball; St Ia's Well

World Pilot Gig Championships, Scilly Isles

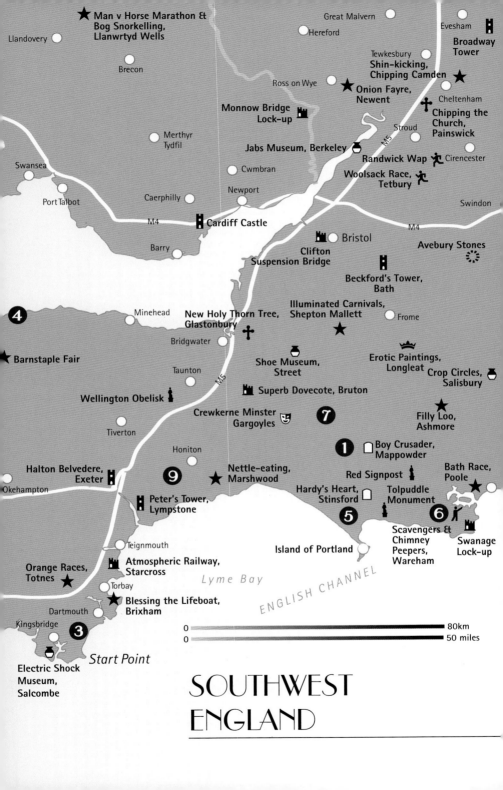

Man v Horse Marathon &
Bog Snorkelling,
Llanwrtyd Wells

Llandovery

Great Malvern

Hereford

Evesham

**Broadway
Tower**

Brecon

Tewkesbury

**Shin-kicking,
Chipping Camden**

Ross on Wye

**Onion Fayre,
Newent**

Cheltenham

**Chipping the
Church,
Painswick**

**Monnow Bridge
Lock-up**

Merthyr
Tydfil

Stroud

Jabs Museum, Berkeley

Randwick Wap Cirencester

Swansea

Cwmbran

**Woolsack Race,
Tetbury**

Port Talbot

Caerphilly

Newport

Swindon

Cardiff Castle

M4

M4

Barry

Bristol

Avebury Stones

**Clifton
Suspension Bridge**

**Beckford's Tower,
Bath**

Minehead

**New Holy Thorn Tree,
Glastonbury**

**Illuminated Carnivals,
Shepton Mallett**

Frome

4

Bridgwater

**Erotic Paintings,
Longleat**

**Crop Circles,
Salisbury**

Barnstaple Fair

**Shoe Museum,
Street**

Taunton

Superb Dovecote, Bruton

Wellington Obelisk

**Crewkerne Minster
Gargoyles**

7

**Filly Loo,
Ashmore**

Tiverton

Honiton

1 **Boy Crusader,
Mappowder**

**Halton Belvedere,
Exeter**

9

**Nettle-eating,
Marshwood**

Red Signpost

**Bath Race,
Poole**

Okehampton

**Hardy's Heart,
Stinsford**

**Tolpuddle
Monument**

6

**Peter's Tower,
Lympstone**

5

**Swanage
Lock-up**

Teignmouth

**Scavengers &
Chimney
Peepers,
Wareham**

**Orange Races,
Totnes**

**Atmospheric Railway,
Starcross**

Island of Portland

Lyme Bay

Torbay

ENGLISH CHANNEL

**Blessing the Lifeboat,
Brixham**

Dartmouth

Kingsbridge

3

0 | 80km

0 | 50 miles

**Electric Shock
Museum,
Salcombe**

Start Point

SOUTHWEST
ENGLAND

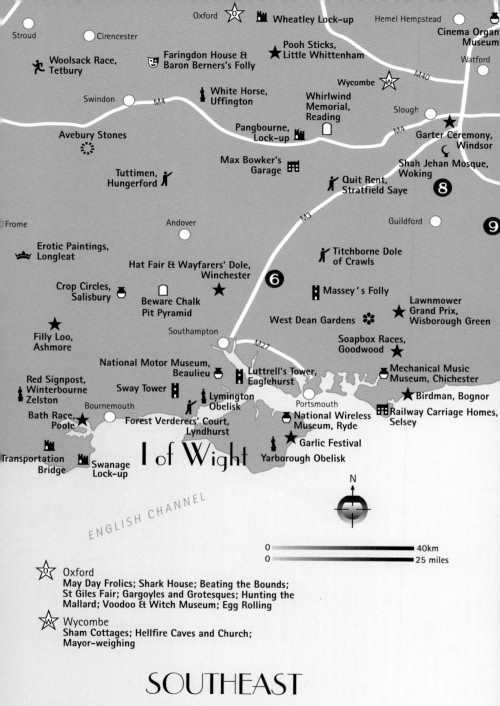

Oxford ☆ 🏰 Wheatley Lock-up   Hemel Hempstead   Cinema Organ Museum

Stroud   Cirencester

Woolsack Race, Tetbury   Faringdon House & Baron Berners's Folly   Pooh Sticks, Little Whittenham   Watford

Swindon   M4   White Horse, Uffington   Whirlwind Memorial, Reading   Wycombe ☆   M40   Slough

Avebury Stones   Pangbourne, Lock-up   M4   Garter Ceremony, Windsor

Tuttimen, Hungerford   Max Bowker's Garage   Quit Rent, Stratfield Saye   Shah Jehan Mosque, Woking   ⑧

Frome   Andover   M3   Guildford   ⑨

Erotic Paintings, Longleat   Titchborne Dole of Crawls

Hat Fair & Wayfarers' Dole, Winchester   ⑥

Crop Circles, Salisbury   Massey's Folly

Beware Chalk Pit Pyramid   West Dean Gardens   Lawnmower Grand Prix, Wisborough Green

Southampton   Soapbox Races, Goodwood

Filly Loo, Ashmore   Mechanical Music Museum, Chichester

Red Signpost, Winterbourne Zelston   National Motor Museum, Beaulieu   Luttrell's Tower, Eaglehurst   Birdman, Bognor

Sway Tower   Lymington Obelisk   Railway Carriage Homes, Selsey

Bath Race, Poole   Bournemouth   Portsmouth   National Wireless Museum, Ryde

Forest Verderers' Court, Lyndhurst   Garlic Festival

Transportation Bridge   I of Wight   Yarborough Obelisk

Swanage Lock-up

ENGLISH CHANNEL

N

0 ——————— 40km
0 ——————— 25 miles

☆ Oxford
May Day Frolics; Shark House; Beating the Bounds;
St Giles Fair; Gargoyles and Grotesques; Hunting the
Mallard; Voodoo & Witch Museum; Egg Rolling

☆ Wycombe
Sham Cottages; Hellfire Caves and Church;
Mayor-weighing

SOUTHEAST
ENGLAND

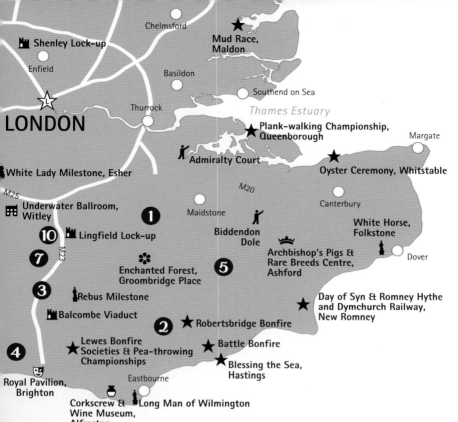

Shenley Lock-up

Chelmsford

Mud Race, Maldon

Enfield

Basildon

Southend on Sea

LONDON

Thurrock

Thames Estuary

Plank-walking Championship, Queenborough

Margate

Admiralty Court

Oyster Ceremony, Whitstable

White Lady Milestone, Esher

M25

M20

Canterbury

Underwater Ballroom, Witley

Maidstone

White Horse, Folkstone

Lingfield Lock-up

Biddendon Dole

Dover

Archbishop's Pigs & Rare Breeds Centre, Ashford

Enchanted Forest, Groombridge Place

Rebus Milestone

M23

Day of Syn & Romney Hythe and Dymchurch Railway, New Romney

Balcombe Viaduct

Robertsbridge Bonfire

Lewes Bonfire Societies & Pea-throwing Championships

Battle Bonfire

Blessing the Sea, Hastings

Royal Pavilion, Brighton

Eastbourne

Corkscrew & Wine Museum, Alfreston

Long Man of Wilmington

Ben's 10

1 **May's Folly, Hadlow**
A jolly good example of total folly – if it hasn't fallen down by the time you visit (see page 276)

2 **Mad Jack Fuller's Follies, Brightling**
Perhaps my favourite set of follies, including himself in his pyramid. Batty (see page 54)

3 **Balcombe Viaduct, Sussex**
The stylish Italianate job with a secret underneath. You'll be well chuffed (see page 238)

4 **Clayton Tunnel House and Church**
Sinister, weird, and with stories to tell of the underworld (Note - private house, see page 203)

5 **Biddenden Dole**
A rather moving and very old custom to honour what we now call Siamese twins (Easter, see page 127)

6 **Dole of Crawls, Titchborne**
This has a hell of a yarn behind it, and still goes forth every year (March, see page 126)

7 **World Marbles Championships**
Like the conkers, eccentric only if you take it very seriously. They do (Easter, see page 16)

8 **Death Railway, Brookwood, Woking**
The other end of an odd yarn that starts at the other Waterloo. Martian death ray machine nearby (see page 160)

9 **Leith Hill Tower, Coldharbour**
A great spot for a picnic, and to read about massacres and buried eccentrics (see page 280)

10 **Wife-carrying Races, Dorking**
Acting like the cliché view of Vikings in – dont-you-know, darling – Surrey, actually! (March, see page 12)

See separate London map for details of London sites.

Ben's 10

1 Horseman's Sunday, Hyde Park
Literally a sermon on the Mount, congregation and priest in the saddle (September, see page 180)

2 Ceremony of the Keys, Tower of London
Ancient, sincere, elaborate, and pointless (Nightly, see page 125)

3 The Bombers' Bridge and a Wronged
Princess of Wales, Hammersmith
Very odd history by the ton (see pages 240-1)

4 Sham Houses, Leinster Gardens, Bayswater
It's always fun tracking down something that isn't there (see page 290)

5 Hero Cat's Grave, Ilford, Essex
This is such a great story, starting in the mysterious Orient – the real one, not Leyton Orient nearby (see pages 157-8)

6 Arab Fantasy, Leighton House, Kensington
'The secret heart of Kensington,' as Lady Lucinda Lambton said (see page 164)

7 Giro's Grave, St James's
The little thing, and it surroundings, tell a huge story. London's only Nazi monument (see pages 156-7)

WEMBLEY

Missing Legs & Tomb Doggerel, St Mary's, Harrow on the Hill

Swaminarayan Hindu Temple, Neasden

WILLESDEN

A40

GREENFORD

EALING

ACTON

PADDINGTON

Executed Earl Obelisk, East Acton

9

First Planes, Science Museum, South Kensington

6

M4

BRENTFORD

Death Railway, Southall

A4

CHISWICK

3 Hammersmith Bridge, and Monument

FULHAM

Clog and Apron Race & Princess's Pagoda, Kew Gardens

Putney to Mortlake, The Oxford and Cambridge Boat Race

FINISH

START

Marc Bolan's Tree, Barnes

Burton Tomb, Mortlake

HOUNSLOW

A316

RICHMOND

PUTNEY

Fireplates Obelisk, Putney Common

TWICKENHAM

A3

Buddhapadipa Temple, Wimbledon

Stag Lodge, Wimbledon

WIMBLEDON

KINGSTON UPON THAMES

SUNBURY

Great British Duck Race, Hampton Court

Leith Hill Tower, Coldharbour

MORDEN

SURBITON

8 I Am The Only Running
Footman, Mayfair
Maddest of London's deeply
mad pub names (see page 143)

9 Cornflakes Packet
Museum, Notting Hill
In fact, the much wider
Museum of Brands, Packaging
and Advertising (see page 102)

10 Blood and Guts Museum,
London Bridge
In fact the Operating Theatre
Museum, London Bridge:
Gruesomely fascinating.
Bleed all about it...
(see page 109)

LONDON

EDMONTON

WALTHAMSTOW

First British Flight,
Walthamstow Marshes

HACKNEY

Annual Clown Service,
Dalston

ISLINGTON

STRATFORD

5

AMPSTEAD

CAMDEN

BETHNAL GREEN

Hot Cross Bun Ceremony,
Widow's Son Pub, Bow

Horseshoe
and
Faggot-
cutting
Ceremony,
High Court

King's Cross
Lighthouse

Guildhall Processions

Great Christmas
Pudding Race,
Covent Garden

4

CITY

Changing of the Quill,
Church of St Andrew, Undershaft, St Mary Axe

WESTMINSTER

Cleopatras Needle,
Embankment

2

Druids meet,
Tower Hill

Indoor Windsurfing,
Excel

Pet
Cemetery,
Victoria Gate
Lodge

1

8

7

Nagging
Museum,
London Bridge

10

ISLE
OF
DOGS

Royal Maundy Money
Distribution,
Westminster
Abbey

BERMONDSEY

NIGHTSBRIDGE

Transportation Bollard, Millbank

CHELSEA

LAMBETH

Brass Crosby Milestone,
Kennington

GREENWICH

Horn Fair,
Charlton

Marquess of Anglesey's Leg,
National Army Museum,
Chelsea

Doggett's Coat and
Badge Race

Severndroog Castle,
Castlewood Park,
Greenwich

Peace Pagoda,
Battersea Park

BRIXTON

CAMBERWELL

Fan Museum,
Greenwich

BATTERSEA

VANDSWORTH

CLAPHAM

PECKHAM

LEWISHAM

N

0   2km
0   1 mile

STREATHAM

BECKENHAM

MITCHAM

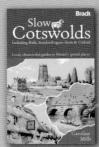
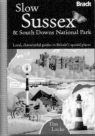
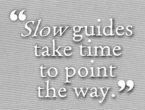

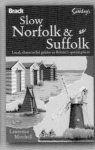
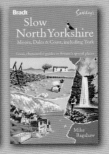

SCARECROW FESTIVAL Wray, near Hornby, Lancashire. Invasion of the scarecrows, many dressed on a theme, appear through this village for a week. Ends with a fair on the bank holiday which usually includes country crafts, rare breeds, geese-herding etc. *Late April–May Day bank holiday.*

BEATING BOUNDS This is a procession to mark parish boundaries, which takes place in many villages including Cannington, near Bridgwater, Somerset, and Oddington, Otmoor, Oxford; originally choirboys were bumped upside down on boundary stones to make a lasting impression. At Lichfield, Staffordshire, the cathedral choir processes with boughs, stopping at eight places to sing a psalm. In Oxford you have the bizarre sight of a bunch of choirboys thrashing the floor in the ladies' underwear department of Marks & Spencer in Queen Street with long canes while a vicar looks on approvingly. But go to St Michael at the North Gate for the morning service on Ascension Day if you want to join in this most peculiar event. At Hayling Island in Hampshire the bounds are beaten by boat, which is a difficult circumnavigation given the tides in the two harbours concerned. *Ascension Day (Thursday, 40 days after Easter).*

WELL DRESSING This takes place in Tissington, Derbyshire, and elsewhere in the Peak District. Village wells are decorated with elaborate floral pictures of religious scenes made of moss, lichens, petals and nuts pressed into damp clay, usually with a procession between the different wells (six at Tissington). Well dressing also takes place in Bisley, near Stroud, Gloucestershire. *Ascension Day (Thursday, 40 days after Easter).*

MAY

MAY MORNING Latin hymn singing, jumping in the river and occasional naked frolicking. Magdalen Bridge, Oxford (see box, page 20). *1 May.*

'OBBY 'OSS This raucous fertility dance takes place in Padstow, Cornwall: there is a similar Hobby Horse, at Minehead, Somerset (see box below). *1 May*; Travel: page 68.

WORLD DOCK PUDDING CHAMPIONSHIP This involves the competitive cooking of a bizarre local delicacy made from nettles and dock leaves (not the common docks), Mytholmroyd Community Centre, Elphaborough, Mytholmroyd, Hebden Bridge, West Yorkshire. (Date varies, often Sunday. The address alone is a good mouthful.) *Early May or late April.*

PEOPLE SOMETIMES COMPLAIN that the May Day bank holiday on the Monday nearest 1 May is a socialist-inspired nuisance – brought in by a Labour government in 1978 to celebrate International Labour Day and suck up to trade unions – although governments of various complexions have given up trying to shift it to the autumn.

But the real May Day, 1 May, is non-political, non-religious, bizarre, bawdy, ancient and usually pagan.

In **Oxford**, for example, crowds block Magdalen Bridge and the High Street from early morning, and at 6am the sweet sound of hymns in Latin floats down from the top of Magdalen College Tower. There are **madrigals and a procession of Morris men** around the city, waving handkerchiefs, sticks and pig bladders in their ancient dance. City pubs are open from 6.30am for pots of ale or cider and hearty breakfasts. Many an Oxford student has stayed up all night drinking and dancing, and usually some jump from Magdalen Bridge into the somewhat shallow River Cherwell.

May Day may be pagan and rude, but not official

20

RANDWICK WAP This is an ancient festival (see page 88) that involves bizarre religious cheese rolling and a procession on the *first Sunday in May*, and a fair, procession and mass cheese-rolling event on the *second Saturday*; Travel: page 69.

INTERNATIONAL FESTIVAL OF WORM CHARMING, Normandy Arms, Chapel Street, Blackawton, near Totnes, Devon, usually 11.30am. *May bank holiday (first Monday)*.

This has sometimes ended in tragedy but not long ago a woman student hit the tabloid headlines by jumping in nude.

Oxford May Day celebrant David Martin said: 'The May Day festivities have been recorded in Oxford since 1650 but we believe it goes back far further than that. Forget the official bank holiday on the nearest Monday: no-one in Westminster can tell Englishmen on which day to celebrate May Day – or when to stop!'

In **London** spring festivities going back to pagan times were uninhibited – the street Mayfair is named after a riotous festival of drinking and womanising held there throughout the 18th century.

The more common maypole, innocently copied in primary school dances today, is believed to go back to a pagan fertility symbol, which is why the Puritans chopped down an imposing maypole that used to stand in the Strand in 1644. May customs in country areas have included maidens gathering the May dew before dawn on 1 May for its alleged healing and beautifying power, and the May Doll dressed in flowers and paraded about by children.

The **May Hobby Horse** or **'Obby 'Oss** dances lewdly around places such as Padstow and Minehead in the West Country and promises fertility to maidens caught in its skirts; there are the more widespread May Garlands, usually carried on sticks, and, of course, school and village May Queens.

All these long predate the workers' holiday beloved of socialists worldwide. **Garland Day** in Abbotsbury, Dorset, for example, when garlands on poles are carried round the village and money collected by children, dates from long before the calendars were changed in the 18th century – hence it is held on 13 May, the 'old' May Day. Either way, it's still not the official government May Day holiday.

NEWBOROUGH WELL-DRESSING Staffordshire, 11am. General village fair to celebrate retreat of plague of 14th century. *May bank holiday (first Monday).*

STILTON CHEESE ROLLING Whole Stilton cheeses are rolled through the village by teams in fancy dress. Dancing follows. Stilton, Peterborough, from 9.30am. *May bank holiday (first Monday).*

WORLD PILOT GIG CHAMPIONSHIP Rowing races in the Scilly Isles, but accommodation likely to be booked out. So get your oar in early. *First long weekend in May.*

FURRY DANCE Couples dance in ball gowns and morning suits with grey toppers through well-decorated Helston, Cornwall, all day (if the 8th is a Sunday or Monday, moves to Saturday before the 8th). Not 'Floral Dance' as a certain London composer had it. *8 May.*

TOWN CRIER COMPETITION Tenby (date varies).

WHIT MONDAY

This is the day after Whit Sunday, or Pentecost, and the date is dependent on when Easter falls. It is usually in late May, or early June, or on Spring bank holiday.

CORBY POLE FAIR Every 20 years (2022, 2042, etc). The town is barricaded off for the fair and travellers are required to pay a toll. Those who won't are carried on a pole (or chair if female) to the three sets of stocks and locked up until someone pays.

GLOUCESTER CHEESE ROLLING This takes place at various very steep hills in Gloucestershire such as Cooper's Hill, Brockworth. Contestants attempt to catch cheese rolled down hills; there are many injuries to runners and spectators hit by flying 8lb Double Gloucesters. This is an ancient and seriously dangerous ceremony and even continued with

dummy cheeses during wartime rationing. The master of ceremonies must wear a white coat, ribbons and a top hat and some in the 20th century were buried wearing them. The event was cancelled recently (and then resumed) to allow safety to be improved because of a mere 33 injuries the previous year. As one outraged local said: 'This is the Nanny state gone mad. If you can't hurl yourself down a steep hill after a few drinks chasing cheeses, what's the point of being British?'

EDAM CHEESE ROLLING Ide Hill, Kent. Much more elegant. Women chase an Edam thrown down the sloping village green during Whit Monday Fair. 'But it's Dutch,' I protested, 'and made backwards'. 'It's an anagram of dame, they pointed out. One lady taking part was so posh that 'rind' referred not to the red waxy covering but the shape. See page 66.

GRUNTY FEN RHUBARB FESTIVAL Mill Close, Burwell, Cambridgeshire. Rhubarb semaphore, Miss Rhubarb Tart, rhubarb combat, that kind of thing.

TETBURY WOOLSACK RACES Racing up and down Gumstool Hill, Tetbury, Gloucestershire (see page 85); Travel: page 113.

GARLAND DAY The Garland King rides through on his horse completely covered in a pyramid of flowers, followed by his retinue, Castleton, Derbyshire. Origins uncertain. *Oak Apple Day (29 May) or if a Sunday, the day before.*

HUNTING OF THE EARL OF RONE Combe Martin, Devon. A weird, wonderful and worrying tradition. *Usually spring bank holiday weekend*; see box, page 24.

ARBOR DAY An apparently ancient fertility rite at Aston-on-Clun near Craven Arms, Shropshire. Villagers dress an ancient black poplar tree with flags, bunting and ribbons, and a ritual wedding scene is enacted by a children's procession. There are also races, and maypole dancing. It seems that it is a combination of three strands: the pagan tree ceremonies associated with the fertility of the crops and people (these were banned along with maypoles by Cromwell in the 1650s after the Civil War); the restoration of the monarchy in 1660, which permitted such rites' revival, and also brought in the celebration of Oak Apple Day on 29 May, to mark the king's birthday and the Restoration, which focused on trees partly because the future king had escaped by hiding in a tree; and

23

Hunting the Earl of Rone: hold the front pagan

O NE OF THE MOST BIZARRE, colourful, sinister, historically and highly charged events to take place in the British calendar is the Hunting the Earl of Rone (Travel: page 23), which takes over **Combe Martin, Devon**, each Spring bank holiday.

Men dressed as grenadiers, with muskets that they fire from time to time, hunt down a fugitive, which may well be based on the Earl of Tyrone, an Irish traitor who was indeed wanted by the government some 400 years ago.

After two or three days of noisy searching, having caught the man, all dressed in sackcloth, he is put backwards on a donkey and marched along with drums and music through this very long seaside village towards the church.

He escapes now and then and is shot and falls to the ground, only to be revived by a fool with a besom, or an 'Obby 'Oss – a dancing figure with a great hooped skirt and a horse's head, complete with clacking, snapping teeth. He's then put back, again backwards on the donkey, and continues his sad journey. Women and maidens are carrying beautiful flower garlands. Eventually the procession reaches the church where people are dancing and the bells ringing and the Earl of Rone is shot once more.

Then it is all the way down to the sea, where the dead Rone is thrown into the waves from the quay, and the women throw their garlands after him. It is an utterly amazing spectacle for what is otherwise a civilised West Country village in the 21st century. Quite weird, wonderful and worrying, possibly.

The thing probably defies analysis, but one thing is for sure – it is not just about hunting the Earl of Rone, who may or may not have been captured here after an attempted flight to France ended in a shipwreck.

Yes, the history seems simple: the Earl of Rone was indeed shipwrecked here in 1607 and the ceremony ran until 1837, when it was banned because of drunken licentiousness (one participant was so drunk he died after falling down steps), and revived in the 1970s.

But the whole story appears to have been grafted on to some very old pagan folk memories blended with medieval Christian teaching in that odd way that gives us, for example, pagan trees, holly and yule logs at Christmas.

On the Christian side you have echoes of the path to Golgotha, Christ's terrible last journey, with the crowd both jeering at the condemned and sympathising. There are elements of Christian medieval folk dramas such as Mummers' plays.

But there are much older pre-Christian British rites included here such as the ritual scapegoating of some poor individual to appease a god or ensure a harvest.

This sinister element is familiar from that very, very strange Edward Woodward film, *The Wicker Man*, or indeed from the antics of the boys in *Lord of The Flies*. It is a basic tribal urge, and a horrible one, to round on some individual or minority and enjoy persecuting them.

Also included are elements of ancient fertility rites, such as the women with garlands, the 'Obby 'Oss (Hobby Horse) and the sacrifice. There is a direct link between the 'Obby 'Oss and fertility in some West Country versions of this dance, where it is said any maiden covered by the horse's skirt will be pregnant within six months.

What we have here is a fascinating and strange blend of prehistory, early Christianity and fairly modern history – whether it has evolved naturally or has been concocted more deliberately – and the result is a colourful oddity that cannot be matched the world over. Eccentric indeed.

a local celebration of a squire's marriage in 1786 when this particular tree, or rather its parent, was first decorated. *Last Sunday in May*; Travel: page 64.

FESTIVAL OF FOOLS Muncaster Castle. Ravenglass, Cumbria. This was the home of the 16th-century jester Tom Fool, as in tomfoolery. Can you be jest as good? *Late May*; Travel: page 66.

SHIN-KICKING WORLD CHAMPIONSHIPS Chipping Campden, Gloucestershire. Just one of the events in Robert Dover's Olimpicks; at least they are centuries older than the more familiar international contest. Marching bands, cannon fire, rustic wrestling, evening torchlit parade, and the vicious shin event (straw-filled wellies and white shepherd's smocks a must). *Friday after Whitsun bank holiday, so sometimes in June*; Travel: page 69.

JUNE

WORLD TOE-WRESTLING CHAMPIONSHIPS
Ye Olde Royal Oak Inn, Wetton, Ashbourne, Derbyshire. This sport has not been recognised at Olympic level despite repeated requests. *Early Saturday.*

CHARLTON HORN FAIR Fair that came about after the king cuckolded someone's wife and sought to pay him off. See box, page 47. *Second Sunday in June.*

GIANT YORKSHIRE PUDDING BOAT RACE People set out in huge Yorkshire puddings at Brawby, North Yorkshire, across the waters of a pond (see box, page 32). *Early June.*

WORLD STINGING-NETTLE-EATING CHAMPIONSHIPS Yes, it's true, at the Bottle Inn, Marshwood, Dorset. *Early June.*

SWAMP SOCCER WORLD CHAMPIONSHIPS Messy, sticky, ankle-deep and Scottish (like porridge). Held in Edinburgh, teams from around the

world get down and dirty – eg: Suffolk Mud Munchers, Blackbum Rovers, Swamp Bog Millionaires, Cowdungbeath… *Usually late June.*

APPLEBY HORSE FAIR The biggest in Europe, it utterly transforms this quiet little town in Cumbria. See box, page 28. *First Thursday, unless that is the 1st, in which case it starts on the 8th, and ends the following Wednesday*; Travel: page 64.

SELKIRK COMMON RIDING One of several mass posse-like excursions of hundreds of riders from Scottish border towns, following a standard bearer, asserting rights to what was lawless unmarked bandit territory in the Marches, the scene of cross-border raids. The Selkirk one ends after about four hours with a gallop back into town and a lament for the dead of the Battle of Flodden. More recent battles have been about whether women can join in. Also held at Linlithgow, West Lothian; and Lockerbie, Dumfries & Galloway. *Friday after second Monday.*

GREAT KNARESBOROUGH BED RACE
Teams of six run beds containing
a seventh member around the
North Yorkshire town at
high speed and through
the River Nidd (the
beds are supposed
to float, the runners
to swim or wade).
Mid-June Saturday;
Travel: page 66.

MAN VERSUS HORSE MARATHON
Can a man beat a horse for £25,000?
Run at Llanwrtyd Wells, Powys (see page 85).
Mid-June Saturday; Travel: page 113.

HOPPINGS FAIR Newcastle upon Tyne (see page 61). Europe's largest. *Third or last week*; Travel: page 67.

GARTER CEREMONY St George's Chapel, Windsor Castle. The monarch and knights of the Order of the Garter process with spectacular robes and hats to mark this oldest order of chivalry (from about 1347) and a useful, if humble, garment. A few tickets can be booked. *19 June.*

APPLEBY HORSE FAIR is a Charter Fair that was instituted by James II in 1685. It is an amazing event that takes place each June, temporarily increasing the human population of this charming Cumbrian market town from 3,000 to around 15,000, and the horse population by a larger proportion.

Thousands of horse dealers – mostly gipsies – flock to the valley by the town to show off their horses, put them through their paces and celebrate gipsy life in general. While many arrive with modern caravans, others travel there for days and weeks in the traditional wheeled wooden wagons.

Here you will see people bidding for horses; running them into the River Eden to wash them down with detergent until the coats are covered in suds and then make them shine like new leather for sale; racing them up and down the narrow Roman road to show them off, pulling carts and traps at frightening speeds past each other on the narrow lane. If you love horses, beautiful scenery and seeing a unique culture surviving against the odds, it's the place to be.

Travelling people have always been viewed as eccentric – to put it mildly – by the rest of the population, and that view has been both romantic and suspicious. The concept of someone with no home, mortage, wages, pensions, bank, etc, has always puzzled the rest of the populace and made some resent gipsies, traditionally supposed to have special powers, such as fortune-telling, and inflicting curses.

Chariots and Chavs: surprising facts about gipsies and aristocrats

There were those secret signs outside your house for the door-to-door hawkers which marked a house as friendly, likely to give a cup of water or tea, likely to buy, or likely to show hostility.

A recent radio documentary on the Appleby Horse Fair came up with a telling remark from an 86-year-old fortune teller called Pearl. She was asked if, having spent her entire life on the road, she'd ever considered living in a house. 'No. It would be like putting a bird in a cage.'

The term 'gipsy' was a mistake made in Tudor times. People supposed they had come from Egypt, hence 'gipsy', although it now seems likely they originally came from India, leaving about 1,000 years ago. In fact, the Egyptians Act of 1530 was supposed to send them packing in 16 days. They clearly didn't go, as an Act of Queen Mary in 1554 complained that 'Egyptians' were plying their 'devlish and naughty practices and devices'. Four centuries later, they are still here.

So where *did* they come from?

The following quote from Zilla Roberts about Appleby Fair is fascinating. Recorded by John Ezard, and showing how Romany terms survived not as a separate language but mixed with English, it says:

> 'When the little chavvies gets up, they take the grails down the pani... then we all have bread and kel and a piece of stinger... Some of the old raklis dodikins to the gorgios. They go out with the jukells shushing and alot of muskros are in the pov.'

It is translated thus:

> 'The little children are asleep in the wagons. When they get up, they water the horses, then everyone has bread and cheese and a little bit of onion. Some of the old ladies tell people's fortunes. They go rabbiting with the dogs and a lot of policemen are in the field.'

Gorgios means non gipsies. Two words stand out to an ignorant layman like me. One is *Chavvies*. In vogue at the moment in mainstream English is the term a chav, meaning someone ill-educated, sometimes, of bad taste, dressing badly and with lots of cheap bling. It does *not* mean gipsy child, but that's perhaps where the word comes from.

The other more fascinating word in that quotation is *pani*, meaning water – a word for water used in India or Nepal.

The 'Indians' in Cowboys and Indians should not be so-called – it was famously a navigational error on the part of European explorers. But maybe the gipsies should be.

In Hertfordshire, back in the 1960s, the gipsies' greatest champion as they battled for a site to park their caravans safely in the county, was none other than local eccentric aristocrat Dame Barbara Cartland, writer of romantic fiction by the ton and Princess Diana's step-grandmother. Cartland would turn up in her white Rolls-Royce, dressed from head to toe in fluffy pink, befriending people who then suffered prejudice and disadvantage and were harried from place to place. She respected them, and they her, so much so that when that first site was established in Hatfield in 1964, it was called Barbaraville. It still is.

Who said fins ain't what they used to be?

SOME OF BRITAIN'S OLDEST, and oddest, ceremonies take place on the ocean wave. Environmentalists warn us that Britain's seas are overfished and we do not take the future of marine life seriously. In fact, Britons never have taken the fruits of the sea for granted, as many ancient ceremonies show.

In late May (usually Rogation Sunday) a lifeboat is used as a pulpit at **Hastings**, Sussex, for the annual **Blessing the Sea**. The thriving fishing community gathers on the shore to say the blessing while three churchmen sail out on the lifeboat and cast a wreath in the shape of a cross into the sea. Nearby **Brighton** has a Mackerel Fair in May at the Fishing Museum, which includes the **Blessing of the Nets**.

For many years fishing boats at **Brixham**, Devon used to gather together for Blessing the Fleet in late May (again usually Rogation Sunday), but Brixham, instead, has a rather moving **Blessing the Lifeboat** service (Travel: page 65) in early August, which takes place in the old fish market with the lifeboat tied up alongside, the sound of stirring old nautical hymns mixing with the cries of seagulls.

At **Whitstable**, Kent, on the high tide of St James's Day (25 July) the clergy and choir of St Peter's Church gather at Reeves Beach for the **Oyster Ceremony** service (Travel: page 68), while fishing boats bob offshore in a watery congregation.

At about the same time of year the **Tweedmouth Feast** (Travel: page 70), across the river from **Berwick-upon-Tweed** near the Scottish

SUMMER SOLSTICE

BAWMING THE THORN This ancient tradition takes place at Appleton Thorn, near Warrington, Cheshire, and involves dancing round a garlanded and beribboned tree, once said to be descended directly from the one that sprang up when Joseph of Arimathea (the man who asked Pontius Pilate for Jesus's body, which he laid in his own tomb) thrust border with Northumberland, sees a week of activities, including the **crowning of the Salmon Queen** on the Thursday. The Feast Service comes on a Sunday around 20 July and the rituals date back to 1292.

At the **Eyemouth Herring Queen Festival**, north of Berwick, about five miles into Scotland, in July, the flag-bedecked fishing fleet escorts the newly chosen Herring Queen from St Abbs, a few miles up the coast, into Eyemouth.

Perhaps the oldest and oddest such ceremony is the **Oyster Proclamation at Colchester**, Essex, on the last Friday in August or the first in September – depending on tides – which sees the spectacle of the mayor and councillors in full regalia setting forth by fishing boat to the oyster beds. These have belonged to the corporation at least since Richard I gave them the town in 1189, and probably longer.

The clerk reads aloud the Proclamation of 1256, which asserts that the rights have belonged to Colchester 'from the time beyond which memory runneth not to the contrary' and the company then toasts the Queen with gin and consumes special gingerbread. The mayor lowers the trawl and eats the first oyster of the season – whatever its condition.

The **Oyster Feast** is held in the town's Moot Hall in late October and up to 12,000 oysters are consumed with much pomp.

his staff in the ground when he landed at the Isle of Glastonbury. The Glastonbury Thorn itself flowers at the old Christmas, 5 January, and a sprig is always given to the monarch for her table. Puritan soldiers cut it down as idolatrous during the Civil War but clergymen secretly saved cuttings. *Saturday before 20/21 June, the longest day.*

DRUID CEREMONY, STONEHENGE The Most Ancient (doubtful) Order of Druids mark the summer solstice. In the past, police entered into the stone-age spirit by clubbing non-violent New Age travellers over the head to stop them partaking or even coming vaguely near (I have

A YORKSHIRE PUDDING, if you come from Tibet or somewhere, is a great British culinary invention (not a phrase that is often assembled, I admit) consisting of flour, water, possibly eggs and milk, and the batter forms a shape like a small bowl about two inches across to eat with roast dinner and fill with the accompanying gravy. Delicious! Some pubs do big ones about a foot across with the whole dinner inside the batter bowl. In Brawby, North Yorkshire, however, they make giant ones that children can sit in (looking rather like coracles) and paddle down rivers. To avoid the gone-soggy fate of normal Yorkshire puddings, they are first coated in several layers of yacht varnish. Many absurd British customs such as this go back into the mists of time. This one goes back to a lazy afternoon in a pub in the 1990s, when local sculptor Simon Thackray dreamed of floating down a river in a giant Yorkshire pudding.

Britain's most surreal boat race

Apparently, the process involves being read some kind of epic poem about a great Yorkshire pudding voyage written by another local character while the puddings float. A Yorkshire Pudding Orchestra sometimes provides entertainment. Sounds deeply eccentric. Critics have raised the question of whether it is right to use many bags of flour and dozens of eggs in this way, when people are starving, to which I say, 'Get a life and get a sense of humour.'

If such critics were donating all the money they waste on their sad existence to the starving, I might listen, but they fail to understand this planet has far too much food, it's just in the wrong hands. A few people having fun in Yorkshire aren't going to make any difference. Personally, I think it could be an Olympic event, possibly with a slalom where you have to dodge giant roast potatoes or else face a dunking in the fast-flowing gravy. Watch out for sausage submarines...

seen this). But in 1998 the Druids, who are arguably from completely the wrong era, were allowed in once more to chant their chants, etc. Midnight, dawn and noon. *Summer solstice, 20 or 21 June.*

FILLY LOO This folk-dancing-related village do at Ashmore, North Dorset (not far from Shaftesbury), involves dancing beside the village pond and features perennial British folk characters, such as the Green Man, Maid Marion, the Fool and the 'Obby 'Oss. There are stalls and food and later, a sinister torch-lit Horn Dance by six antlered deer-men is performed to eerie music. The atmosphere returns to the convivial with *Auld Lang Syne*-style dancing round the pond, virtually the entire village joining hands. *Friday nearest summer solstice.*

MIDSUMMER WATCH PARADE A strange carnival-like procession wends its way round Chester, including, typically, a family of giants, dragons, angels, fire-eaters, the Chester raven, a unicorn, hobby horses, the tree of life, green men, elephant and castle, camel, drummers and dancers. *Weekend nearest summer solstice.*

WORLD WORM-CHARMING CHAMPIONSHIPS Global worming comes to Willaston primary school, near Nantwich, Cheshire. Each of 144 teams of two gets a three-metre square plot in a field and half an hour to charm up the worms. The first year saw Tom Shufflebotham charm up 511 (still the world record) but most years have seen the winner count more than 300. Dancing, music and wiggling a fork are allowed but watering or drugs aren't. There's no worm abuse. 'It's a nice day out for them, they meet relations they haven't seen for a year. They're not bothered,' I was told. Nothing to writhe home about, then. *Late June Saturday.*

GOLOWAN FESTIVAL A Cornish cornucopia of music, drama, maritime stuff and mayhem based on Penzance. It culminates with Mazey Day, which offers anarchic street theatre, an 'Obby 'Oss, a well over-the-top

33

carnival parade featuring monsters, giants, enormous banners, etc. *A week around summer solstice*; Travel: page 66.

DUNMOW FLITCH TRIALS A flitch of bacon is awarded to a couple who do not repent of their marriage within a year and a day, after a long-winded trial (see page 118). *Every leap year, June, date varies*; Travel: page 130.

KNOLLYS ROSE Mansion House, City of London. An odd quit rent ceremony (see page 115). *24 June.*

WORLD TIN BATH CHAMPIONSHIPS 70 competitors race across the middle harbour in Castletown, Isle of Man, paddling tin baths. Been running for 40 years. *Date varies, could be June, July or August.*

JULY

HAT FAIR Held in Winchester, this is the biggest collection of street theatre in the south. If you want to see someone dressed as a gorilla unicycling along playing *Waltzing Matilda* on a mouth-organ while juggling with plastic exploding iguanas, this is the most likely place. People do wear a lot of hats, but it's more to do with the one on the ground with coins in. *First weekend in July*; Travel: page 67.

MUCH WENLOCK OLYMPIAN GAMES
The revival of Olympic Games in the modern era in 1896 is usually credited to Frenchman Pierre de Courbetin, and bully for him. Total rubbish, of course. In 1850 Dr William

Penny Brookes, a local magistrate and doctor, started the Olympian Games in this lovely Shropshire village. They still go on and include running, hurdling, archery, etc, and have from time to time had events such as 'blind wheelbarrow racing' and 'old woman's race for a pound of tea'. *Three day weekend early July*; Travel: page 68.

SOAPBOX CHALLENGE Downhill racing at Goodwood, West Sussex, in homemade carts reaching 62mph. Sadly, it's no longer scruffy urchins putting a set of wheels on a wooden soapbox, but serious whizzo designers

trying to get the last ounce of speed within the £1,000 per car budget. But it's still driven only by gravity and still dangerous. Part of the Goodwood **Festival of Speed**, an annual posh, petrolhead thingy with vintage cars, celebrities, etc. You usually can't go without advance tickets. *Early July.*

WORLD PEA-SHOOTING CHAMPIONSHIPS Contestants at the Village Green, Witcham near Ely, Cambridgeshire, fire a pea (by blowing it) down a 12-inch tube 12 feet towards a 12-inch target. Some entrants have fitted sights to their tubes and even – really, I have seen them – laser sights. *Early Saturday.*

WORLD PEA-THROWING CHAMPIONSHIPS Every July, at the Lewes Arms, Lewes, Sussex. Record at time of writing 44 metres. Injecting peas or varnishing them is not allowed, but growing special varieties is. At the same pub later in July: **DWILE-FLUNKING**, a local spelling of dwile-flonking (see page 90). *Early*; Travel: page 71.

BLACK CHERRY FAIR Windsor Street, Chertsey, Surrey (see page 62). *Second Saturday.*

WORLD VIKING LONGBOAT RACES CHAMPIONSHIP Peel, Isle of Man. Hairy types in horned helmets re-enact the race of raiding Norsemen to land. Pillage no longer compulsory. The Peel team ought to enter the orange races at Totnes next month. *Usually second Saturday.*

WORLD SNAIL-RACING CHAMPIONSHIPS The hallowed Centre Court, as it were, of snail racing is a damp circle of cloth at Grimston Cricket Pitch, Congham, near King's Lynn, Norfolk. The snails race from an inner circle to an outer circle on the command 'Ready, steady, slow!' Snailmaster Neil Riseborough says he can tell good racers when he selects them from what he calls his stud farm by the way their shells curl. 'They usually take two-and-a-half to three minutes, but the going depends on the humidity and strength of daylight. The world record owner was Archie, who did it in two minutes. We were gobsmacked, I've never seen a snail move like that.' Sounds thrilling. The winner gets a pewter tankard, filled with the best wet Norfolk lettuce. Snail heaven. Plus fete and barbecue. *Mid July Saturday.*

LAMMAS FAIR Exeter, Devon (see page 61). Mayoral procession, then craft fair and festival. *Tuesday before third Wednesday (sometimes earlier).*

HONITON FAIR Honiton, Devon (see page 61). *Tuesday after 19 July.*

TRAM SUNDAY Fleetwood, Lancashire. Vintage transport affair; it is best to arrive by tram from Blackpool (see page 95). *Third Sunday.*

SWAN UPPING This astonishing complex ritual starts from the premise that all swans in Britain are royal birds and belong to the Queen. Except those belonging to the Dyers' and Vintners' companies, of course. The ritual involves a parade of boats catching all the swans on the Thames, marking them to identify to whom they belong (as if it mattered); weeks of work by officials in archaic uniforms swanning about in special boats and impossible to justify for any purpose whatsoever. Some British traditions need no justification other than being traditional. *20–24 July.*

KNILL CEREMONY Virgins prance round pyramid, St Ives, Cornwall, every fifth year: 2011, 2016, etc (see page 155). *25 July.*

KINGSBRIDGE FAIR Kingsbridge, Devon (see page 61). *Late July week.*

SCARECROW FESTIVAL Muston, near Filey, North Yorkshire. Thoroughly off-putting for crows, but not crowds, for a week when the surreal, the humorous and even the macabre effigies take over the place. *Late July weekend.*

MARLDON APPLE PIE FAIR Marldon, Devon (see page 62). *Last weekend.*

BRITISH LAWNMOWER RACING GRAND PRIX Bat and Ball Pub, Wisborough Green near Billingshurst, West Sussex. *Date and month varies (ticket only).*

AUGUST

ALTERNATIVE SCOTTISH GAMES At Castle Douglas, Dumfries & Galloway. Normal Highland Games are odd enough, but here we have games such as Gird 'n' Cleek (bowling a large metal hoop along with a rod, and this is the world championship final) and Spinning the Peerie (whirling a top with string), plus Hurlin' the Curlin' Stane, Flingin' the Herd's Bunnet and Balmaclellan skittles. You suspect they might be making them up. *First Sunday, unless the first is a Sunday.*

BLESSING THE LIFEBOAT Brixham, Devon (see box, page 30). *Early August;* Travel: page 65.

SOUTH QUEENSFERRY FAIR AND BURRY MAN Bizarre, rather frightening figure of a man totally covered with burdock burrs, who stalks around the day before the fair leaning on striped poles collecting money. South Queensferry, at Forth bridges southside. It is good luck to meet him, despite his gruesome appearance (see box, page 38). *Second Saturday, Burry Man the day before;* Travel: page 69.

HENGISTBURY HEAD KITE FESTIVAL Bournemouth, Dorset. Past highlights have included man-lifting kites and parachuting teddy bears. *Usually third Saturday;* Travel: page 67.

CHILLI FIESTA West Dean, near Chichester, West Sussex. More types of chilli than are imaginable. Chilli beer, chilli pictures, chilli pottery, chilli lamps, chilli sauces and salsas, chilli growers and chilli seeds. *Three-day weekend mid-August.*

LAWNMOWER 12-HOUR ENDURANCE RACE Brinsbury Agricultural College, Wisborough Green, near Petworth, West Sussex (see page 75). Ride-on and run-behind classes. Advance ticket admission only. *Mid-August.*

ORANGE RACES Contestants race through the streets of Totnes, Devon, kicking oranges while trying to keep them intact to the finishing line (otherwise they'd be pipped at the post). Claimed to commemorate the visit of the great sailor and victor against the Spanish armada Sir Francis Drake (so they'll be navel oranges then) when an orange-seller dropped

FEB MAR APR

S COTLAND'S SOUTH QUEENSFERRY on the Firth of Forth is a fascinating place at any time. The quiet former fishing village and ferry landing for those coming from the kingdom of Fife has the two enormous Forth bridges leaping high over its rooftops across the sky.

But sometimes, as you stand on the waterfront marvelling at science fact, science fiction seems to arrive. An alien stalks round the town – or is it a terrifying Thing From The Swamp? It cannot be human, this puffy figure walking strangely and covered in what looks like rough brown-green fur.

You are lucky, local legend has it, if you meet this creature, the **Burry Man**, and to mark it you must give a coin to one of his attendants. The Burry Man is central to **South Queensferry festival week** (Travel: page 69). The festival starts on the second Saturday in August but he tours the streets the day before, but who, how or why is he?

Why? is quickest to answer. Nobody has a clue. Fertility figure, pagan scapegoat, fishing good-luck charm – take your pick, the festival is far too old for anyone to remember. There is a mention of the Burry Man as if he were already long established from 1740.

Who and how it is done are remarkable. The volunteer who has the honour of being the year's Burry Man must first spend days scouring the hedgerows for burrs, the bristly hooked balls that are the fruit of the burdock, a common British weed. These burrs with their hundreds of tiny hooks fasten themselves to your clothing as you pass the plant, and Nature would have long ago sued the makers of Velcro for

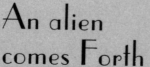

An alien comes Forth

copying the idea, if Nature had a lawyer. Getting them out of a child's hair, or sheepdog's fur, is not amusing.

At 7am of the appointed day it all starts at the pub where the volunteer is wrapped in thick clothing including a balaclava helmet and thick woollen tights (often a hot August day!), then layers upon layers of burrs are applied until only his eyes and mouth are showing. The Burry Man cannot put his legs together or his arms by his side all day, lest they stick together, so he sort of wades around, using his two flowery beribboned staffs to support himself.

A flag is tied around his waist like an apron and a hat of flowers on his head. He sets off on his rounds of the town at 9am, preceded by a bell-ringer and helped by two attendants, collecting money and whisky (sipped through a straw) wherever he calls. He cannot possibly go to the toilet, so he can drink nothing besides the obligatory whisky all day. Somehow he carries this on till returning to the pub at 6pm. The volunteer has to be fit, alcohol- and heat-tolerant, and keen, as he usually does it once a year for around 25 years before handing on the flowery staves.

No one has yet suggested feminism requires a Burry Woman (sponsored by Velcro, possibly) for the good reason that if they embraced, you could never get them apart. Anyway, the Burry Man appears to have no particular sex, given his shapeless bulk.

An old participant recalled that the Burry Man was so grievously scratched by evening, that he had to be dabbed all over with iodine. Today, thicker materials help to prevent this.

Then it's back to the waterfront to have a beer and watch cars and trains soaring as high as aircraft above you. When the enormous cantilevered arms of the railway bridge were reaching out to meet each other in 1890, they were so huge that they couldn't exactly meet. The reason was that although perfectly made and aligned, they were so big that the effect of the sun on the eastern side in the morning, and the west in the afternoon, could bend the structure enough to prevent perfect alignment. The solution was to send men inside the massive tubes, each large enough to take an express train, to light bonfires to trick the bridge, as it were, into thinking that it was sunny on both sides. The ends aligned perfectly, the bolts were dropped in and the last plates riveted up. But did all the men get out of the smoke-filled tubes? Is the bridge haunted?

a load of oranges in the steeply sloping main road. Probable twin town: Peel, Isle of Man. *Mid-August.*

CORACLE RACING Cilgerran, near Cardigan, Pembrokeshire. Pre-Roman form of transport thrives on a Welsh river (see page 86). *Mid-August Saturday*; Travel: page 112.

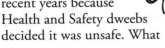

GARLIC FESTIVAL Isle of Wight. Garlic cheese, garlic soup, garlic beer, even garlic ice-cream, and many other goodies for garlic gourmands. Plus a massive funfair. But no snogging for three days. *Mid-August weekend.*

WORLD PLANK-WALKING CHAMPIONSHIPS In a muddy creek at Queenborough on the Isle of Sheppey, Kent, people queue up to walk the plank and make a splash in fancy dress. *Mid-August Sunday*; Travel: page 71.

ILLUMINATED CARNIVAL PROCESSIONS The start of a West Country seasonal obsession of amazing complexity. *The Wessex Grand Prix Circuit: Sturminster Newton, the third Thursday in August/weekend before Bank Holiday.* See September and November for processions later in the season.

BURNING OF T'OWD BARTLE An ugly effigy with lit-up eyes is paraded round West Witton, Wensleydale, Yorkshire, and burnt spectacularly for reasons totally forgotten (see box, opposite). *Nearest Saturday to 24 August*; Travel: page 65.

BIRDMAN, OR BOGNOR BIRDMAN (As successful as that of Alcatraz.) Dozens of hopefuls in various serious (hang-gliders etc) or joke (skateboarding cow, Mary Poppins outfit) one-man gliding outfits try to win a cash prize by reaching a set distance after jumping off the end of the pier in Bognor Regis, West Sussex, cheered on by huge crowds. Oddly it was relocated to Worthing twice in recent years because Health and Safety dweebs decided it was unsafe. What

The ugly old enemy

IF YOU HAPPEN to meet a hideously ugly giant lurching through the streets with its eyes weirdly lit up and accompanied by strange incantations, don't worry, it's not an alien life-form – at least not if it's on the Saturday nearest 24 August (St Bartholomew's Day) in **West Witton**, in Wensleydale, Yorkshire. The effigy is used in a custom called **Burning of t'Owd Bartle**, which involves a march round the village chanting an old verse about Bartle's doom:

> At Pen Hill crags he tore his rags,
> At Hunter's Thorn he blew his horn,
> At Capplebank Stee he brak his knee,
> At Grassgill Beck he brak his neck,
> At Waddam's End he couldn't fend,
> At Grassgill End he made his end.

The procession ends with his being hurled onto a massive bonfire stuffed with hidden fireworks. Quite who Bartle was that he still deserves such ire has been forgotten – St Bartholomew did little to offend and the date near the saint's day is thought to be a coincidence. The commonest theory is that he was an evil robber who was chased to his doom, as described in the verse, by a gang of outraged villagers. Either way, it makes an excuse for a weekend of village festivities including a tug-of-war and fancy dress parade.

– a bunch of nutters jumping to the sea in home-made contraptions not *safe*? Why on earth didn't somebody say? So check which to go to. *Mid or late Sunday*; Travel: page 64.

BECA MOUNTAIN RACE Men dress up as women, run up hills and chop down gates. Near Fishguard, Wales (see page 83). *Last Saturday in August.*

SCARECROW FESTIVAL About 100 life-size scarecrows on a theme take over the village of Kettlewell in Upper Wharfedale, Yorkshire Dales, for

a week. Also many other villages including Hayling Island, Hampshire. Children love them. Pet crows probably not. *Mid-August.*

Day of Syn The Kent village of Dymchurch re-enacts the days of 1780 when smugglers with their contraband outwitted the beach patrols of dragoons (see box, page 47). *Every second August Bank Holiday Monday;* Travel: page 66.

Bog-snorkelling World Championships Swimming 60yds through stinking black water, outside Neuadd Arms Hotel, Llanwrtyd Wells, Powys. Dress 'smart, no jeans, plus flippers and snorkel of course'. *Last weekend (bank holiday);* Travel: page 63.

English Open Chainsaw Competition Sounds noisy and dangerous, which it is if you don't know what you're doing. The insane buzz of contestants going at logs like demented beavers on drugs while woodchips fly everywhere is the speed carving event, but there are some terrific sculptures produced, most of which are auctioned off for charity (if punters can stump something up). Usually at Cheshire Game & Country Fair, Tatton Park, Manchester. *Last weekend (bank holiday).*

Plague Sunday Service Cucklet Church, Eyam, Derbyshire (see page 180). *Last Sunday in August.*

Sussex Bonfire Society Marching Season Starts in Rotherfield. Procession of dramatic figures in horned helmets, Roman armour, topical enemies built in effigy, etc. First of many until 21 November (see box, page 52). *Last Monday (bank holiday).*

The Water Game A rather wet five-a-side football game at Bourton-on-the-Water, Gloucestershire, because the pitch is the bed of the river Windrush. Coincides with the local fete. *Last Monday (bank holiday).*

SEPTEMBER

BONFIRE SOCIETIES Sussex. See *Sussex Bonfire Society Marching Season* opposite. *August–November, various.*

THE GREAT BRITISH DUCK RACE Another world-record holder, for the number of plastic ducks chucked in a navigable waterway. At Molesey Lock, near Hampton Court, Surrey. If we think tipping quarter of a million toy ducks into a river where they slowly spread like some insane blue oil slick is a great idea, we must be quackers! Well it's for charity, there are huge cash prizes, and the ducks get scooped up and recycled. Not in orange sauce, sadly. *First Sunday*; Travel: page 67.

ILLUMINATED CARNIVAL PROCESSIONS A West Country seasonal obsession of amazing complexity, involving floats costing up to £20,000 with hundreds of bulbs forming an astounding mile-and-a-half long procession of garishly lit floats to defy the darkness of this time of year. It's like Mardi Gras with scrumpy (strong cider). There may be *squibbers* carrying strings of exploding fireworks or pouring flammable liquid along the route and lighting it. The floats, or carts, are just sensational. No fewer than 70 towns and villages have clubs with thousands of volunteers to build these things. Arranged in three official leagues (you will have to check further locally): *The Wessex Grand Prix Circuit:* Sturminster Newton, the third Thursday in August/weekend before Bank Holiday; then Trowbridge; Mere; Frome; Shaftesbury; Gillingham; Castle Cary & Ansford; Wincanton; Warminster. *The South Somerset Federation Of Carnival Committees Circuit:* Wellington last Saturday in September; then Ilminster; Chard; Taunton; Yeovil. See November for carnivals later in the season.

WORLD BLACK-PUDDING-THROWING CHAMPIONSHIPS The Royal Oak pub, Ramsbottom, Bury, Lancashire. Contestants bowl three black puddings each at 21 Yorkshire puddings set on a platform 20ft high, attempting to knock down the most (see page 44). *First or second weekend*; Travel: page 64.

THE BLACK-PUDDING-THROWING World Championships (see page 64) take place each year at a pub in or near Ramsbottom, Lancashire. You'd imagine the rest of the world hasn't many competitors at this arcane sport, and that it was really Lancashire's for the taking (like the Americans' so-called World Series, a sport virtually no-one else plays) but you'd be wrong. The sport is throwing black puddings (a kind of sausage made from blood, which like the haggis, is an acquired taste) up to a mound of Yorkshire puddings placed on a platform, with the aim of knocking as many as possible of the latter over with the former.

I was invited to the '140th World Championships' and began to suspect some serious leg pulling when a self-styled 'Black Pudding historian' offered the following rationale for this amiably daft sport.

'It started in the War of the Roses [the civil war between the Houses of Lancaster and York] when the two sides had run so low on ammunition they were reduced to throwing food at each other. This would be Yorkshire puddings and black puddings.' This ignores the fact that a Yorkshire pudding is so light it can't possibly hurt the enemy (except those served at Midhurst Grammar School circa 1967, which were deadly).

The truly bizarre world of black-pudding-throwing

ST GILES FAIR Oxford (see page 63). *Monday and Tuesday after first Sunday*; Travel: page 69.

CHEESE AND ONION FAIR Newton Abbot, Devon (see page 62). And no, it's not followed by a Salt 'n' Vinegar or Smokey Bacon Fair. Take it seriously, *please*! *First or second Tuesday.*

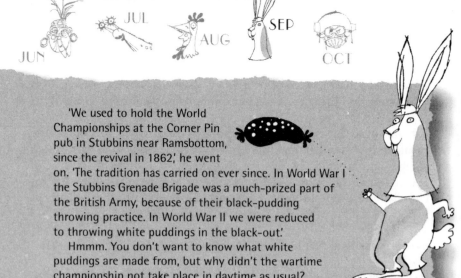

'We used to hold the World Championships at the Corner Pin pub in Stubbins near Ramsbottom, since the revival in 1862,' he went on. 'The tradition has carried on ever since. In World War I the Stubbins Grenade Brigade was a much-prized part of the British Army, because of their black-pudding throwing practice. In World War II we were reduced to throwing white puddings in the black-out.'

Hmmm. You don't want to know what white puddings are made from, but why didn't the wartime championship not take place in daytime as usual? Weren't Yorkshire puddings rationed?

Leaving aside such doubts, I can attest to making the journey to Ramsbottom, where I was fed black pudding for breakfast as feverish excitement mounted on the day of the World Championships. On arrival at the pub, I was told I was to present the World Championship prizes, a great honour.

Battle commenced, although some contestants who came out of the bar seemed rather tired and emotional as their black puddings soared hopelessly off target. Rather worryingly good was a character dressed as a giant rabbit, and I stood there wondering how hallucinogenic black pudding could be and hoping the rabbit wouldn't win.

Eventually I had to award the prize jointly to an Australian chap who was extremely tired and emotional (so much so he kept forgetting what was going on) but had a deadly aim, and a local boy. They both won a Gold Pudding mounted on a display board. When I say 'gold' and 'mounted', I should add that it was a normal black pudding hastily nailed to a bit of wood in front of them and then sprayed gold and handed over while still dripping wet. Still, how many people have got a trophy like that, eh? I gave the giant rabbit a prize for being best-dressed tosser. What a deeply strange day, I thought, as I trammed back to Manchester.

HORN DANCE Abbots Bromley, Staffordshire (said to be oldest in Europe). Old reindeer horns mounted on dancers' wooden heads prance round the parish, to celebrate hunting rights in Needwood Forest (see box, page 47). *Monday after first Sunday after 4 September.*

RAW-ONION-EATING CONTEST Part of Newent Onion Fayre, near Gloucester. It'll bring tears to your eyes, obviously. *Second Saturday.*

RUSHBEARING FESTIVAL Sowerby Bridge, Calderdale, Yorkshire. The rush cart pulled by 60 men in traditional garb travels ten miles through villages accompanied by dancers and street entertainment, calling, of course, at all the pubs. Celebrates ancient bearing of fresh rushes for church floor every autumn; takes place in about 40 other villages at various dates but with less razzmatazz. *Early weekend.*

WIDECOMBE FAIR Widecombe, Devon (see page 60). *Second Tuesday.*

BARNSTAPLE FAIR Barnstaple, Devon. *Wednesday nearest 17 September.*

WORLD GURNING CHAMPIONSHIPS These involve pulling vile and frankly unbelievable faces, at Egremont Crab Fair, Cumbria – an event which has neither crabs nor fairs, but includes the Applecart Parade, where children vie for apples thrown from a cart, and sports such as Cumbrian wrestling. It's been legal only since a 1267 charter. In the early 21st century, grown men were having all their teeth removed, to compete better. *Saturday nearest 18 September;* Travel: page 71.

CLIPPING THE CHURCH Embracing the church, in lovely Painswick, Gloucestershire (see page 179). *Sunday on or after 19 September.*

HORSEMAN'S SUNDAY Service on horseback, St John's, Hyde Park, London W1 (see page 180). *Third Sunday.*

GREAT BRITISH CHEESE FESTIVAL Includes cheese-tossing, which could be messy with a ripe Somerset brie. The haughty French President De Gaulle said that you couldn't hope to govern a country with 250 cheeses. At the last Cheese Festival here there were 450 British cheeses, so perhaps we've again beaten the French at their own game (being ungovernable, that is). Tough cheddar, vieux fromages. Cardiff Castle (or Blenheim Place or similar; www.thecheeseweb.com). *Last weekend.*

MOP FAIR Marlborough, Wiltshire (see page 63). Little Mop, then a week later Big Mop. *Saturday before and after Michaelmas (29 September).*

UNBRIDLED LUST MAY have been expunged from many a ritual, but in Abbots Bromley, Staffordshire, they have a good old fertility dance on the first Monday after 4 September. The dancers collect the horns from St Nicholas Church at 7.30am in the morning. The **Horn Dance** involves six men with reindeer horns, plus Maid Marion (a man in drag), a Hobby Horse (as at Padstow and Minehead), a jester and a musician with an accordion. The vicar blesses them, then they dance lewdly all round the village until 8pm when they return to be blessed again, just to be on the safe side. This is folk-dance royalty, going back at least to the 11th century.

Another horn ceremony based on lustiness is the **Charlton Horn Fair** in the London SE7 suburb, held on the second Sunday in June. It dates from when King John had his wicked way with the local miller's wife, and in desperation at facing the cuckolded husband, said he could hold an annual fair, which locals naturally called the Horn Fair. It's an ordinary sort of fair today, with stalls and so on, but there's a procession involving King John, the miller and some horn decorations.

The vicar and the lewd – from horn to syn

The **Day of Syn** (Travel: page 66), which overcomes the Kent village of Dymchurch, down on Romney Marsh, has little to do with sins of the flesh, but is named after Dr Syn, the smuggling rector of Dymchurch. The event, held every second August Bank Holiday Monday, returns the village to the days of 1780 when smugglers with their contraband outwitted the beach patrols of dragoons. All this is re-enacted in costume with a fleet of smuggling boats under the command of the Scarecrow (as Dr Syn was known off duty). There is street theatre all morning and a fair in the afternoon in this village best known for the splendid miniature steam railway, the **Romney, Hythe and Dymchurch Railway** (the quickest engine being called, of course, *Dr Syn*). And don't miss Hythe's gruesome secret: the stacks of bones in St Leonard's Church (see page 169).

APR MAY JUN

OCTOBER

BONFIRE SOCIETIES, Sussex, see *August*, page 42.

ILLUMINATED CARNIVALS West Country, see *September*, page 43.

HORSESHOE AND FAGGOT-CUTTING CEREMONY Bizarre quit rent (see page 116). High Court, London. *Date varies.*

WORLD MANGOLD-HURLING CHAMPIONSHIPS In which the humble mangold or mangelwurzel (a root crop that features in local band, The Wurzels' hit *Whur be yon blackbird be?*) is hurled at 'the Norman' (another

Donkers? No Ma'am, it's conkers, and bonkers

IF YOU HAPPEN TO hear cries of 'iddley, iddley ack, my first smack' or 'hobily, hobily honker, my first conker' one October, you should either check your medication isn't excessive or you're on the village green at Ashton, near Oundle, Northamptonshire. These, I'm told, are traditional cries at the **World Conker Championships**.

Well, they weren't at my school, although I do have happy memories of throwing sticks up into horse chestnut trees to gain the shiny brown nuts, which we Brits call conkers, used on the ends of bits of string to battle with rivals in playground attrition. You hold your conker up and the other guy tries to smash it to pieces with his. When he misses or tangles your string (which causes a yell of 'Strings!') it's your go to bash hell out of his. The history of 'oners' becoming 'sixers' through successive victories, the feared 'cheesers' (a hemispherical twin conker but with a sharp edge) ... has it all gone the way of penny-for-the-guy as our children instead play electronic games?

In fact, the usual hopeless bureaucrats and compensation culture are getting in the way. Certain humourless prats running schools

mangelwurzel). Sherston, Wiltshire. Where's it near? 'Nowhere, really. A bit near Old Sodbury, and a bit near Malmesbury,' said a villager. You get the picture. Turnips allowed if you can't find mangelwurzels? 'You are *joking*? Quite unsuitable for sporting purposes.' *First Sunday in October.*

GOOSE FAIR Held in Nottingham. It's huge (see page 60). *Starts Wednesday before first Thursday.*

HONEY FAIR Callington, Cornwall (see page 62). *First Wednesday.*

GOOSEY FAIR Tavistock, Devon (see page 62). *Second Wednesday.*

WORLD CONKER CHAMPIONSHIPS Village Green, Ashton, near Oundle, Peterborough, Cambridgeshire (see box, below). *Second weekend.*

have banned conker fights, or insisted children wear goggles to prevent eye injuries from flying debris. And even more stupid council jobsworths have cut down conker trees in case pedestrians are injured by conkers falling, or more likely by the sticks thrown up to get them down or small boys falling out of the branches. May their nuts shrivel and fall off. Actually, it's like banning the old-fashioned double-decker buses because so many people were allegedly injured falling off the open platform. When you ask the creeps in charge for actual figures of injuries, they go, 'Er...'. Do you know anyone who has been thus injured? Mind you, when I was at school the conkers game would continue on the platform of the No 3 bus going up Crystal Palace hill, which was probably pushing our luck.

Conkers is such a familiar game if you're a native that it didn't at first strike me as particularly eccentric but, looked at globally, it certainly is. An American woman asked me at a lecture I gave over there: 'What's that strange game you guys play with your nuts?' It took me an embarrassingly long time to realise she was talking about good old British conkers, after she suggested 'Donkers or something?'

PACK MONDAY FAIR Sherborne, Dorset (see page 63). *First Monday after 10 October.*

MOP FAIR Stratford-upon-Avon (see page 63) and **Runaway Mop Fair** on the following Friday week. Also Abingdon, Oxfordshire. *12 October, unless a Sunday, then 13 October.*

MOP FAIR AND ROAST Warwick (see page 63). *Friday and Saturday following 12 October, Runaway Mop a week later.*

HERRING DAY Odd to celebrate a smelly and perhaps dull fish but, in fact, the story of Great Yarmouth's 'silver darlings' is rather fascinating. Eat the things, make rope, learn how they launched 1,000 ships. But don't bring your pet fish. They'd be gutted. *Third Sunday approx*; Travel: page 67.

THE BIG APPLE IN MUCH MARCLE Weekend celebration of apple orchards, rare varieties, cider making and much marcling in general, at Much Marcle, on A449 between Ross-on-Wye and Ledbury, Herefordshire. Similar events at Binstead, Isle of Wight; Sandling, near Maidstone, Kent; Sulgrave, Oxfordshire; Gressenhall, Dereham, Norfolk; and Blackmoor, near Petersfield, Hampshire at about same time. *Mid-October.*

MINCE-PIE-EATING COMPETITION Wookey Hole, Somerset. It makes you feel queasy to think about it! Someone ate 46 in ten minutes to win £1,000 recently. It wasn't John Prescott, but a woman called Sonya Thomas who has also eaten 65 hard-boiled eggs in 6min 40 sec. Respect! *Late October or, often, mid-November*; Travel: page 68.

NOVEMBER

ILLUMINATED CARNIVAL PROCESSIONS A West Country seasonal obsession of amazing complexity. *The Somerset County Guy Fawkes Carnival Association Circuit* (correct from 2012): **Bridgwater**: *first Saturday in November*; **Weston-super-Mare**: *the following Friday*; **North Petherton**: *second Saturday*; **Burnham-on-Sea**: *following Monday*; **Shepton Mallet**: *following Wednesday*; **Wells**: *third Friday*; **Glastonbury**: *third Saturday*. See September for carnivals earlier in the year.

STICKLEPATH FIRESHOW Play enacted by 10-foot puppets ending with the villain being consigned to flames. Finch Foundry Field, Sticklepath, near Okehampton, Devon, 19.30. Numbers limited. *5 November.*

BONFIRE SOCIETIES AND SPECTACULAR PROCESSIONS Lewes *5 November* (Travel: page 68), Battle *Saturday near 5 November* (Travel: page 64) and throughout Sussex; Ottery St Mary, Honiton, Devon (see box, pages 52–3).

TURNING THE DEVIL'S BOULDER Shebbear, near Holsworthy, Devon (see box, page 54). *5 November.*

HATHERLEIGH FIRE FESTIVAL Devon (see box, page 53). *First Wednesday after 5 November.*

FIRING THE FENNY POPPERS Vicar firing weird cannons, Fenny Stratford, Bedfordshire (see page 179). *11 November.*

WROTH SILVER RENT PAID Knightlow, Derbyshire (see page 116). *11 November.*

MOP FAIR Cirencester, Gloucestershire (see page 63). *Mondays before and after Martinmas (11 November)* or three Mondays if that day is a Monday.

BIGGEST LIAR IN THE WORLD COMPETITION The Bridge Inn, Santon Bridge, Holmrook, Cumbria, evening; includes 'tatie pot' supper (and bright green beer served by 8-ft tall barmaids). Date can vary. *17 November.*

The burning passions
that come out at night

REMEMBER, REMEMBER THE FIFTH OF NOVEMBER? Citizens of several English towns where Guy Fawkes Night is celebrated with more than usual blazing ferocity have not had much chance to forget it since the old conspirator was caught in 1605.

Lewes, East Sussex, normally one of Britain's sleepiest county towns but once the scene of fiery executions, literally explodes into action with five very serious bonfire societies parading in armour or full costume and carrying flaming torches. They take various routes, race blazing tar barrels into the river, have a mass procession at 7.45pm then split off for rival and spectacularly sculptural bonfire creations and salvoes of fireworks.

Religious zealotry, perhaps more often associated with Ulster, surfaces: 'No Popery' banners are carried and, until recently, an effigy of the Pope was burnt along with Fawkes. Here, however, the slogans are echoes of historical rather than present enmity – after all, the Catholic Gunpowder Plot in 1605 was just a few years after 17 Protestant martyrs were burnt at the stake in Lewes during the brief, Catholic reign of Mary I. Their names are proudly hung from banners across the streets.

Be in town early (Travel: page 68) and leave late to avoid road closures and traffic congestion, and, to fit in with the rowdy locals as the pubs close, it's best to learn the words of 'Sussex by the Sea', which is sung lustily as the bonfires die down. In recent years the town has been so crowded that some pubs haven't opened at all on the night. Shops are boarded up against the scrum.

Topical hate figures have often been burnt in effigy, such as Hitler or Napoleon at various dates, or even the editor of a local paper who was foolish enough to criticise the whole bonfire society shenanigans.

Not that Lewes is unique. Thirty Sussex villages share this ritual, based on a distant pagan past with fantastical sculptures, untraceable symbols and costumes better than the Mardi Gras. The **Sussex bonfire season** is ignited at **Rotherfield** on the last Monday in August, and burns through **Uckfield** in September, **Fletching** on the third Saturday in October, before exploding at **Littlehampton** on the last Saturday.

The anti-Catholicism is little evident outside Lewes, and at Littlehampton Guy Fawkes isn't much mentioned – but then the event (motto: 'We burn, to do good') takes place on land donated by

the Duke of Norfolk who owns the nearby splendid Arundel Castle. The duke is traditionally England's premier Roman Catholic and landlord of many of those taking part in the celebrations.

At **Battle** near Hastings an amazing and politically topical sculpture, built over at least a month, is blown to smithereens in a piece of noisy street theatre near Battle Abbey on a Saturday near 5 November. Other towns, such as Guildford, Surrey, had their celebrations banned after 19th-century rioting between bonfire societies and troops, but in Battle they proudly tell of how the authorities were outwitted in the 1920s. They tried to stop the fire being lit, so decoy rubbish fires were started at the other end of the town; while police were dealing with those, the bonfire supporters threaded through the alleyways and footpaths with great bundles of wood and barrels of tar and set a proper blaze going. It was too late for the authorities, who wisely gave up.

Robertsbridge (Travel: page 69) has the last of Sussex's spectacular celebrations on the third Saturday of November, with a procession comprising a thousand costumed people from 23 bonfire societies.

Topical enemies are set ablaze – recently it was the fat cat bosses of privatised utility companies and the National Lottery. As a member of the Robertsbridge Bonfire Society explained: 'It hasn't got all that much to do with Guy Fawkes but, as I understand it, goes back to a pagan festival. It was just lucky that Fawkes made his attempt to blow up parliament within three weeks of the old celebration.'

A Sussex fire festival with a dramatic difference is held at **Rye**, usually on a mid-November Saturday, where a boat was traditionally burnt on the Saltings, in memory of burning the boats of captured French raiders.

Blazing tar barrels are also much in evidence at the culmination of a day of celebrations at **Ottery St Mary**, Devon, near Honiton (Travel: page 65), on 5 November, or the 4th if the 5th is a Sunday. Nine are carried through the village on prescribed routes, men with their hands and arms swathed in sacking carrying each until the heat becomes unbearable. This goes on until around 11.45pm and ends in a huge bonfire. **Hatherleigh**, near Okehampton, Devon, has another fire festival, usually on the first Wednesday after 5 November.

(CONTINUED OVERLEAF)

JUN

The burning passions that come out at night

Britain's oddest 5 November ceremony can also be found in Devon – at **Shebbear** near Holsworthy. **Turning the Devil's Boulder** dates back to well before Guy Fawkes. The massive stone lying outside the churchyard is said to have been dropped by the Devil on his way to harm the village, and it is turned by the villagers each 5 November after a deliberately discordant peal of bells is rung to drive Old Nick away – making a clamour to drive out devils is an almost worldwide folk custom. The Turning has gone on for centuries, but during World War II it was felt that it might be inappropriate and was dropped in 1940. The desperate war news only got worse, so the custom went ahead after all, a week late. It was felt no stone should be left unturned to help Britain's fortunes. The fortunes of war slowly improved.

SUSSEX BONFIRE MARCHING SEASON CLOSES Robertsbridge (see box, page 53). *Usually third Saturday*; Travel: page 69.

BLACKSMITH'S PROCESSION To celebrate St Clement, patron saint of blacksmiths, an anvil is dragged around Mayfield, East Sussex, and fired with gunpowder at various points, with an effigy of 'Old Clem'. There is a re-enactment in the church of the temptation of St Dunstan by the Devil, dressed as a woman, who is grabbed by the blacksmith's tongs on the nose and leaps all the way to Tunbridge Wells, making a hole to start the famous spring of sulphurous waters. 6.30pm. *Last Saturday*.

ETON WALL GAME Pointless, brutal and incomprehensible and therefore much loved at the great Berkshire public school (see page 86). *Saturday nearest St Andrew's Day (30 November)*.

SANTA RUN Every year, thousands of Santas descend on sleepy Newtown in mid-Wales to make a 4.5-mile charity run. No reindeer or sleighs allowed, just a sea of red-and-white Santas. *Saturday in late November or early December*; Travel: page 69.

SCOURING OF THE CHRISTMAS TREE The Wimborne Militia blast muskets over the Dorset town's tree. It was banned for making children cry in 2008, but later decided children *should* be frightened by the unexpected from time to time if their parents were too stupid to take them away when warned. The Militia also blamed some serious disasters in the town on the ceremony being stopped (it's like wassailing in that regard), so it was resumed in 2009. A spokesman said (and don't analyse this too closely): 'The Wimborne Militia are delighted that this tradition can be re-established and a sensible solution has been found to ensure evil spirits lurk no longer in this town.' *Last Saturday afternoon in November.*

DECEMBER

MISTLETOE DAY This is part of the Mistletoe festival held in Tenbury Wells, Worcestershire, which is, it seems, the mistletoe capital of Britain and the producer of the world's best-quality mistletoe, a seasonally important parasite that preys on apple tress around here. There are three days of mistletoe auctions (usually three Tuesdays over three weeks) for the trade. On Mistletoe Day a procession, street entertainment, a druid, blessing of the crop, a mistletoe Queen, crowned by, in recent years, the best-known mistletoe vendor in Britain, Eddie Grundy of radio soap *The Archers* (or rather Trevor Harrison, the local actor who plays him). 'I'm just popping over to Tenbury, Clarrie, love…' *Usually first Saturday*; Travel: page 68.

GREAT CHRISTMAS PUDDING RACE Teams of competitors in great fancy dress – reindeer, the Queen, Jordan – hurtle round the West Piazza of London's Covent Garden Market, tackling insanely difficult inflatable or watery obstacles while trying to keep a Christmas pud on a plate. They have to add eyes, holly, etc at certain points but sadly no flaming brandy. Silver sixpence detectors are not allowed. Cracking fun, for charity. There may also be one in Brighton the following Sat. There was in 2010. *First Saturday, usually at 11.00am.*

BURNING THE CLOCKS A bizarre ritual in Brighton, Sussex, which involves a rather magical procession, through the town to the beach, of paper clock lanterns and time-themed figures, such as the Grim Reaper, the Four Seasons, the Hours and the Years. They are set on fire at the beach amid a massive firework display. There are also giant Roman clock numerals. Mother Time Keeper presides over the proceedings. The day is important: the winter solstice, after which the days get longer. Feels like an ancient ritual, but invented in 1993. *21 December.*

TOM BAWCOCK'S EVE Mousehole, Cornwall. Locals celebrate when their hero set forth in a storm to save the fishing village from starvation just before Christmas, and returned with a huge catch of fish. Includes children proceeding with huge fish lanterns, Starry Gazy Pie in which the fish heads poke through the pastry crust, and singing the Tom Bawcock Song about his feat. *23 December.*

TOLLING THE DEVIL'S KNELL Every year, the tenor bell is rung in Dewsbury, Yorkshire, once for every year since Christ was born, to remind the Devil of his defeat. The last bong must sound at midnight, so the ceremony starts a little earlier every year. It's been going on since the 13th century, when Sir Thomas de Soothill who gave the bell to the church, started it in penitence for a murder. *24 December.*

UPPIES AND DOONIES Kirkwall, Orkney Islands. A massive 200-a-side communal scrum lasting four hours (see box, page 11). *25 December and 1 January.*

WALRUS DIP Members of the shivering public come along in fancy dress to take the plunge into the sea at Cefn Sidan beach, Pembrey Country Park, Carmarthenshire. Usually at 11am, or just watch the other f-f-fools rush in, and instead walk off the Christmas pud on the eight miles of golden sands. *Boxing Day;* Travel: page 70.

MARSHFIELD PAPER BOYS An elaborate play is performed in the streets of this Gloucestershire town not far from Bath, involving people bizarrely dressed from head to toe in strips of newspaper. Usually starts at Marshfield Market Place at 11am and moves towards the Elias Crispe almshouses. *Boxing Day.*

SEP OCT NOV DEC JAN FEB

Spectacular year-ending ceremonies include:

— **ALLENDALE GUIZERS** Allendale, Northumberland (see box, page 58). *11.40pm, 31 December;* Travel: page 65.
— **FLAMBEAUX PROCESSION** Comrie, Perthshire (see box, page 58). *Midnight, 31 December;* Travel: page 66.
— **NE'ERDAY BONFIRE** Biggar, Lanarkshire (see box, page 58). *9pm, 31 December.*

Tall, dark lumps of coal: New Year customs

NO, LIZ HURLEY, Liz Taylor or even Liz Windsor simply wouldn't do, according to the sexist **First Footing tradition** at New Year, which insists that, for a household to have good luck in the coming 12 months, the first person over the threshold after the chimes at midnight should be a tall, dark man, if possible bearing tokens of warmth and wealth such as a lump of coal. Preferably, the man should be a stranger, and – even harder to arrange – born foot first. Women should use the back door.

Women are not barred, however, from another New Year custom – **Sipping the Cream of the Well**, the first water drawn after midnight, said to bestow wealth and happiness. Indeed, in the north of England and Scotland its qualities were thought to be magical and that a lonely maid would be wed within a twelvemonth if she tasted it.

A third, West Country custom not yet quite snuffed out, the practice of making a globe of thorn briars and mistletoe, dousing it in cider and hanging it near the door, is to prevent evil and diseases from entering the house all year. After the midnight chimes the old one must be burnt outdoors while a new one is hung up. On some farms it was considered essential to carry the burning globe over the first-sown furrows.

At the old water mill at Putley, west of Ledbury, Herefordshire, this **Burning the Bush** ceremony is still carried out with a ring of 13 bonfires, a crowd growling 'auld cider' nine times, and, of course, a new globe, which is doused with the drink, scorched a little in the fire and then hung up for the coming year.

Biggar eccentrics on New Year's Eve

T HE SCOTS' HOGMANAY has always beaten plain old New Year's Eve as such peaceful festivities go. But many English would be surprised to know that the year end sees Britain's most violent, dramatic and colourful ceremonies, which literally set things ablaze in many a northern town.

Most are in Scotland, but in **Allendale**, Northumberland (Travel: page 64), at about 11.45pm the brightly dressed 'guizers' go marching through the town, led by a band. Each bears a blazing half barrel on his head, filled with tar and wood shavings, and these are eventually hurled on a huge bonfire in the marketplace, the ancient ritual being linked to the rebirth of light in the coming year.

Similarly, in **Comrie**, Perthshire, the flambeaux procession (Travel: page 66) starts from the square on the last stroke of midnight. Every corner of the village is visited 'to drive out evil spirits' and the procession ends with the flaming torches being thrown from a bridge into the River Earn and all dancing round.

The **Biggar** Ne'erday Bonfire (see page 68) at the South Lanarkshire town sees a marching band and an enormous bonfire in the High Street (9pm–midnight). Sparks also fly at **Stonehaven**

STONEHAVEN FIREBALL CEREMONY Stonehaven near Aberdeen, *11.30pm, 31 December;* Travel: page 70.
NOS GALAN MIDNIGHT RACE Mountain Ash, Mid-Glamorgan, *31 December.*

VARIOUS DATES

BUN-THROWING CEREMONY On certain key occasions – such as Coronations, Royal Jubilees, that kind of thing – the Mayor of Abingdon, a charming

(Travel: page 70) near Aberdeen in the fireball ceremony, which starts at about 11.30pm and involves a couple of dozen men marching down the High Street whirling round their heads balls of fire, made of flammable material in wire netting, on the end of wire ropes. As the men march down to the harbour, the circles of fire make a startling sight.

Not far away, in **Burghead**, Burning the Clavie (Travel: page 65) takes place on the old calendar's New Year's Eve – 11 January. An old whisky barrel is filled with tar and wood chips and set ablaze, then run up and down the street, bringing good luck to anyone who can seize a firebrand. It is set on a special stone pillar to burn, then brought to earth and smashed to pieces by hundreds of spectators.

Lerwick, Shetland, must take the prize for the most spectacular New Year pyromania, although **Up Helly Aa** (Travel: page 70) doesn't take place until the last Tuesday in January. Again, guizers in gaudy dress parade through the town with blazing torches, but in keeping with the Shetland Islands' Norse heritage, they draw a replica Viking galley with them, complete with dragon's head on the prow and dozens of beefy Vikings in horned helmets.

The procession, which starts at 7.30pm, ends at the King George V playing field where, after certain rituals, the guizers hurl their flaming torches high in the air to rain down on the Viking galley, which blazes fiercely, to the cheers of the crowds. The night is then spent dancing, dining and partying.

Oxfordshire market town, will don his full regalia, ascend the roof of the magnificent 17th-century Town Hall and then, like a naughty schoolboy, throws buns at passers-by. Or rather *to* them, for the custom is well established and much-loved. In fact, as there are 4,500 to throw, the fellow councillors help in pelting the passing populace with pre-cooked patisserie, a bizarre bakery barrage, after a musket shot starts the fun. No cream-filled chocolate éclairs or rock cakes allowed.

BRAMBLES BANK CRICKET Once a year a sandbank in the middle of the Solent appears above water, by an inch or two, thanks to an extreme tide. When it does, yachtsmen from rival clubs either side of the water race out there wearing full cricket whites, set up stumps and play cricket. Spectators are bobbing about in boats, or come ashore (if that's the term for something that's awash) to visit The Brambles Inn, a hastily erected bar. The Brambles is the reason why huge supertankers and cruise liners heading for Southampton perform a wide almost circle before they turn north. As they do so, those on board, and those on passing ferries, are presented with the surreal spectacle of people in cricket whites playing in all seriousness, with umpires, while apparently standing on the open sea. They get swamped by said ships' wash. Also the buxom Brambles mermaid turns up only on this occasion (well, she's in some of the photos, don't know what she does the rest of the year).

EVERY DECADE

GREAT KNUTSFORD RACE A penny-farthing cycle race held every ten years (2020, 2030, etc) in the Cheshire town. As one entrant says: 'You need ten years to forget about falling off last time.' Also an event for bone-shakers, the ones with wooden wheels and no tyres. See also page 104.

FAIRS

Whether it was Simple Simon going to the fair or Uncle Tom Cobbley (or Cobbleigh) and all off to **Widecombe Fair**, the great fairs of Britain go back in folk memory to the dawn of time, or at least to medieval charters granting the right to hold them.

For those used to common country fairgrounds, the older fairs have downright peculiar customs – such as the lawless, mop and runaway mop or fairs named after foods – while others are just huge and spectacular.

Britain's biggest is Nottingham's four-day **Goose Fair** (Travel: page 66) starting on the Wednesday before the first Thursday in October. This has its origins in a centuries-old tradition of up to 20,000 geese being driven to the city in great flocks, coming from as far away as Norfolk or Lincolnshire, their feet dipped in mud and then grit to give them concrete boots to protect them during the journey.

As the 19th century changed society, so the entertainment section of the Goose Fair became more important, with freak shows such as the Fattest Lady in the World or the Ugliest Dwarf or the Three-headed Chicken giving way to spectacular steam-powered rides with fantastic organs, wall-of-death motorbikes and modern white-knuckle rides of every kind.

Traders still offer all kinds of goods on stalls, and the whole fairground sprawls for a mile or two of riotous colour and cacophony. There are plenty of Goose Fair folksongs and justice on the fairground at the Forest Recreation Ground was once dispensed by Pie Powder courts (the term coming from the French *pied poudre*, dusty feet, meaning the people at the fair).

If you miss the geese there are sheep not so far away, usually the following Monday (in fact the first Monday after the 4th), at the **Corby Glen Sheep Fair** in Grantham, Lincolnshire. This is more of a real sheep-trading affair but has fairground fun, albeit in much smaller quantities.

Another truly massive fair is the **Hoppings** at Newcastle upon Tyne, in the third week in June. The Hoppings is said to be the biggest travelling fair in Europe as a coming together of various showmen; but don't go just for the beer. It was started by the North of England Temperance Society in 1882 to show that the working man can have fun without booze, and it's still dry and still fun.

If, on the other hand, you prefer lawless fairs, with the gloves off so to speak, then Devon might seem the place. On the Tuesday after 19 July, **Honiton Fair** opens with the town crier proceeding up the High Street, followed by a gaggle of excited children, and then ringing his bell and making this proclamation: 'Oyez, oyez, the Glove is up, the Fair has begun, no man shall be arrested until the Glove is taken down, God save the Queen', with the children repeating every word as in a church.

The gilded leather glove is held up for all to see on the end of the crier's garlanded and beribboned pole, which is displayed on the balcony of the pub. Then hot coppers are thrown for the children to scramble for in an unseemly mêlée (as in Hungerford and Lanark); but a sense of sadistic humour assures that there are no fancy gloves for them as they burn hands and scrape knees. Some wrap rags around their palms. (The fair takes place on the Wednesday and Thursday.)

A similar amnesty for minor crimes is promised in Exeter at the **Lammas Fair** – on the Tuesday before the third Wednesday in July or sometimes earlier. The mayor proclaims a charter and the gilded glove is hoisted, then a procession to the Cathedral Green opens a craft fair and festival.

Kingsbridge, also in Devon, has a four-day fair towards the end of July, complete with white glove hoisted to indicate that petty crime is

OK (it isn't), plus a picturesque Floral Dance through the main street. It's all laid down in the 1461 charter.

FAIR GAME FOR EVERY KIND OF FOOD

On the food theme, the **Marldon Apple Pie Fair** takes place at the Devon village on the last weekend in July, with said confections for sale and an Apple Pie Princess to be crowned; there's a **Goosey Fair** at Tavistock, Devon on the second Wednesday in October; and nearby, across the Tamar in Cornwall, the much smaller **Honey Fair** at Callington in the first week of October (beekeeping does come into it, but it's mainly a funfair); the **Cheese and Onion Fair** – again in Devon at Newton Abbot – is on the first or second Tuesday in September (this dates back to Edward II and deals in enormous cheeses and onions, but today is more of a funfair). The centuries-old **Onion Fayre** at Newent, Gloucestershire each September could bring tears to your eyes. Events include a raw onion eating contest, a prize onion competition, onion-related stalls, books, tea-towels, mugs featuring said alliums and competitions.

One more food festivity is the **Black Cherry Fair** in Windsor Street, Chertsey, Surrey, on the second Saturday in July. This is ancient, dating from a charter granted by Henry VI to John de Harmondesworth, abbot of Chertsey Abbey; and although it originally celebrated St Anne's Day in August, it now coincides with the supposed cherry harvest. And, being Surrey, there's no white glove indicating freedom to misbehave.

HIRING AND FIRING, AND RUNAWAY MOPS

The reason so many of the ancient and more spectacular fairs fall in the autumn is simple. It was the time of the harvest, so the farm workers received their annual pay and went to hiring fairs to bargain with farmers for the next year's work.

Workers, including servants, would have attended hiring or mop fairs with a few pence in their pockets, so the tradition of providing sweetmeats and entertainment grew up. Each type of worker would gather at a particular corner bearing the sign of his or her job – a crook for a shepherd, a whip for a carter, perhaps even a mop for a domestic servant – and if taken on by a farmer would receive a fastenpenny to keep him loyal to the employer. Nevertheless, this could soon be spent at the fair, and a Runaway Mop fair was held a week or two later for those who changed their minds.

Mop Fairs – now more for fun than for seeking work – are still held at Marlborough, Wiltshire, on the Saturday before and after Michaelmas (the Big Mop and the Little Mop); at Cirencester, Gloucestershire, on the Mondays before and after St Martin's Day (11 November) or three Mondays if that day is a Monday; and at Warwick (the Mop Fair and Ox Roast) in mid-October. Stratford-upon-Avon has had not only a Mop Fair (12 October unless a Sunday in which case 13 October) for 600 years, but also the **Runaway Mop Fair** on the Friday week.

Similarly, **Pack Monday Fair** at Sherborne, Dorset (first Monday after 10 October) was once the Pact, or hiring, fair for the whole region. At midnight on the evening before, 'Teddy Roe's Band' processes through the town banging on saucepans and blowing horns and whistles. This bizarre cacophony commemorates the completion of 15th-century repairs to the town's abbey, under a foreman named Teddy Roe.

Equally, nearby Abingdon, Oxfordshire, has an annual **Michaelmas Hiring Fair** and a **Runaway Fair** a week later. Another massive October festivity is the **Hull Fair**, at Walton Street Fairground, which covers 23 acres of rides, with a mile of stalls in Walton Street itself. It is down this street at 18.00 on the first Friday that a procession of the Lord Mayor and councillors in their robes, plus the leaders of all Britain's guilds of showmen in their glittering chains of office, ends up, perhaps a little surreally, on one of the rides for prayers. Then, as for the last 700 years, the Lord Mayor rings the Hull Fair Bell and festivities run until the following weekend (according to the royal charter, it must close on Sunday but must include 11 October). It is also billed as the largest travelling funfair in Europe (a pedant could wonder, as with occasional tables, what it does the rest of the time, but of course it is various groups of showpeople coming together). Recent years have seen a million people attend.

Among other autumn fairs are the great **Charter Fairs**, usually instituted under Royal Decree, such as the great **St Giles Fair** at Oxford, which goes back at least 400 years, in the specially wide thoroughfare north of the city centre.

TRAVEL INFORMATION

ALLENDALE GUIZERS, Northumberland NE47 9BY
🦶 01434 322002
🚗 From A1 near Newcastle, or M6 J43 at Carlisle, take A69 across country to Haydon Bridge, then south on A686 and B6295 🚂 Nearest station: Haydon Bridge

APPLEBY HORSE FAIR, Cumbria CA16 6XE 🦶 017683 51177
💻 www.visitcumbria.com
🚗 M6 J40, then east 14 miles on A66, or west from Scotch Corner on the A1 37 miles. Traffic will be heavy and slow, so be patient and careful of horse-drawn vehicles 🚂 Appleby is on England's most scenic rail-line, the Settle-Carlisle. Services usually start from Leeds

ARBOR DAY, Aston on Clun, Shropshire SY7 8EW 🦶 875053
💻 arbordayuk.co.uk
🚗 Off A49 which runs up Welsh border, turn west just south of Craven Arms 🚂 Broome via Shrewsbury, or Craven Arms via Newport

BACUP NUTTERS DANCE, Bacup, Lancashire OL13 9NR 🦶 01282 664421
🚗 From M6 J29, take M65 east to J5, B6232 to A690, turn right and onto A681 to Bacup 🚂 Nearest station Burnley or Rawtenstall (East Lancashire Railway, steam, change at Bury from Manchester)

BATH RACE, Poole, Dorset BH15 1NE 🦶 01202 253253
💻 www.pooletourism.com
🚗 M3, west on M27, A31, A350 south 🚂 Poole, from London Waterloo

BATTLE BONFIRE, East Sussex TN33 0AT 🦶 01424 773721
🚗 From London or M25, take A21 south and it is signed on right just before Hastings 🚂 Direct from London Charing Cross

BIRDMAN 🦶 01903 210022 (Worthing) 💻 www.visitworthing.co.uk
🚗 Both off A27 coast road 🚂 Both from London Victoria

BLACK-PUDDING-THROWING WORLD CHAMPIONSHIPS, Ramsbottom, Lancashire BL0 9JE 🦶 0161 253 5111
🚗 M60 onto M66 (north towards Burnley) to Ramsbottom turning and head north for 1 mile, drop down into Ramsbottom, over railway and river 🚂 Ramsbottom (East Lancashire Railway, steam, via Bury or bus from that

station). Ramsbottom offers, up the hill, a wonderful Peel Tower, well worth the steep climb to enjoy the view. This will work up an appetite for some more black pudding

BLAZING BARRELS, Ottery St Mary, Devon EX11 1BZ ☎ 01404 813964
🚗 From M5 J29 at Exeter, take A30 east towards Honiton, look for turn-off 🚂/🚐 Nearest station Honiton (London Waterloo–Exeter line), then bus 398

BLESSING THE LIFEBOAT, Brixham, Devon TQ5 8AW ☎ 01803 852861
🚗 M5 to Exeter, then A38 for 5 miles, A80 towards Torbay and A3022
🚂 Nearest station: Paignton, bus 12 to Brixham

BOG-SNORKELLING WORLD CHAMPIONSHIPS, Llanwrtyd, Powys LD5 4RB ☎ 01591 610666 🖥 www.llanwrtyd.com
🚗 M4 to end, A483 north 🚂 Llanwrtyd, via Swansea

BURNING OF T'OWD BARTLE, West Witton, Yorkshire DL8 4LS
☎ 01748 828747
🚗 Turn off A1 at Leeming, take A684 west 15 miles

BURNING THE CLAVIE, Burghead, Moray Firth IV30 5YN ☎ 01463 234353
🚗 From south, A9 to Inverness, then A96 🚂 Nearest station: Forres

CLOG COBBING WORLD CHAMPIONSHIPS, Roebuck Inn, Waterfoot,
Lancashire BB4 9JR 📞 01706 223550
As Bacup Nutters, but nearer Rawtenstall (ELR station or bus from Bury)

CLOWN SERVICE, Holy Trinity, Beechwood
�';, Dalston, East London E8 3DY 🚂 Dalston Kingsland, Hackney Downs
🚌 30 from Oxford St and King's Cross; 38 from Piccadilly and Victoria

DAY OF SYN AND ROMNEY, HYTHE AND DYMCHURCH RAILWAY,
Kent TN28 8PL 📞 01303 258594; RHDR: ☎ 01797 362353
🚗 From M20 J11, turn south to Hythe 🚂/🚌 London Charing Cross
to Folkestone Central then bus 10, 11 or 12, or get off at Sandling for
a downhill walk of just over a mile

EDAM CHEESE ROLLING, Ide Hill, Kent TN14 6BU 📞 01732 450305
🚗 Two and a bit miles west of the A21 London-Hastings road, as it
bypasses Sevenoaks, on the B2042

FLAMBEAUX PROCESSION, Comrie, Perthshire PH6 2LZ 📞 01764 652578
🚗 From Edinburgh, Forth Bridge and M90 to Perth, then A85 west
🚂 Nearest station: Perth

FESTIVAL OF FOOLS, Muncaster Castle, Ravenglass, Cumbria, CA18 1RQ
☎ 01229 717 614 💻 www.muncaster.co.uk
🚂 Ravenglass

GOLOWAN FESTIVAL, Penzance, Cornwall TR18 4EF ☎ 01736 369686
💻 www.golowan.org
🚗 End of M5 to Exeter, then A30 through Cornwall 🚂 Penzance, from
London Paddington

GOOSE FAIR, Nottingham NG7 4AW 📞 08444 775678
🚗 Off M1 (J24–26) 🚂 From St Pancras, London, and many other centres

GREAT BRITISH DUCK RACE, Molesey Lock, Hampton Court, Surrey KT8 9AJ
💻 www.thegreatbritishduckrace.org
🚗 A309 west and then north from A3 at Hook 🚂 Hampton Court, from
London Waterloo

GREAT KNARESBOROUGH BED RACE, North Yorkshire, HG5 9AY
📞 01423 866886 💻 www.knaresborough.co.uk
🚗 A59 west from A1(M) 🚂 Knaresborough on the York–Leeds line

HARE PIE SCRAMBLE AND BOTTLE KICKING, Hallaton, near Market Harborough, Leicestershire LE16 8UB 🦶 01858 821270
🚗 From Leicester (M1 J21) ring road, A47 towards Peterborough. Hallaton is signed on right at East Norton

HAT FAIR, Winchester, Hampshire SO23 9LJ 🦶 01962 840 500;
🖥 www.hatfair.co.uk
🚗 M3 J9, or A34 from Midlands 🚂 Winchester, from London Waterloo, or Midlands direct

HAXEY HOOD AND SWAY, Haxey, near Gainsborough, Nottinghamshire DN9 2HY 🦶 01724 296296
🚗 From A1(M) south of Doncaster at J34 take A614 to Bawtrey, A631 east towards Gainsborough, A161 north (left) to Haxey

HENGISTBURY HEAD KITE FESTIVAL Bournemouth, Dorset 🦶 01202 471780
🚗 M3 to end, M27, A31, A338 towards Bournemouth, turn left on A3060, left onto A35 towards Christchurch, right at lights onto B3059, over 2 roundabouts, look for left turn signed Hengistbury Head
🚂 Christchurch, from London Waterloo

HERRING DAY, TIME AND TIDE MUSEUM, Blackfriars Rd, Gt Yarmouth, Norfolk NR30 3BX ☎ 01493 743942 🖥 www.museums.norfolk.gov.uk
🚗 From Norwich on A47 follow brown signs for Historic South Quay
🚂 Great Yarmouth, via Norwich, then walk or bus

HOPPINGS FAIR, Grandstand Rd, Newcastle upon Tyne NE2 2NH
🦶 0191 277 8000
🚗 Off A1 London–Edinburgh road, on A167 to Town Moor 🚂 On London King's Cross–Edinburgh line, then bus 10 to Town Moor

HUNTING THE EARL OF RONE, Combe Martin, Devon EX34 0ET
🦶 01271 863001
🚗 M5 J27, A361, A399 north

HURLING THE SILVER BALL, St Columb Major, Cornwall TR9 6AA
🦶 01208 76616
🚗 From end of M5, A30 to Indian Queens, A392 right to St Columb Rd, then A39 right (north)

HURLING THE SILVER BALL, St Ives, Cornwall TR26 1LP 🦶 01736 796297
🚗 End of M5 to Exeter, A30 through north Cornwall, then, before Penzance, A3074 to St Ives 🚂 Short branch off London Paddington–Penzance main line

LEWES BONFIRE SOCIETIES, East Sussex BN7 2JU ☏ 01273 483448
🖳 www.lewes.gov.uk/visit/htm
🚗 From London or M25, take M23 and A23 towards Brighton, then just before Brighton A27 to Lewes 🚂 From London Victoria, or from Brighton

MALDON MUD RACE, Promenade Park, Maldon, Essex CM9 5HN
☏ 01621 856503 🖳 www.maldonmudrace.com
🚗 signed from A12 Chelmsford

MAPPLETON BRIDGE JUMP, Derbyshire DE6 2AB
🚗 From M1 J24 or J25, enter Derby, go round ring road and leave on A52 for 13 miles to Ashbourne, then take A515 exit from Ashbourne, and look for signs to the left

MINCE-PIE-EATING COMPETITION, Wookey Hole, near Wells, Somerset, BA5 1BA ☎ 01749 672243 ☏ 01749 672552 🖳 www.wookey.co.uk
🚗 From M5 J22 follow brown signs

MISTLETOE DAY, Tenbury Wells, Worcestershire, WR15 8AE ☏ 01584 810136
🖳 www.visitworcestershire.org
🚗 From M5 J3, take A4546 west

MUCH WENLOCK OLYMPIAN GAMES, Shropshire TF13 6HR ☏ 01952 727679
🚗 M6 J10a, M54 west to J6, south on A5223, right (west) on A4169

NE'ERDAY BONFIRE, Biggar, South Lanarkshire ML12 6BE ☏ 01555 661661
🚗 From A74(M) J13, or Edinburgh ring road, take A702

OLNEY PANCAKE RACE, Bedfordshire MK46 4AA ☏ 01234 221712
🚗 From M1 J14, take A509 north 🚂 Nearest station: Bedford, from London St Pancras

OYSTER CEREMONY, Whitstable, Kent CT5 1AB ☏ 01227 378100
🚗 From London/M25, M2 to J7, then A299 🚂 From London Victoria

PADSTOW 'OBBY 'OSS, Cornwall PL28 8AF ☎ 01841 533449
🚗 M5 to end, A38 to Bodmin, then A389 via Wadebridge 🚂/🚌 Nearest station: Bodmin Parkway, from London Paddington and other centres

POOH STICKS WORLD CHAMPIONSHIPS, Days Lock, Little Wittenham OX14 4RB ☎ 01235 522711 💻 www.pooh-sticks.com
🚗 M4 J13 or M40 J9, to Didcot via A34, stay on A4130 round north side of town, take B4016 then lane to Long Wittenham first. Parking in narrow lanes a problem; get there early 🚂 Appleford, just north of Didcot on London Paddington-Oxford line. A nice walk east two miles, or taxi from Didcot station

RANDWICK WAP, Randwick, Gloucestershire GL6 6JA ☎ 01453 760960
💻 www.randwick.org.uk
🚗 M5 J13, A419 east to Stroud, sharp left west at Cainscross roundabout onto B4008, but immediately turn right onto Cashes Green Road, follow to end, left and right into Randwick 🚂 Stroud, but a two-mile walk (go west 600 yards on A419 Cainscross Road to roundabout and follow route as above)

ROBERTSBRIDGE BONFIRE, Sussex TN32 5DG
Same as Battle but 4 miles closer to London

ROYAL SHROVETIDE FOOTBALL, Ashbourne, Derbyshire DE6 1EU
☎ 01335 343666
🚗 From M1 J24 or J25, enter Derby, go round ring road and leave on A52 for 13 miles to Ashbourne

SANTA RUN, Newtown, Powys SY16 6JG ☎ 01686 625580
💻 www.santarunnewtown.org.uk
🚗 A489 west from Craven Arms, reached on A49 which runs up Welsh borders 🚂 Newtown, via Shrewsbury

SHIN-KICKING WORLD CHAMPIONSHIPS, Chipping Campden, Gloucestershire GL55 6HB ☎ 01789 868191 💻 www.olimpick.games.co.uk
🚗 M40 J15, A429 towards Stow, B4035 to Chipping Campden

SOUTH QUEENSFERRY FESTIVAL AND BURRY MAN, EH30 9PP
☎ 0845 22 55 121
🚗 From Edinburgh on A90 take Dalmeny turning before reaching the bridge 🚂 From Edinburgh to Dalmeny station, which is in South Queensferry

ST GILES FAIR AND MAY DAY, Oxford ☎ 01865 252200

STONEHAVEN FIREBALL CEREMONY, Aberdeen AB39 2AA 📞 01569 762806
🚗 15 miles south of Aberdeen on A90 which comes north from Edinburgh as M90 🚂 On London King's Cross–Aberdeen via Edinburgh line

STRAW BEAR FESTIVAL, Whittlesey, Cambridgeshire PE7 1DR
📞 01945 583263 💻 www.strawbear.org.uk
🚗 A1(M) J17, east on A1139 then A605 🚂 Whittlesea, via Peterborough or Ely

TWEEDMOUTH FEAST, Berwick-upon-Tweed TD15 2XF 📞 01289 330733
🚗 The A1 London–Edinburgh road bypasses the town 🚂 Berwick-upon-Tweed is on the London King's Cross–Edinburgh line

UP HELLY AA, Lerwick, Shetland ZE1 0LU 📞 01595 693434
⛴ From Aberdeen

WAKEFIELD RHUBARB FESTIVAL, Wakefield Cathedral Precinct, Wakefield, WF1 2HQ 📞 0845 601 8353
🚗 J41 off the M1 will lead you straight into the city centre 🚂 Wakefield Kirkgate or Wakefield Westgate

WAKEFIELD WESTGATE WALRUS DIP, Cefn Sidan beach, Pembrey Country Park, Carmarthenshire SA16 0EJ
🚗 On A484 Llanelli to Carmarthen coast road. Follow brown signs off M4 J48. *Further information on the park* ☎ 01554 833913

WASSAILING THE APPLE TREE
Further information:
Butcher's Arms, Carhampton, Minehead, Somerset TA24 6LP
☎ 01643 821 333 or 01643 821333; **Somerset Rural Life Museum**, Chilkwell Street, Glastonbury, Somerset BA6 8DB ☎ 01458 831197;
Victoria & Albert Inn, Stoke Gabriel near Totnes, Devon TQ9 6RF
☎ 08721 077 077

WIFE-CARRYING RACES, The Nower (open space), Dorking, Surrey RH4 3JT
📞 01306 879 327 💻 www.trionium.com/wife/
🚗 M25 J9, A24 south 🚂 Dorking from London Waterloo or Victoria; Dorking Deepdene from Guildford or Redhill on North Downs Line

WORLD COAL-CARRYING CHAMPIONSHIP, Ossett, West Yorkshire
📞 0113 242 5242
🚗 Just west of M1 J40 south of Leeds

WORLD GURNING CHAMPIONSHIPS, Egremont Crab Fair, Cumbria
CA22 2DW 🦶 01946 820693
🚗 M6 to Carlisle, A595 coastal road south

WORLD MARBLES CHAMPIONSHIP, Greyhound pub, Tinsley Green,
near Crawley, West Sussex 🦶 01403 211661
🚗 From London/M25, M23 to J10, then turn right and right to double
back north on B2036; Tinsley Green is on the left

WORLD PEA-THROWING CHAMPIONSHIPS, Lewes Arms, Mount Place, Lewes,
East Sussex BN7 1YH ☎ 01273 473152
🚗 A27 east from Brighton about 5 miles 🚂 Lewes, from London Victoria
or Brighton

WORLD PLANK-WALKING CHAMPIONSHIP, Queenborough, Isle of Sheppey, Kent
🦶 01795 417478 💻 www.captaincutlass.com
🚗 M2 J5, A429 🚂 Queenborough, from London Victoria or St Pancras,
change Sittingbourne

Orkney
Islands

Thurso

ECCENTRIC PASTIMES

Isle of Lewis

Isle of
Skye

Inner
Hebrides

Inverness

SCOTLAND

Aberdeen

NORTH
SEA

One-hole Golf Course,
Oigh-Sgeir Lighthouse

Island of
Mull

Islay

Glasgow

Elephant's Toe Nail Museum,
Edinburgh

N

Arran

ATLANTIC
OCEAN

0 — 80 km
0 — 50 miles

Newcastle
upon Tyne

Carlisle

Pencil Museum,
Keswick

Middlesbrough

Isle of
Man

Stan Laurel Museum,
Ulverston

Tramp Museum, Ripon

Tram Sunday,
Fleetwood

York

IRISH
SEA

Lawnmower Museum,
Southport

Bradford   Leeds

Kingston-upon-Hull

NORTH
SEA

Anglesey

Liverpool

World Coal-carrying
Championship,
Ossett

Bottle Museum,
Elsecar

Holyhead

Catalyst Museum,
Widnes

Manchester

Sheffield

Grimsby

Penny Farthing Museum,
Knutsford

Lavatory Museum,
Stoke-on-Trent

ENGLAND

Cardigan
Bay

Tile Museum,
Ironbridge

Nottingham

Derby

Mustard, Radar &
Teapot Museums, Norwich

Man v Horse Marathon,
Llanwrtyd Wells

Birmingham

Gas Museum,
Leicester

Coracle Racing & Beca Mountain Race,
Cilgerran

Needle Museum, Redditch

Coventry

Cambridge

Fishguard

WALES

National Teddybear Museum,
Stratford-upon-Avon

Ipswich

Midnight Race,
Mountain Ash

Randwick Wap

Voodoo & Witch
Museum, Oxford

Cinema Organ Museum,
St Albans

Jabs Museum,
Berkeley

Nagging, Cornflakes, & Operating
Theatre Museums, London

Swansea

CARDIFF

Woolsack Race,
Tetbury

Clog Race,
Kew

London Fan Museum

Bristol
Channel

Bristol

Biscuit
Museum, Reading

Dover

Shoe Museum,
Street

Mechanical Music Museum,
Chichester

Witchcraft Museum,
Boscastle

Southampton

Brighton

Corkscrew & Wine
Museum, Alfreston

ATLANTIC
OCEAN

Exeter

National Motor Museum,
Beaulieu

National Wireless Museum,
Ryde

Penzance

Electric Shock Museum,
Salcombe

ENGLISH CHANNEL

ECCENTRIC
PASTIMES

COLLECTIONS
OF ECCENTRICS

Collecting is a slightly introverted hobby, even obsessive, solitary or self-absorbed, which seriously cool and street-cred trendy fashion victims would perhaps dub 'sad'. That puts me firmly on the side of collectors, who at least have an original thought in their heads, at least if they collect odder things than coins, stamps, matchboxes or beer mats. And believe me, they do.

Take David Morgan of Burford, Oxfordshire, who collects cones – parking cones, those much-loathed plastic objects which have multiplied endlessly up and down the nation's highways, perhaps contributing to safety but appearing merely to deprive drivers of mile after mile of lanes devoid of any visible repair work.

Mr Morgan, on the other hand, venerates cones. His garage holds 530 or so variations. There are metre-high jobs for the fast lane, small ones, black ones for undertakers, blue ones for water companies, flashing ones, barber-pole swirling striped ones, wooden ones, midget Italian ones, recycled ones, and five-sided ones.

His interest is understandable, perhaps, when you realise that his company, Inotech, based in nearby Broughton Poggs, manufactures perhaps 25,000 cones a week for use around the world. He tends to see a cone-dominated world: 'The really exciting bit of the First Gulf War coverage was, when they were filming how the cruise missiles attacked Baghdad, there was one of my cones standing in the street!'

His obsession is more than simply commercial. He keeps standard cones in his car boot to trade for any interesting ones he may encounter

and won't let pressing family matters get in the way of his interest: he found the rare rubber Lindvale model, which has pride of place in his collection, being used by funeral directors at his uncle's burial. Perhaps understandably, he says he didn't go on about cones to his fiancée until he was married, but on his honeymoon he left his wife at baggage reclaim to nab the 'fascinating' Adaptaform model at Corsica airport.

His four children have grown up in a beconed environment. 'It saved a lot of money on toys really,' he says. 'The kids can always cycle round cones in the garden.'

Actually, he is the history of the British traffic cone. He believes he made the first experimental plastic one when working at ICI in 1961, so he's got a lot to answer for. There were wooden ones before that, but strictly speaking they were usually pyramids, not cones. But where do all the cones go? Why do police forces have to re-order hundreds? Are they abducted by cone-headed aliens?

'It's a strange thing but if a road repair involves laying 400 cones, only about 390 come back. Students wear them as hats. They screw police ones upside down on ceilings as lightshades so they can read ECILOP on the wall. People use rows of them as flowerpots. They lie under hedges for a bit then end up propping open the village hall door. Hippies even burn them in braziers at West Country pop festivals.'

This may be cone sacrilege but it's all good business replacing them. Still, Mr Morgan's collection continues to grow. He found a lonely deserted cone in the middle of Exmoor once, miles from a road. And ask him where he found the Malaysian police number … would you believe on a Scilly Isles beach?

CUTTING EDGE OF OLD TECHNOLOGY

He's not barmy, but he's often on the verge. Brian Radam of Southport, Lancashire, loves lawnmowers and is quite happy to come out of the closet, or rather garden shed, about his obsession. But then he has 400 of the things, including 150 fully restored in the museum he and his wife Sue run above their garden machinery business in Shakespeare Street, Southport (see page 108).

He says: 'I'm someone who can't let bygones be bygones. I saw these beautiful examples of old British engineering being thrown away by people who couldn't get spares or wanted new models and I thought it was a shame.' He bought his first veteran mower for 2 shillings (10p) as a teenager and did it up. Now, particularly when the seasonal mower business is quiet, Brian and Sue lovingly restore machines – making unobtainable spare parts and faithfully following original paint styles – not just for the museum but for customers who have come to appreciate fine examples of great names such as Ransome's, Atco, Royal Enfield, Perkins or Hawker Siddeley.

There are horse-drawn Shanks models, water-cooled jobs one can boil an egg in, specialist graveyard models, even the early hover numbers. Brian and Sue also have a Rolls-Royce mower, or rather a JP, which was the brand name Rolls used for a while. It gives a different edge to 'getting out the lawn Roller'. Like-minded members of the Old Lawnmower Society hold rallies around the country where models are as proudly displayed as vintage cars, and aficionados can tell a mower's make just by the sound.

Lawnmower racing and endurance grands prix are no joke either. There's an **annual 12-hour event** at Brinsbury Agricultural College, Wisborough Green, West Sussex, each August and speeds can reach 70mph in the ride-on class, the walk-behind models travelling at a more sedate 4–8mph. Blades are removed for the duration and admission is by ticket. (Incidentally, when I pointed out to a local mower fan that the Wisborough Green Mower Grand Prix was actually some way from that village, he retorted angrily: 'Well, Le Mans isn't run through the centre of Le Mans, is it?' Quite.)

Brian used to race himself, but fate cruelly intervened when he developed hay fever. But as with Beethoven going deaf, Brian wasn't going to let this obstruct his great passion. 'I've even found abandoned mowers with trees growing through them and rescued them.' Brian and Sue's museum features celebrity mowers such as one from Prince Charles and another from Hilda Ogden of Coronation Street (the actress Jean Alexander). Sue says: 'We have tourists from America calling in because they can't believe we have such a museum. We also had a chap from the empty desert of Saudi Arabia – we had to explain to him about grass cutting and lawns first.'

CRATE EXPECTATIONS

There is little outwardly odd about Mike and Naomi Hull's house and garden overlooking the beautiful Golden Valley near Stroud, Gloucestershire, until you notice the flagpole is topped with a milk bottle. And you may spot an oil painting of a milk bottle as you enter the stone-built house. A few ancient-looking milk bottles hove into view, but it is not until you enter their sanctum holding 1,300 different milk bottles that their passion for dairy glassware becomes transparent. One thousand three hundred different milk bottles? Aren't they all the same?

They are not, and this is where the fascination soon begins. For one thing there are different types, from 19th-century ones with wire spring and ceramic stopper closures like some Continental beer bottles have today, to the wide-necked pint bottle with the recessed waxed-cardboard disc which dominated the first half of the 20th century, to the aluminium-foil-covered tall bottles of my own childhood, to the dumpy glass bottles of today's few dairies which haven't surrendered to cartons, plastic bottles or, horror of horrors, plastic bags.

As Naomi says: 'In the process of development less and less glass was used to make the bottle, from a 29oz quart bottle of before the First World War to about 8oz of glass in the modern dumpy pint ones.'

Milk bottles, one can soon see, were relatively elegant and made far more interesting by the embossed name of the dairy that owned them (plus the usual warning to rinse and return, and sometimes even threats to other milkmen who might use them with STOLEN in huge type). From the early 1920s the addition of colour printing gave dairymen the opportunity for garish artwork, rough doggerel and slogans and even advertisements for completely different products.

It wasn't so bad when pictures of cows or ads for breakfast cereal appeared, but pink sausages on milk bottles seemed wrong somehow. As for the slogans, one W J Pickford's dairy of Downend, Bristol, had a picture of Mickey Mouse plus the somewhat dated:

> *Mickey Mouse is always gay,*
> *He drinks two pints of milk a day.*

For Clyde Higgs of Leamington Spa, corny puns were a speciality:

No milk for seven days makes one WEAK

Or try this rival's rhyme:

Old Pat Russell has a farm Ee-aye-ee-aye-oh
At Yerbeston Farm he keeps good cows Ee-aye-ee-aye-oh
Friesians here, Jerseys there
Red top, gold top
You should drink a good drop
Have your milk from Russell's Farm Ee-aye-ee-aye-oh.

Naomi explains that she and Mike began collecting in 1975 when they were living in Highgate, London, but had a bottle delivered embossed with the name Cricket Malherbie. 'This aroused my curiosity because malherbie was obviously Norman French for bad grass, so what was it doing on a milk bottle?' Actually, these kinds of thoughts puzzled millions of people in the returnable bottle era, when they wondered how far bottles could stray from home and how they were ever returned. However, Naomi was motivated to find out that Cricket Malherbie was a dairy in Somerset taken over by the Express Dairy and their bottle stocks had been mixed. 'A couple of days later another bottle from a different part of the country turned up on our doorstep and I was hooked,' says Naomi.

'We looked at older, pre-motorway maps, and calculated where people would be likely to stop for a picnic or snack on a long journey. A woodland layby with a bit of a view, usually.' The Hulls struck glass as frequently as the best prospectors strike oil. 'We picked a wood on the A303 road to the West Country and there within chucking distance was a treasure trove barely concealed. Bottles from all over the country – Cornwall, Scotland even, so you could tell which towns people came from and when and where they were going not just by the obvious direction but the resort dairy bottles they chucked there on their way home. Social history, really.'

There were so many in this one find that four car trips were needed to ferry them home. Other finds were made by checking under hedges at a likely cycling distance from major towns. The bottles, built for recycling whole, were virtually everlasting if dumped intact. And so the collection grew. There are kosher bottles from north London with the Star of David; Hindi scripts from northern immigrant areas; an anagramatic 'Liropalfo Dairy' bottle for use on 1 April; beautiful French ones with delightful script printed on them; and pukka colonial ones from Hong Kong, Rhodesia, and elsewhere.

The Hulls are not alone in their hobby. They run a newsletter, *Milk Bottle News*, for the perhaps 750 fans who indulge in bottle rallies to swap and sell rare examples, and the Hulls' collection is far from the largest. 'There's a chap on the Isle of Wight with 7,000 different ones,' says Mike. 'Then if you start on American milk bottles, they had hundreds of thousands of different dairies. Then there's the cream bottles ...'

IT'S A MAIL THING, BUT HE REALLY WANTED A GAS LAMP

When I discovered that the greatest collector of pillar boxes and letter boxes in the world was electrician Arthur Reeder, now of Newport, Isle of Wight, I just had to go and see him.

At the time of my first visit he had 107 of them and when I last checked, he had 148, which probably explains why he moved (with great difficulty) from a tiny London terraced house, where the pillar boxes were wedged in like sardines, to one with a couple of acres of space round it to display the bright red cylinders, squares and ovals.

Actually, one of them is air-mail blue. In the early days of powered flight the concept of air mail was so exotic that special post boxes for air mail were set up in key business centres. 'There's still one in Windsor, although it's the wrong blue. Too dark,' says Arthur. Today's aerogramme letters are still that colour. 'They used special blue vans and air mail sacks to collect this mail.' Note the attention to detail that marks the true, even slightly obsessive collector, rather than the general junk lover.

This air mail box originally had an enamel price list of postage to every corner of the globe on the front, and this was missing from the one Arthur obtained, so he went to the National Postal Museum to borrow an original and have a replica expensively made. It offers postage to the Straits Settlements for 0s 5d a half ounce, or Transjordan for only fourpence halfpenny. Fabulous, but expensive in those days.

His house itself is crammed with those little letter boxes that fix to lampposts or telegraph poles – lamp boxes, apparently – and the ones set in walls (wall boxes, unsurprisingly).

There are different designs and makers, the key giveaway being the royal cypher on the front. 'Except for one period in the 19th century. They had gone to the hexagonal, Penfold boxes for a while and when they went back to cylindrical they forgot to put the royal cypher on the front for a few years, so these "anonymous" boxes are a collectable rarity.

'Then you get situations like the South of Ireland and Hong Kong where the post boxes are covered in royal insignia and the British withdrew, so they want to get rid of them.' Naturally, Arthur's got a Hong Kong box in his garden, and no end of Irish ones. He showed me one Irish one that had an Irish Free State door on it, replacing the British one, but contradictorily retained VR for Queen Victoria and the crown on the top. 'A bit Irish?' I ventured. 'I'm not even going to think about Irish history, but this is a real gem. I swapped two pillar boxes for it. It was well worth it.'

So how did it all start?

'It's about a love for old things that shouldn't be scrapped willy-nilly. Actually, what I really wanted was a gas lamp, a real working one like those they still have in the Royal Parks in London. This started an interest in what they call street furniture and I started to photograph out-of-date road signs, mileposts, that kind of thing. Then I realised with post boxes that they're not all the same, and started travelling to look at rare ones.'

This part is like birdwatchers or train spotters. In fact, when I heard that his aim was not just to find one Penfold box, say, but to locate all of them I was reminded of small boys – and grown men – who had to 'clock' every one of a particular class of steam locomotive. 'Yes. I've travelled from Land's End to John o'Groats and photographed every single Penfold box, about 100 of them, the whole set,' admits Arthur cheerfully.

Sometimes he'd be on holiday with his family and they'd be diverted to look for rare boxes. On one of these occasions they went to look for a rare wooden box on Rhyl station in North Wales when he found it had been vandalised and thrown in a skip. The children were squeezed up in the car and the letterbox was their prized companion on the rest of the tour. Now it's fully restored and takes pride of place in the collection (with seemingly billions of other pieces of Post Office trivia and ephemera such as arm bands, telegrams, rule books, uniforms, stamp machines).

That was what started it all and when word got around that he was keen, Post Office workers scrapping old boxes would get in touch and offer him them in return for a donation to charity.

But why are they ever scrapped? Surely there's nothing to wear out? 'The door hinges go after a few hundred thousand times of a postman

flinging the door open and slamming it shut. Sometimes they're not worth repairing. Other times cars hit them, or thieves damage the doors, so a more secure one is erected.'

Another one came to him after a phone call from a friend who had seen it lying around in a garden. It turned out to be the oldest he has yet collected, 1869 – and you can see why the design was changed, as the rain would easily get in.

Actually, Arthur doesn't really want to collect them all. He'd rather that the old ones were left where they are. 'Some of them are listed structures so cannot be moved, but there is a tendency in the Post Office to say people have got to be able to post A4-size letters so the old boxes with small slots must go. This is a shame, but if this happens I'd rather collect them than see them go for scrap.'

Arthur hopes one day to be able to present them all as a proper museum, but hasn't the ready cash that the authorities would want him to spend on disabled toilets, coach parking, ticket booths, insurance, refreshment area, etc, etc. 'I'm an electrician and have work to do. But I'll gladly show anyone round by appointment who is interested.' I'd give it a cast-iron recommendation. Details: End of chapter.

For the Pillar Box Group and another collection, see page 98.

GIVEAWAY SIGNS, KEY RINGS AND AIR RAID SIRENS

There are as many peculiar collectors as things to collect, but some of the things collected are decidedly odd, whether it be the road signs collected by a Bromsgrove man or the world-beating collection of **airline sickbags** (unused, thankfully) amassed by Dr David Bradford of Richmond, Yorkshire. He had 1,112 at the last count.

A **key-ring collector**, you may not often need to know, is a copoclephilist and one of them – a lady in Southsea, Hampshire – has 7,000 of the things, all different, and possibly she should meet collectors of ancient keys, of which there are several. I even heard indirectly of an **air raid siren collector** from the North of England, from a near neighbour, who heard of him directly. Apparently he was upset when the air raid sirens, which used to wail when German bombers were coming (and later, practising for the arrival of Russian ones), were scrapped and started saving them. And, like letterboxes and road cones – they're not all the same.

Some other obscure words for collectors include: archtophilist (teddy bears), scripophilist (bonds and shares), notaphilist (paper money), deltiologist (picture postcards), philgraphist (autographs), vexillologist (flags) and conlectionomenclatologist (collector of obscure names of types of other collectors). Just a tick… Pauline West of Chandler's Ford, Hampshire, has **4,500 clocks** crammed in her little house. Twice a year, when the time changes, it takes her two and a half days to put them right again. 'I enjoy it,' she told a reporter. I don't think it was a wind-up, either. I just hope they don't all chime on the hour.

Then there is the **Cast Iron Implement Seat Society** who collect those elaborate iron seats featuring manufacturers' names that used to adorn farm equipment. The chairman, called Dennis, wants a DENNIS seat bolted to his coffin. Crackers? Absolutely, as his wife collects nutcrackers. Certainly, there are more truly odd collectors out there than anyone could believe. Perhaps someone should start a collection of them …

ECCENTRIC INTERESTS

John Blashford-Snell is a man who has been explosively eccentric from an early age. Literally. The great explorer and former Royal Engineers Lieutenant-Colonel (a rank particularly attractive to eccentrics, it seems), 'Blashers' ('the bloody Daily Mail made up that name' he said) started off in the style in which he has carried on.

His father, a Hertfordshire country parson, thought it quite reasonable to clear the church gutters of rooks with rifle fire, gradually destroying the roof in the process. A visiting master of foxhounds, after a glass of port too many at the vicarage, thought he was dying when he woke up and saw the family's pet foxes come in and curl up round the hearth. 'Oh my God, Vicar,' he said, 'damn foxes everywhere!' The young Blashers took after his father by carrying out his chore of ringing the early morning communion bell at a distance – with a .303 rifle. At 11, John shot himself in the thumb, trying to force a cartridge into his gun in his bedroom. 'Fortunately, I didn't feel a thing because it blew out my nerve, but bits of nail, bone and blood covered the wall my mother had just painted and she was furious.'

An army commission and a publicly funded supply of explosives set up the young eccentric. Take the way he dealt with a guardsman who kept using his field lavatory in Cyprus, for example. He boobytrapped the 'thunderbox' and the next guardsman who sat down was met by a deafening blast. The guardsman and plastic loo seat were hurled one way, the loo paper another, but there were no injuries.

In 1977 the Fleet Street papers were full of stories about a giant perch – nicknamed Jaws – terrorising a Kentish village pond. The army, unwisely, chose Blashers to deal with it. He took an armoured car and plenty of explosives. The resulting bang was so loud that a duck flying overhead laid an egg in fright. An old lady who had been near-deaf for years said: 'I think I heard something.' One of Blashers's men bellowed helpfully: 'That's only the atom bomb they've dropped on London.' 'Oh dear,' said the old lady in concern. 'Does that mean I won't get my paper in the morning?'

Another time, when Blashers was asked to clear a rubbish dump of rats, the explosives he used landed the rubbish up to a thousand yards away and a chapel roof was covered in dead rats.

Not that it's all been light-hearted stuff. The Colonel has widened scientific knowledge with his numerous expeditions, and saved at least one life – that of a British climber in Mongolia. It was an extraordinary saga of hopping across country, a borrowed helicopter, bribery for fuel and improvised surgery using the operating table for splints. Blashers's whole life has been one extraordinary saga after another, as his autobiography *Something Lost Behind the Ranges* can testify.

ONE FLING LED TO ANOTHER

Many a small boy confronted by those history-book drawings of medieval siege weapons must have thought: 'That'd be fun.' And contemplating the impractical-looking sling-like trebuchet, a sort of giant tripod the size of a house with an ungainly seesaw and sling, they might wonder: 'But did it really work?'

For a long time no one knew because the things hadn't existed for hundreds of years. The question also intrigued former cavalry officer and Shropshire landowner Hew Kennedy, so he set about building a trebuchet with his friend Richard Barr. First there was a small Meccano model. 'Bloody hopeless,' he said. The next small trebuchet worked and was used to fire blazing lavatory bowls. Then came the monster full-sized version fashioned out of pine trunks and using a 60ft beam and a heavy counterweight. In the Middle Ages, vast boulders were said to have been fired into besieged castles, and alternative missiles were rotting carcasses, blazing objects, heads of prisoners, or plague-ridden corpses – the usual stuff of medieval neighbourly disputes.

'I'm interested in ancient weapons,' Mr Kennedy said, 'and some historians said these machines could only fire small stones and wouldn't be able to batter down walls and gates in a siege. We had to test this out.' Now Mr Kennedy and Mr Barr have proved that the trebuchet was indeed the heavy artillery of its day. They happily fired an exploding piano, which landed with a satisfying Peyoing!!!, a dead pig – 'very aerodynamic' – and the tour de force, an exploding Yugo car stuffed with petrol cans, which flew 150 yards before exploding on impact. 'Well, it worked,' said a satisfied Mr Kennedy afterwards. 'Pity about the car, it went quite well, I drove it up here.'

THIS RATHER ECCENTRIC RACE

The eccentric British race could well describe the decidedly odd sports indulged in annually around the country. These include men who don women's clothing and take axes to smash down gates; a horse race without a course that crosses a busy trunk road; Londoners running in clogs and aprons or rowing for a full-skirted coat; paddling Iron Age craft through rapids; or running up hills carrying heavy sacks of wool or coal. And then, for good measure, there is the re-running of an arduous race where the original entrant dropped dead.

The **Beca Mountain Race** held in Mynachlog-ddu in the Preseli Hills near Fishguard, Pembrokeshire, recalls the Rebecca riots of 1843 when local bands of men, dressed as women with leaders called 'Rebeccas', smashed down hated tollgates after the roads were handed to fee-charging turnpike trusts to improve them for stagecoaches. The military had to be called out to quell the rioters, who took their name from the biblical Rebecca, who was sent by her father and brother to become Isaac's wife with the words: 'Let thy seed possess the gates of those that hate thee.'

Late in August, the modern race involves climbing steep hills and then, on return, donning women's clothing and smashing down a gate. Another annual race with a dressing-up tradition is the **Clog and Apron Race** (Travel: page 112) at the Royal Botanic Gardens, Kew, London, where late in September dozens of horticultural students thus garbed have to clatter their way down the 373yd Broad Walk.

The third Thursday in March sees one of the world's oddest and oldest horse races, the **Kiplingcotes Derby**, take place on a peculiar uphill route – there is no proper course, although many old maps show the route – along lanes and across fields off the A163 near Market Weighton, Yorkshire. The road is closed by police as the riders cross it at full tilt. The start and finish of the race, first held in 1519, are out of sight of each other, so the only spectator ever to see the whole race was a man who once had a helicopter waiting.

Until recently, the second prize was worth considerably more than the first, due to the income from a poor investment in 1618 paying the winner and the second taking the entry money, which once led to an unseemly 'you go first' tussle at the finish. Locals are proud that the race has never been stopped, neither by war, plague, famines nor storms. 'There were dreadful snow drifts in 1948 and to keep the tradition alive, a lone farmer fought his way through on foot, leading his horse.'

Another uphill struggle is the **World Coal-carrying Championship** (see page 16), which sees the nation's coalmen converge on Ossett, West Yorkshire, on Easter Monday for a back-breaking event. Like a lot of slightly loopy things the British do, this started with a conversation in a pub, the Beehive Inn at Gawthorpe, Ossett, Yorkshire, one day in 1963 to be precise. Mollie Oldroyd kindly produced this record of the vital exchange:

Reggie Sedgewick and one Amos Clapham, a local coal merchant and current president of the Maypole Committee, were enjoying some well-earned liquid refreshment whilst stood at the bar lost in their own thoughts. When in bursts one Lewis Hartley in a somewhat exuberant mood. On seeing the other two he said to Reggie, 'Ba gum lad tha' looks booggered!' slapping Reggie heartily on the back. Whether because of the force of the blow or because of the words that accompanied it, Reggie was just a little put out. 'Ah'm as fit as thee,' he told Lewis, 'an' if tha' dun't believe me gerra a bagga coil on thi back an ah'll get one on mine an ah'll race thee to t' top o' t' wood!' (Coil, let me explain, is Yorkshire-speak for coal.) While Lewis digested the implications of this challenge a Mr Fred Hirst, Secretary of the Gawthorpe Maypole Committee (and not a man to let a good idea go to waste) raised a cautioning hand. 'Owd on a minute,' said Fred and there was something in his voice that made them all listen. 'Aven't we been looking fer some'at to do on Easter Monday? If we're gonna 'ave a race let's 'ave it then. Let's 'ave a coil race from Barracks t' Maypole.' (The Barracks being the more common name given by the locals to The Royal Oak Public House.)

And so a great new sport was born.

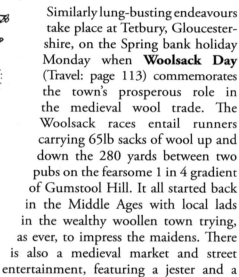

Similarly lung-busting endeavours take place at Tetbury, Gloucester-shire, on the Spring bank holiday Monday when **Woolsack Day** (Travel: page 113) commemorates the town's prosperous role in the medieval wool trade. The Woolsack races entail runners carrying 65lb sacks of wool up and down the 280 yards between two pubs on the fearsome 1 in 4 gradient of Gumstool Hill. It all started back in the Middle Ages with local lads in the wealthy woollen town trying, as ever, to impress the maidens. There is also a medieval market and street entertainment, featuring a jester and a witch ('gumstool' means ducking stool for testing witches – if they drowned they were innocent) as the town goes back in time hundreds of years for the day. There's a Gumstool pub a couple of miles away.

Someone who did drop dead after a race was Guto, a local hero born in 1700 who lived at Nyth Bran farmhouse in mid-Glamorgan. Local people said Guto could outrun a horse, but when he took on an Englishman named Price over a 12-mile course, Guto won handsomely, only to drop dead. His memory is kept alive by a torchlit **midnight road race** on New Year's Eve at Mountain Ash, mid-Glamorgan. This question of can two legs ever beat four is also addressed at the annual **Man versus Horse Marathon** at Llanwrtyd Wells, Powys, Wales, on a mid-June Saturday (Travel: page 113). Amazingly, in 2004 the answer was found to be yes, and the £25,000 prize was paid up to Bedford IT consultant Huw Lobb who covered the gruelling course in 2 hr 5 min

19 sec. The contest had been run for 25 years, with £1,000 uncollected human prize money added to the fund each year the horses won – so don't count on the cash being that much in future.

A much older Welsh sport is **coracle racing**, which still takes place in Cilgerran, near Cardigan (Travel: page 112). These Iron Age oval boats made from animal skins, light enough to be carried on a man's back, are still used for fishing on several Welsh rivers. The course runs over a rocky stretch of the River Teifi every August. The National Coracle Centre is nearby at Cenarth, a few miles upstream on the Teifi.

A river race of precisely datable origins is the **Doggett's Coat and Badge Race**, held every July (the date depends on tides) between London Bridge and Chelsea on the Thames. Comedian Thomas Doggett launched the race in 1716 to celebrate the accession of George I to the throne. Prizes from money left by Doggett include a splendid full-length red coat with a tight waist and a silver badge for the best oarsman, who looks rather odd thus dressed in today's London. Again, there's a pub named after the race, right on Blackfriars Bridge.

LIKE SEX AND SHOPPING: THE ETON WALL GAME

'The Battle of Waterloo was won on the playing fields of Eton,' said the Duke of Wellington once, and he may have been thinking of the bizarrely brutal **Eton Wall Game**, played each year on the Saturday nearest St Andrew's Day (30 November).

No such game had resulted in a goal since 1909 at the time of writing, but the great heaving mass of tightly packed boys goes at it with all seriousness each year (and in many practices). You can spectate but as it nearly always ends up where it started, with nothing to see but a bunch of boys wrestling in the mud in the meantime, it can be a little tedious, being described as the Most Boring Sport in the World. Actually someone wittier than I described it as like sex and shopping: a lot of pushing and shoving and very little to show for it.

What *is* the Eton Wall Game? A strange cross between a mass punch-up and rugby football. (In fact, most old public schools once had ludicrously violent and complicated games of their own, and so the famous incident of William Webb Ellis picking up a football and running with it and thus inventing the sport of rugby at Rugby School in 1823 may not be as eccentric as it seems today. Ellis has the Rugby World Cup and a pub named after him.)

At around that time, the Eton Wall Game in 1825 – only ten years after Waterloo – was recorded as lasting 60 rounds over three hours and causing only one death. The game has a pitch 125ft by five yards alongside a not very straight wall. The two sides are the 'collegers' (scholars) and 'oppidans' (fee-payers).

Prince Harry played in 2002 and scored a '*shy*', which isn't as good as a goal and involves holding the ball against the wall with your foot raised against it and then touching it with your hand, I think. This has to take place in an area near the end called the *calx*, past a chalk line on the said wall (calx being the Latin for 'chalk'). The game starts with a 'bully', as frankly do many public school games, but is a kind of heaving scrum here. Once you've scored a shy you can take a throw at the goal, which is pretty impossible to hit, being a thin tree or a door, depending which side you are on.

Many of Britain's greatest politicians have learned the joys of pointless extreme effort and suffering here, including David Cameron, Douglas Hurd and Alan Clark.

But one bloodthirsty Eton game no longer continues. This was the Ram Hunt, run until 1747, when a ram was hunted down and butchered by the scholars. It all makes Quidditch in Harry Potter seem totally sane and sensible.

I reproduce with permission a letter to a newspaper on Eton Wall Game tactics which gives something of the flavour:

SIR – In discussing football punch-ups, your Eton wall game correspondent could have mentioned two particular forms of torture that it is legitimate to inflict. In one, when an opponent's torso is locked in a horizontal attitude, you run your elbow up and down his spine, as on a washboard, applying as much weight as possible to his vertebrae.

In another, you insert a knee between his head and the wall and lever sideways. If, because of the general pressure, he is unable to move, this soon makes him reconsider.

Your correspondent rightly says that conditions in the middle of the bully can become extreme. If a player is desperate, he can cry 'Air!' – at which the umpire is supposed to halt play.

But in my day one master who regularly umpired proceeded according to a simple formula: if a player was still capable of calling for air, he did not need any – so the game could continue.

DUFF HART-DAVIS, Uley, Glos.

FEELING TIDDLY, PROFESSOR? (WINK, WINK)

It's reassuring to know that Oxford and Cambridge universities vie with each other to excel, to be the elite, to lead the world – in tiddleywinks, a game where little plastic counters are flipped by pressing them down with other ones at one side across a carpet towards a target cup. It's all taken very seriously. Here's an extract from the many rules of the sport at varsity level:

3) Players shall tiddle in strict rotation, members coming from alternate sides.
4) Touching a tiddleywink with anything other than the tiddler is strictly prohibited.
5) Touching any other player's winks is strictly forbidden.

The Duke of Edinburgh awards a Silver Wink to the winner.

A REMOTE CHANCE OF A ROUND OF GOLF

If you ever get fed up with how crowded golf courses have become, don't worry. All you need to do is cycle to the most westerly point of the UK mainland, Ardnamurchan Point in Scotland. Then, somehow, to a lighthouse on an uninhabited rock called Oigh-Sgeir, about 10 miles west of Rum in the Hebridean Sea, where there is a one-hole golf course. It was built by the lighthouse keepers, before it was automated, to relieve the tedium. It is the smallest golf course in the world, some say, although others say it has three holes. I haven't been to check, but if you do, let me know. By the way, take plenty of balls. Any that roll off go into deep water teeming with sharks.

CHEESE AND CRACKERS IN DEEPEST GLOUCESTERSHIRE

It would be truly hard to come up with anything more deeply, deeply eccentric in terms of village life than the **Randwick Wap** in the sleepy village of the same name, near Stroud, Gloucestershire.

It's not just that the rituals involve bizarre dressing-up, and deeply odd titles for the officials. Nor just that it involves doing very strange things with cheeses. Nor indeed that it involves the mayor and the vicar taking part in all seriousness in something that would be judged, well, crackers elsewhere. It's that they haven't a clue what it all means or why they do it, but do it they must year after year.

Do what? Well, it's complicated. There's the cheese rolling on the first Sunday in May, which involves a procession to the church of the Wap Mayor, the Wap Queen, the High Sheriff, the Sword Bearer, the Mop Man, the Flag Boys and the Bearers of the Cheeses carrying three Double Gloucesters covered in floral garlands. The officials are wearing 17th-century frock coats and tricorn hats or full dresses. The cheeses are then blessed by the vicar at the altar in the church.

Now, the Double Gloucester is an aristocrat among cheeses, up there with Stilton and Wensleydale in the nobility of cheesedom, but does it deserve this much respect? Or, possibly, as much disrespect as follows?

They are taken outside where the congregation forms a ring around the church (not unlike the ceremony at nearby Painswick). The vicar, the Wap Mayor and the Wap Queen each set a cheese rolling and they are rolled around the church three times, returning to the official who started it. It must be anticlockwise, looking from Heaven. One cheese is diced and gobbled up by the crowd while the other two are kept for stage two of the proceedings on the following Saturday (and this is the bit visitors are encouraged to come to).

This is the Wap Fair in the streets, with the Wap Queen and Wap Mayor carried shoulder high with the Mop Man going on in front flicking water over the crowd. The Wap Mayor's chair is then put in the Mayor's Pool, and if it should happen to be tipped up, so be it. The Wap Song is sung and the procession continues to Well Leaze Hill, where the remaining two cheeses are rolled three times down the slope, then sold to onlookers who also consume a strange local delicacy known as Wiput Cake. A fair then ensues. It's all very, very strange. As Wap stalwart Stan Giles said: 'Why do we do it? Well, its origins are lost. One theory is that when they finished the church many centuries ago the foreman got tipsy, so they took him and threw him in the pond. But whatever it means, it's an important link with the past that brings the community together. It's easy to stop doing these things and rare for them to start again, so we must keep going.'

In fact the Randwick Wap, like the Tichborne Dole, was banned for rowdiness once, but luckily many decades later there still existed some very old people who remembered it, and a book detailing the ritual.

OH NO, THE DRIVELLER HAS DONE A SWADGER!

If you've ever thought of country people as easily amused, slow-witted bumpkins living in another era, then the ludicrous sport of dwile flonking might reinforce your prejudices. Unless, that is, they have invented it to take the mickey out of the rest of us.

Basically this game, particularly popular in Suffolk and Norfolk pubs, involves dancing in a circle while someone in the middle tries to hit you in the face with a beer-soaked knitted dishcloth. Of course, being deepest East Anglia (where they find snail racing thrilling), the language and the rules are deeply, deeply strange.

The pub side whose turn it is not to flonk, hold hands and dance round in a ring – an activity called *girting*. One of the other side stands in the centre of the ring holding a broom handle called a *driveller* and he or she fishes the *dwile* – a knitted grey dishcloth – out of a chamber pot filled with beer and tries to fling it at the members of the circling team. A hit on the head is a *wonton*, worth lots of points, a hit on the chest a *mowther* (worth fewer) and on the legs and nether regions a *ripper*, worth just one point. A complete miss is a *swadger*, at which point the *flonker* must drink the chamber pot full of ale (or sometimes another one) before the wet dwile can be passed from hand to hand round the circle while the opposing team make a strange chant.

The whole thing is overseen by the *jobanowl* who starts each game by calling 'Here y'go t'gither!' and referees the above-mentioned rules.

'How do you get to be a jobanowl?' I foolishly asked once. 'By being the most stupid person in the team of course, stupid,' was the reply.

The game either goes back to time immemorial or merely to the 1960s and some boozy printers in Beccles, which seems more likely given the suspiciously short trail of documentary evidence. But the game spread around the globe for a short dwile, with flonking recorded in Jakarta, Hong Kong, Singapore, St Andrews and wherever a group of inebriated East Anglians might end up.

ON THE ROAD TO ECCENTRICITY

Should you be out driving and be overtaken by a garden shed, of the plain wooden variety, or a chap sitting on a sofa steering with a pizza pan on a coffee table in front of him with a standard lamp behind flapping in the wind, or a giant lobster-cum-Morris Minor, complete with snapping claws, then there are three possibilities. You are asleep and dreaming; you are far too drunk or drugged to drive; or you have encountered some of Britain's motoring eccentrics, a truly bizarre collection. There is also a motorised orange, a 70mph dodgem, and even a high-speed fireside armchair.

The Morris crustacean, named Claude by its owner at the time of writing (he was trying to sell it), probably outrages as many folk as it amuses, such is the reverence these cars are held in by some people, but the crustacean conversion is well done. It has a head made out of an old crash helmet, complete with antennae, above the windscreen. The claws are the best bit, for they actually snap open and shut as the car drives.

Brilliant as it is, don't Morris fans object to one of their treasured cars being mutilated, I asked owner Phil Vincent of Burton Joyce, near Nottingham. 'Not when I explain it was done for a television series,' explains Phil, who has used the 150,000-mile car as a local runabout for so long that people in the village don't even turn round when a giant, pink, snapping lobster drives past. 'They used it in a children's TV series Professor Lobster during the 1980s. When the series was over I bought it back and have been taking it to shows all round the country ever since. It's a bit heavy, with the tail full of filler and old inner tubes, but Claude goes all right with a tail wind,' he quipped. And goes better on Shell, no doubt.

SHED INHIBITIONS

The garden shed, built on a quad-bike frame and capable of 56mph, is fully roadworthy and street legal, as are the sofa-cum-living room, a motorised rubbish skip and a huge Outspan orange, which all met for a race at Donington Park racing circuit in Leicestershire in 1998, organised by the *Sun* newspaper.

The shed, complete with trailing pot plants in a window box and rattling watering cans hung up, can zip along at 56mph, but the skip,

despite its 1300cc engine, turned out to be, well, rubbish on corners. The giant orange, built for a fruit company, could manage 61mph, but was pipped at the post by Edd China's 79mph couch.

Edd, a 27-year-old inventor-designer when I spoke to him, said it all started when he had to raise £4,500 to go on an Operation Raleigh adventure training trip to Belize. 'I thought I could raise sponsorship and so on, so I made it out of the front end of a Mini, and the front wheel of a Reliant Robin plus some bits of wood from the garage. Being a three-wheeler it tends to go on only two wheels on bends if you're doing the full 85mph but then it just planes down the wood underneath a bit more!' Edd's odd approach to motoring started two years before. 'We were sitting round in the pub talking about slobs who order pizzas from home, and we said it would be great it you could just drive down to the Pizza Hut in your living room, so we did it.'

As a fund-raising exercise, the Sitting Room was a complete flop. Pizza and cola companies, etc, approached for sponsorship, couldn't see what he was on about. But after the trip to Belize, more publicity began to earn appearance money at various arena events, and now Edd China is setting himself up as an agent for other wacky cars:

'The oranges – there were about four – were made for advertising back in the Sixties, but they made them too well. There's one in the National Motor Museum at Beaulieu (which also has a 1924 Daimler beer bottle; Travel: page 113) but the other ones have started to come out of storage.

'The guy with the shed – which is on a quad bike so it's quite stable – is George Shields of Derbyshire, and, like the living room, it's completely street legal. He's working on a high-speed grand piano, and I've got commissions for a bathroom and a four-poster bed.'

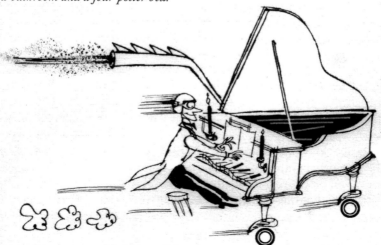

Just try not to lose control of your own car if you see one of them coming round a corner...

Then there's Mini-mad maverick Tony Anchors of Didcot, Oxfordshire, who does very strange things with the tiny British cars. He's made a Mini-Bus, an open-top Mini with stairs up the back (so he can go down bus lanes), a Mini with a garage on the roof that unfolds around itself (so he can avoid wheel clampers), a floating Mini with stern paddle wheel, called the Minisippi (which was last seen in a lake at Birmingham), a Mini with only one wheel at the back, which looks like a boat (called the Trimini) and his *tour de force*, the world's only half-timbered thatched Mini cottage (or Minisuckle Cottage as he calls it).

Then there was Winchester art student Daniel Lobb who built a stately home inside a caravan in 2000. Inside, it has a chandelier, elegant balustrade, marble fireplace, quality wood panelling and an elegant staircase to an upstairs balcony, and is thoroughly eccentric.

'Caravans have become very boring and this is to show how something can be bigger inside than out, like the Tardis,' he told bemused reporters. It was called The Grange but quickly gained the nickname Towed Hall.

Neither is this madcap mad car stuff particularly new. Slightly batty British engineer Robert 'Scotty' Matthewson, who lived in Calcutta, in 1909 commissioned a Swan Car from Brooke's car builders of Lowestoft, Suffolk. The radiator and bonnet of the car were concealed in a swan's body surmounted with an elegant neck and head at the front. It was all done in carved feathers, which stopped by the driver's door.

It caused an absolute sensation in Calcutta in 1910. Matthewson sat in the rear as he drove around Calcutta, playing chords and bugle calls on the multi-note horn, which worked off the exhaust via a keyboard. The swan's eyes would glow orange at night and if the streets of Calcutta were crowded, the chauffeur could spray hot radiator water, hissing out of its beak, to clear the way. It amused him to press a valve so splats of whitewash would be left like droppings behind the one and only Brooke Swan Car. I believe the wonderful motor vehicle later went to a maharajah but where it ended up I don't know. More recently, collectors have been buying models of it because it was so very, very extraordinary.

Get a move on, Grandad!

Have you ever cursed the slowness of mobility scooters, those motorised armchairs that the less able use (usually festooned with carrier bags and a dog on a lead) to get around?

Well, Lincolnshire plumber Colin Furze has the remedy. He has souped up a mobility scooter so that it looks the same on the outside – but does nearly 70mph on the road.

He did this, gaining an entry in *Guinness World Records 2011*, by installing a compact petrol engine instead of using batteries. Mind you, he had already produced flame-throwing mopeds that look like a fire eater's night out, so we should have expected something impressive from the then 31-year-old.

So, mobility scooter problem solved. Or maybe not, if hundreds of pensioners get hold of them. Mind you, imagine the coppers' faces when the speed camera picture, saying a mobility scooter was doing 70mph, comes up...

FLEETWOOD MAX AND FISHERMEN'S FRIENDS

Fleetwood, the Lancashire port and home to the rather extraordinary Tram Sunday on the third Sunday of each July, has several other oddities about it. The town – dubbed Fish City locally – is home to the Fisherman's Friend throat pills, an unbelievably strong throat lozenge that can't really be put into words: it has to be experienced to be believed. Like most extreme things, it has a small but fanatical following.

Cynics may think if fishermen really eat these things, lozenges would be the only friends they ever have. Actually, they're rather good and I wouldn't be surprised if off the coast of Iceland a fisherman is even now de-icing a trawler's rigging by breathing the fumes on it, or maybe converting a hold full of herrings into kippers by leaving a lozenge down there...

The Fisherman's Friend is also responsible for the surprising **statue of Eros** near the factory, paid for by philanthropic lozenge queen Doreen Lofthouse. And as it's also near the sewage works, which takes Blackpool's effluent, and the fishing port, I imagine the direct intervention of the God of Love is indeed required to sniff any romance in the air at all.

However, you would be quite wrong to think the place unromantic. First there are the trams. Then there's the town's impressive **North Euston Hotel**, which tells a forgotten story. The idea was that the line from Euston, London, would terminate here, it being then inconceivable that the railway could haul itself over the fells and gorges of the Lake District and the hills beyond to Carlisle, Dumfries and Glasgow. Thus, thousands of Cumbrians and Scots would spend the night here before embarking in steamers of the sea-going variety for points north.

And how did the tram festival come about? North Euston Hotel manager Jim Cowpe was looking out of his window in 1985 when he realised that Fleetwood was the only town left in Britain with trams running down the main street (many have restored them since, of course, but Fleetwood to its credit never stopped).

Probably with an eye to business, he figured that this could be made a virtue, not a nuisance. **Tram Sunday** sees half-a-dozen vintage trams cruising the streets, some of them from the connected system of Blackpool, some imported specially from the National Tramway Museum at Crich, Derbyshire, or from as far afield as Hong Kong, where ancient four-wheeled British trams improbably rattle and roll the length of the island.

The Fleetwood day usually sees vintage steam traction engines, veteran transport of every sort, a funfair, steam galloper roundabouts, old motorbikes. 'It's grown and grown beyond my dreams,' said Mr Cowpe. And now that Manchester, Croydon and all sorts of other places have replaced the tram tracks they ripped up 50 years ago, we can see that Fleetwood was right all along.

CREATING CROP CIRCLES

Making crop circles is not at all eccentric for aliens, as my book *Eccentric Treens from Planet Tharg* makes clear (not for sale on this planet). Or would do, if it were true. But it *is* eccentric for humans, and it is, in fact, an undercover Wiltshire sport that has garnered huge publicity all over this planet, and maybe beyond.

If any little green men were involved, it must have been ones on pedestrian crossings on the way from a certain Wiltshire pub after closing time. Nearly all these fantastic art works were within 50 miles when the phenomenon began in the 1980s. There were great swathes of wheat fields in East Anglia and acres of barley in Scotland where not a circle ever appeared. Not to mention vast prairies of golden grain across Canada, the United States and Australia, some fields almost as big as Wiltshire. Did the UFOs, so common in these countries according to some Americans, stop there and make crop circles? Did they heck! But millions of people wanted to believe in them.

Meanwhile the giant designs advanced in line with the advance of humans' computer graphics. Odd that if you could manufacture a transgalactic hyperwarp drive to get you from Planet Tharg to Salisbury in a couple of hours, you couldn't design a nice geometrical pattern until the Apple Mac appeared. And as the symbols improved, so the subjects changed. Native North Americans designs, Celtic brooches, ancient medical symbols. Not from alien culture, but from ours. All vaguely right-on in a credulous hippie kind of way – no bank logos or McDonald's arches. Then people confessed to making some of them with computer graphics and planks on long ropes to get the grain flattened in the right way.

And the phenomemon is by no means over. 2009 produced a bumper, er, crop with websites of believers in all this talking of 'many of these having mysterious meanings and messages'; summer 2010 saw these massive things still being created and logged at a rate of almost 20 a month.

A cracking hoax, but about as mystic as a pint of scrumpy. Yet another eccentric British sport dreamed up in a pub.

BRITAIN'S GREATEST LIVING ECCENTRIC?

It's *Chitty Chitty Bang Bang* come to life. Or possibly the cartoonist Heath Robinson, or even Emmet, the 1960s creator of fantasy machinery.

Deep in rural Buckinghamshire or along the nearby Thames you may encounter **Lyndon Yorke**, a fifty-something bespectacled gent. He'll be the one driving a wickerwork car, operating a mechanical folly sculpture, sailing an Edwardian tricycle down the river, or possibly a floating Bath chair. When he is out on the road in a contraption he didn't make, it could well be his favourite 1928 Model A Ford he found with a tree growing through it in a New Zealand farm, which he rebuilt and drove home.

In short, he's a creative mechanical tinkerer. 'It all started when I was a teenager and there were still lots of 1920s cars and motorbikes lying around in barns. I loved taking things to bits, even if I couldn't always get them going,' said Lyndon, who conducts aerial survey work when he's not tinkering. Somewhat worryingly, his workshop has the gun turret from a bomber on the roof.

His creative use of what other people would call junk became well known locally – he was invited to make mechanical flowers for an Oxford Arts Week – but he decided he'd like to make things that he could use himself.

The amphibious Edwardian tricycle, called the *Tritania*, was the first. 'It's a two-seater Edwardian trike mounted on twin floats. There's a double chain sprocket at the back driving a propeller through the gears of a hand drill.'

He takes care not to spoil any old machines he uses, so they can be returned to their original form, and uses period pieces of scrap for the construction. 'The *Tritania* was for Henley Regatta – I thought it might get a few laughs and be worth a few free drinks!'

Then Lyndon saw a picture of an Indian tea planter driving a wickerwork car, and immediately wanted to make one. Luckily, he soon came across a burnt-out 1922 Citroën. 'I couldn't possibly spoil a complete one, so this was a godsend.'

He found the Model A Ford in a field at Tauranga, New Zealand, when Lyndon was working on aerial surveys out there. 'There were quite a few of them around, all abandoned. My friend and I bought five, got three going and restored from the parts, sold one, and drove the other two home via Sydney, Melbourne, Colombo, Delhi, Pakistan, Afghanistan, Iran, Turkey, Greece, Yugoslavia, across to the Channel, and back to his home at Marlow Bottom.'

Did the cars break down? 'Every day, but they're easily fixed.'

He calls his own style of machinery 'Retrotech' and there is a serious side to it all: 'Not many years ago in this country, you could see how everything worked, with gears, sprockets, levers, whether it was a car or a signal box, and you could fix it.

'It's very sad that people are losing this ability, although they've still got it in the Third World. We probably used to laugh at them, they didn't have the knowledge to fix a car or a steamship. Now it's gone full circle – our kids play on computers and have no idea what's inside the box. A kid nowadays finds his bike doesn't work so it's regarded as broken and is discarded. They wouldn't know how to change a brake block.'

ODD ASSOCIATIONS

There are societies for everything if you know where to look. Where do you start? Well, there are specialist groups who would of course not consider themselves eccentric in the common sense of the word. The Left-Handers Club (☎ 08458 723272) runs **Left-Handers Day** and there is also the **Left 'n Write** at shop 5 Charles Street, Worcester (☎ 01905 25798), where sinister (in the Latin sense, not the English) lefties can buy scissors,

The Top Ten British Eccentrics

WHEN, FOR SOME REASON, Kellogg's Fruit 'n' Fibre (why them? Does it have nuts in it?) asked me to run a national televised awards ceremony for the top ten eccentrics, I found I had the great honour of hosting it with Sir Norman Wisdom, the veteran British comic, who sadly died in 2010. He stole the show, of course, but it was a bizarre day with the ten most eccentric people we could find gathered in one room. In fact it was surreal.

They were, for the record, with their then eccentricities (they may have moved on to new extremities), and the order we put them in:

1. **Lyndon Yorke** from Marlow Bottom, Bucks, with his bizarre contraptions (see page 96). He had his crackpot creations at the awards ceremony.
2. **Alan 'the Dominator' 'Nasty' Nash** of Stoke-on-Trent, world toe-wrestling champion and chicken whisperer. He wears a Marigold rubber glove on his head when talking to his chickens (or 'girls' as he refers to them) to put them at their ease.
3. **Arthur Reeder** of the Isle of Wight, who has the world's biggest collection of post and pillar boxes (see page 78).
4. **Captain Beany** from the Planet Beanus (actually Port Talbot, South Wales, but an understandable mistake), who is obsessed with baked beans and dresses as one (see page xi). He told a newspaper that his

corkscrews, potato peelers, etc. It applies to a lot of stuff, really – why do microwave ovens always open on the right?

What other odd groups can one send a letter off to? To begin with, there is the **Pillar Box Group**. (This is a more serious affair than you might think. I once met author Jon Wynne-Tyson, a king of a tiny uninhabited Caribbean island who lived near Fontwell, Sussex, and had a remarkable complaining at coming merely fourth wasn't 'just sour beans' but was justified.

5 **Ted Hannaford** of Kent who loves French knitting (it produces a rope-like tube like the fingers of a glove for no obvious purpose). He has ten miles of it in a huge box and has to keep going to stop an Australian rival catching his world record.

6 **Ann Atkins** who runs a gnome reserve in Devon (see page 217).

7 **Neil Riseborough** of Norfolk. Neil is snail master and commentator of the World Snail Racing Championship (see page 35) who somehow makes it very exciting.

8 **Phil Taylor** of Lancashire who runs the Black-Pudding-Throwing World Championships in Ramsbottom, Lancashire (see page 44).

9 **Captain Cutlass**, aka Adrian Collins, of Kent. Captain Cutlass says he is a swashbuckling pirate and dresses like one. Captain Cutlass is the leading light in the World Plank-walking Championships held in a muddy creek on the Isle of Sheppey, Kent, every August, which involves people getting very, very wet.

10 **Josef Kollar**, born and bred in Southampton, a board-game champion extraordinaire. He was, at the time, World and UK champion at Cluedo, for which he wore a yellow Colonel Mustard outfit, and is Scottish Champion at Monopoly, for which he wore a Monopoly board coat, complete with Monopoly money fluttering down the tails.

collection of 30 or so boxes standing around his garden.) Have you seen a rare Edward VIII box? Try Chorleywood in Hertfordshire. A Queen Victoria hexagonal? Kensington, London, has plenty. A Victorian vertical slot octagonal with bad weather flap? The only one is at Barnes Cross, Holwell, Dorset.

Then there are the elaborate pseudo-Tudor postboxes donated to the villages of Rous Lench and Radford, Worcestershire, by the eccentric local squire and parson, Dr Chaffy, at the end of the 19th century. Either you find this sort of stuff fascinating or you don't, but it is undeniably fascinating that some people, like train spotters or bird twitchers, will drive hundreds of miles to bag a rare pillar box. Pillar boxes were the idea of novelist Anthony Trollope, then a clerk for the General Post Office. The standard Victorian colour for them was green, the first red ones not appearing in London until 1874. They often have details of collections on the front, and the oddest of these was recalled by politician Tony Benn on Osea Island, Essex, connected to the mainland by a causeway across which a postman would cycle. The plate said 'Letters collected according to the tide'. Electrician Arthur Reeder has the world's biggest collection of postboxes, (see page 78).

There is even a **Talbot Society**, which holds reunions for anyone called Talbot. The Talbots travel to Port Talbot, Wales, in their Talbot cars, stopping off at the innumerable Talbot hotels (a talbot was a Norman hunting dog, if you must know).

Other oddities include a **Test Card Circle** that sits around watching tapes of those things that used to go between programmes; a **Tall Persons' Club of Great Britain & Ireland** (☎ 07000 TALL-1-2, or 07000 825512 with a numbers-only phone), for people probably unkindly nicknamed 'Shorty' at school, meets in a Docklands tower block, where they have a high old time telling their kind of tall stories; the **Bald-Headed Club of Great Britain** recently had the bare-faced cheek to write to a leading Labour politician who is alleged to wear a wig, offering him a prominent position in the club; and then there's the **Handlebar Club**, which meets in London and celebrates those great Jimmy-Edwards-style moustaches. Marvellous.

And finally, I'd like to give a quick mention of a group formed in London recently: the **Cloud Appreciation Society**. You might have thought given the British climate that the lack of clouds would be appreciated more, but this society believes the beauty of clouds needs to be looked at with more organised enthusiasm, and the members travel to places such as Australia to look at the unusual clouds they have there. They would probably be beyond cloud nine. Maybe, on the other hand, they prefer there always to be a cloud on the horizon …

ECCENTRICITY ON DISPLAY: BRITAIN'S TOP ODD MUSEUMS

1 **CHAIR MUSEUM, HIGH WYCOMBE, BUCKINGHAMSHIRE**
More interesting than you expect when you get furnished with the details. For instance, bodging is the art much practised in the woods hereabouts of spinning a bit of wood on a forest lathe to make ornate chair legs. Hence the Bodgers Arms pub nearby. You wooden credit it. Local council meetings could be confusing, however. 'The sitting chair chair is going to table a motion…'

> **WYCOMBE LOCAL HISTORY AND CHAIR MUSEUM,** Castle Hill House, Priory Avenue, High Wycombe, Buckinghamshire HP13 6PX ☎ 01494 421895 🖥 www.wycombe.gov.uk/museum ☏ 01494 421892
> 🚗 Off M40. 🚆 High Wycombe, from London Marylebone

2 **CINEMA ORGAN MUSEUM, ST ALBANS, HERTFORDSHIRE**
See and hear a couple of those amazing organs such as the Wurlitzer from the great days of giant 'dream palaces', mostly now demolished, and four gaudily decorated mechanical organs which, like those in fairgrounds, work automatically but equally rousingly off cards with the music punched on them.

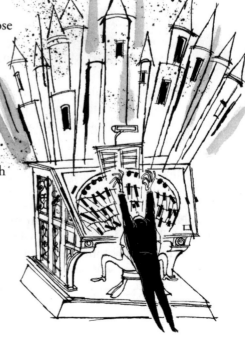

> **ST ALBANS ORGAN MUSEUM,** 320 Camp Road, St Albans ☎ 01727 851557 ☏ 01727 864511 🚗 Off M1, A1 or M25 🚆 St Albans City, from London St Pancras

101

3 CORNFLAKES PACKET MUSEUM, NOTTING HILL, LONDON

In fact, the much wider Museum of Brands, Packaging and Advertising, which founder Robert Opie, with admirable foresight – although his friends may have thought him a little odd – started at the age of 16 in 1963, collecting, dating and pricing ordinary packaging of then contemporary household goods. A tad boring in 1963, but by 2010, absolutely fascinating. Since then his collection has mushroomed and gone back in time to the fascinating and unlikely origins of the things on all our kitchen shelves. His greatest wish? Winning the Lottery, perhaps? 'Probably an early Heinz baked bean can, dating back the end of the 19th century. Mine only go back to the 1930s,' he says wistfully.

> **MUSEUM OF BRANDS, PACKAGING AND ADVERTISING,**
> 2 Colville Mews, Lonsdale Road, Notting Hill, London W11 2AR
> ☎ 020 7908 0880 🖥 www.museumofbrands.com
> ⊖ Ladbroke Grove, Notting Hill Gate 🚌 23 from Oxford
> Circus and Piccadilly

4 CORKSCREW MUSEUM, ALFRISTON, SUSSEX

Actually just a display that's part of the English Wine Museum at the English Wine Centre, near Drusilla's Zoo. There is also an extensive corkscrew collection, not always on display, at the Victoria & Albert Museum, Kensington (☎ 020 7938 8500).

> **ENGLISH WINE MUSEUM** at the English
> Wine Centre, Alfriston Road, Berwick, East
> Sussex BN26 5QS ☎ 01323 870164
> 🖥 www.englishwine.co.uk 📞 0871 6630031
> 🚗 Off A27 coast road between Brighton
> (M23 from London/M25) and Hastings
> 🚂 Berwick, from London Victoria, 1 mile walk south

5 NAGGING MUSEUM, LONDON

Really the Clink Museum, where macabre medieval implements of punishment include a scold's bridle, which made speech impossible. I know, sexist, not funny, don't tell me off …

> **CLINK MUSEUM,** Clink Street SE1 9DG ☎ 020 7403 0900
> ⊖ London Bridge (Northern, Jubilee and main lines)

6 **ELECTRIC SHOCK MUSEUM, SALCOMBE, DEVON**

There is actually just the one shock machine, Overbeck's Rejuvenator, which made a huge fortune of £3 million for Otto Overbeck in the 1920s. The eccentric inventor of Bovril and alcohol-free beer left his peculiar collection of curios and his home at Overbecks to a shocked nation.

> **OVERBECKS MUSEUM (NATIONAL TRUST)**, Sharpitor, Salcombe, Devon TQ8 8LW ☎ 01548 842893 ▦ www.salcombe-online.co.uk
> ☀ 01548 843927
> 🚗 From end of M5, A38, then A382 to Newton Abbot, A381 to Salcombe

7 **GAS MUSEUM, LEICESTER**

Not so much the gas itself, which would be rather difficult to pin down or display, but the history of the gas industry from the grimy Victorian coal gasworks to a 1920s kitchen full of appliances to modern natural gas piped from the North Sea. Which of these is feasible: gas iron, gas hairdryer, gas fridge, gas curling tongs, gas projectors, gas radio? Answer: all of them and they're all on display. In the Victorian gatehouse of an old gasworks.

> **GAS MUSEUM**, 195 Aylestone Road, Leicester LE2 7QH
> ☎ 0116 250 3190 ▦ www.gasmuseum.co.uk ☀ 0844 888 5181
> 🚗 Off M1 (J21/22). From town centre ring road take Aylestone Road (A426) and look out on right just after rail bridge 🚂 Leicester, from London St Pancras. Walk south on ring road and then as above

8 **JABS MUSEUM, BERKELEY, GLOUCESTERSHIRE**

This includes the hut where poor local children received jabs free from the great Dr Edward Jenner, whose work on the now-eradicated scourge of smallpox means he saved more lives than anyone else on earth. He liked to call the hut the Temple of Vaccinnia, which could equally indicate a sense of humour or a complete lack of one. His study and medical equipment may be viewed in his former home. Open afternoons except Mondays.

> **EDWARD JENNER MUSEUM**, Church Lane, Berkeley, Gloucestershire GL13 9BN ☎ 0145 3810631 ▦ www.jennermuseum.com
> ☀ 01452 396572
> 🚗 Signed west of A38 midway between Bristol and Gloucester

9 **LAUREL AND HARDY MUSEUM, ULVERSTON, CUMBRIA**
The local boy was the thin one in the globally famous comedy duo.
The films, the music, the custard pies – another fine mess, in fact.
And have a drink afterwards at the Stan Laurel Inn.

LAUREL AND HARDY MUSEUM, Brogden Street, Ulverston, Cumbria
LA12 7AH ☎ 01229 582292 📠 www.furness.co.uk/on-line/
laurelandhardy.htm 📠 01229 587120
🚗 A590 west from M6 J36 🚆 Connecting services to Ulverston
from London Euston–Glasgow line

10 **BOTTLE MUSEUM, ELSECAR, YORKSHIRE**
If you thought bottles were boring and just about their contents,
what about the brilliant bottles invented by Hiram Codd in the
19th century for fizzy drinks, which had a marble wider than its
neck somehow inserted inside and which, thanks to the pressurised
lemonade, jammed up against a washer to make a seal? I've
got one at home with its marble and washer still rattling
around and with the maker's name proudly embossed on
the glass, which is a miracle, as millions of small boys
smashed them to get the marbles out. So many that
Codd designed a pear-shaped marble before the whole
design went, well, pear-shaped, as easier-to-clean crown
cap bottles arrived in the 20th century. It's all part of the
much wider Elsecar Heritage Centre, which includes
steam railway, etc...

ELSECAR HERITAGE CENTRE, Wath Road, Elsecar, South
Yorkshire S74 8HJ ☎ 01226 740203 📠 01226 206757
🚗 Follow the brown Elsecar Heritage signs from M1 J36
🚆 Hoyland about 1 mile. Or Barnsley then bus 66

11 **PENNY-FARTHING MUSEUM, KNUTSFORD, CHESHIRE**
The bicycles, not the coins after which they were named (being
one big and one small). The main wheel, above which one sat,
could be 54 inches high, with a small trailing wheel behind, so
falling off was painful. This museum with around 70 machines on
display is, in fact, the Courtyard Coffee House. Free tea to anyone
arriving on a penny-farthing. See race, page 60.

PENNY-FARTHING MUSEUM, at the rear of 92 King Street, Knutsford,
WA16 6DX ☎ 01565 653974 📠 033001235500
🚗 M6 J19 🚆 Knutsford on the line from Manchester to Chester

12 TILE MUSEUM, IRONBRIDGE, SHROPSHIRE

A lot of it is to do with those glorious Victorian loos, or rather their way of making a virtue of a necessity and going for decoration in a huge way that we perhaps don't have the confidence to do today. The Jackfield Tile Museum shows how the fantastically ornate tiles were made, and there are walk-through reproductions of tilework at its most fancy (a Victorian pub and Covent Garden Underground station). Young people, if they can be persuaded to spend a day on the tiles, end up fascinated and making their own tiles, which are later fired and posted on to them. Part of ten attractions on the Ironbridge Gorge Passport Ticket, mostly relating to the birthplace of the Industrial Revolution.

JACKFIELD TILE MUSEUM, Telford, Shropshire TF8 7LJ; ☎ 01952 882030 📧 www.ironbridge.org.uk 🖶 01952 884391
🚗 M54 J4, follow brown signs to Ironbridge or Blists Hill Victorian Town

13 CATALYST MUSEUM, WIDNES, CHESHIRE

Four rather good galleries dedicated to the science that gave this area its prosperity (and a lot of pollution). You can take refreshment in the Elements café where you may indeed ponder the importance of chemistry, in that it's all right to sprinkle sodium chloride (salt) on your chips but not sodium chlorate (which might make them explode and would certainly poison you). Not recommended: chatting up the staff with the line 'I think there's a certain chemistry between us.' The whole area and the river have, of course, been much cleaned up since the height of the Industrial Revolution. Or as the Bard would have put it: 'The quality of Mersey is somewhat strained.'

CATALYST MUSEUM, Mersey Road, Widnes, Cheshire WA8 0DF
☎ 0151 420 1121 📧 www.catalyst.org.uk 🖶 0151 709 3631
🚗 M6 J20 then M56 westbound to J12, follow signs for Widnes and pick up brown signs for the museum 🚂/🚌 The main station is Runcorn, across the river, whence you can catch a bus across (or back across) or a great walk of just over a mile if it's a good day. Ask for Irwell Street and walk down through the underpass. Also buses from Warrington Bank Quay station

14 LAVATORY MUSEUM, STOKE-ON-TRENT

Set amidst the Potteries, principal source of the world's plates, mugs, etc, and also the khazi capital of the empire, is the Gladstone

Pottery Museum. Here the Flushed With Pride gallery lifts the lid on the illustrious history of the brilliant British bog, or water closet, which freed the world from perilous pongs. It's a subject that affects everyone, so there's plenty to go on (groan!). There are fascinating Victorian contraptions with their strange embellishments. Were the ones marked Crapper the origin of the verb? (No, it was a coincidence.) How do you make a lavatory bowl in one piece? There's even a section called Triumph of the Water Closet, which boggles the mind somewhat, plus a fascinating complete Victorian pottery factory. Plus, if you don't pooh-pooh the whole concept, there's the guided walk at York. The **Historic Toilet Tour of York** is a sanitary experience, but a guided walk happens only at their convenience. 'It's come and go,' said a spokesman. Quite.

GLADSTONE POTTERY MUSEUM, Uttoxeter Road, Longton, Stoke-on-Trent ST3 1PQ ☎ 01782 319232 ✆ 01782 236000 🚗 From M6 J15 follow A50 to Longton 🚂 Blythe Bridge station is within walking distance (change at Crewe or Derby) YORK WALK ☎ 01904 622303

15   ELEPHANT'S TOE NAIL MUSEUM, EDINBURGH

OK, OK, I can't produce a whole museum dedicated to this subject. But there are indeed some elephant's toe nails on display in a most unexpected place: in a military museum in Edinburgh Castle. The elephant in question was adopted as a mascot by the 78th Regiment while serving in Ceylon (Sri Lanka) in the 1820s and was shipped home as it proved so disciplined at leading regimental parades. But after moving into stables at the castle its discipline slipped a little and it adopted the local love of a little too much booze, aided and abetted by its keeper Private McIntosh, who was lucky not to be charged with being trunk in charge of an elephant (tusk, tusk). In the end, neither of their livers was up to the vast amounts of beer they consumed and the elephant's toe nails are all that remains, sawn off and retained in the National War Museum of Scotland. The castle, of course, in itself well worth a visit, is also home to an eccentric **Dogs' Cemetery** (see page 244) and the Scots are also rather good at elephant polo (see page

143). To quote my book *Eccentric Edinburgh*, 'You don't visit Edinburgh, you fall in love with the place'.

EDINBURGH CASTLE, EH1 1SH 📞 0845 2255 121 🖥 www.edinburgh.org
🚗 A1 London to Edinburgh 🚂 London King's Cross and many other centres to Edinburgh Waverley

16 SHRUNKEN HEADS, VOODOO AND WITCH MUSEUM, OXFORD

Again these are contents, not the official title of Oxford's extraordinary, eclectic and eccentric Pitt Rivers Museum, one of those everything-in-the-world collections that curious rich people used to put together. Where else will you find: shrunken heads; mummified people; a witch in a bottle; whole boats; American Indian skin shirts decorated with porcupine quills? The place is crammed and many of the items are still labelled in the handwriting of the original curator. Pull open a drawer (under the display cases) and there may be magic objects, including amulets and charms; an intriguing collection of locks and keys; tools and weapons; voodoo dolls; weird musical instruments; mummified toads; severed fingers. The opening hours are limited to afternoons at the time of writing, but it's free and fascinating. Don't make the mistake of thinking the Natural History Museum, through which you must pass, is it.

PITT RIVERS MUSEUM, South Parks Road, Oxford OX1 3PP
☎ 01865 270927 🖥 www.prm.ox.ac.uk 📞 01865 252200
🚗 M40 London or Midlands. Parking hopeless – use Park & Ride.
🚂 Oxford 🚌 Fast coaches from London Victoria

17 BISCUIT MUSEUM, READING

Reading, Berkshire (pronounced Redding, not like the activity you are doing now) is famous for many things, including being home to Huntley & Palmer, major manufacturers – in fact the world's biggest in 1900 – of biscuits (cookies, if you will). The place was called Biscuit Town colloquially and the football team the Biscuit Men. These biscuits are held with great affection by the British, and the highly decorated tins they used to be sold in are collectable in themselves. It's in fact just a section of The Museum of Reading at the Town Hall (style: twiddly bits Gothic Revival). This also has, strangely, a full-sized copy of the Bayeux Tapestry made by Victorian ladies, which doesn't have to be viewed in near-darkness like the original (yes, I know that's an embroidery, not a tapestry, and was probably made in Kent, not Bayeux, but we're not going to change that now). Plus you can buy biscuits to take away or nibble in the Biscuit Tin café. Huntley & Palmer's biscuits were taken to the South Pole by Captain Scott in his disastrous expedition. Not enough Oates probably. Does that take the biscuit, bad-joke-wise? What about the fact that in 19th-century Italy, Garibaldi helped push out the Bourbons? Lets stop before we go crackers.

MUSEUM OF READING, Town Hall, Blagrave Street, Reading, Berkshire RG1 1QH ☎ 0118 939 9800 🖳 www.readingmuseum.org.uk, 🖳 www.bayeuxtapestry.org.uk 🖳 www.huntleyandpalmers.org.uk. 🚗 Off M4 🚌 Reading, from London Paddington and other centres

18 **LAWNMOWER MUSEUM, SOUTHPORT, LANCASHIRE**
Above Brian and Sue Radam's lawnmower shop, this is mower interesting, containing 150 vintage and celebrity machines (see pages 74–5). There is a smaller display at Trerice, a National Trust manor house near Newquay, Cornwall TR8 4PG (☎ 01637 875404), which has a mere 87 mowers.

LAWNMOWER MUSEUM, 106–114 Shakespeare Street, Southport, Merseyside PR8 5AJ ☎ 01704 501336 🖳 www.lawnmowerworld.co.uk 📠 01704 533333 🚗 M6, follow signs 🚌 Southport, 15-min walk or Birkdale 🚌 42, 43

19 **MUSIC BOX AND DOLL MUSEUM, CHICHESTER, SUSSEX**
One hundred china- or wax-headed Victorian dolls amidst the cacophony of 100 automatic music boxes, curios and mechanical dance organs from the same period.

MECHANICAL MUSIC MUSEUM AND DOLL COLLECTION, Church Road, Portfield, Chichester PO19 4HN ☎ 01243372646 📠 01243 775888 🚗 A3 from London then A27 east 🚌 Chichester, from London Victoria

20 **MUSTARD MUSEUM, NORWICH, NORFOLK**
Hotter than the Spice Girls ever were, Norfolk's mustard industry has a fascinating history illustrated here through the history of the Colman family, plus, of course, oodles of products to buy. And if that leaves you thirsty, try the Teapot Museum nearby (see page 110).

MUSTARD MUSEUM, in the Mustard Shop, The Royal Arcade, Norwich NR2 1NQ ☎ 01603 627889 🖳 www.norwich.gov.uk/tourism/ museums 📠 01603 727927 🚗 A11 from London, A47 from Midlands 🚌 Norwich from London Liverpool Street or Midlands

21 NEEDLE MUSEUM, REDDITCH, WORCESTERSHIRE

An interesting remnant of a once-huge local industry that helped stitch the Empire together. This is in fact a water-powered needle scouring mill but you'll have to go along to see the point. One could naturally follow this with the Button Museum, Ross on Wye, but I believe the owners have retired and closed it ('Sell our collection? Never!').

NEEDLE MUSEUM FORGE MILL, Needle Mill Lane, Redditch, Worcestershire B98 8HY ☎ 01527 62509 ✆ 01527 60806
🚗 Off M40 London–Birmingham at J2, south on A441, signed at first roundabout 🚂 Redditch, on branch line from Birmingham
🚌 The free shopper bus from Redditch bus station to Sainsbury's takes you near, then walk under dual carriageway to museum.

22 OPERATING THEATRE MUSEUM, LONDON BRIDGE

Return to the land of hope and gory when conscious, screaming patients endured butchery, which often killed them, in front of an audience (as in operating theatre), while sawdust soaked up the blood. The Old Operating Theatre and Herb Garret, near London Bridge, dates from 1822, before antiseptics and anaesthetics. If this makes you feel faint, there's always the **London Fan Museum** at Greenwich.

OLD OPERATING THEATRE AND HERB GARRET, 9A St Thomas's Street, near London Bridge, London SE1 9RY ☎ 0207188 2679
🖳 www.thegarret.org.uk
🚂/🚇 London Bridge
LONDON FAN MUSEUM, 10–12 Crooms Hill, Greenwich SE10 8ER
☎ 020 8305 1441 🖳 www.fan-museum.org
🚂 Greenwich from London Charing Cross 🚇 Greenwich (DLR)

23 PENCIL MUSEUM, KESWICK, CUMBRIA

To be blunt, some may not see the point, but it's quite a draw on a rainy day in the Lake District where graphite mines provided the 'lead' for the famous Cumberland pencils. How about the world's biggest pencil, or spy pencils with secret maps in them? Plus all the 4Bs or 3Hs you can carry.

PENCIL MUSEUM, Greta Bridge, Keswick, Cumbria
CA12 5NG ☎ 017687 73626 🖳 www.pencils.co.uk
✆ 017687 72645
🚗 From M6 J40, A66 west

24 SHOE MUSEUM, STREET, SOMERSET

The home of Clark's shoes, but this family business is not the sole subject. It has the last word on footwear back to the 16th century and, on the way in, some early shoemaking machines.

SHOE MUSEUM, Street, Somerset BA16 0EQ ☎ 01458 842169
🔥 01458 447384 🚗 Off M5 J23, A39 towards Glastonbury

25 TEAPOT MUSEUM, NORWICH CASTLE, NORFOLK

This features a selection of the world's largest collection of British teapots – 3,000 varieties from short and stout to ancient and priceless, including the world's largest. The fascinating **RAF Air Defence Radar Museum** is nearby.

NORWICH CASTLE MUSEUM AND ART GALLERY, Market Avenue,
Norwich NR1 3JQ ☎ 01603 493650 📟 www.museums.norfolk.gov.
uk 🔥 01603 727927 🚗 A11 from London, A47 from Midlands 🚌
Norwich from London Liverpool Street or Midlands
RADAR MUSEUM, Neatishead NR12 8YB ☎ 01692 631485
📟 www.radarmuseum.co.uk

26 TEDDY BEAR MUSEUM, MELROSE, BORDERS

A fur bet for the right kind of child. There's another one in Worcestershire.

TEDDY MELROSE, The Wynd, Melrose, Scottish Borders TD6 9PA
☎ 01896 823854 📟 www.theteddybearmuseum.com
🔥 0870 608 0404 🚗 Melrose is between A7 Edinburgh–Carlisle road
and A68 Edinburgh–Darlington on A6091 🚌/🚗 Edinburgh, from
London King's Cross, then bus
TEDDY MUSEUM, 76 High Street, Broadway, Worcestershire WR12 AJ
☎ 01386 858323 📟 www.jks.org
🚗 On A44 between Oxford and Worcester

27 TRAMPS, VILLAINS AND PAUPERS MUSEUM, RIPON, NORTH YORKSHIRE

There are three linked museums: the Prison and Police Museum, which includes stocks and chains in an 1816 extension to a house of correction; the 18th-century Courthouse Museum; and the Ripon Workhouse Museum, in an 1854 building. Curator Anthony Chadwick says: 'This place has a remarkable effect on people. About 90 per cent of visitors to the prison approve of everything that they see and wish to go back to those times, then they see the workhouse and their reaction is exactly the opposite.'

RIPON MUSEUMS, Allhallowgate, Ripon HG4 1LE ☎ 01765 690799
🖳 www.ripponmuseums.co.uk ✆ 01765 604625
🚗 Off A1 north of Wetherby, then A61 southwest 🚂/🚌 London
King's Cross to Leeds, then to Harrogate, then frequent bus 36

28 WIRELESS MUSEUM, RYDE, ISLE OF WIGHT

Marconi transmitted from here to the mainland, first installing his
equipment on the Titanic, which saved so many lives. There is a
good collection of early radios and televisions, if that kind of thing
is on your wavelength.

NATIONAL WIRELESS MUSEUM, Puckpool Park, Ryde PO34 5AR
☎ 01983 567665 ✆ 01983 813813
🚗 On A3054 on east edge of Ryde (towards Seaview). Car ferry from
Portsmouth (reached by A3 from London/M25) lands 3 miles west on
same road at Fishbourne 🚂 Ryde Esplanade, from London Waterloo,
including ferry from Portsmouth Harbour

29 WITCHCRAFT MUSEUM, BOSCASTLE, CORNWALL

Wizard during a wet spell on holiday. But think about it: either
witchcraft is real, or all those women burnt alive or drowned on
ducking stools were terribly wronged. In fact this museum itself
was pretty drowned in the shock Boscastle floods of 2004, but is
back on form now, as if someone waved a magic wand. Don't miss
staggeringly beautiful Tintagel nearby.

THE MUSEUM OF WITCHCRAFT, Boscastle, Cornwall PL35 0HD
☎ 01840 250 111 🖳 www.museumofwitchcraft.com ✆ 01840 250010
🚗 M5 to Exeter, A30 to Launceston A395 and then pick up B road
signs

30 VACUUM CLEANER MUSEUM

If you think this idea sucks (sorry), you'd be right, literally. More
than 70 vintage Hoovers, Electroluxes, Kirbys, Dysons, etc. 'All
I've ever wanted is to work with vacuum cleaners,' says James Brown.
It's actually a shop in Eastwood, Nottinghamshire, called Mr
Vacuum Cleaner, which sells and repairs machines. But the further
into the shop you go, the more vintage and strange machines come
into view. And don't call them Hoover when they are not or –
crime of crimes – use 'Hoovering' as a verb. James started young:
'When I was four and my Mum was poorly, I used to help out with
her Electrolux 345 Automatic,' James says. 'When I was eight, my
Dad found a little Goblin 800 that had been thrown away. We

fixed it and that was my very own vacuum cleaner.' Note the early attention to detail. James's biggest treat was visiting the factory of the Rolls-Royce of vacuums, Kirby, in Ohio. He was quoted as saying 'I was so excited, I could barely speak.' Hoover didn't invent the vacuum, but bought it off a sucker called Spangler (and then really cleaned up), so perhaps one should Spangler the carpet. This is a shop, so no admission charge, but do buy something, even if it's just some bags for your old upright. A few yards away from D H Lawrence's Birthplace Museum … I wonder which women were more grateful for at the time – *Sons & Lovers* or the vacuum?

MR VACUUM CLEANER, 58 Nottingham Road, Eastwood, Nottingham NG16 3NQ ☎ 01773 712 777 💻 www.mrvacuumcleaner.co.uk
🚲 08444 775678
🚗 A610 from M1 J26 and Nottingham 🚂 Langley Mills station is less than a mile away. Walk east down Station Road and cross the A610 into Derby Road.

TRAVEL INFORMATION

ARTHUR REEDER, Last Post, Fairlee Road, Newport, Isle of Wight PO30 2JX ☎ 01983 825193 (by appointment only)
🚗/🚄 Convenient for the Southampton–Cowes or Portsmouth–Fishbourne ferries 🚂/🚄 London Waterloo to Ryde via Portsmouth and connecting ferry. Then bus to Newport, or rail to Smallbrook Junction, change to Isle of Wight Steam Railway to Wootton Bridge

CLOG AND APRON RACE, Kew Gardens, Surrey
☎ 020 8332 5655 💻 www.kew.org
🚗 South of Kew Bridge on the north/
south circular roads and north of
the A316 which links the M3 from
the M25 to Chiswick 🚂 Kew
Gardens, North London main
line 🔵 Kew Gardens

CORACLE RACING,
Cilgerran, near Cardigan
🚲 01239 613230

From west end of M4, A48 to Carmarthen, then A484. Cilgerran is on left before Cardigan

MAN VERSUS HORSE MARATHON Llanwrtyd Wells, Powys, Wales
☎ 01591 610666 💻 www.llanwrtyd-wells.powys.org.uk

NATIONAL MOTOR MUSEUM, Beaulieu, Hampshire
☎ 01590 612345 📠 01590 689000
Signed from M27 J2 🚂 From London Waterloo to Brockenhurst, then taxi. Keen walkers or cyclists could use Beaulieu Road (3 miles).

WOOLSACK DAY, Tetbury, Gloucestershire
From M4 J17, north on A429 then west on B4014 📠 01666 503552

PS ... high-voltage eccentricity

TRAIN SPOTTERS ARE TWO-A-PENNY in his line of work, but West Country railwayman Harvey Brant is a little different – he's a pylon spotter. Electricity pylons, that is, those dull grey things that march uninvited across the countryside.

Mr Brant spends hours roaming the countryside to photograph the towering metal structures and record their serial numbers. And no, they're not all ugly and all the same, he says.

'Electricity pylons can really enhance the beauty of a landscape,' he claims. 'They are sadly unappreciated and are quite stunning feats of engineering. They provide a comforting reminder of Man's harnessing of the forces of nature.'

Mr Brant took up pylon-hunting in 1999 after being bored by his workmates' talk about train spotting. He has now set up a website 💻 http://users.tinyonline.co.uk/bigh/bigh/pylonof.htm – to log his findings. There's a Pylon of the Month – a sort of pin-up page. When I checked, it was, if you're interested, TP23 at Hindlip in Worcestershire. His favourite, however, is 4YX183 near the M4–M5 junction at Almondsbury, south Gloucestershire.

'Its design and backdrop are superb,' he enthuses.

BARMY BUREAUCRACY

ATLANTIC OCEAN

Orkney Islands

Thurso

Isle of Lewis

Isle of Skye

Inner Hebrides

Inverness

Aberdeen

SCOTLAND

Island of Mull

NORTH SEA

N

Islay

Glasgow

EDINBURGH

Arran

ATLANTIC OCEAN

Newcastle upon Tyne

Carlisle

0   80 km

0   50 miles

Middlesbrough

Tynwald Ceremony, St John's

Isle of Man

ENGLAND

IRISH SEA

York

Kingston-upon-Hull

NORTH SEA

Leeds

Anglesey

Bradford

Holyhead

Liverpool

Manchester

Grimsby

Sheffield

Cardigan Bay

Stoke-on-Trent

Nottingham

Norwich

Derby

Horseshoe Tax, Oakham Castle

Wolverhampton

Birmingham

Fishguard

Court Leet, Bromsgrove

Coventry

Cambridge

WALES

Ipswich

Big Court Night, Laugharne

Milo's Dole, St Briavels

Swansea

CARDIFF

Dunmow Flitch Marriage Trials

Mayor-weighing, High Wycombe

Ceremony of the Keys, Tower of London

Oxford

LONDON

Guildhall Processions

Bristol Channel

Bristol

Hungerford & the Tuttimen

Quit Rent, Strathfield Saye

Admiralty Court, Rochester

Lady Marvyn's Dole, Ufton Nervet

Biddendon Dole

Tichborne Dole of Crawls

Wayfarers' Dole, Winchester

Southampton

Dover

Portsmouth

Brighton

ATLANTIC OCEAN

Exeter

Scavengers & Chimney Peepers, Wareham

Forest Verderers' Court, Lyndhurst

Penzance

ENGLISH CHANNEL

BARMY BUREAUCRACY

PAYING THE RENT IN ROSES, NAILS AND PARSNIPS

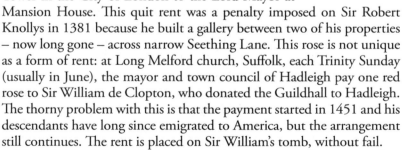

Paying the rent might be one of life's less amusing chores, yet for some this droll routine is curiously colourful and the rent is even paid for centuries after the property in question has disappeared.

Every 24 June a single red **Knollys Rose** is carried on a velvet cushion by churchwardens of All-Hallows-by-the-Tower in the City of London to the Lord Mayor at Mansion House. This quit rent was a penalty imposed on Sir Robert Knollys in 1381 because he built a gallery between two of his properties – now long gone – across narrow Seething Lane. This rose is not unique as a form of rent: at Long Melford church, Suffolk, each Trinity Sunday (usually in June), the mayor and town council of Hadleigh pay one red rose to Sir William de Clopton, who donated the Guildhall to Hadleigh. The thorny problem with this is that the payment started in 1451 and his descendants have long since emigrated to America, but the arrangement still continues. The rent is placed on Sir William's tomb, without fail.

That this is not merely a medieval hangover was demonstrated in 1995 by the start of a 99-year lease of land by Mrs Mary Cornelius-Reid of **Sutton Scotney**, near Winchester, Hampshire. The rent is a dozen red roses payable each Midsummer's Day. The land was to be used by the Wessex Children's Hospice Trust.

Initially difficult to understand is the annual rent for the **Rose and Lion pub** in Bromyard, Hereford and Worcester, first paid in January 1997: a kilo of home-grown parsnips. Landlady Fran Hurdman handed over the token amount after Wye Valley Brewery owner Peter Amor decided to charge her in vegetables instead of cash, as a way of ensuring that the pub garden was kept full of crops to put off greedy developers.

Much harder to understand and more than 700 years older are the **Horseshoe and Faggot-cutting ceremonies** held at the High Court, London, on a Wednesday afternoon late each October ('between the morrow of St Michael and the morrow of St Martin'). The City Solicitor cuts hazel rods with two knives, which he then presents to the Queen's Remembrancer, who pronounces 'Good service'. This is the rent for a piece of ground called The Moors at Eardington in Shropshire. Six very large horseshoes and 61 nails are then counted out and the Remembrancer pronounces 'Good number'. This was the rent agreed after Walter le Brun was granted land in 1235 for a forge in St Clement Danes parish, probably where Australia House now stands. This may be the oldest surviving English ceremony, apart from the Coronation.

In Warwickshire, the **Wroth Silver** is paid by the 25 parishes of Knightlow Hundred (a hundred is an old rural district) to the Duke of Buccleuch, Lord of the Hundred. The rent must be paid before sunrise each St Martin's Day (11 November) at Knightlow Cross near Dunchurch. The representatives gather in the dark to hear the duke's agent read the Charter of Assembly. They walk three times round the stone, say 'Wroth Silver' and drop coins (worth between a penny and about 12p) into the hole where the cross used to be. The company then repairs to a pub and drink the duke's health in rum and milk.

Although the duke must make a loss on the whole operation – he receives less than 50p in total Wroth Silver – non-payment is rigorously penalised at a rate of £1 per old penny unpaid, or a fine of a white bull with red ears and a red nose. Such old English cattle are now hard to find, yet this fine was imposed at least once in the 19th century.

Some quit rents certainly seem a good bargain for both sides. The Duke of Wellington's enormous **Stratfield Saye** estate on the Hampshire–Berkshire border is paid for each 18 June with the presentation of a memento of the Iron Duke's victory at Waterloo in 1815 – a small silk tricolour flag is given to the monarch before noon and is hung on the duke's bust in the Guard Room at Windsor Castle. Stratfield Saye (Travel: page 130) is also home to the grave of Copenhagen, the Iron Duke's famous horse.

Even royalty get involved in this eccentric quit rent business. The Prince of Wales, as **Duke of Cornwall**, used to receive 40 puffins a year in rent from certain Scilly Isles, and an annual greyhound from one Cornish manor. (Absurd? One Somerset farmer was, until recently, compelled to accompany the prince with a bow and 12 arrows whenever he entered the county.) Even today the prince receives a daffodil each year as a quit rent from an environmental trust for the uninhabited bits of the Scilly Isles.

Perhaps the most exclusive rent – or tax – in the kingdom is applied only to peers of the realm passing through Oakham, Leicestershire, each of whom must give a shoe from his or her horse, or money to have one made, so they may be hung in **Oakham Castle hall** (Travel: page 130) to go with the 218 others to be seen today – including one from the queen.

BRITAIN'S WEIRD COURTS THAT COURT DISBELIEF

The rule of law is often upheld as one of those great British virtues – like sporting fair play – spread by the Empire to the four corners of the globe. But when you examine the peculiar way some of Britain's oldest and oddest courts actually operate, you could be forgiven for thinking them not much of a role model.

There is the **Big Court Night**, for example, at Laugharne, Carmarthenshire, where, on the first Monday of each October, the new Portreeve is elected with much pomp and ceremony, then adorned with a fabulous three-strand chain of golden cockleshells (engraved with the names of the previous Portreeves) and carried three times round the town hall shoulder-high by the constables. This is just part of the paraphernalia created in the 13th-century charter, including not only the Portreeve, but a Grand Jury, Recorder, Common Attorneys, Constables, Halbardiers and a Bailiff.

Older and yet odder is the **Court of Arraye** at Lichfield, Staffordshire, each Spring bank holiday, which dates back to before 1176 in the reign of Henry II and was once part of a nationwide array of men-at-arms, to assess all men between 14 and 60 years of age and inspect their arms and armour. Today the High Constable still presides but the Bowers Procession is a less warlike event, with the crowning of a local maid as Bower Queen, plus a market and a fair.

PUTTING YOUR MARRIAGE ON TRIAL

One of the oldest, oddest, yet ever-relevant courts in the country must be the **Dunmow Flitch trials** (Travel: page 130), held in June or July every leap year at Great Dunmow, Essex. It dates from 1104 when the lord of the manor, Robert Fitzwalter, established a priory there. To test it he and his wife went in disguise and asked for a blessing on their marriage, according to the local legend. The prior quizzed them about it closely and was so impressed he gave the couple a side of bacon. After that Sir Robert gave the priory some lands, on condition that they offered a flitch of bacon to whichever man could show that within a year and a day of his marriage he did not repent of his wedding, nor quarrel nor dispute with his wife in any way. The claimants – or the pilgrims as then termed – were for centuries required to swear the oath of their testimony while kneeling on sharp stones in their churchyard.

By the 14th century the Dunmow Flitch, meaning a good marriage, was well known enough for Chaucer's ribald character, the five-times married Wife of Bath, to make reference to it without further explanation.

Today, the proceedings take the form of a properly argued trial, presided over by the Flitch Judge and with a jury of six maids and six bachelors. There is often a well-known figure as counsel for the couple and another as counsel for the bacon. In fact there are two sessions, in the afternoon and evening, with two couples in each. The trials are held at Talberds Ley in a marquee – tickets are sold for charity – at the same time as a special fair, and end with a procession to the marketplace, the couple being carried shoulder-high in the Flitch Chair, accompanied by Morris dancers, the bachelors, maids and the flitch in a frame like a gibbet, all amidst much merriment. Finally they make their oath and take home the bacon.

DO THESE JOBS REALLY EXIST?

Other ancient local courts are largely ceremonial talking shops, although a few retain real powers. There is one ancient type of court dating back to baronial times called the **Court Leet** which was once aimed at preserving local liberties and ending grievances (although at times it worked vice versa).

The Court Leet, with a whole gamut of frankly unbelievable office-holders and titles, should have been abolished many times over as the court system went through its evolution into Assizes, Quarter Sessions, County and Crown Courts. Somehow a few weren't, and stubbornly survive, such as the Court Leet at Southampton on the first Tuesday after Michaelmas; at Ashburton, Devon, on the fourth Tuesday in November; at Wareham, Dorset, on the four evenings before the last Friday in November; and at Bromsgrove, Worcestershire (Travel: page 130), on the Saturday nearest to Midsummer's Day, where it involves a procession through the town at 10.30am, the proclamation of the 1199 charter, the assize of Bread, Ale and Leather and the Walking of the Fayre, a carnival that begins at 2pm.

Probably the best collection of these comic-opera titles is at **Lichfield**, Staffordshire, at the St George's Day court, which sees two High Constables, four Clerks of the Market, two Dozeners for each street, two Pinners or Pound Keppers, four Commoners, an Ale Taster and a Gamekeeper. All these courts hear local grievances or nuisances, sometimes lightheartedly, and few do anything about them. But each town's right to hold these courts, however meaningless to the outsider, has been jealously guarded down the centuries.

In the last week of June at **Ashburton**, Devon, the Portreeve and the official Ale Tasters visit every tavern in turn to taste the beer. If it is of good quality, the landlord is handed an evergreen bough to put over the pub door. The Ale Tasters' procession includes the official Bread Weighers, who visit all the town's bakeries, weighing two loaves in each.

At **Wareham**, the Court Leet goes on patrol in its strange garb with ancient bread scales and an 18th-century ale measure, but is accompanied by officers such as the Leather Sealer, the Scavengers – for enforcing refuse removal – and the Surveyors and Searchers of Mantels and Chimneys or Chimney Peepers. The fine for having an unswept chimney is a double whisky.

Mugwort, Deemsters, Tynwald: Yes, it's Mad Manx

If you see a procession involving curious characters such as the First Deemster and the Second Deemster, Yn Lhaider, a Sword of State, trumpeters, a bishop, soldiers presenting arms and His Excellency the Lieutenant Governor, you could be forgiven for thinking you are watching a Gilbert and Sullivan operetta, are on powerful medication or watching a Hollywood film about some Ruritanian country.

It is, in fact, a very real and particularly powerful court, although it takes place on an open hillside. It is fenced in, legally speaking, by a strange process. On one side the aforesaid Yn Lhaider proclaims:

> *Ta mee cur yn whaiyl shoh fo harey ayns ennym Chiarn Vannin, nagh jean peiagh erbee troiddey, baghart ny jannoo boiranys erbee, as dy jean dy chooilley pheiagh freggyrt tra vees eh er ny eam...*

That's got my spellchecker totally freaked out. Still puzzled? On the other side of the hill the same proclamation is being made in English:

> *I fence this court in the name of Our Most Gracious Sovereign Lady The Queen, I charge that no person do quarrel, brawl or make any disturbance and that all persons do answer their names when called...*

So we've got a British crown possession within the British Isles, clearly with its own Celtic language, and a powerful set of independent institutions. If you haven't worked it out, the flag flying shows three legs joined together and the hill concerned is called Tynwald.

Yes, it's the **Tynwald Ceremony** on the Isle of Man, where all the island's officials, such as coroners and captains of parishes, receive their authority. Members of the House of Keys, which makes the island's laws, are very much involved, and the official instruction says the officials should all wear bollan bane. This is not some Dark Age clothing but a plant called mugwort, which is Manx's own way of warding off evil spirits. Even when the queen opened the Tynwald not long ago – in her local role of Lord of Man, not a bad title – she had to wear bollan bane too. It seemed to work as the flypast of two jet bombers managed to miss the hill she was standing on.

It's a big deal for the island, with troops lining the route from a church – the Royal Chapel of St John the Baptist, no less – and even the Scouts, Guides, coastguard, prison service and fire brigade have members lining the route. It is the island's greatest ceremony, well worth watching if you are there, and totally fascinating in its mad Manxness. As long as you don't 'quarrel, brawl or make any disturbance'.

New laws are not legal unless they are declaimed from this hill, for the Vikings who set up this parliament – the oldest unbrokenly held democratic parliament in the world – did not write things down. The word Tynwald comes from the Norse *Thing-Vollr* meaning 'parliament field'. The legendary Viking raping, looting and pillaging probably doesn't tell the whole story of what were clearly here an advanced and civilised people.

Equally legendary at the time of the queen's visit was the truly great Manx resident, veteran British comedian Sir Norman Wisdom, who treated Her Majesty to one of his gags where he shakes your hand and shakes it and shakes it, refusing to let go. A lady-in-waiting had to be called to separate them, but the queen didn't seem to mind.

The Isle of Man, otherwise famed for a tailless cat and the insanely dangerous annual TT motorcycle races along the ordinary roads, is deeply annoying to Brussels Eurocrats because it has its own laws, language, parliament, banking system and money, and is thus not only deeply eccentric but for many people a Good Thing.

It can be clearly seen from the hills of four countries – the Lake District of England, southwestest Scotland, north Wales and Northern Ireland. It is a tantalising, magic distance – not so close, like the Isle of Wight, that it's basically part of the same country, and not so far, like the Channel Islands, that they logically ought not to be.

NOT ANY OLD COURT

'New' and 'from time immemorial' are relative terms but when it comes to two specialist courts still held in England, complete with eccentric traditions, they mean much the same thing.

One, the **New Forest Verderers' Court**, is held in Lyndhurst, Hampshire, on the third Monday of odd-numbered months. The word 'New' refers to the laws of William the Conqueror who, after 1066, sought to establish a new royal hunting domain. This is a real court, in effect a specialised magistrates' court dealing with forest bylaws, and is opened with the proclamation: 'Oyez! Oyez! Oyez! All manner of person who have any presentment or matter or thing to do with this Court of Swaincote let him come forward and he shall be heard. God Save the King!' The court starts at 10am and is public.

The **Admiralty Court**, held at Rochester Pier, Kent, on the other hand, is supposedly the opposite of new – it has been in operation since 'time immemorial'. This phrase, also referred to as 'time out of mind' in the law confirming the procedure in 1727, actually means in English law before 1189. A procession is held of the mayor, aldermen and civic bigwigs, notably the Principal Water Bailiff carrying a large silver oar to the civic barge, where the court is held to regulate the fishery. Twelve jurymen and a chamberlain are sworn in to oversee the oyster and floating fishery for the coming year. It takes place on the first or second Saturday in July, according to the tides.

YOUR TAXES OR A KISS

Not many people smile and dance, or sport flowers, blue ribbons and balloons when the taxman comes, nor offer him foaming pints of ale. But they do in **Hungerford**, Berkshire (Travel: page 130), at Hocktide – the Monday and Tuesday of the second week after Easter. Actually most towns and villages have forgotten that Hocktide was the date for collecting tithes or church and parish taxes, and maybe the fact that Hungerford's Tuttimen ('tutti' is a West Country term for flowers) collect only the 13th-century penny per household makes them less feared than the Inland Revenue. Or is it because they usually throw all the taxes – including larger coins donated – for local children to scramble after?

In fact Hocktide is the day Hungerford goes to town. Proceedings start at 8am on the Tuesday with a blast from the Lucas horn summoning the commoners to the **Hocktide Court** in the gloriously over-the-top town hall. The original horn was donated by John of Gaunt in 1343 and is kept in a bank vault, so a modern replica is used. John of Gaunt gave the town certain rights over fisheries. The Hocktide Court is called in 14th-century style to regulate these ancient rights and appoint officers.

The Constable sends the Tuttimen round the town at 9am, carrying their tutti poles and accompanied by the Orangeman who wears a hat decorated with pheasant feathers and gives an orange in exchange for the penny, or kiss, collected. The Tuttimen's work goes on all day and they have been known to return at dusk in wheelbarrows, such is the exhaustion caused by drinking the health of many a commoner.

The burghers of Hungerford also have a way of dealing with those characters who do anything to avoid buying a round of drinks but always partake of one bought by others. (Such individuals employ tricks such as dropping to tie a shoelace while a group approaches the bar and then catching up while the round is being bought.) This isn't a problem in Hungerford, where, after a civic lunch, newcomers are approached by a blacksmith in apron and another man with a box of farrier's nails. The initiate's foot is pulled up – even if this means being heel over head – and a nail is driven into the heel in a custom called 'Shoeing the colt'. The 'colt' can stop the process by crying 'Punch!', which is taken as an order for a round of drinks, and is thus admitted to the company of Hungerford men.

WORTH THE WEIGHT

If MPs really are getting too many free lunches, then an ancient method of checking such things in **High Wycombe**, Buckinghamshire (Travel: page 130), each May could provide the proof of the pudding.

Outside the Guildhall in the High Street at 6.30pm the outgoing town mayor is publicly weighed and the results compared to those of a year before. If he or she is heavier, the mayor is given a good-natured round of boos and cries of 'Shame!', the traditional assumption being that this means a lazy year. If the mayor is lighter – and the police chief, certain councillors and various council officials also go in the balance – then resounding cheers will be heard. Needless to say, the incoming mayor and others are carefully weighed.

The ceremonial weighing is carried out with the full pomp the Chilterns town can muster, with berobed processions before and after, led by a Beadle carrying a mace. It is his job to proclaim the weight after crying: 'Oyez, oyez, oyez!' It could make the State Opening of Parliament worth the weight.

BRITAIN'S MOST ECCENTRIC JOBS

Britain has the most ludicrous set of job titles in the world. Even remote African tribes with Third Fly Whisk to the King or whatever couldn't have dreamt up the eccentricities that abound here.

One of my favourites is the post of **Lord Warden of the Cinque Ports**. Cinque Ports, as the French suggests, refers to Five Ports, a league of ports in the part of England nearest to the Continent. Except that there are not five, but 14, and they are not ports, having 'moved' inland due to silting. The late Queen Mother was Lord Warden and she got a jolly good castle at Walmer near Deal, Kent to go with her other half dozen (so she rarely used it). Actually the job has certain other perks, as I noticed when her successor, Admiral the Lord Boyce, a former Chief of the Defence Staff, was appointed Lord Warden of the Cinque Ports. Under the 850-year-old laws, he has the right to:

> *soc and sac, tol and team, bloowit and fledwit, pillory tumbril infangentheof, outfangentheof, mundbryce waives and strays, flotsam and jetsam and ligan.*

Edward Lear couldn't make it up. When you try to translate this medieval gibberish, it means basically he can plunder and pillage anyone who comes near the Straits of Dover by sea or by land. I think.

The meetings of the Cinque Ports are called the Courts of Brotherhood and Guestling, though nobody knows why. It could be something to do with guests or the village of Guestling, near Hastings.

Other insane-sounding jobs, more fully detailed in my book *Eccentric London*, include:

1 **Queen's Remembrancer.** His job is to remember to conduct pointless ceremonies for which any purpose has been forgotten. For example, the Horseshoe and Faggot-cutting (see page 116).
2 **The Lord Great Chamberlain,** who has to walk backwards in front of the monarch carrying a long wand, and has to break his wand over the monarch's grave when he/she dies.
3 **The Queen's Swan Marker,** who runs the totally bonkers but charming Swan-upping ceremonies (see page 36).
4 **Royal Ravenmaster.** More raven nonsense to do with the Tower of London.
5 **Groom of the Stool.** A royal job that did once exist, but given that the stool was the sort you'd rather not sit on, I don't think anyone would do it nowadays.
6 **Searcher of the Sanctuary,** *also* **Silver Stick in Waiting, Gentleman Usher of the Black Rod, Blue Mantle, Rouge Dragon.** I could go on, but you'd think I was making them up. I'm not. The uniforms and the pay (12 pence a year for life in one case) are ludicrous too, but they do have functions. And they confirm Britain as indelibly eccentric.

KEY TO ECCENTRICITIES

Locking a door or a gate would seem to be a fairly simple matter. Not, however, if the gates are of the **Tower of London** (Travel: page 130) and the strange ceremony is more than 700 years old. At 9.53pm each day for all those centuries the Chief Warder, in Tudor uniform, carrying a lantern and the keys, has set off from the Byward Tower to meet the Escort of the Key, all bedecked in Beefeater garb. They tour the various gates, ceremonially locking them.

On returning to the Bloody Tower Archway, however, the party is challenged by a sentry with the words:

'Halt! Who comes there?'
'The Keys.'
'Whose Keys?'
'Queen Elizabeth's Keys.'
'Advance Queen Elizabeth's Keys.'
'All's well.'

The party passes through the arch and the chief warder raises his hat, saying: 'God preserve Queen Elizabeth.' All reply: 'Amen.' A bugler plays the Last Post and the keys are carried to the Resident Governor of the Tower for the night.

The only time the Keys were late in 700 years was in September 1941 when the Tower suffered several direct hits from Nazi bombs. No doubt to their great consternation, they were delayed by half-an-hour. Amazing, eh?

The same Yeomen of the Guard make a ceremonial search of the Houses of Parliament before the monarch arrives for the **State Opening of Parliament**, recalling the Gunpowder Plot, which nearly succeeded in blowing king and parliament to pieces in 1605.

The State Opening involves another ritual challenge when Black Rod, the monarch's messenger sent to summon the House of Commons to the House of Lords to hear the monarch's speech outlining coming legislation, has the Commons' door slammed in his face. He has to bash his black staff three times on the oak door to overcome this show of hard-won independence.

CURSE OF THE UNDERGROUND MUTTON

Please don't read this paragraph aloud on **the Isle of Portland**, a strange stone outcrop into the English Channel off Dorset only just connected to the mainland. Local superstition forbids the mentioning of the word rabbit, which brings bad luck. Portland is riddled with quarries (facing all those white buildings in London), and a quarryman was once killed when a crane toppled over thanks to rabbit warrens underneath. Since then the long-eared critters must be referred to as 'underground mutton' or 'furry things'. Portlanders are splendid people, of course, although hearing them talking of 'going to England' (that is Weymouth, three miles away across a causeway) is a little odd. But when the Wallace and Gromit film *The Curse of the Were-Rabbit* was shown in 2005, it had to be advertised as above. The film company produced a poster with the R word missing, and the slogan 'Something bunny is going on.'

GETTING THE DOLE

Around Britain's countryside some bizarre, moving and curious older systems still operate from the days before the welfare state.

These range from little-known tales, such as that of the agonised Hampshire wife who went through torture to make her skinflint husband help the poor, to the relatively well-known customs, such as the monks of **Prinknash Abbey** in the Vale of Gloucester, who have been serving free meals to poor wayfarers since 1096. They hit the headlines in 1993 when feckless wastrels who arrived in luxury cars abused their hospitality. After that, the splendid three-course roast dinners were replaced by a more humble soup, bread and tea. But the monks are not alone in offering a hospitality dating back to the Middle Ages. At the **Hospital of St Cross**, Winchester, the first few callers of the day at the porter's lodge have received the 'wayfarer's dole' of bread and beer daily since 1136.

Nearby, real pathos can be found with the curious story of the **Tichborne Dole**, distributed each 25 March at the Hampshire village.

Given to the needy since the 13th century, the dole consists of a gallon of flour and dates from the time a dying Lady Tichborne asked her skinflint husband to leave food for the poor in her memory.

The heartless Sir Roger said he would give grain grown on as much land as the bedridden Lady Mabella could go round before a burning firebrand went out. She managed to crawl round a 23-acre field, still called The Crawls, and every Lady Day villagers assemble at Tichborne House to be given a gallon of flour per adult, and half a gallon for children ... a life-saver in famines past.

There's nothing like a good curse to ensure that the terms of a will are observed, and there was one in this case. If ever the Tichbornes failed to give the dole, the curse said, the house would fall down and there would be a generation of seven daughters, the family name dying out. In 1796 the dole caused such a commotion, with riffraff from other villages trying to muscle in – a precursor of the more recent row over Prinknash Abbey's dole – that alarmed gentry had the local magistrates ban it in following years. Part of the house did subside in 1803 – you can see that it still leans – and Sir Henry Tichborne produced seven daughters but no male heir, which in turn led to Britain's longest-yet court case at 291 days in 1874 (only displaced by the 'MacLibel' trial of 314 days in 1996), when an Australian impersonator claimed to be the rightful heir. The dole was resumed to stop the whole house and family name collapsing. The court case had fascinated and divided the whole country. The Tichborne Dole subsequently became the name of a pub, a play and a film. The dole takes place a mile south down a pretty lane from New Alresford, a charming 18th-century small town, which is worth a visit.

Another poignant tale of suffering is remembered in the **Biddenden Dole** (Travel: page 130), given each Easter Monday. It recalls the 12th-century Siamese twins Mary and Elisa Chulkhurst who, despite being joined at the hips and shoulders, lived happily in the Kent village until one of them died at the age of 34. Friends of the survivor begged her to save herself by having the 'ligaments' joining her to her dead sister cut, but the tale is told how she refused, saying as they had come into the world together so they must leave together. Six hours later, they did. The sisters left land to provide for bread and cheese to be handed out to the poor of the parish. Widows and pensioners still receive this, together with tea, butter and a special biscuit bearing an image of the twins and their names.

In 1566 Lady Elizabeth Marvyn became lost when trying to find her way through the woods of Berkshire in bad weather and poor light. She was befriended by the poor villagers of **Ufton Nervet** who gave her food, although they had hardly any, and helped her to her destination.

Lady Marvyn never forgot this kindness and when she died in 1581 she left money for an annual bequest every Maundy Thursday for 'the poore of Ufton'. The original terms of the will, which you can see still inscribed in Ufton Nervet church, granted '10 bushels of wheat to be made into household bread, 12 and a half ells [a medieval measurement] of at one shilling per ell for shirts and smocks 12½ ells of narrow blue cloth for coats and cassocks.' I don't think a shopkeeper today would know what the ell you were talking about and if he did, wouldn't sell it to you at those prices. Lady Marvyn's two loaves of fresh bread and sometimes bed linen are still handed through the window of Ufton Court by the Lord of the Manor at 2.30pm in a tradition that hasn't stopped for civil war, plague or world wars for well over 400 years. In past centuries this dole could have made the difference between life and death for a starving village child (coming, like the Tichborne Dole, at the thinnest time of the year), but now it's driven by that great British reverence for tradition.

On the evening of Whit Sunday at **St Briavels** in the Forest of Dean, Gloucestershire, pieces of bread and cheese are thrown into the air outside St Mary's church as a 'dole'. There are no rules about who gets what: parishioners wear large hats or unashamedly lift their skirts to catch a bigger share. Like other doles this goes way back – to Milo, Earl of Hereford in the 12th century. Like other doles its original purpose – the bread and cheese were exchanged for a penny and this gave the right to cut timber in Hudnalls or Hucknolls Wood – has long been forgotten. And like other doles, it has been met with rowdiness and drunkenness and been banned or moved from time to time. Like the others, local people are determined it shall continue. Indeed, the morsels are considered blessed and instead of being eaten, some have been carried by miners or fishermen to keep them safe, or kept under pillows to ensure dreams that foretell the future.

Those who moan about social security benefits being too easily given out to today's idle, ill-educated young people might approve of a graveside dole in **Wotton**, Surrey, intended to benefit local youths – on one condition. In 1717 William Glanville left 40 shillings each (then a considerable sum) to five poor boys on condition that they each lay their hands on his tomb, recite the Lord's Prayer, the Apostles' Creed and the Ten Commandments from memory, read aloud from Corinthians and write two verses in a clear hand. Older villagers in Wotton can remember the dole was held each 2 February, but it is now seldom given out.

Another dole that should have ceased 500 years ago at **Selborne**, Hampshire, sees the village's old people receive a loaf each on St Thomas's Day (21 December), although the priory that ordered this closed in 1486. Magdalen College, Oxford, took over because of its interest in priory lands, for the next 500 years, but recently sold the lordship of the manor. The new owner continues the tradition, however.

St Thomas's Day also sees the inhabitants of the Cathedral Close, **Lichfield**, Staffordshire, each receive a loaf from the Dean's Vicar after a special service.

Another St Thomas's Day charity was actually a fine imposed on the Swan pub, Ipswich, in 1664, for having a murder on the premises. It was 40 shillings a year (£2, then six months' pay) in perpetuity, for fuel for the poor. When the charity concerned rediscovered it in 2006, the publicans happily paid up, including backdating.

George Carlow's gravestone in the back garden of the Bull Hotel, **Woodbridge**, Suffolk, is inscribed with directions of how penny loaves – Carlow's Bread – are to be given to the poor from his gravetop from 1738 'for ever'. Landlord Neville Allen said: 'We mark it some years with children coming from one of the local schools to get rolls which we have baked. Of course, they're not that poor nowadays, but it's very educational.'

'For ever' was the hopeful term also used in Peter Symonds's will of 1587, instructing that 60 Christ's Hospital boys receive a packet of raisins and a new penny on Good Friday.

Similarly, 21 coins are supposed to be laid on a tomb in St Bartholomew-the-Great in **Smithfield**, London, also on Good Friday, for 21 poor widows to pick up as they step across the unnamed grave. As a church spokesman says: 'Not so many people live round here any more, so we've run out of poor widows in the parish. We still have the open-air service, then spend the money not picked up on hot cross buns for children.'

Such bequests are by no means all in the distant past. In 1997 farm worker Jack Palmer, 83, died and left money to buy the pensioners of **Great Massingham**, Norfolk a slap-up Christmas dinner for ten years – even though Jack had left the village 50 years earlier.

TRAVEL INFORMATION

BIDDENDEN DOLE, Kent TN27 8LW ☎ 01580 762558
🚗 On A274 south from Maidstone, accessed from J7 of M20 which links London/M25 with Dover 🚂 Nearest station: Headcorn, on main line from London Victoria to Dover

BROMSGROVE COURT LEET AND CARNIVAL, Worcestershire ☎ 01527 831809
🚗 Off M5 at J4A, or from London via M40 then M42. Some motorway junctions are limited in direction, so follow signs 🚂 Bromsgrove

DUNMOW FLITCH TRIALS, Essex ☎ 01799 510444
🚗 M11 from London/M25 to J8, then A120 east 🚂 Bishops Stortford from London Liverpool St, then bus

HUNGERFORD HOCKTIDE AND TUTTIMEN, Berkshire ☎ 01635 30267
🚗 From M4 J14, take A338 south for 3 miles 🚂 From London Paddington

KEYS CEREMONY, Tower of London, EC3N4AB ☎ 0844482 7777
🚇 Tower Hill (Circle and District lines)
NB: Admission to the Keys Ceremony is only by written application and invitation. Apply to Ceremony of the Keys, HM Tower of London, EC3N 4AB

MAYOR-WEIGHING, High Wycombe, Buckinghamshire ☎ 01494 421892
🚗 On M40 between M25 and Oxford 🚂 From London Marylebone

OAKHAM CASTLE, Rutland LE15 6HW ☎ 01572 758440
🖥 www.rutlandgov.uk ☎ 01572 724329
🚗 In town centre, east of church. From A1 near Stamford, take A606 west for 11 miles 🚂 Oakham, on Peterborough–Leicester line

STRATFIELD SAYE, Hampshire RG7 2BT ☎ 01256 882882
🖥 www.stratfield-saye.co.uk 🚗 Off A33, south from Reading M4 J11

TICHBORNE DOLE, Hampshire ☎ 01962 840500
🚗 A31 to New Alresford, which connects with J10 of the M3, linking Winchester with Guildford and A3 from London. Then follow signs to Tichborne (1 mile).

'I think for my part one half of the nation is mad – and the other not very sound.'

Tobias Smollett

Part Two

ECCENTRIC
PEOPLE

ATLANTIC
OCEAN

Orkney
Islands

Thurso

Isle of Lewis

Inverness

Aberdeen

Isle of
Skye

Inner
Hebrides

SCOTLAND

NORTH
SEA

Island of
Mull

Islay

Glasgow

Arran

EDINBURGH

Fairbairn's Folly, Fordell

N

ATLANTIC
OCEAN

0   80 km
0   50 miles

Newcastle
upon Tyne

Carlisle

Isle of
Man

Middlesbrough

Fyling Hall Piggery,
Robin Hood's Bay

Lille Cottage and
Gleaston Mill

ENGLAND

IRISH
SEA

Anglesey

Leeds

York

Bradford

Kingston-upon-Hull

NORTH
SEA

Holyhead

Liverpool

Manchester

Sheffield

Grimsby

Newborough's Cannon,
Beland Fort

Duchess's Pig,
Chatsworth House

Tunnelling Duke,
Welbeck Abbey

Cardigan
Bay

Stoke-on-
Trent

Nottingham

Stateley Pig Bath & Gossip,
Shugborough

Derby

Norwich

Wolverhampton

Birmingham

Mad Marquess,
Ickworth

Coventry

Fishguard

WALES

Cambridge

Ipswich

Castell Coch,
Tongwynlais

Blenheim Palace,
Woodstock

Swansea

Oxford

Reading

LONDON

Bristol
Channel

Cardiff
Castle

Bristol

Dover

Unique Marquess,
Longleat

Archbishop's Pigs,
South of England
Rare Breeds Centre, Ashford

Southampton

Portsmouth

Brighton

ATLANTIC
OCEAN

Exeter

Cupid's Obelisk,
Mount Edgcumbe

Penzance

ENGLISH CHANNEL

ARISTOCRATIC
ECCENTRICS

ARISTOCRATIC ECCENTRICS

THE TUNNELLING DUKE AND OTHER ODD ARISTOS

One might assume that the reputation for eccentricity of British aristocrats is because their wealth, and general mischief-making idleness, meant their whims had a more lasting impact than those more modest extravagances of more lowly Britons. This would be a simplification of a much more fascinating phenomenon than mere excess. Although fabulous riches obviously played their part in the legacy of flamboyant characters such as the **third Marquess of Bute** (1847–1900), who left Cardiff with the quite extraordinarily embellished **Cardiff Castle** (Travel: page 278) and the almost Bavarian fantasy retreat of **Castell Coch** some five miles to the north, there is no denying that many a British aristocrat has been deeply strange as well as rich and powerful (or, sometimes, just deeply strange).

Take the **fifth Duke of Portland**, the eccentric Lord William John Cavendish-Scott-Bentinck (1800–75), who was shy to Howard Hughes extremes. When travelling, he would have his curtained carriage unhitched from the horses and then hoisted aboard a railway truck with himself inside it. He wore a 2ft-high silk hat and carried a deep umbrella when out walking to shield himself from strangers' eyes. The penalty if any of his 500 workmen doffed a hat to him was instant dismissal. He used only four rooms in **Welbeck Abbey**, Nottinghamshire, his ancestral seat – now the Army's Welbeck College for educating would-

be officers. Each room had two letter boxes on the door – one for incoming and one for outgoing messages – so he need not see anyone. A roast chicken was passed through every day, one half for lunch and one for supper. All other rooms were painted pink and left bare except for an unscreened lavatory pan in the corner of each room.

In old age the duke went to ground by constructing a vast network of underground rooms. Miles of passages, stables and kitchens were all hewn out by hand, together with a 1½-mile-long gas-lit tunnel wide enough for two carriages to pass, a vast underground ballroom, the largest in Europe, where no-one danced, and even a riding school – at 400ft by 600ft the second-largest in the world, supported by 50 pillars and lit by 40,000 gas jets – where no-one ever rode.

Those recruited to be estate workers were surprised to find mushroom-like ventilators in their cottage gardens, and were told these were for underground washrooms so his lordship would not have to see washing rudely displayed.

Rumour has it that the duke's curtained carriage went all the way to Worksop station by underground tunnel, so it could be hoisted aboard the train, but this is not quite true. The main 1½-mile Skylight Tunnel from the abbey to the outskirts of the estate has an exit at the estate's northern boundary, known as the Tunnel End. From here the duke, in a covered coach, travelled a further 3½ miles overland, through the Duke of Newcastle's Worksop Manor estate, to reach Worksop station.

Incidentally, he caused a crisis for the prime minister Benjamin Disraeli in 1857 when he demanded the repayment of huge loans he had made to him, presumably to finance further mad mole-like behaviour. The suggested reasons for the underground extravagance by the former MP vary from being thwarted in love to wanting to create work for local unemployed labourers, but a true eccentric needs no reasonable explanation.

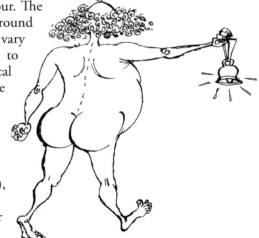

Another aristo who did not appreciate the presence of his servants was the **third Lord Wallscourt** (1797–1849), who had few peers in terms of eccentricity. He used to wander round his draughty stately home stark naked, ringing a cowbell to warn maidservants, who ran screaming from the sight. He died – whether of a chill or not is not recorded – in 1849.

The **second Baron Rokeby** (1712–1800), at one time Matthew Robinson, MP for Canterbury, should have been a duck. He much preferred water to dry land. He became an enthusiast for the foreign habit of bathing after a visit to the spa town of Aix-la-Chapelle. On his return to Kent, he began to make daily trips to the seashore to swim regardless of the weather, walking all the way. He preferred the water so much that his servant waiting on the beach had a hard time ever getting him out of it. Sometimes he fainted from the cold and had to be rescued. He had a hut built on the sands at Hythe and drinking fountains set up along his route to the beach. If he found people drinking from one of his fountains, he gave them a valuable coin. In Lord Rokeby's old age he built a pool at his home and spent nearly all his time there. He did not allow heating of any sort in his house, whatever the weather, but he rarely suffered colds and chills and lived to the grand old age of 88.

If the so-called working class turns out to be sometimes lazy nowadays, as is often claimed, you can see where they learned idleness from: the upper class. In 1770 two earls bet each other that one could ride from London to Edinburgh and back before the other had drawn a million dots. The dotty one became bored and lost the bet.

More fun was **Lord Delaval Beresford** (1862–1906), although it was sadly ironic that he died in a train crash, since his uncle, the third Marquess of Waterford, once asked a railway company to crash two railway engines just for fun. But then Beresford once put aniseed, a scent loved by bloodhounds, on the hooves of a parson's horse before hunting with the terrified clergyman and placed a donkey in the bed of a traveller at a wayside inn as another jolly jape. Lord Beresford's brother Admiral Lord Charles Beresford had a love of the chase too – he had a hunt in full cry tattooed down his back, with the fox going to earth at the appropriate aperture. It was one of the Beresfords, **Lord Charles Beresford** (1846–1919), who when invited to dine with the Prince of Wales and unable to think of an excuse, telegraphed:

VERY SORRY CAN'T COME. LIE FOLLOWS BY POST.

Talking about brilliant telegrams we should recall writer Robert Benchley's to his editor on arriving in Venice:

STREETS FLOODED. PLEASE ADVISE.

And, of course, the most brilliant one ever sent, the one-word cable sent by **General Sir Charles Napier** (1782–1853, whose statue stands in Trafalgar Square) to the Foreign Office in London:

PECCAVI.

It means in Latin, 'I have sinned.' It was instantly understood that the British conquest of Sindh province in India was completed.

The Beresfords' penchant for railways and hunts was also shared by the **ninth Earl of Lanesborough** (1918–98). This seemed to run in the family, judging by his recollections of childhood holidays in the 1920s:

> *'We used to travel through the night down to the French Riviera. My grandfather, Sir Anthony Abdy, would not spend the night in the sleeping car with us, however, because he would have had a word with the driver in Paris and would the next morning step down from the loco footplate at Nice, black with soot, but most pleased.'*

Lord Lanesborough himself trained as an LNER engine driver during the war and, before he lost his fortune and had to sell his family house, Swithland Hall in Leicestershire, had 600ft of toy track running through the house with detailed scenery, including a miniature Quorn Hunt in full cry.

Many years before that, also in Paris, the **eighth Earl of Bridgewater** (1756–1829) used to hold formal banquets at his Paris mansion for his best friends who were required to wear full evening dress and polished shoes. Nothing odd in that, except that the guests were all his favourite dogs. The earl put on a brand-new pair of shoes every day and he arranged each year's worn shoes into rows, so he could see how much of the year had gone. He loved animals, yet when his eyesight started failing, he had the wings clipped on the partridges and pigeons in his garden so he could walk up to them and shoot them. Not surprisingly, you may think, he never married and so the title died out on his death in 1829.

Moving on about a century, it was appropriate that Dame Edith Sitwell wrote a book called *English Eccentrics*. Her father, **Sir George Sitwell** (1860–1943), was a fully paid-up member of that group. He invented a musical toothbrush and a tiny revolver for killing wasps, which he liked to do while talking to visitors. He wrote a guide for insomniacs called *The 27 Postures of Sir George R Sitwell* and hunted his own children on horseback when foxes weren't available. When he ran out of money, he paid his sons' school fees in live pigs. He told his daughter to take up gymnastics because 'there's nothing a young man likes so much as a girl who is good on the parallel bars'.

HELLFIRE AND HEROISM

The eccentricity of the British upper classes, if we are allowed to use such a politically incorrect but honest term, seems to be nothing new. A couple of centuries ago, **John Mytton, Sheriff of Shropshire** (1796–1834) despite having been expelled from Westminster and Harrow schools, went hunting naked, owned a thousand hats and drank eight bottles of port a day. He once astounded his dinner guests by riding into the dining room astride a bear, which became so excited it bit part of his leg off. He died after he set his shirt alight to 'show how Jack Mytton cures the hiccups'. His last words are said to have been: 'Well, the hiccups is gone, by God.'

The 18th century saw the debauched excesses and whimsical creations of the **Hellfire Club** (see page 168), with their satanic caves, very strange church and odd mausoleum. But what of the 20th century? Did the upper classes retain their eccentricities?

Sometimes it was a question of mere direct pragmatism, which could be amusing in small ways. The former prime minister Sir Anthony Eden's father Sir William was in the habit of tapping the barometer in his hall each morning. Once, when it was pouring with rain, but the barometer forecast sunshine, he hurled the instrument outside, yelling: 'Go on, you damned fool, go and see for yourself.'

In the 1930s, conductor **Sir Thomas Beecham** (1879–1961) met a woman he vaguely recognised in the exclusive emporium of Fortnum & Mason's. After exchanging greetings, he asked: 'What's your husband doing nowadays?' The answer was: 'Oh, he's still king.' But he could be more forthright as a conductor. To a cellist he once thundered: 'Madam, you have between your legs that which could give pleasure to thousands. All you do is sit there and scratch it.'

The **seventh Lord Newborough** (1917–98), was a war hero of the first order and a true eccentric to boot. His war record included rescuing men in five trips to Dunkirk with a yacht, taking part in the incredibly brave and successful St Nazaire raid in 1942, where he was wounded and captured when stopping under the German guns to rescue men in the water; and various escapades at the notorious Colditz prison, from where he, of course, escaped. His post-war record, which concerns us here, included various cannon-firing incidents at his family estate in Denbighshire, north Wales. He liked to fire his cannon (plural) from Beland Fort for special occasions, such as birthdays, and was convicted of firing a 9lb cannonball through the spinnaker of a yacht passing through the Menai Strait, which he denied. He hit the headlines for removing the roof of the home of a gamekeeper to whom he had taken a dislike.

His parting shot was to have his ashes blasted from a gun fired by his son, the eighth Lord Newborough, in front of 700 guests. His remains hurtled through the air in a canister he had designed himself into one of his favourite places, the Big Wood, to resounding cheers from his many friends. The family motto is 'Gentle in manner, vigorous in action.'

A somewhat different attitude to war was demonstrated by the eccentric laird of Dundonnell, a Scottish Highlands estate in Wester Ross, one **Neil Munro 'Bunny' Roger** (1911–97). He minced through enemy lines during World War II wearing a chiffon scarf and carrying a copy of *Vogue*. Asked what to do when Germans attacked, the conspicuously rouged Bunny answered: 'When in doubt, powder heavily.' However, the Scots soldiers in general were far from girlish: the Germans called them the 'ladies from hell' not just because they wore kilts but also because they were ruthlessly aggressive with bayonet, rifle and grenade.

The flamboyant 'Bunny' Roger's eccentricity has clearly rubbed off on Dundonnell's modern owner, the millionaire lyricist Sir Tim Rice. When he heard that a Scottish island was set to exterminate the hedgehog population because the imported creatures threatened some local wildlife, Sir Tim offered all 200 prickly hogs asylum on his 33,000-acre estate.

One of my favourite eccentric aristos of World War II was **Lady Helen Gleichen** (1873–1947) of Ross-on-Wye who, early in the war when the threat of invasion was high, formed her estate workers into the Much Marcle Warriors to fight the Germans. She sent a message to the local Battalion Commander of the Local Defence Volunteers demanding 'eighty rifles, ammunition and two machine-guns if you have any'. She was turned down, not only because she was a lady in her 60s, German-born with the title Helena von Gleichen, and was totally outside the Home Guard command structure, but also because there weren't any weapons available in the grim days after Dunkirk. So she armed and drilled her force with pitchforks, pikes, swords, halberds and flintlock guns that would have been better suited to the Battle of

Waterloo. She then formulated plans to 'protect' Wales with this motley crew. I don't know if as this old battleaxe, a would-be Boadicea, rose for the attack, sword in hand and shouted 'Forward the Much Marcle Warriors!', that the Panzer crews would have died laughing. But she would, surely, have died fighting.

BONKERS, AND BONKING, MPS

Modern politicians are not so colourless, either. **Sir Nicholas Fairbairn** (1933–95), the flamboyant Tory MP for Perth and Kinross, designed his own clothes, the results sometimes execrable, leaving him wearing what looked like a skirt and patent leather high-heeled boots. A member of his family recalled: 'He once wore a see-through négligé top, with a huge black cross beneath it and white flared trousers: that was especially vile.' When he had a German guest at his ruined Fife castle, Fordell, he even insisted on the guest goose-stepping through the house wearing a spiked German helmet: about as subtle as Basil Fawlty in the *Fawlty Towers* television comedy.

He rarely said the right thing and often the horribly wrong one – such as lecturing his daughter about gonorrhoea on her wedding day. He once summed it all up in *Who's Who* when he described his recreations as 'making love, ends meet, people laugh'. In a later edition he changed this to 'drawing ships, making quips, confounding Whips, scuttling drips'.

David Mellor (born in 1949), the philandering former member for Putney turned media moneyspinner, was famous as Minister for Fun for supposedly making love to an actress in a Chiswick flat while wearing Chelsea football kit (which he now denies). Eventually Mellor, who clearly had something to offer besides good looks (he was memorably described as having an 'ideal face for radio'), ran off with the Viscountess Cobham, whose husband was distant heir to the second Lord Lyttleton, a Hellfire Club member (see page 168) and Jack-the-lad, who ate himself to death 200 years ago in a three-day binge at Hagley Hall.

To maintain a semblance of balance, a third example was not a Tory MP at all but a baron, and half-brother to a Tory minister. The late **third Baron Moynihan** of Leeds, Anthony Patrick Andrew Cairnes Berkeley Moynihan (1936–1991), died from a stroke while running a chain of brothels in the Philippines, leaving a string of small boys in the Orient whose mothers claimed him as their father and at least three

Lady Moynihans in Manila. He had fled there in 1970 to evade a string of arrest warrants concerning 57 charges over gambling debts and other frauds, building up a £3 million sex industry fortune and acquiring himself the soubriquet, the Ermine Pimpernel.

Meanwhile he took out an advertisement in *The Times* to call the British police 'one of the most corrupt forces in the world'. His half-brother Colin Moynihan, a former Olympic rowing medallist, who while a Tory sports minister was himself controversially photographed with the exotic Pamella Bordes, witnessed an extraordinary court battle in 1996 when one of the third baron's alleged offspring tried to claim the title. In the event, the lawsuit failed and Colin became the fourth Baron Moynihan.

Another dotty peer, Rufus Alexander Buxton, **second Baron Noel-Buxton** (1917–80), was convinced that he could wade across the Thames to the Houses of Parliament, and tried to do so at a very low tide in 1952. He claimed it must be possible because that's how the Romans did it. Despite being 6ft 3in, he became out his depth and floated away, to the derisive jeers of the large crowd that had gathered on Westminster Bridge.

Undaunted – his family motto was 'Do it with thy might' – he forded the Severn and the Humber in the following years. He almost became a pier of the realm.

Oh just one more: the motorcycling peer, the **second Lord Strathcarron** (1924–2006), used to tour Europe with his wife Eve strapped to him with rope (in case she fell asleep, he told chums) and a butler following behind in a three-wheeler, accompanied by his favourite parrot, which would squawk loudly at foreign customs officials. He rode almost every kind of motorbike, owned every Jensen car ever made and flew many types of plane (including in combat Wellingtons during the war) despite having a 'claw hand' that made it difficult to grip the controls. 'I can manage,' he said after corrective surgery, 'but it's a bit of a bugger getting out of the bath.' The Strathcarrons had their own railway station of the same name – it's still there, now used by the public too – and their own signal levers to pull to stop the trains.

Once, arriving at the headquarters of BP in leathers, helmet and goggles, Strathcarron was turned away by a functionary with the customary cockney riposte of disbelief. He turned up a few minutes later in business pinstripes, looking every inch a peer of the realm. 'I'm Lord Strathcarron,' he announced, 'and *that* (pointing at said functionary) is the f***ing queen of Sheba.' He died a few weeks after colliding with a dustcart.

MODERN MARQUESSES OF B

Not all today's aristocrats live up to their eccentric heritage; some confuse mere spoilt-brat bad behaviour with truly creative craziness.

To limit a rather wide field, let's take modern eccentrics with the title of Marquess of B. The mildly misbehaving (for drugs and motoring offences) **Marquess of Blandford**, heir to Blenheim Palace (Travel: page 148), turns out to be rather bland: most people would think him from his record in the 1980s and 1990s somewhat spoilt and silly.

The **seventh Marquess of Bristol**, also a partaker of substances, whose main achievement seemed to have been to quit one of Europe's most astounding stately homes, **Ickworth** in Suffolk (Travel: page 149), and flog off the treasures therein, was eccentric only in a negative way – he managed to lose a real fortune more unwisely. He looked like Rick Mayall playing a heartless toff and died in January 1999, aged 44, having achieved only notoriety. He'd carried a hint of Marquis de Sade cruelty from his schooldays at Harrow to his arrogant, sneering adulthood. He would set his dogs on innocent visitors to Ickworth; he drove at speed through screaming visitors in his fast playboy cars; he sent an American woman visitor out on the lake at Ickworth in a rubber dinghy and shot at it with an air-rifle until it sank; he read out begging letters from parents of very sick children to amuse his dinner guests.

Are all marquesses of Bs as vile, or as dull? Far from it: the **Marquess of Bath** (born in 1932) upheld the fine tradition of aristocratic eccentricities. He openly maintained a set of 'wifelets' – put by some commentators at a number hard to credit, around 62 – and had a predilection for mad murals on sexual themes, rhino horns and suchlike, at his family seat, **Longleat** (Travel: page 149), made famous by his father for the Lions of Longleat. Predictably, Fleet Street christened the current marquess 'Loins of Longleat', which I imagine delighted him.

Was the eccentricity – favourite dish: squirrel in mushroom sauce – merely a convenient persona for Bath, who when he inherited the title proved himself a canny businessman, allowing Center Parcs to build a holiday village at Longleat (without even correcting their spelling)? Not entirely. The 'hippy peer' was just being honest about his unconventional love life, and those murals dripping off miles of corridors ('pornographic pizza' as a family member put it) represent hundreds of hours of dedicated daubing. A truly eccentric Marquess of B, but not a crackpot.

WANTED: HERMITS, RUNNING FOOTMEN, GOSSIPS

Eccentric British aristocrats create deeply eccentric job opportunities from time to time. There was the 18th-century obsession with picturesque landscapes, which had to contain a folly, a ruin, and a grotto or cave with **a hermit** in it.

The hermit had to be authentic, the pampered aristocrats decreed, even though the whole thing was basically to amuse their friends. So although he was hired to do the job, he would not be allowed to speak to anyone, or wash, or shave or cut his hair for *years*. Billy Connolly is halfway there already, although he hasn't mastered the silence yet (sadly, you may think). The hermit was not allowed to speak to servants who would leave food for him, and although the whole thing was conceived as romantic, if the people who applied for the job weren't already deeply strange misfits, they must have become so.

One of their jobs was to converse with a skull when nobility was nearby. You'd think that some would sneak off to the pub for a bit of company when the nobs were away, but in the quest for authenticity they would be sacked for speaking to anyone even when the people in the big house were away on holiday. And, as in at least one case they didn't get paid for seven years, there would be some incentive to see the thing through after about six-and-a-half years.

Of course, this was a different age when lunatics were mocked and visited as a spectacle, when public hangings were popular events, when deformed people were exhibited as freaks and when children died labouring in mines and chimneys or else starved. Servants were cheap and the lords and ladies could use them trivially.

A classic case of the latter is recalled by a Mayfair pub name, I Am The Only Running Footman (see also page 231). An odd name on three counts. First, it is Britain's second-longest pub name and London's longest. Second, it is initially totally incomprehensible (actually, that isn't so unusual for pub names). Third, it has been taken wholesale for the title of a book by Martha Grimes – a murder mystery, no less.

Difficult though it is to imagine today, the nobs of Mayfair's early days required a **Running Footman** in full livery to run before the coaches or sedan chairs of their masters, opening gates, paying tolls or whatever. Of course, the real reason for them was to increase the pompous self-importance of the grandee concerned: 'Make way, here comes the Duke of Bombast! Make way!' That kind of thing. There was also a group of footmen in livery who walked behind bigwigs to emphasise their importance. These equally pointless characters were known to Londoners as '**fart-catchers**'.

The fashion for running footmen declined except for one poor sweating booby, whose Mayfair master would not change with the times. Hence the pub name. Another character in 18th-century stately homes was the **gossip**. I don't know if it was a profession back then, but in 2004 the Earl of Lichfield's stately home, **Shugborough Hall** (Travel: page 149), was advertising for one. A newspaper advert, which in 21st-century style didn't actually say it had to be an old woman, offered a small wage and a gallon of ale a day. A spokesman said: 'This estate thrived for centuries on gossip. We want to bring that back to life and celebrate the role of the wittering scandalmonger.'

THE DUKE WHO GOES TO THE POLO BY JUMBO

Scotland's **13th Duke of Argyll** (born in 1968) likes to play polo, as do many aristocrats and rich playboys. Except that the duke and his team do it on elephants. Real ones.

In December 2004 they brought back to Scotland the world title, having beaten all comers at the tournament in Nepal. And as Scotland weren't doing that well in rugby or soccer, the duke was proud to quip: 'No-one can deny Scotland is now one of the world's sporting heavyweights.'

The thrilling, and thundering, final was won 12–6 against the National Parks of Nepal side. The elephants seem to know what they are doing and are controlled by mahouts sitting on their necks, so the player is merely using the beast as a massive platform to hit goals from.

Elephants sometimes score goals themselves, by picking the ball up with their trunk and carrying it, which is allowed, but then the peeved jumbos on the other side can lie down across the goal mouth, which is a foul. (I suppose the charge could be being trunk and disorderly.)

'It sounds slow but they can get up some speed. The elephants really get into it, they follow the ball without being told,' said a spokesman. 'They charge down the pitch with their trunks in the air and trumpeting.'

In fact, one contestant says that even the umpire who threw the ball in at the start, was an elephant. The sport was invented by a Scot, James Manclark, in 1983, although it tends to be played in countries where there are enough mounts. 'You canna play polo astride a haggis,' quipped one fan (aye, but have they tried Highland cattle?).

So is it all just silly fun? 'It's fun all right, but it's a serious sport, registered with the Nepal Olympic Association. 'We're playing for Queen and country. We played to win and we did,' said a victorious Scot.

STY SOCIETY: STATELY PIGS OF OLD ENGLAND

That pigs and aristocrats have much in common is no mere fancy of novelist P G Wodehouse. Lord Emsworth's devotion to Empress of Blandings in the Wooster books merely represented the esteem held between many a noble family and their porkers of equally good breeding.

This symbiosis of swine and toff goes back a long way. On a hill overlooking Plymouth Sound, a massive obelisk (Travel: page 149) is said to record Cupid the pig, social darling of Devonshire in the 18th century, who followed the **Countess of Mount Edgcumbe** everywhere. The aristocrat and her pig were inseparable – even on her visits to London.

Things aren't that different today. The **dowager Duchess of Devonshire** (born in 1920), for example, the youngest of the five sisters belonging to the somewhat eccentric Mitford family, had a soft spot for a 36-stone

Gloucestershire Old Spot called Primrose, whose perfect and massive proportions complement the vast 365-windowed **Chatsworth House** in Derbyshire (Travel: page 148). As the duchess confided: 'One can grow very affectionate towards pigs – there is something comforting about them.'

The late Archbishop of Canterbury, **Lord Runcie** (1921–2000), agreed: 'I wish I could turn my attention to such things as tranquil as my Berkshires.' The Berkshire is one of several breeds of British pig threatened with extinction, and good breeding has been a concern of aristocrats since at least 1884, when the Earl of Ellesmere started the National Pig Breeders' Association to look after such pearls among swine as the Large Black, the Middle White, the Tamworth and the British Lop. Today there are fewer than 100 Berkshire boars left, so Lord Runcie's contribution was vital.

He first met the breed in the 1940s at a country rectory, which was backing the war effort by having a Pig for Victory. Later, in the 1970s, he created a Berkshire herd, albeit in Hertfordshire, when he was Bishop of St Albans. Later still the herd moved to the **South of England Rare Breeds Centre** in Kent (Travel: page 149). But Lord Runcie's delight in the animal was almost paternal: 'They are splendid and their skin shines. The tiny piglets are like advertisements for polish.' He modestly described himself as a 'bogus pig-keeper'.

Royalty, too, values pigs: the **Princess Royal** (born in 1950) keeps Gloucestershire Old Spots at Gatcombe Park, and the **Earls of Lichfield** have long kept pigs in appropriate splendour at **Shugborough**, their Staffordshire seat. They – the pigs – occupy a splendid lead pig bath designed by Samuel Wyatt in the 18th century, and the farm itself is now open to the public. The fifth Earl, who died in 2005, recognised the pigs' special charm: 'I find them relaxing. Contemplating pigs can be a peaceful occupation. In this regard I identify with Lord Emsworth.'

Even the Shugborough pigs cannot aspire to the 'porcine poshness' of **Fyling Hall** (Travel: page 149) in North Yorkshire (near those more famous golf balls that were supposed to give us four minutes' warning of being turned into pork scratchings ourselves during the Cold War). In the 19th century, Squire Barry decided to build his pigs a sty, and

built them a veritable Grecian temple complete with pillars, pediment and portico ... a shrine to swine, perhaps.

Whether he considered his pigs had divine qualities or whether it was simply to improve his view is not recorded, but Fyling Hall surely offered the world's most exclusive sty. Broadcaster John Timpson described this sty as 'piggery jokery' in his book *Timpson's England*, but the splendid view the beasts enjoyed over Robin Hood's Bay can now be appreciated instead by weekenders in search of somewhere different to stay, thanks to the Landmark Trust's conversion of the piggery.

On the opposite side of the country there's a former piggery that has been converted into 'the poshest pigsty in Cumbria' and, again, is a listed building. **Lile Cottage and Gleaston Mill** near Ulverston have all mod cons including a PC (not a pork chop), and the pig-loving owner has a piggy shop in the nearby mill, worth a visit if you are equally soppy about our porky chums.

Of course, affection for porkers is not confined to the upper classes. In 1998 two Tamworth pigs hit the headlines when they fled the butcher's knife in a Wiltshire slaughterhouse, barged their way under a wire fence, swam a river and disappeared in thick vegetation, evading a huge search, only emerging to snack on gardeners' vegetables at night. Their story earned the admiration of the nation, partly due to headline writers who dubbed the duo Butch and Sundance. Tabloid newspapers fell over themselves to bid for the **Tamworth Two**, and when they were recaptured, they were installed in a centrally heated thatched piggery, with private pool, mudbath, closed-circuit TV and the best possible food. It all made for good reading over your breakfast sausages and bacon, I suppose.

In Blandings-Castle country, at Elmstone near Cheltenham, the **Gloucester Old Spot** pub reveres the name that keeps bringing home the bacon. And, not so far from Wodehouse's fictional Blandings Castle, at the village of **Pillerton Hersey** in Warwickshire, **Glascote Dictator XVIII**, a 58-stone Essex boar, hit the headlines a few years back for not only having his own bank account but also visiting the branch in question. Not to make a deposit, you understand – perish the thought. It was in protest at the closure of the branch where he held his prize money (£31 plus interest) that the great Dictator's owner, eccentric barrister Iain Whitney, decided to take him along to withdraw his funds. Piggy banks are not, after all, adequate for the posher porker.

Well, well, well: Tissington is typical of Derbyshire welldressing (GW) page 19

ECCENTRIC EVENTS

Every week of the year, something utterly amazing happens in Britain. And if it happens twice, that's it... it's a tradition!

Inspector Clous-stack, or Strawlock Holmes: Wray Scarecrow Festival (CC) page 19

Poignant but fun: At east London's Widow's Son pub, another hot cross bun for the sailor who never came back (PGP) page 16

A creature comes Forth: It's considered lucky to meet the Burry Man, who stalks the streets of South Queensferry, Lothian, in August (JAIL/A) page 38

A lawn unto themselves: The British Lawn Mower Racing Grand Prix in Sussex is on the verge (JMT/P) page 36

STRANGE SPORTS

No other country has so many world championships for daft things: bog snorkelling, black-pudding-throwing, marbles, conkers, pea-shooting, worm-charming, mangold-hurling...

Ugly turn of events: Gurning is a highly competitive face-making sport in Cumbria (BV/P) page 46

You'll get a rind to it one day: The Stilton Cheese Rolling is suitably sedate (PB) page 22

Sting for your supper: The World Stinging Nettle Eating Championships in Dorset (JMT/P) page 26

Ready, steady, slow: The World Snail Racing Championships in Norfolk (MS) page 35

Equestrian of sport: Who will win the man versus horse marathon in Wales? (KW/P) page 85

A penny-farthing for your thoughts: The Great Race in Knutsford (JF) page 60

The geometry of devotion: The fascinating, cryptic Triangular Lodge, Rushton (AW/TTL/P) page 285

An apparition in white on London's North Circular: The stunning Swaminarayan Temple, Neasden (E&EIL/P) page 193

Someone dropped Jaws from a plane: Oxford's astonishing shark house (MM/P) page 197

Twisted: The Devil bent the spire in fury that a virgin married at St Mary's, Chesterfield, say locals. And it will untwist if it ever happens again! (PE/D) page 189

Stony-faced in Oxford: As pedants and readers of this book will know, this is a grotesque not a gargoyle (T/D) page 291

BARMY BUILDINGS

Forget the tourist honeypots, and find around the kingdom astounding architecture, usually with no crowds, admission charges or parking hassles

Shall I wrap it up? The Chinese pagoda, Kew Gardens, was a birthday present for a spoiled princess (YB/D) page 275

Frankly, they went bananas: Britain's best architectural joke is The Pineapple, Dunmore (S/D) page 281

Ideal gnome show: You must don a red hat to visit Devon's Gnome Reserve (SD/P) page 217

Wooden't credit it: A Narnian touch at the Enchanted Forest, Groombridge Place, Kent (SH/P) page 221

Where all woads lead to: The Druid's Temple, Ilton Moor, Yorkshire (KN/A) page 223

Cumbria's secret hedge fund: Levens Hall has a somewhat spooky collection (PT/P) page 223

Standing out like an orange in a slag heap:
Portmeirion fantasy village (GJ/D) page 247

PECULIAR PLACES

If you are in search of the truly odd, Britain has the compellingly curious, completely charming and insanely inexplicable in abundance

Viagra Falls: Throw yourself on the Cerne Giant, Dorset, and you won't need fertility treatment, locals claim (AW/P) page 268

Pity the poor signwriter: This Anglesey village is understandably often shortened to Llanfair PG (CPL/P) page 228

If it floats your boat: the *Tritania* is one of Lyndon Yorke's contraptions (LY) page 96

No has-bean: Captain Beany from Planet Beanus, aka human bean Barry Kirk from South Wales, has his own museum (DL/APA) page xi

POTTY PASTIMES

It's the British people who make the country eccentric: inventors, humorists, enthusiasts, explorers and – we mean this affectionately – complete crackpots

F-f-f-firth of F-f-f-forth: You'd have to be nuts to jump in the sea on New Year's Day for the Loony Dook. Or British. (MG) page 4

Towed hall: A stately home interior in a caravan, created by Daniel Lobb (DL) page 93

Dictator eventually headed for the pigsty in the sky, but his stuffed head will embellish Mr Whitney's cottage for years to come. Mr Whitney spent ten years in a one-man campaign to have the Essex saddleback breed of pigs reinstated after an

ill-starred attempt to merge them and Wessex saddlebacks into one breed, 'Now I've won, the Essex is saved and I've won the Royal Show Supreme Champion too,' he said with satisfaction.

Mr Whitney even followed in Lord Emsworth's footsteps in 1996 with a classic Wodehouse-style ding-dong with the village bobby. This involved an allegedly truculent police sergeant who owned land next to Mr Whitney's piggery and seemed to dislike the animals. The force farce ended with police waiting for Mr Whitney outside a pub and Mr Whitney lying prostrate and speechless when stopped from driving his car as if he was having some kind of fit.

The jury believed his story and Mr Whitney's bacon was saved. It's rather curious when you consider his job… prosecuting in police cases in the courts. 'I only do it to pay for my hobby with the pigs,' he avers.

Perhaps, as W H Hudson noted, it's the hail-fellow-well-met air of the pig that endears him to the British, particularly the aristocracy, surrounded as they are by cap-doffing or forelock-tugging envy. And as Churchill said, 'Dogs look up to us, cats look down on us, but pigs treat us as equals.'

THOSE PESKY TITLES

For those who believe that the British class system has disappeared, try entering your details in these two websites: easyJet (flights for plebs like me, simplistically), Royal Opera House (music for toffs, simplistically). EasyJet's drop down menu for the person's title extend to:

Mr
Mrs
Miss
Ms

And that's it.

The Royal Opera House's title box offers 133 drop down title options, including these:

Countess
Dowager Marchioness
President
His Serene Highness The Prince of
The Rt Hon Viscount

AND WHEN IT COMES TO CHRISTIAN NAMES

Puritan names for girls that are based on virtues have never quite died out: Felicity, Joy and Prudence, for example, even if Chastity isn't quite in vogue. But a look at a Sussex church late-16th century register of baptisms reveals these: Bethankful, Bestidfast, Renewed, Repent, Goodgift, Sindinye, Givethanks, Humilitie, Obedeence, Repentence, Fearnot, Confidence, Feargod, Fayntnot, Renued and Replenish. Perhaps the least pleased with his middle name might have been Nicholas If-Jesus-Christ-Had-Not-Died-For-Thee-Thou-Hadst-Been-Damned Barebone, son of Praise-God Barebone, (the man who gave his name to the Barebones Parliament of 1653 simply by being first on the register).

TRAVEL INFORMATION

BLENHEIM PALACE, Woodstock, Oxfordshire OX20 1PP
☎ 01993 811091 🖳 www.blenheimpalace.com
🛎 01865 726871
🚗 M40 to J9, then A34 towards Oxford, then A44 to Woodstock
🚂/🚌 From London Paddington to Oxford, walk or taxi to Gloucester Green bus station, then bus S3 to Woodstock

CHATSWORTH HOUSE, Bakewell, Derbyshire DE45 1PP
☎ 01246 565300 🖥 www.chatsworth.org 📠 01246 345777.
🚗 Signed from M1 J29 🚆 Chesterfield, then bus

CUPID'S OBELISK, Mount Edgcumbe House and Country Park, near
Plymouth, Devon PL10 1HZ ☎ 01752 822236;
🖥 www.mountedgcumbe.gov.uk 📠 01752 266030
🚗 From M5 end at Exeter, take A38 to Plymouth, through city to
Devonport for ferry to Torpoint, then follow signs 🚆/🚌 Plymouth
station, from London Paddington and many other centres, then walk to
Royal Parade and catch bus 33 to Admiral's Hard in Stonehouse district.
Then Cremyll foot ferry (a great, inexpensive ride) direct to country park

FYLING HALL PIGGERY, above picturesque Robin Hood's Bay, near historic
Whitby, North Yorkshire YO22 4QD 📠 01947 602674
🚗 Off A1(M) at Thirsk, take A61, A19, A172, A171

LILE COTTAGE AND GLEASTON MILL, Cumbria LA12 0QH
☎ 01229 869244 🖥 www.lilecottage.com 📠 01229 894784
🚗 North of the A5087 coast road between Ulverston and Barrow-in-Furness

LONGLEAT, Wiltshire BA12 7NW ☎ 01985 844400
🖥 www.longleat.co.uk 📠 01985 218548
🚗 From M4 J17, take A350 south, join A36 near Warminster and follow
signs 🚆/🚌 Nearest station: Warminster (on the Salisbury–Bath line, or less
frequently, Waterloo–Cardiff). Then Lionlink bus, not Sun (check times)

ICKWORTH, Suffolk IP29 5QE ☎ 01284 735270
🖥 www.nationaltrust.org.uk 📠 01284 764667
🚗 A14 turn-off at first Bury St Edmunds exit then follow signs

SHUGBOROUGH HALL, Ilford, Staffordshire ST17 0XB ☎ 01889 881388
🖥 www.shugborough.org.uk 📠 01785 619619
🚗 From M6 J13, follow signs 🚆/🚌 Stafford or Lichfield City stations,
then Arriva North Midlands bus 825

SOUTH OF ENGLAND RARE BREEDS CENTRE, Woodchurch, Ashford, Kent
TN26 3RJ ☎ 01233 861493 🖥 www.rarebreeds.org.uk 📠 01233 629165
🚗 On B2067 Tenterden–Folkestone road. From London and M25, take
M20 to J10, A2070 to, appropriately, Hamstreet, turn right on B2067 and go
west for 3 miles 🚆/🚌 Nearest mainline station: Ashford (from London
Victoria, Paris or Brussels). 🚌 295 leaves Ashford International direct to
centre at 10.52 weekdays with two return options. Hamstreet also has a
railway station on Ashford–Hastings branch, but then 3-mile walk or cycle

DEAD ECCENTRIC

ATLANTIC OCEAN

Orkney Islands

Thurso

Isle of Lewis

Isle of Skye

Inner Hebrides

Island of Mull

Islay

Inverness

SCOTLAND

Aberdeen

NORTH SEA

Logierait Mortsafes

Fraser Mausoleum, Arbroath

Perfect Pyramid, Dean Cemetery, Edinburgh

Glasgow

Hamilton Mausoleum

Heart Burial, Melrose Abbey

Byzantine Mausoleum

Arran

Drumlanrig Castle

Johnnie Turner's Grave & Sculptures, Glenkiln

Sweetheart Abbey

Carlisle

Newcastle upon Tyne

ATLANTIC OCEAN

Corpse Road, Haweswater

Middlesbrough

Wainwright's Ashes, Haystacks

Corpse Trail, Swaledale

Dracula Trail, Whitby

Isle of Man

ENGLAND

Otley Church & Tunnel of Death

York

Kingston-upon-Hull

IRISH SEA

Bradford

Leeds

NORTH SEA

McKenzie's Pyramid, Liverpool

Anglesey

Holyhead

Manchester

Grimsby

Sheffield

Marquess's Missing Leg, Plas Newydd

Stoke-on-Trent

Cardigan Bay

Derby

Nottingham

Bonomi Pyramid, Blickling Hall

Norwich

Wolverhampton

Birmingham

WALES

Fishguard

Coventry

Cambridge

Ipswich

Tomb Doggerel, Ely Cathedral

Railway Grave, Bromsgrove

Bandaged Heart, Woodford

Wheatley Lock-up

Dashwood Mausoleum & Hellfire Caves, West Wycombe

Tomb Doggerel, St Mary's Church, Harrow-on-the-Hill

Swansea

CARDIFF

Whirlwind Memorial, Reading

LONDON

Giro's Memorial, Waterloo Place

Bristol Channel

Bristol

Brookwood Cemetery & Death Railway, Woking

Army Museum, Chelsea

Leighton House, Kensington

Dover

Beware Chalk Pit Pyramid, Farley Mount

'Boy Crusader', Mappowder

Southampton

Mad Jack Fuller's Pyramid, Brightling

ATLANTIC OCEAN

Exeter

Portsmouth

Brighton

Hardy's Heart, Stinsford

Wrong Hardy Memorial

Knill Monument, St Ives

Penzance

ENGLISH CHANNEL

0 —— 80 km
0 —— 50 miles

N

DEAD ECCENTRIC

BIZARRE LAST WISHES

Most people settle for burial or cremation. The odd eccentric asks to be frozen or mummified. Brian Crombleholme, 28, announced in 1994 he'd like the services of a good taxidermist. The father-of-two shocked his neighbours in Blackpool with his wish to be stuffed and put on display after death, but he would not be unique if his wishes were carried out.

But it's nothing new. Hannah Beswick, presumably terrified of waking up in her coffin, left a fortune to her physician in 1758 on condition that he regularly checked her for signs of life. To save himself trouble, the Lancashire doctor had her embalmed and mounted inside a glass-fronted grandfather clock on his landing so he could check her along with the barometer on his way out each morning. It was only 110 years later that her trustees decided she was safely dead and could be buried at last.

People still make strange requests about their deaths. A Bristol housewife astonished tabloid readers in 1994 by asking to be buried with her faithful gas cooker, appropriately a New World model. This gave plenty of scope for headline writers: Roast in Peace, or possibly, Rust in Peace.

People also make odd last requests for their ashes. When scientist Jeff Thorp died aged 72 in 1992, his family were determined to honour his last wishes to go out with a bang. In fact, in the form of specially made rockets, his ashes lit up the night sky for miles around. And, as befits a brilliant biochemist who invented a major heart drug, he took the preparations seriously and researched rocket propulsion and the specific gravity of human ashes before calculating the best trajectory. He even staged a test run with coal fire ashes.

On the day, it took 28 rockets to blast all his remains into the sky from Kerridge Hill, near Macclesfield, Cheshire. Planes from nearby Manchester airport were diverted from the airspace as silver, red and green stars exploded in the heavens. A fellow scientist was quoted as saying: 'I came to this unusual event to honour Jeff. He was a fine colleague and an outstanding scientist – and he had a wicked sense of humour.' He got his last laugh. It *is* rocket science.

But could anything beat, for happy aptness, the great Lake District fell walker A W Wainwright's last request? He asked for his ashes to be scattered on **Haystacks** (Travel: page 176), one of his favourite fells, and so they were in 1991. It is a place of pilgrimage for latter-day Wainwrighters, the be-backpacked followers of the goat-like guru, and it is indeed wonderful on a half-decent day. If you walk up from Buttermere, where you will have looked at the window to his memory in the church, go round the far side of this incomparably lovely lake and up through Scarth Gap round Haystacks to the peaceful Innominate Tarn; you can come back down Warnscale Beck to the lake, completing the circuit of Haystacks, perhaps seven miles in all.

The great man wrote with his dry humour of this place: 'Should you get a bit of grit in your boots as you are crossing Haystacks, please treat it with respect. It could be me.' It would be going too far, as I usually do, to say if you get a bit of grit in your eye, shed a tear for him. But don't be too sad on his behalf. He said of Buttermere church, where his memorial is: 'Buttermere is a foretaste of heaven.'

At the **Hatters Arms**, Marple, Greater Manchester, by contrast, one regular drinker's ideas of heaven was somewhat different. He has been interred, as it were, in the form of ashes, in the pub's hanging baskets. 'You could set your clock by the time old Ernie came in bang on 9pm every night and picked up his pint of mild', the landlord said. He added: 'Occasionally I pour half a pint of mild in to keep him happy and it's done wonders for the flowers. It's safe to say Ernie has done a blooming marvellous job.' Talk about hanging round the bar…

Other people ask to be deposited in the goal of their favourite football team, whizzed round in pneumatic message carriers or blasted from the chimneys of their favourite steam locomotives. Wanting to be buried with a much-loved car is unlikely to find favour in the average churchyard. Grieving relatives of Jaguar-owner Ian Ashton of County Durham made a compromise by screwing his personalised numberplate to his coffin before his burial in 1996. All these characters were in a fine tradition that has been long-lived.

Britain is littered with bizarre relics of the dead eccentric, delightfully dotty deceased and buried buffoons. Some even had the last laugh *en route* to the grave.

The 17th-century English eccentric **Jemmy Hirst** (1738–1829), who during his life had ridden round town on a bull and printed his own 5*d* banknotes, directed in his will that his coffin should be carried by 12 elderly local virgins. No doubt he would have chuckled to know that his executors, at their wits' end, could find only two.

Perhaps the oddest case concerns a woman who never reached her grave at all. When the first wife of the king of 18th-century eccentrics, **Martin van Butchell** (1735–1814) died in 1775, he had her embalmed with turpentine and camphor, fitted with glass eyes, coloured to appear lifelike and mounted in a display case in the front room of his Mayfair home. She was wearing full wedding dress and van Butchell charged the public to see her. Van Butchell, who made a fortune supplying dentures and trusses to the gentry, although qualified in neither field, refused to visit his rich clients despite, in one case, being sent a horse and carriage and the small fortune of 500 guineas. On the other hand, he regularly visited Newgate jail to treat prisoners free of charge.

His bizarre preservation of his first wife's corpse may have been brought on by her will, which stated that her fortune was to go to a distant relative 'the moment I am dead and buried'. She had been offered, incidentally, the choice of wearing black or white for the rest of her life on her wedding day – she chose black – and when van Butchell married his second wife (in fact, his maid Elizabeth, perhaps so he no longer had to pay her a wage) she chose white. Still the first wife was not buried, and in 1815 his son Edmund offered the body to the Royal College of Surgeons. There she remained unburied until blown to bits by a Nazi bomb in the Blitz of 1941. From dust to dust.

LAND OF ODD PYRAMIDS

The Pyramids have fascinated our nation since Briton Howard Carter discovered the tomb of Tutankhamun in 1922. But the British interest in things Egyptian goes back much further than that. There are a surprising number of old pyramids dotted around this country, often connected with death in some bizarre way.

At **Brightling** in East Sussex, for example, local eccentric 'Mad Jack' Fuller (1757–1834) has been entombed in a fair-sized pyramid he built in the churchyard in 1811. Village lore has it that his 22-stone corpse sits in an iron chair with a bottle of port and a roast chicken before him, waiting for the Resurrection. The floor of the pyramid is said to be covered in broken glass to deter the Devil from trying to snatch him away in the meantime.

A similar, surprisingly large, pyramid is the grave of Dr Francis Douce in the Hampshire village of **Nether Wallop**, where again it dominates the churchyard. Another handsome 18th-century pyramid, somewhat smaller, is in the churchyard of St Mary's Church, Painswick, Gloucestershire, famed for its strange clipping rituals (see page 181).

One pyramid you can enter is at **Farley Mount Country Park** (Travel: page 174) near Winchester. The deceased is buried in the mound beneath – it is the favourite horse of Paulet St John who, while hunting in 1733, survived an amazing leap over a hedge on the horse's back and down into a 25ft-deep chalk pit. In the following year the horse won the Hunters' Plate at Worthy Downs races, again ridden by St John, under the somewhat cautionary name Beware Chalk Pit. Another fine pyramid you can enter is the Obelisk Lodge at **Nostell Priory,** Yorkshire, a National Trust stately home near Wakefield (Travel: page 176).

And the perplexing plethora of pyramids extends north of the border. In the Dean Cemetery, **Edinburgh**, there is the most perfectly polished example you could imagine, down the far end near the gate to the Dean Gallery.

A cautionary tale attaches to a probably unique pyramidical village lockup still to be seen in the centre of **Wheatley**, near Oxford (Travel: page 177). It was, local legend has it, used to detain 'loose women'. **Swanage**, Dorset, has yet another pyramid, a tomb for the 19th-century entrepreneur-builder John Mowlem (1788–1868); and there is a fine bunch of pyramids at **Castle Howard**, Yorkshire (Travel: page 175).

One is stunningly mounted above an arch in the massive fortified wall through which passes an approach road to the great house, with an obelisk perfectly aligned to be visible through the arch.

Perhaps the most elegant pyramid in Britain is the sizeable one at **Blicking Hall**, Norfolk (Travel: page 174), built by Bonomi as a tribute to the Earl of Buckingham who died in 1793. The great house is run by the National Trust.

Definitely unique is the ceremony attached to a splendid pyramid that takes place at St Ives, Cornwall. At the **Knill Monument** (Travel: page 176) of 18th-century mayor John Knill, on every fifth anniversary of his death – 25 July 2011 and so on – ten virgins dressed in white must dance for 15 minutes and then sing a psalm. Two elderly widows in black must supervise, says his will, and the mayor and town council attend for good measure.

We've got more pyramids than Egypt, frankly. One more: in **St Andrew's Church**, Rodney Street, Liverpool, there is an eye-catching pyramid memorial to William McKenzie (1794–1851). McKenzie was a successful Victorian railway engineer and Liverpool's most notorious gambler who won and lost several fortunes. He commissioned this tomb before his death and the story – evocative of Mad Jack Fuller, above – is that he made a pact with the Devil that if he could win a certain game, the Devil could have his soul as soon as he was buried. He is, therefore, locals say, sat upright in the tomb at a card table, a winning hand of cards in his grasp. And not buried.

LEG-END IN HIS OWN LIFETIME

One of the odder possessions of the National Trust, along with the stately homes and beauty spots, is a part of its heritage that should not be forgotten – the **first Marquess of Anglesey's leg**.

During the Battle of Waterloo, as the cannon roared, the marquess (then merely Lord Uxbridge but later elevated for his heroism) cried out: 'My God, Sir, I've lost a leg!' The Duke of Wellington remarked: 'Have you, by God!' and carried on observing the French lines through his telescope. It is not recorded whether the Iron Duke dismounted to lend a hand, as it were – the two were hardly friends and later were political enemies – but amputation was performed in the field and the leg buried under a willow tree with full military honours.

The marquess (1768–1854) later had the world's first articulated artificial limb made and the patented 'Anglesey leg' may be seen at the National Trust's neo-Gothic **Plas Newydd** on the Menai Straits, north Wales (Travel: page 177). The house was given to the Trust by the seventh marquess in 1976 and contains a military museum, including a sprig of willow from the tree at Waterloo where the real leg was buried. That spot was marked with a monument and gave the marquess the peculiar prospect of being able to visit part of his own tomb.

Not only was the wooden leg only one of three made for the marquess – there was a riding leg, a walking leg and a best leg – but the National Trust's leg is just one of three monuments to the historic limb. At the **National Army Museum** in Chelsea (Travel: page 176) a somewhat grisly display re-creates the scene as the leg was detached on a farmhouse table, with the surgeon's 15-inch bloodstained saw and his once-white glove. The Waterloo site has been recently redeveloped and the real leg disinterred and reburied in a nearby cemetery alongside whole people, the spot being marked by a plaque.

What about the rest of the marquess, minus his leg? Is he forgotten? Not at all: there's a one-legged but 91ft-tall monument on the island of Anglesey. The monument, at the exhaustively named spot of Llanfairpw-llgwngyllgogerychwyrndrobwllllantysiliogogogoch (see page 228), is a column ascended by an internal spiral staircase, with a statue on top. The hero's loss was others' gain: the marquess's pioneering limb enabled thousands of disabled people worldwide to stand on two feet, if not their own.

LONDON'S ONLY NAZI MEMORIAL

For how many more years will someone put a flower, as they have every February for decades, on the only Nazi memorial in London? In February 1934, **Giro**, the faithful hound of the German ambassador Leopold von Hoesch, was buried complete with tombstone near the then German embassy at 7 Carlton House Terrace (Travel: page 175).

The memorial, with touching epithet *Ein Treuer Begleiter* ('a true companion'), is tucked under a tree at the top of the steps from the Institute of Contemporary Art on the Mall to Waterloo Place, perhaps somewhat cheekily given that the area is laden with vast monuments to heroes of the British Empire. Indeed, the statues of Field Marshal Lord Clyde and the mounted Edward VII show serious bomb damage inflicted by Giro's master's master less than ten years later. Giro's tombstone, however, was undamaged – as was the splendid Nazi interior nearby designed by Hitler's architect Albert Speer – and has been encased in glass to preserve it further.

PIGEONS AT WAR AND ANIMAL HEROES

There is a splendidly conceived and charming, if somewhat stained, war memorial for pigeons in Worthing, Sussex. It consists of inscribed boulders and a pond on a mound in **Beach House Park** and is perfectly serious. One stone reads: 'In memory of warrior birds who gave their lives on active service 1939–45 and for the use and pleasure of living birds.'

Hundreds of homing pigeons were dropped into Nazi-occupied Europe to the Resistance and many made it home. Others were with troops on secret missions. Naturally, the Germans tried to shoot down any pigeons they thought might be carrying messages. An astounding 31 of the 53 Dickin medals, the 'animal VCs', went to pigeons, so these brave creatures were not, when it came to war, doves.

My all-time favourite of Britain's decorated animal war heroes – even though it included collie dogs that were parachuted into Italy and returned home to their farms after years of fighting the Nazis and still knew their masters, even though it included the stoical war horses of both wars – is a cat.

A black and white moggie called Simon was hero of the **Yangtze Incident** of 1949, when a British ship HMS *Amethyst* was trapped up the Yangtze river by Communist forces (during the civil war in China). Although Britain had not taken sides and the ship was on an evacuation mission, *Amethyst* was mercilessly shelled for days, causing death and injury, but then boldly escaped down river by night.

Simon, having been smuggled aboard by a rating, was a cheeky cat, curling up in the captain's cap to sleep. But when one shell hit the captain's cabin he was terribly wounded, and although he was treated and four pieces of shrapnel extracted, he was terribly burned and not expected to live. He recovered, however, and returned to duty (promoted to Able Seacat from Ordinary Seacat) and fought off the commie rats, as it were, in the potato store, occasionally bringing one of the dead enemy to a sailor in triumph.

He and the ship's company returned as heroes. Simon's citation when presented with the Amethyst campaign ribbon in Hong Kong on the way home: 'Be it known that on April 26, 1949, though recovering from wounds, when *HMS Amethyst* was standing off by Rose Bay you did single-handedly and unarmed stalk down and destroy "Mao-Tse Tung" a rat guilty of raiding food supplies which were critically short.'

The officer saluted Simon, and the assembled crew gave three cheers. Simon the cat, with predictably stiff upper lip, said nothing...

As the story spread, a sailor had to be detailed to answer the burgeoning fan mail, which Able Seacat Simon declined to read.

Back in Britain, as the crew went ashore to be feted as heroes, Simon stayed aboard on guard, and can be seen briefly in archive Pathé newsreel of the event. The cat was awarded the Dickin Medal, (and the Blue Cross Medal) but died before the planned presentation (by the Lord Mayor of London) as a result of complications from his war wounds.

He received obituaries in newspapers and magazines and the British wept when they read one telling in Dickensian style of the moment of his death: '...the spirit of Simon slipped quietly away to sea.'

Thousands, including the entire crew of *HMS Amethyst*, attended his funeral. People were in tears as the little coffin came past, draped in a miniature Union Jack. His grave may be seen at the **PDSA Ilford Animal Cemetery** in East London (a rather fascinating place, Travel: page 177). It has a proper headstone remembering him, ending with the lines carved in granite:

THROUGHOUT THE YANGTZE INCIDENT
HIS BEHAVIOUR WAS OF THE HIGHEST ORDER.

He also has a memorial bush at the National Arboretum in Staffordshire. That and two medals and a campaign ribbon.

Only in eccentric Britain...

PICKLED BRAINS AND RESTLESS HEADS

A controversial exhibition at London's Serpentine Gallery in 1995 included, beside a naked actress asleep in a box, the pickled brain of mathematician **Charles Babbage** (1791–1871).

Babbage's brilliant ideas on calculating machines in the early 19th century laid the groundwork for today's computers more than a century before such machines were actually made to work. But the bizarre preservation of his brain – it normally resides at the Royal College of Surgeons of England – isn't unique.

Not far away the embalmed body of philosopher **Jeremy Bentham** (1748–1832) sits in state within a glass case in University College, Gower Street, London. In the 19th century his head was replaced with a replica, as disrespectful students had the macabre habit of playing football with the real thing, even if this followed his famed principle of utilitarianism – matters should be arranged to be useful for 'the happiness of the greatest number'.

People can become very pompous when writing their wills and Bentham was no exception. He directed how his body was to be displayed in great detail, including:

> my executor will cause the skeleton to be clad in one of the suits of black occasionally worn by me. The body so clothed shall together with the chair and staff in my later years bourne by me he will take charge of and for containing the whole apparatus he will cause to be prepared an appropriate box or case and will cause to be engraved in conspicuous characters on a plate to be fixed thereon and also on labels on the glass cases in which the preparation of the soft parts of my body will be preserved ... etc, etc

This suggests not only that Bentham's lectures might in real life have been less than riveting, but also that he had that delusion of the self-appointed great and the good that the world's fascination with them cannot end with their death. Now of whom does that remind me today?

Like Bentham's, the Lord Protector **Oliver Cromwell**'s head has not had a restful time in the three centuries since it was ripped from his remains in the 1660 Restoration and impaled on a pole at Westminster Hall. It supposedly blew down in a storm and was buried in various places before ending up in the grounds of Sidney Sussex College, Cambridge. Its location is unmarked in case Royalists, still angry after all those years at his part in chopping off the head of King Charles I, dig it up again.

SURREY'S MYSTERY MOSQUE AND A DEATH RAILWAY

Generations of commuters, schoolchildren returning from boarding school and holidaymakers using the main railway line from London's Waterloo will have all, momentarily, wondered exactly the same thing. Why, just before Woking, in the leafy gin and Jag belt beloved of stockbrokers, is there a sizeable mosque, complete with handsome dome and crescent moon?

After all, it is an area where few Muslim immigrants have ever lived and religion is more likely thought of in terms of old ladies cycling to evensong. The eccentric character behind this puzzle can be found a couple of miles further down the main line in the massive **Brookwood Cemetery** (Travel (Shah Jehan Mosque): page 192), itself a rather bizarre answer to Victorian London's burial space crisis. Both stories are most peculiar.

Things in the capital were so bad in the early 19th century that the poor were buried in shallow graves on top of one another. The poor scavenged coffin wood from the inadequately buried, whom they were often doomed soon to join in a capital rife with disease and lacking basic sewerage systems.

Human bones were shipped north to be used as fertiliser. Churchyards even today bulge higher than the paths through them, such was the burial upon burial, often after an indecently short interval. One solution to this, along with the great Victorian cemeteries such as Hampstead, Kensal Green and West Brompton, was the macabrely fascinating **Brookwood Necropolis Railway**, which started running in 1854.

It was exclusive in that you only travelled once, and then only in one direction. The service was run for the dead, so the 'coffin tickets' issued right up to the 1950s were not available as returns. Funeral trains ran from the discreet London Necropolis station near Waterloo, where steam-powered hoists would raise coffins to the level of the hearse vans. In the spirit of the age, there was segregation between Anglicans and the rest, as there was in the mourners' waiting rooms and carriages.

At Brookwood, a part of Woking, a vast city of the dead was laid out with every possible nationality and creed catered for (and indeed, judging by the number of graves marked 'resting' or 'fell asleep', waking Woking might still be a possibility). If today you take the pleasant and fascinating walk along the route of the long siding that these mournful trains took from Brookwood station, to two truly terminal stations (one Anglican, one for the rest).

On the right of the tracks, the solution to the mosque puzzle comes with an impressive monument to **Gottlieb William Leitner** (1840–99), featuring a noble bust framed by an arch inscribed 'The Learned are Honoured in their Work' (as untrue for him as for many another forgotten eccentric). Undoubtedly a gifted linguist, Dr Leitner, who had been born in Budapest in 1840, was the kind of self-obsessed, self-driven, self-publicising oddball who would make little impact today, unless he could find a sponsor for an expedition by yak to the South Pole or host a television show.

After creating an Oriental section at King's College, London and becoming its professor by 1861, Leitner saw a job advertised running Government College, Lahore, then in British India. Although only 21, he was appointed, a decision the authorities came to regret. He started a bank and other organisations for 'native people' in a way that annoyed the authorities who believed they had run India perfectly well for years without him.

His expeditions for linguistic researches into remote parts of the North-West Frontier, the Hindu Kush and Ladakh produced some scattered information, which few took any notice of, about languages and peoples he encountered, sitting, as he put it, by a camp fire with a pen in one hand and a revolver in the other.

On his trips back to Europe, Leitner not only brought Oriental artefacts but several native people who were paraded like specimens before learned societies' soirées. On leave in 1884 he purchased the Royal Dramatic College, Woking, and eventually made it into the Indian University Institute affiliated to his own Punjab University.

Like many of his creations, the Indian University at Woking did not outlive him. But the beautiful **Shah Jehan Mosque** (Travel: page 192), built in its grounds in Oriental Road, still surprises and delights passengers of the adjacent railway line.

HOW THE LIVING CAN FOLLOW THE DEAD

The increasingly popular Coast-to-Coast walk across the most beautiful bits of the north of England – from the Lakes across the Pennines to the North Yorkshire Moors and the North Sea – has the merit, and I write from footsore experience, of making a hiker feel really alive. But, oddly enough, the route has often been rather popular with the dead.

'**Corpse roads**' feature strongly in the pre-motor road days of these then-remote areas, when some settlements could only be reached by foot or packhorse. The dead from remoter farms and hamlets still had to be buried in consecrated ground and, as parishes in these thinly populated areas could be huge, the church might be a dozen miles away. There were set routes for the dead to reach these graveyards, the corpses being slung over packhorses, or being carried by mourners or bearers.

One of the more tiring but rewarding days of the Coast-to-Coast walk brings the hiker down to **Haweswater**, a reservoir that today fills Mardale, once home to a pretty village and a more modest natural lake. Across the lake from the hiker's long track, beside the road on the other side, a trail can be seen zigzagging up the hill. This is the corpse road that once led from Mardale Green up and over the hill to consecrated ground at Shap. The dead would have been strapped to a horse and carried across in all weathers, followed up the fellside by windswept mourners. This happened until 1729, when Mardale Green at last gained its own church and consecrated ground.

In 1936 the church was taken down and used in building the dam that was to flood the valley. That left the awkward question of the dead, and whether being under 100ft of water as well as 6ft of earth would cause problems. It certainly would have done for those wishing to visit graves without diving gear – although in times of drought the eerie remains of the village, the lane and drystone walls emerge as the water levels fall. So the dead were exhumed and reburied at Shap, where they would have gone anyway up the corpse road, had no church been built. It is all fuel for thought for hikers who also feel pretty near dead when, exhausted, they reach Shap's welcoming pubs.

Two days further along the Coast-to-Coast walk, which by now has crossed the Pennine watershed heading east, the walk follows the length of lovely **Swaledale**. This entire valley was the prescribed route for those carrying – often on a mourner's back – their dead to Grinton, a journey that could take two or three days. Side routes led from other hamlets in the bleak and sparsely populated upland. The corpse stone at Ivelet, where there is now a handsome bridge, was the spot for laying down the body for the bearers to rest before fording the river, and at Blades a dead-house, now ruined, provided the overnight stop for those who started way up the valley. Eventually, today's hiker passes St Andrew's, Grinton, the dead end for that particular corpse trail.

The macabre theme goes on. As the North Yorkshire Moors are reached, the route converges with that famous route of the dead, the **Lyke Wake Walk**, immortalised by the *Cleveland Lyke Wake Dirge*, a dialect folksong about death and the Devil, naming several features along the route. There is a tradition among trekking fanatics to do the whole thing in one go, right through the bleak windswept night.

Despite all this, and despite the fact that a party in recent years made the 40-mile trek carrying a coffin, the authors of the dirge admit that the song and the route were created in the 20th century as a bit of instant folklore, albeit representative of the customs in the hills all around. After all, there was no reason to take bodies *away* from the perfectly adequate graveyards at either end of the trail. Dead peculiar, one might think, heading on towards the North Sea.

Yet further along the Coast-to-Coast walk for the dead, near Grosmont, on a track not open to cars, walkers pass an old tollhouse sign still saying: 'Hearses, 6*d*'. After all that, if you end up at **Whitby**, even its Dracula Trail (Travel: page 175) might seem a little dead.

GONE FOR A BURTON: THE ARAB TENT IN DEEPEST MORTLAKE

The most eccentric tomb in London must be that of **Richard Burton** (1821–90). Not the Richard Burton who kept marrying Elizabeth Taylor – surely rather eccentric behaviour in itself – but the

great explorer who opened up the vast and unknown lands of Arabia to the eyes of an enchanted Western world. Thus, a full-scale Arab sheik's tent – complete with stone folds of cloth frozen in mid-flap of a desert breeze as if touched by a Narnian witch's wand – stands somewhat incongruously in a sleepy corner of suburban Mortlake.

Aptly, finding **Burton's mausoleum** (Travel: page 175) is something of an exploration in itself. It is not in the vast municipal Mortlake Cemetery, nor in the graveyard of the confusingly named St Mary the Virgin church fronting Mortlake High Street near the Thames. But behind there, through a labyrinth of paths such as Tinderbox Alley, lined by Victorian cottages, lies St Mary Magdalen, a Catholic church, where the extraordinary monument can be found by following a well-worn track through the undergrowth.

Close up, one can see an iron star romantically hidden in the foliage above the tent, a valedictory poem typical of the era and, behind, the most fascinating aspect: a window in the tent's roof with a handy steel ladder, enabling one to peer at the coffins of Burton and his wife. They are surrounded by some of their favourite objects from his explorations and well-withered wreaths, a century of dust and decrepitude having failed to spoil the oddly cosy, domestic scene.

Another half-forgotten gem in London from this era of exotic Arabists is the home of the great Victorian artist **Frederic, Lord Leighton** (1830–96). The creator of the familiar *Flaming June* picture lived at the extraordinary **Leighton House** (Travel: page 176), in a quiet road off Kensington High Street, where one can experience heady incense in the exotic, bejewelled Arab hall where Leighton's unique collection of Moorish tilework is employed, complete with tinkling fountain and the lofty dome described in its day as the eighth wonder of the world.

Lord Lloyd-Webber (born in 1948) and Lady Lucinda Lambton (born in 1943) are great fans of what the latter calls 'the secret heart of Kensington'. Leighton, whose career received a huge boost when Queen Victoria bought one of his pictures, was made a peer – the only artist so honoured – shortly before his death in 1896.

TOMBS ALONG ODD LINES

Railwaymen whose lives are ruled by unemotional iron and steel have often been strangely sentimental, as their bizarre tombs dotted around the country, adorned with fantastic if not appalling doggerel, testify.

One of the most elaborate rhymes is on the memorial to William Pickering and Richard Hedger in the south porch of **Ely Cathedral**, Cambridgeshire (Travel: page 175). They were killed on Christmas Eve 1845 aged 30 and 24 respectively on the Norfolk Railway near Thetford. An inquest blamed their deaths on excessive speed, although some of the jury thought the engine construction deficient – these were very early days and the technology primitive, although Norfolk jurors can't have known much about it.

Their memorial, however, happily compares the newfangled railway journeys to the trip to heaven in a wonderful poem known as the *Spiritual Railway*. Either the Norfolk accent was then a lot stronger or the writer was an atrocious rhymer, but the conclusion was clearly on the right lines:

> *The Line to heaven by Christ was made*
> *With heavenly truth the Rails are laid …*
> *God's Love the Fire, his Truth the Steam,*
> *Which drives the Engine and the Train …*
> *In First and Second, and Third Class,*
> *Repentence, Faith and Holiness …*
> *Come then poor Sinners, now's the time*
> *At any station on the Line.*
> *If you'll repent and turn from sin*
> *The Train will stop and take you in.*

Train-surfing, an insanely dangerous American game of riding train roofs or sides, and the mass roof-riding phenomenon that Indians euphemistically call ticketless travel, are nothing new, judging by an 1838 tombstone at **St Mary's Church**, Harrow-on-the-Hill, northwest London (Travel: page 177). But one hopes that the gruesomely detailed doggerel is not copied elsewhere. The inscription says that Thomas Port, who used to ride wagons on the nearby London and Birmingham

Railway, lost his legs in 1838 after falling from the train. 'With the greatest fortitude he bore a second amputation by the surgeons and died from loss of blood.'

The macabre doggerel goes as follows:

> Bright rose the morn and vig'rous Port,
> Gay on the train he used his wonted sport
> Ere noon arrived his mangled form they bore
> With pain distorted and overwhelmed with gore
> When evening came to close the fateful day
> A mutilated corpse the sufferer lay.

Another fine piece of railway disaster doggerel, at **St John's Church** in Bromsgrove, Worcestershire (Travel: page 177), also dates from the very early days. It is a memorial to Thomas Scaife, 28, and Joseph Rutherford, 30, engineers on the Birmingham and Gloucester Railway, who were killed by a boiler explosion in November 1840. As the tombstone of Scaife records:

> My engine now is cold and still
> No water does my boiler fill
> My coke affords its flame no more
> My days of usefulness are o'er.
> My wheels deny their noted speed
> No more my guiding hands they heed
> My whistle too has lost its tone
> Its shrill and thrilling sounds are gone …
> No more I feel each urging breath
> My steam is now condens'd in death …

Brilliant stuff, but the detailed carvings on the graves wrongly show one of the American-built Norris engines used near here to bank (push) heavy trains up the notorious Lickey Incline. In fact, poor Scaife and Rutherford were using an experimental locomotive that was blown to pieces and therefore could not be copied. Its name was, aptly, *Surprise*.

Another railway disaster is commemorated in the churchyard at **Otley** (Travel: page 177), near the Leeds to Harrogate line. This time there is no verse, but a splendid miniature tunnel portal, stone-built and crenellated with towers. It would grace the best garden train layout and one can happily imagine puffing models bringing truckloads of scones to ladies at vicarage tea parties. However, the truth is somewhat more sombre. The miniature is a replica of the portal of nearby Bramhope Tunnel, and a memorial to the 23 men who died in its appallingly troublesome construction, 280ft beneath the ridge between Leeds and Wharfedale. Some 1,500 million gallons of water had to be pumped out to prevent flooding during construction.

Surely one of the oddest railway memorials must be that in **St Lawrence**'s churchyard at Reading, Berkshire, where a wooden memorial marks the peculiar fate of one Henry West who was killed by a whirlwind that blew the roof off Reading station in 1840. He was aged only 24.

Naturally this board offers suitable doggerel:

> *Sudden the change, and in a moment fell,*
> *had not time to bid my friends farewell*
> *Yet hushed be all complaint, 'tis sweet, 'tis blest,*
> *to change Earth's stormy scenes for endless rest,*
> *Dear friends prepare, take warning by my fall,*
> *so you shall hear with joy your Saviour's call.*

SOME VERY STRANGE ORGANS

Just as rushing living hearts around to save lives in transplants seized the imagination of late 20th-century society, so the location of even dead people's hearts has been thought in the past to have immense significance.

The explorer Livingstone's heart is buried where he was searching for the source of the Nile in his beloved Africa, while **Thomas Hardy's heart** can be found beneath a tombstone at Stinsford near Dorchester, Dorset (Travel: page 176) – appropriately, as Dorchester was the Casterbridge of Hardy's great novel.

Hardy actually wanted to be buried whole at Stinsford next to his wife, but against his wishes the rest of him was cremated and the ashes taken to Poets' Corner in Westminster Abbey. Local legend has it that the 'heart' was another bit of meat, as the cat got in and stole the real organ. But a spokesman for the Thomas Hardy Society said sniffily: 'We've never lent any credence to this local gossip. It's just a myth which probably had its origin in the fact that Hardy wasn't very popular locally.'

By the way, the nearby ugly factory chimney-style **Hardy Monument** uphill from Portesham near Weymouth (Travel: page 177) is often assumed to commemorate Thomas Hardy the author. But actually it remembers

the other Thomas Hardy – the 'kiss me' or *kismet* ('fate' in Arabic) Hardy of Trafalgar fame, not the writer of a century later. The view, nevertheless, is fantastic. You can see the Isle of Wight, 35 miles away.

A yet stranger story can be traced at **St Paul's Church**, Hammersmith, West London. At the back of the nave stands an urn in which Sir Nicholas Crispe requested his heart be put on his death in 1665. The urn is below a bronze bust of 'that glorious martyr Kinge Charles the first of blessed memory' and symbolises Crispe's role as a 'loyall sharer in the sufferings of his late and present majesty'.

Curiously, the urn is empty. In 1898 the Royalist knight's body was moved to Hammersmith from St Mildred's, Bread Street, London, and someone with a strong stomach took the two-centuries-old, and probably crisp, heart from the urn and reunited it with Crispe's body in the churchyard. There it lies today, beneath the thundering A4 flyover.

Another heart missing from its urn is at that altogether amazing collection of eccentricities at **West Wycombe**, Buckinghamshire, where Sir Francis Dashwood and his **Hellfire Club** (motto: 'Do What You Will') met for feasts (some say orgies), deep in labyrinthine caves he had had carved hundreds of feet inside West Wycombe Hill. The club had an initiation rite that involved a naked woman lying on a table and, on one occasion, a dozen 'vestal virgins' were ordered from a London brothel. They were plied with champagne and danced with leading members of parliament, while a band played behind a screen.

A typical Hellfire Club practical joke was the one played by MP John Wilkes on Lord Sandwich, First Lord of the Admiralty. During a Black Mass, Wilkes released a baboon dressed as the Devil. The creature leapt on to the shoulders of Lord Sandwich who fled screaming into woodland, convinced he was being chased by Satan.

Today, the caves can be toured and their colourful past is illustrated deep in the hill. Above, the church of St Lawrence, with its extraordinary golden ball 646ft above sea level, forms a dramatic landmark along the A40 from High Wycombe, a road built on chalk dug from the caves. Sir Francis and nine of his pals could sit drinking on seats within the ball, accessed by a curved trapdoor let down as if from a spaceship. Until 1950 the public could enter too, but now you can reach only the top of the tower a few feet below, drinking in merely the exceptional view, heady enough after climbing the 113 steps.

Between the church and A40 leading to London sits the extraordinary **Dashwood Mausoleum** (Travel: page 175), a vast flint hexagon open to the skies. One of Dashwood's greatest fans was the poet Paul Whitehead, Steward of the Hellfire Club, who left his heart plus £50

Britain's most gruesome churches

THE GHASTLIEST GATE in London is definitely that at **St Olave's Church** in Hart Street, EC3, not far from Tower Hill tube station. The gate is grimly festooned with skulls, bones and spikes. Dickens uses it for a fictional location in *The Uncommercial Traveller* as 'St Ghastly Grim' and describes how 'the skulls grin aloft horribly, thrust through and through with iron spears. Hence, there is attraction of repulsion for me in Saint Ghastly Grim'. This, however, has nothing on the crypt of **St Leonard's Church** at Hythe in Kent where more than 1,000 real skulls and 8,000 thigh bones are neatly stacked. Visitors, who may have to pay a small fee to see the bones, reel with astonishment, locals tell me. They are not plague victims, merely the medieval parishioners organised in a space-saving way. In the churchyard is the grave of one Lionel Lukin who is credited with inventing the unsinkable lifeboat and discredited with being a smuggler on the side, like a lot of people round here.

for an urn, with a request for it to be placed in the mausoleum. This was done with much pomp, six soldiers carrying the heavy urn up the hill and firing a salute. But visitors to West Wycombe had a habit of taking out poor Whitehead's heart and disrespectfully throwing it around. In about 1820, someone failed to replace the heart in its urn. Heartless.

The **11th baronet**, another **Sir Francis Dashwood** (1925–2000), also had his foibles. There was once staged a re-enactment of the Battle of Trafalgar on West Wycombe's lake complete with rockets and cannon, and in 1996 he was noted regularly catching the Green Line bus to London, despite being 'England's premier baronet'. On hospitality, he said: 'You can stick caviar' and served Marmite sandwiches instead. The separate, but not nearly so eccentric, house at **West Wycombe Park** and the quite remarkably preserved village either side of the main road are in the care of the National Trust.

BROKEN HEARTS AND A VISIBLE ORGAN

Another heart that tells a story can be found at **West Parley Church**, Dorset, just north of Bournemouth, the rest of the lady's body being buried at Lydlinch, about 20 miles away. Her name is modestly not recorded, but it is thought that in the 14th century a lady of the manor of West Parley was compelled on her marriage to leave her home village to live at Lydlinch. She said before she died that as her heart had always been at West Parley, she wished it be buried there. The heart was buried in an urn under a circular stone, but the urn was excavated in 1895 and can now be seen behind an iron grille on the east wall of the church.

Of course, in the days before refrigeration there was no way of moving the dead around unless they were thoroughly embalmed, and even then it was, frankly, dead difficult over long distances. In **Mappowder**, another Dorset village, can be seen a small stone effigy of a crusader with chain mail, sword and shield, his legs crossed, indicating that he died in action. This led to a local legend of a 'boy crusader', but in fact it is the heart of a knight, who died fighting in the Holy Land, which is buried here, his embalmed heart having been sent back to his grieving family – the body bag of its day.

This tradition even involved the heart of one of the late Princess Diana's ancestors. In the crypt at **St Mary the Virgin** at Great Brington, near the Spencer family home at Althorp, lies the embalmed heart of the third Baron Spencer, who died at the Battle of Newbury in 1643. The ashes of Diana's father are also in the crypt, entered by lifting a heavy stone slab embedded with an iron ring. Diana would have been buried there – and not on a lake island on the estate – had not her global fame meant that the tiny village would have been overwhelmed.

At **St Mary's Church**, Woodford, Northamptonshire, a bandaged heart may be seen, and, again, its spooky story is convoluted. It is a reminder of John Styles, a 16th-century priest who refused to accept the Reformation and fled to the Low Countries, taking with him a valuable chalice that belonged to the church. A later minister hunted down the chalice, and brought it back with Styles's heart; later still, both were lost. Then in the 19th century, after a ghost, apparently, pointed the way, the chalice was rediscovered concealed in a wall at the vicarage. It did not contain the heart, but it did contain a letter saying where the heart was hidden in a church pillar. There it may still be seen, through a glass panel.

FAITH GIVEN A HAND

It may seem rather bizarre and macabre nowadays, but going even further back, relics of the saints such as alleged bits of their bodies were venerated. Most of these were destroyed by the Puritans, but at **St Peter's Church**, Marlow, Buckinghamshire, may be seen a mummified hand, said to have belonged to St James the apostle.

Another saint's hand is in the reliquary at **St Etheldreda's Church**, Holborn, London, a beautiful church dating back to the 16th century. In this case it is a 'portion' of her hand. Portion? I don't mean to be offensive, but we're not talking about chicken nuggets here. What happened to the rest, and have other churches got more 'portions'? Such taking pieces of saints would be seen as macabre or disrespectful nowadays, but in the Middle Ages small parts of saints, or of something related to them, such as a garment, would be thought to have miraculous powers.

One hand that apparently reached from beyond the grave to help today's faithful is that of 17th-century martyr St John Kemble (1599–1679). The Roman Catholic was hanged, drawn and quartered in Hereford at the grand old age of 80 after the Titus Oates plot – a conspiracy to kill King Charles II – was exposed. After the execution, the severed hand of Kemble was picked up by a woman sympathiser and for the past three centuries the relic has been at **St Francis Xavier's Church**, Hereford.

In July 1995 a local Catholic priest, Father Christopher Jenkins, lay in a coma after a stroke and doctors said that only 'the hand of God' could save him. This gave churchmen the idea of taking the relic – Kemble's hand – from the church to the hospital bedside. Father Anthony Tumelty took the relic from its oak casket and placed it on Father Jenkins's forehead. The 63-year-old priest made an astonishing recovery.

BRAVE HEART INTO BATTLE

A heart that went into battle without its body in the crusades can be found at **Melrose Abbey**, in Scotland's Borders (Travel: page 296). It belongs to Robert the Bruce, best known for thrashing the English at Bannockburn in 1314. A month before his death he wrote to his son asking to be buried at the abbey, but on his deathbed asked his loyal friend Sir James Douglas to take his heart to the Holy Land to fight the Infidel. Sir James, the 'Black Douglas', was mortally wounded in battle despite carrying the heart as protection. As he died, he hurled the casket at the enemy with the cry: 'Forward brave heart!' Everywhere in **Drumlanrig Castle** (Travel: page 175), built in Dumfries & Galloway on the site of Sir James's stronghold, can be seen the emblem of the winged heart.

As for Robert the Bruce's heart, a lead casket was excavated at Melrose in 1921, and a further archaeological dig in 1996 saw it reburied without being opened, but with a new marker stone locating it easily for the visitor. 'Good' Sir James Douglas's heart can similarly be found at **St Bride's Chapel**, Douglas, Lanarkshire, in a lead casket, as can that of Archibald, fifth Earl of Angus.

In fact some recent historical detective work found that Robert the Bruce has at least three official burial sites. Yes, his heart is at Melrose and his body at Dunfermline but – and this gets a bit gooey here – his viscera or innards were removed and buried at **St Serf's Kirk** at Dumbarton, where he died of leprosy in 1329. This was so he could be embalmed. So while Robert the Bruce was a greater Scots hero than William Wallace (despite Hollywood's version) and he escaped the latter's indignity of being hanged, drawn and quartered by the English, he ended up in bits too. In fact, if you want to visit his graves, you may as well get an all-routes rover ticket ...

A GREAT SCOTTISH LOVE STORY

Perhaps the most poignant heart burial is the one behind the romantic red stone ruin of **Sweetheart Abbey**, near Dumfries (Travel: page 177). This is one of many relics of a renowned 13th-century beauty, Lady Devorgilla, and her enduring love for her husband John Balliol (c. 1205–68), founder of Balliol College, Oxford. They lived at Buittle Castle near Dalbeattie and were devoted to each other. Balliol's early death in 1269 caused his wife a grief not unlike Queen Victoria's, six centuries later, for her husband Albert. Devorgilla had his heart embalmed and placed in an ivory casket bound with enamelled silver bands. She kept this 'silent, sweet companion' with her until she died in 1289, aged 81. The casket was buried with her in the monastery that she had founded and which the Cistercian monks came to know as Sweetheart Abbey. Her tomb-top effigy showed her still clasping the heart to her bosom.

Devorgilla's beauty and bounty were sung of by minstrels and renowned by poets in Scotland for centuries afterwards. She also left the handsome Devorgilla Bridge in Dumfries, set up friaries in Wigtown and Dundee and confirmed and endowed Balliol College – enduring testimonies to one of Scotland's greatest love affairs.

EVASION OF THE BODY-SNATCHERS

Edinburgh having been the setting for Burke and Hare's grave-robbing exploits – they were hanged in 1829 – the Scots could be forgiven for being cautious about their mortal remains.

In Perthshire, at **Logierait** (Travel: page 176), the churchyard contains three mortsafes – coffin-shaped iron cages whose grilles extend above and below the ground to prevent digging. By a low wall, there are two adult mortsafes and a child's. (Similar iron hoops can be seen in Edinburgh graveyards.) It is likely that coffins were left here until the body was in no condition for the medical students (who paid the grave robbers so well) and then buried.

At **Udny Green** in Aberdeenshire, the churchyard contains a circular stone building erected as a mortsafe in 1832 to combat the body-snatching hysteria. A turntable in the centre facilitates the handling of coffins.

Perhaps the most extreme example is the remote grave of eccentric shepherd **Johnnie Turner** high above Glenkiln Reservoir, seven miles west of Dumfries. Turner, terrified of body-snatchers, hewed his own grave out of solid rock at an altitude of 1,300ft, and it is now marked with a monument (Travel: page 176). This is rather eccentric country, with some of the greatest sculptures by Rodin, Moore, Epstein and Renoir gazing around the bleak landscape. This has to be God's own wonderful art gallery. The superb Moore *King and Queen* were beheaded by morons in 1995, and the sculpture was away being mended when I visited but they left Turner's remains alone, so perhaps he was right.

When the great and the powerful in Scotland wanted to be buried, however, they built some of the most magnificent mausoleums in Europe. In Hamilton, Lanarkshire, the **Hamilton Mausoleum** soars 120ft high with its glass-topped cupola (Travel: page 176). It was designed by the tenth Duke of Hamilton in 1840 for his own funeral in 1852. The entrance is flanked by two huge stone lions. The interior is marble floored and has bizarre acoustic qualities. The duke, it was said, was obsessed with a classical sarcophagus he had brought to Hamilton and frequently lay down in it to ensure he would fit when the time came. However, he forgot the thickness of the necessary casket, so his feet had to be cut off and put in beside him.

The duke's Hamilton Palace has long been demolished but the mausoleum remains, as does the Chatelherault Hunting Lodge and Country Park.

A far more attractive and artistically eccentric mausoleum is that of Patrick Alan Fraser of Hospital Field at **Arbroath** in Angus (Travel: page 175). Beautifully detailed carving adorns the extraordinary building to the rooftops. It was begun in 1875 and took local stonemason James Peters 25 years to execute. The exquisiteness of his sandstone carvings deserves greater recognition. It is in Western Cemetery, and is opened once a year (in September) for visitors to inspect the interior.

Another attractive Scottish mausoleum worth stopping to inspect is on the A68. It has an attractive **Byzantine** dome, glazed stars in the roof and, as at Hamilton, two lions guarding the door, one sleeping and one awake. This is the resting place of one General Sir Thomas Monteath Douglas, who died in 1868 (Travel: page 175).

TRAVEL INFORMATION

BEWARE CHALK PIT PYRAMID, Farley Mount Country Park, Hampshire SO22 5Q ✆ 01962 840500

🚗 On back roads west of Winchester, which is off M3 J12. Take B3049 and then turn south (left) through Sparsholt. Postcode SO21 2NF is for Sparsholt College nearby

BONOMI PYRAMID, BLICKLING HALL, Norfolk NR11 6NF

☎ 01263 738030 (National Trust) ✆ 01263 733903

🚗 Just north of Aylsham, off A140 Norwich–Cromer road. Norwich is reached from London/M25 by A11

BROMPTON CEMETERY, Earl's Court, London SW5 9JF

🚆 West Brompton (District Line and main line from Clapham Junction)

BURTON TOMB, Mortlake, Surrey SW14 8PR

🚗 Off High Street, Mortlake, accessed from south end of London's

Chiswick Bridge, or approach from White Hart Lane along North Worple Way 🚆 Mortlake station (from Waterloo), then walk back 200yd towards Barnes on north (left) side of railway 🚌 419 from Hammersmith to Mortlake High Street

BYZANTINE MAUSOLEUM, Nether Hindhope, Borders TD8 6TY
📞 01835 863170. 🚗 On A68 going towards Edinburgh between Jedburgh and St Boswells, on the left just after Lilliardsedge

CASTLE HOWARD, York YO60 7DA ☎ 01653 648333
🖥 www.castlehoward.co.uk
🚗 From the North: from A1 take A61 to Thirsk, then A170 to Helmsley. Before Helmsley, turn right onto B1257 and follow brown signs. From the South: take A1M to J45 and follow A64 east to York. Go past York and pick up brown signs for the castle. 🚆/🚌 To York from London King's Cross, then catch a Stephensons of Easingwold bus and you can use the ticket for a part refund of entry (www.stephensonsofeasingwold.co.uk)

DASHWOOD MAUSOLEUM, Hellfire Caves, etc, West Wycombe, Buckinghamshire HP14 3AH 📞 01494 421892 🖥 www.hellfirecaves.co.uk
🚗 Off M40 J4, then A4010 towards West Wycombe
🚆/🚌 High Wycombe, then bus

DRACULA TRAIL, Whitby, (and *en route* Grosmont), North Yorkshire YO21 1YN 📞 01723 38363
🚗 Off A1(M) near Thirsk, then A61, A19, A172, A171
🚆 Whitby, on picturesque Esk Valley branch line via Darlington and/or Middlesbrough

DRUMLANRIG CASTLE, Dumfries & Galloway DG3 4AG
☎ 01848 330248 📞☎ 01387 253862
🚗 Off A76 about 18 miles north of Dumfries. From M6 Carlisle take A74, A75

ELY CATHEDRAL, Cambridgeshire CB7 4EJ
📞 01353 662062 🖥 www.elycathedral.org
🚗 From London or M25 take M11 to J14 near Cambridge then A14 east, A10 north. 🚆 Ely, from London King's Cross and Midlands

FRASER MAUSOLEUM, Arbroath, Angus DD11 3RA 📞 01241 872609.
🚗 Take A92 towards Dundee from town centre, right on to Westway after a mile or so, then left into Keptie Road 🚆 Arbroath, on King's Cross and Edinburgh–Aberdeen line

GIRO'S MEMORIAL, Waterloo Place, London SW1Y 5AH ⊖ Piccadilly Circus

HAMILTON MAUSOLEUM, Lanarkshire ML3 6BJ ☎ 01698 426213 (book a tour)
🚗 Near Carlisle–Glasgow M74 J6 🚂 Hamilton Central from Glasgow
then 10-min walk

HARDY'S HEART, Stinsford, Dorset DT2 8PX 🌿 01305 267992
🚗 M3 to south end, M27 west, A31 and A35. Stinsford is on the left just
before Dorchester

HAYSTACKS, Cumbria CA13 9XA 🌿 01768 772645
🚗 From M6 J40 take A66 west to past Keswick, fork left on B5292 over
Whinlatter pass to Lorton, through village and then B5289 left (south, up
valley) to Buttermere. Don't consider this on an August weekend or a fine
bank holiday because of congestion. Take precautions as for all hill walking
(maps, clothes); a walk around the lake is much easier stroll in about 2 hours

JOHNNIE TURNER'S GRAVE AND SCULPTURES, Glenkiln, near Dumfries
DG2 9SL 🚗 Take the A75 west from Dumfries and after about 7 miles
turn right for Shawhead (postcode above). In the village a quick right and
left will lead you to a left fork marked Glenkiln. Fork left when you reach
the reservoir and you can park next to a Rodin at the far end. Walk onwards
to see a Hepworth with cows grazing around

KNILL MONUMENT, St Ives, Cornwall TR26 1TG 🌿 01736 796297
🚗 End of M5 to Exeter, A30 through north Cornwall, then, before Penzance,
A3074 to St Ives 🚂 Short branch line off London Paddington–Penzance line

LEIGHTON HOUSE, Kensington, London W14 8LZ ☎ 020 7602 3316
🚗 Off Kensington High Street, north up Melbury Road, then left into
Holland Park Road 🚌/🚂 High St Kensington (Circle and District lines)
and walk west, or many buses such as 9, 10 to Commonwealth Institute. It
is a little beyond here

LOGIERAIT MORTSAFES, Perthshire PH9 0LG 🌿 01796 472215
🚗 One mile off A9, north of Perth, on A827 towards Aberfeldy. Ignore the
cemetery sign to the right and the churchyard is on the left

MAD JACK FULLER'S PYRAMID, Brightling, East Sussex, see page 295

MELROSE ABBEY, Borders, see page 296

NATIONAL ARMY MUSEUM, Chelsea, London SW3 4HT ☎ 020 7730 0717
🚇 Sloane Square (District and Circle lines) then short walk

NOSTELL PRIORY, Nostell, Wakefield, Yorkshire WF4 1QE ☎ 01924 863892
🚗 A638 5 miles SE of Wakefield towards Doncaster

OTLEY PARISH CHURCH, Yorkshire LS21 3HW

 In hills northwest of Leeds. From A1, take A659 west from Wetherby

PDSA ANIMAL CEMETERY, Woodford Bridge Road, Redbridge, Ilford, Essex IG4 5PS. For a guided tour, contact Gill Hubbard ☎ 15952 290999

Just off A406 North Circular, take A1400 Southend Road, then fifth road on the right ●/🚂 Central Line to Redbridge, bus 366 towards Falmouth Gardens, ask for Roding Lane South stop and follow that on foot

PLAS NEWYDD, Menai Straits LL61 6DQ ☎ 01248 714795 (National Trust) 🌿 01286 672232

Slow but picturesque A5 from English Midlands (M6 J10A) then M54 to end, or quicker A55 along north Wales coast from Chester 🚆 Llanfair PG (from London Euston)

SHAH JEHAN MOSQUE and **BROOKWOOD CEMETERY**, see page 192

ST JOHN'S CHURCH, Bromsgrove, Worcestershire B61 7JW 🌿 01527 831809

In the town centre. Off M5 at J4A, or from London via M40 then M42. Some motorway junctions are limited in direction, so follow signs 🚆 On Birmingham–Hereford or Cardiff–Nottingham route (if your engine doesn't blow up on the hill), then 15-min walk to town

ST MARY'S CHURCH, Harrow-on-the-Hill, Middlesex HA1 3HL

From London, take A4005 from A406 (north circular) junction with A40 at Hanger Lane 🚆/🚌/● to South Harrow (Piccadilly Line), turn right out of station, walk half a mile to traffic lights and turn right up Roxeth Hill; turn left at top into old village centre, Church Hill being on left. Or take 258 bus from tube

SWEETHEART ABBEY, Dumfries & Galloway DG2 8BU ☎ 01387 850397 🌿 01387 253862 A75 to Dumfries from Gretna at top of M6/bottom of M74, then A710 south

WHEATLEY LOCK-UP, Oxfordshire OX33 1JH 🌿 01865 252200

Off A40 London–Oxford road 3 miles before Oxford 🚆/🚌 Oxford, then local bus

WRONG HARDY MONUMENT, Portesham, Dorset DT3 4JL 🌿 01305 267992

From Dorchester bypass southwestern corner roundabout (reached from M3 via M27 west, A31 and A35), take minor road through Martinstown over the top towards Portesham and it's on the left at a high point

CHURCH ECCENTRICS

ATLANTIC OCEAN

Orkney Islands

Thurso

Isle of Lewis

Isle of Skye

Inner Hebrides

Inverness

SCOTLAND

Aberdeen

NORTH SEA

Island of Mull

Islay

Arran

Glasgow

EDINBURGH

✝ Whuppity Scourie, Lanark

Samye Ling Buddhist Monastery, Eskdalemuir

Newcastle upon Tyne

ATLANTIC OCEAN

Isle of Man

Carlisle

Middlesbrough

ENGLAND

IRISH SEA

Anglesey

Holyhead

✝ Preston Temple

Leeds

York

Kingston-upon-Hull

NORTH SEA

Bradford

Manchester

Liverpool

Sheffield

Grimsby

✝ Plague Service, Eyam   ✝ Devil's Spire, Chesterfield

Stoke-on-Trent

Cardigan Bay

Fishguard

Wolverhampton

Derby

Nottingham

🛕 Leicester Temples

Norwich

Birmingham

Coventry

Cambridge

Ipswich

WALES

St Non's Well, St David's ✝

Clipping the Church, Painswick ✝

Swansea

CARDIFF

Peace Pagoda, Milton Keynes 🌲

Tree Cathedral, Whipsnade

Oxford

🌲 Firing Fenny Poppers, Fenny Stratford

Swaminarayan Hindu Temple, Neasden

Mystic Stones, Avebury

Little India, Southall

LONDON

Bristol Channel

Bristol

Reading

Shah Jehan Mosque, Woking

Peace Pagoda, Battersea Park

St Nectan's Well, Hartland Point & Morwenstow Vicarage ✝

New Holy Thorn Tree, Glastonbury ✝

Buddhapadipa Temple, Wimbledon

Southampton

Portsmouth

Brighton

Dover

Exeter

ATLANTIC OCEAN

I of Wight

St La's Well, St Ives ✝

Penzance

ENGLISH CHANNEL

N

0 — 80 km
0 — 50 miles

CHURCH ECCENTRICS

BEYOND BELIEF

Those who think the Church is redolent with tedious traditions might be surprised how bizarre, obscure and fascinating some continuing ecclesiastical customs are.

In **Fenny Stratford**, near Woburn, Bedfordshire, for example, cannonfire rings out on 11 November as the vicar of St Martin's, the verger and churchwardens take part in **Firing the Fenny Poppers** – three salvoes of miniature tankard-shaped weapons that the churchwarden primes with gunpowder. The tradition, every St Martin's Day, was started by Dr Browne Willis who founded St Martin's in 1730 in memory of his grandfather who worshipped at St Martin-in-the-Fields, London, and died on St Martin's Day in St Martin's Lane.

A more ancient and less noisy ritual is the gift each Christmas to the reigning monarch of a clipping of the thorn tree in the grounds of St John's Church, **Glastonbury**, Somerset. Legend has it that when Joseph of Arimathea, having arrived in Britain carrying the Holy Grail, first saw the Isle of Avalon (Glastonbury Tor), he thrust his staff into the ground, and it flowered as a hawthorn.

Clipping the Church, on the other hand, is a form of embracing the church by dancing round it, a once widespread ritual. At **St Mary's** in Painswick, near Gloucester (Travel: page 193), hundreds of children wearing flowers still link hands to 'clip' the church on the third Sunday each September, and after the Clipping Hymn has been sung each child is given a bun and a silver coin. St Mary's, by the way, has a remarkable 99 topiary yews in the churchyard and the other sort of clippings – of the yew trees – are given by the church to fight ovarian cancer because

of the rare chemical they contain. (For a real tree cathedral, you need to go to **Whipsnade**, Bedfordshire (Travel: page 194), which has a nave and transept of trees laid out on the floor plan of a traditional cathedral; an annual service is held there in late June.)

Similar customs are recorded in Yorkshire, Berkshire and Sussex, and clipping still takes place at **Burbage**, near Buxton, Derbyshire, on the Sunday nearest 2 August.

An annual service where the packed congregation comprises dozens of horses sounds too bizarre to be true, but for a sight of a priest in his vestments on horseback intoning to the gathered horses – or, perhaps, their riders – make the trip to **St John's**, in Hyde Park Crescent, London W2 (tube: Lancaster Gate) for **Horseman's Sunday**.

Usually the third Sunday in September, it is the occasion when the assembled posse can be seen bursting into a stirring blast of the hymn *Jerusalem*, after a rather strange sermon on the mount, before the horses take a trot round the block and are then announced one by one and given a rosette.

Things are more frenetic north of the border, at St Nicholas Church in **Lanark**, each 1 March when **Whuppity Scourie** involves dozens of children, each wielding a tightly packed paper ball on the end of a piece of string, dashing three times round the church on a signal from a bell, hitting each other over the head and then scrambling wildly for pennies thrown from a platform by local bigwigs.

But the most poignant of Britain's odd church customs does not involve a church building at all. When the Great Plague of 1665 arrived at **Eyam**, Derbyshire, the people, led by the rector, decided not to flee, to stop the disease spreading. They put themselves in voluntary quarantine, leaving money for supplies at the parish boundaries in bowls of vinegar and shouting messages to well-wishers who kept their distance.

Four out of every five villagers died, including the rector's wife and one entire family of seven. Each August a **Plague Sunday Service** is held at Cucklet Church, a rocky spot where open-air services – with the congregation standing well apart – were held during the heroic village's ordeal.

CLERGY'S STRANGE URGES

The clergy – like aristocrats, press barons, the military, and colonials – have always provided Britain with a rich seam of eccentricity, an inexhaustible reserve of batty barminess.

The **Revd F W Densham**, the vicar of Warleggan in Cornwall who died in 1953, for example, had so offended his parishioners that they refused to attend church. He installed a row of cardboard cut-outs and preached at them instead.

There must be something about Cornwall and off-the-wall clerics. Take the **Revd Robert Hawker**, vicar of Morwenstow, who, one night in July 1825, decided to play a trick on the superstitious people of Bude, who were always going on about sea serpents and mythical creatures. Under a full moon he rowed out to some rocks, plaited himself a wig from seaweed and wrapped his legs in more weed to resemble a tail. He sang and crooned to awestruck crowds, returning each night as the 'mermaid' story spread. Eventually Hawker tired of this, sang 'God Save The King' and plunged into the waves.

When entering church to take services, he was always accompanied by nine cats; he rode a mule bareback around the parish, followed by a pet black pig called Gyp. **Morwenstow Vicarage**, which he built, is embellished by odd chimneystacks that are miniatures of various church towers that took his fancy. When his first wife Charlotte died – at 20 years older, she was also his godmother – he was so bereft he decided to eat nothing but clotted cream, morning, noon and night. He is also credited with inventing the modern Harvest Festival church service in 1843.

A modern Cornish priest and poultry enthusiast, the **Revd Ray Trudgian**, has been known to take a Maran hen with him into the pulpit. He now lives in Lincolnshire but keeps preaching (about poultry, at any rate). He says: 'I have been lucky as I have travelled around the country with my job and have always been able to find people who love their poultry and make friends.'

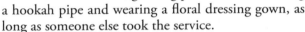

Back in Cornwall, one Bishop of Truro, checking up on his ministers, found one curate chained to the altar rail. He was so nervous that the slightest noise – such as the congregation making a liturgical response – would send him fleeing from the church, so the churchwarden had padlocked him there until the end of the service.

Luckily it was not this minister who had the misfortune to be the preacher in a Lancashire church where the pulpit exploded. It seems the churchwarden had been making elderflower champagne in the small cupboard underneath the steps.

In another church, the vicar point blank refused to enter the church, but was happy to stroll around outside, greeting parishioners, smoking a hookah pipe and wearing a floral dressing gown, as long as someone else took the service.

Parson Pike of Kirkby Mallory, Leicestershire, on the other hand, did want to get into the pulpit but was so gargantuan he could not ascend the narrow stairway. He had to be lowered in by a special crane, revolving slowly like some corpulent archangel.

Another vicar who loved his food was gourmet the **Revd Edward Bragge** of Charmouth, Dorset. His affection for his dining table was such that he asked to be buried with it. His friends obliged in 1747 by cutting the table up and making it into his coffin. His memorial may be seen in the church chancel.

A vicar in Manchester in about 1850 habitually used what would come to be known as mass production by marrying a dozen or more couples simultaneously. He once married the wrong pair, but they fancied the new partners more than the intended and ran off to Blackpool, despite the fury of four sets of relatives.

The early 19th-century cleric and wit **Sydney Smith** so feared for his health that he used to go about in a suit of armour, each part of which could be filled with hot water. It was Smith who retorted once: 'Quaker baby? Impossible! There is no such thing, there never was. They are always born broad-brimmed and in full quake.'

Another minister, recalled by Canon Wilfred Pemberton of Derby, would set his congregation singing all 176 verses of Psalm 119. He would then pop out to feed the chickens and finish his housework, invariably returning just as the panting singers exhaustedly reached the last verse, appropriately, 'I have strayed like a lost sheep. Seek your servant, for I have not forgotten your commands.'

At the beginning of the 20th century, the **Revd Francis Waring**, the vicar of Heybridge in Essex, put a small clock in front of him at the beginning of every service, which he delivered at speed, allowing the congregation no time to make any of the responses, before running out of the porch, and jumping on a horse to take two similar services nearby. Waring was also known for his eccentric garb. Once, when a bishop remonstrated with him: 'But you're wearing purple!' he replied: 'How very good of you to notice. Do let me recommend my tailor to you.'

The eccentricity of the former rector of Calthorpe in Leicestershire, **Revd William Stanesmore**, lay in making the collection. Not just the coin collection from the faithful, but – as was discovered in the rectory after he died – 58 dogs, 60 horses, 50 saddles, 130 wheelbarrows, 200 pickaxes, 74 ladders and 400 pairs of shoes. Imelda Marcos would have been proud of him.

Such eccentricities can be found among present-day clergymen. The **Revd Father B J Eager** of St Catherine of Siena Church, Lowton, Warrington, admitted in a letter to *The Times* in December 1995 not only that he made his dog collars from slices of plastic detergent bottles but that at least once he wore his the wrong way round, so that the word 'Fairy' stood out on his collar. 'Either nobody noticed or they were too polite to mention it,' he added.

And in 1997 **Father Tim Williams**, Anglican vicar of Knighton on the Shropshire border with Wales, was quoted as saying about himself: 'Vicars are often seen in frocks, but not often in frilly dresses, false eyelashes and a bra.' True, his appearance was odd indeed, even for a priest who has ridden down the aisle on a motorbike or on a camel borrowed from a circus. The last two were to make a point to the congregation, but the cross-dressing was less controversial. The village production of *Aladdin* had lost its Widow Twankey at the last minute and the game vicar stepped into her high heels.

The wackiness of West Country clergy continues into the 21st century. In 2006, the **Revd Louise Courtney**, 58, was spotted whizzing about her Cornish parish on a quad bike. The Vicar said she uses it to reach remote parts of her parish, which stretches from Bodinnick to Lansallos.

The **Revd Roly Bain**, a Bristol priest, has a second job: Clown Priest. With the slogan 'Let us play' he takes the Gospel message with a dollop of slapstick. Not many people can say, as he does, that he's custard-pied ten bishops.

The still astonishing Rector of Stiffkey

ANY SUCH SURVEY of eccentric clergymen would not be complete, Britons over a certain age would say, without the Rector of Stiffkey, also known as the 'prostitutes' padre'. His life and death were so very, very headline-hittingly outrageous that they are undoubtedly right.

In brief, the Rector of this Norfolk parish (pronounced 'Stew-key'), Harold Davidson, made many trips to Soho, London's red-light district, to collect fallen women – supposedly to rescue them from vice. He would buy them meals and tap dance in the street to amuse them, but would not shove religion down their throats. He would take them back to his rectory, and in 1932 he was sensationally accused of molesting several of them there.

Oddly, his congregation were very much on his side in the ensuing scandal, but even today there are suggestions that part of the evidence against him was fabricated by his hostile bishop.

Davidson would preach 'Has not Christ Himself walked with scarlet women?' The bizarre ensuing court case included an absurd cross-examination in which the rector maintained he did not know what a buttock was. To persistent questioning, he replied on oath: 'It is a phrase honestly I have never heard. So far as I remember it is a little below the waist.' On another occasion he approached a girl in her room in her pyjamas. He didn't find this odd, the court was told, because: 'Pyjamas are perfectly respectable clothing. I know people of the highest character who sit around in pyjamas.'

Daily evidence such as this was by now spilling out of the teleprinters of newspapers around the world, particularly when a set

Then there's **Dave Bishop** – Bishop by name, minister by nature – of Sidley Baptist Church, Bexhill-on-Sea, Sussex, who loves to add drama to his talks to local schools. He eats out of a tin of dog food – actually it is something palatable with the labels swapped – to shock the children, of photos of the rector with a nude 15-year-old girl were produced. He was convicted and defrocked, the Church equivalent of a doctor being 'struck off'. So far, so normal kinky priest, you may think (by modern standards, although it was absolutely sensational back in the 1930s) but now the story gets really weird.

He took to living in a barrel in the beach at Blackpool, where people paid to see him through a small window while he supposedly was on hunger strike. Posters accused the Church of England of failing him: 'The lower he sinks, the greater the crime'. He would tell the visitors: 'Every fibre of my being revolts against the indignity of this procedure.'

Davidson was arrested for taking part in the 'Fast to Death' for attempting suicide, which was then illegal. He said in court he was doing nothing of the sort and it turned out he was regularly given secret supplies of food.

His displays at fairgrounds around the country became more and more crazy. He was exhibited in or beside a dead whale, frozen in an icy chamber, roasted in an oven while he was prodded in the buttocks by a 'devil', and lying on a bed of nails. Finally he went on show in 1937 at Skegness in the cage of two lions. He would make a speech about the injustices he had borne, and then enter the lions' den for three minutes. After all, hadn't such beasts famously spared Androcles the Christian in ancient Rome?

On 28 July as he entered the lions' den, he thought he would liven up the sleepy lions with his whip to make a better show for the paying public. It did liven them up, because they ate him. Or rather they tossed him around in their mouths, in front of the horrified crowd, until he was so badly injured that he died soon after being rescued.

Next day the showman, never one to miss a trick, altered the poster to say: 'See the lion that mauled and injured the rector! And the plucky girl who went to his rescue!' After that, the newspapers that for five years had filled so many column inches with sensational reports about the Rector of Stiffkey had to write about something else. Like the looming crisis with Nazi Germany.

puts rubber gloves over his head and blows them up until they shoot off like a rocket and chainsaws a chair in half. All his stunts have a reason – to encourage people to seek God – but one where he munched off the flowers of a bunch of daffodils backfired rather in 2001. The idea was about belief: he argued that their parents wouldn't believe that a minister had eaten a bunch of flowers. Unfortunately, some 16 pupils copied him later and forgot that he had warned them never to eat the green leaves, which are poisonous, like the bulb. According to the Press, probably exaggerating as usual, a fleet of ambulances took several children to hospital, after what they called the 'Vicar's daffy trick' ('minister' doesn't fit in 36pt across a single column). Fortunately, the children recovered.

Has the good reverend learnt to be more, well, churchy? I saw this question on a science website recently, which made me think he is still at his madcap ways: 'When I shake a can of Coke and bang the base of the can on the floor and then open it – the distance that the liquid goes is amazing. I use this illustration when I talk in school assemblies and today was asked what the pressure value was that had built up in the can before I pulled the ring pull. Can you help?' Can you indeed, and possibly clean the ceiling afterwards?

I emailed the Revd Bishop the other day to see if he was still on his mayhem mission, and he mentioned his latest ways of reaching out to schoolchildren:

- Setting up a popcorn maker without the lid on in the middle of 500 children (the caretaker dreads my visits)
- Throwing 2lb of maggots into audience
- Setting off a water fire extinguisher
- Setting a Bible on fire (don't know if that's a sackable offence!!)
- Holding squirty cream races up the length of the hall

Mind you, the children would pay attention and remember his message, wouldn't they? Pity our RE teacher wasn't like that ...

The laity, too, can be somewhat peculiar about religion. The Victorian diarist **Augustus Hare** (1834–1903) used to delete any words from the prayer book, before reading to his family, that he felt were too favourable to God. 'God', he said, 'is undoubtedly a gentleman, and no gentleman cares to be praised to his face.'

Equally direct was *Sunday Express* diarist **Lord Castlerosse** (1891–1943) who once drove his golf ball into a bunker and dropped to his knees to pray for divine intervention. He was overheard saying: 'But don't send Jesus – this is no job for a boy.

For the vicar of Farringdon's folly and a bid to keep out Methodists, see page 284.

WELL, WELL, WELL – ECCENTRIC SAINTS

Villagers at Bradninch, near Exeter, appear to have been revering a holy spelling mistake for 196 years. They were told in 1831 that their church was dedicated to St Disen, assumed to be a medieval Irish missionary who might have brought Christianity to heathen Cornwall. St Disen was thereafter mentioned with all due respect, but it should have been St Denis all along, it was revealed recently. (St Penis they probably would have queried.)

But as residents and tourists in the West Country and Wales will know, the area is already riddled with plenty of oddly named saints and their legends are such that you couldn't make them up. There are those associated with ancient wells, for example.

St Nectan was beheaded in the 6th century and miraculously carried his head a mile to cast it into St Nectan's Well, Hartland Point, Devon. Where the blood dropped, the first foxgloves sprang up, a story recalled by the anniversary mass sometimes held there on St Nectan's Day (17 June), which includes a procession of children bearing foxgloves, which decorate the church at this time every year. They should, perhaps, wear gloves, for the poison digitalis is found in that beautiful plant.

St Neot, Cornwall, also has a holy well where the legendary 15-inch high saint kept three fish given to him by an angel, who said that if he ate just one a day, there would always be three the next day. One day when he fell ill, *two* were cooked for him. Praying for forgiveness, he returned one from the frying pan to the well, where it came back to life.

A third well, at **St Keyne**, near Liskeard, Cornwall, bears the legend that the first of a couple to drink from it after their wedding will dominate the marriage. The 19th-century ballad *The Well of St Keyne* by Robert Southey tells of a bride who outwitted her bossy groom by smuggling a bottle of the well water to church under her dress. It was just as well, because after she drank it, she wore the trousers in that marriage.

The delightfully named **St Endellion** was a Welsh princess who lived like a hermit near Wadebridge, Cornwall, in the 6th century, living on only the produce of her cow. When the beast wandered on to Lord Tregony's land, he killed it, and he was in turn killed by enraged friends

of hers. Endellion not only brought Tregony back to life, but asked that when she died her body be put on a cart and drawn by another cow to wherever the beast chose as a last resting place. This was where her church, and today's village named after her, stand. Perhaps unaware of the gruesome story, Prime Minister David Cameron named his daughter, who was born there, Endellion – a middle name – in 2010.

St Ives, Cornwall (Travel: page 194), is in fact named after an Irish virgin, **St Ia**, who landed there after fleeing pursuers in Ireland. She needed to be a saint because, legend says, she crossed the sea on a leaf. She is remembered when the extraordinary Hurling The Silver Ball takes place (see page 10) and the ball has to be dipped in St Ia's well. It all makes St Disen seem positively dull.

Across the water in the rather magical peninsula of **St David's**, Pembrokeshire (Travel: page 193), another mystic well marks the birthplace of that Welsh patron saint. Near the tiny city of St David's, if you take St Non's Road off Goat Street and head southeast towards St Non's Bay, you reach St Non's Well, still credited with great powers of healing.

St Non was St David's astoundingly beautiful mother. His father, a prince of Ceredigion, came across the maiden while out hunting and, the legend says, one thing led to another (supporters of St Non said it must have been rape). The pregnancy meant that Non was cast out from her family. Indeed, after Non's father was told by a prophet that a baby was coming who would one day have power over all the land, he had vowed to kill Non and her unborn baby. She gave birth in an ancient cromlech (group of standing stones) and gripped the stones so hard that they split and a terrible dark storm sprang up all around to protect her during the labour. Yet she and the infant David were in the eye of this storm, bathed in a serene light. As he was born, a spring of pure water sprang up, and it is this St Non's Well that one can visit.

One of the things known about the ascetic St David is that he drank just water all his long life. Near the well are the ruins of St Non's Chapel, a popular place of medieval pilgrimage, and also a more modern chapel to her, set in a place of peaceful beauty.

The story embodies three strands of Celtic culture. One is that disturbing the ancient stones disturbs the elements all around. Another

The mystery of twistery

CHESTERFIELD'S ST MARY'S Church has a fantastically twisted spire and, as any local will tell you, it was twisted by the Devil when a virgin married there (and God will put it right as soon as another virgin weds there). It was not caused, as some may think, by Tony Benn becoming MP in the Derbyshire town (he was merely eccentric, not twisted, in the name-shortening department, starting off as Viscount Stansgate, then becoming Anthony Wedgwood-Benn, then Tony Benn). Here are some spire facts you probably didn't know:

- The 100ft spire isn't attached to the church, but is kept in place by 150 tons of timber and lead. On a windy day it sways.
- The 14th-century spire constantly twists and untwists slightly. Experts measured a one-and-a-half inch twist in a recent year.
- A hi-tech dendrochronologist of Nottingham University's tree-ring dating laboratory took a pencil-sized core sample from beams in the spire and fixed the construction date precisely at 1362.
- Chesterfield is one of no fewer then 79 spiral steeples in Europe, some built that way on purpose, but most having twisted of their own accord due to faults in construction or, as probably happened at Chesterfield, unseasoned timber being used.
- Spiral spire towns regularly hold twisted European conventions and tie themselves in knots discussing the cause of accidental spiralisation – for instance, one spire at Puiseaux in France was straight until vinegar was used to put a fire out in 1785.

is the interconnection of Celtic cultures even at this early date – before AD500 – as in the story of St Ia above. For St Non fled after the birth to Brittany, where for the next 1,300 years her story was annually re-enacted in a passion play. Plus, of course, Christianity.

TOP TEN MOST SURPRISING PLACES OF WORSHIP

Amidst Britain's truly wondrous heritage of mainstream Christian churches, there are, here and there, some astounding, beautiful, surprising or just curious edifices of other religions. Here is a selection:

1 **AVEBURY**, Wiltshire SN8 1RF ☎ 01672 539425
Why Stonehenge is so much better known than this more interesting site, the remains of Europe's largest stone circle, perhaps 4,000 years old, is a total mystery. Equally obscure are the origin and purpose of a whole collection of extraordinary prehistoric monuments around the village of Avebury, which is on the Swindon to Devizes road. Nearby is the enigmatic Silbury Hill, an artificial earth cone 130ft high – again the largest in Europe. There are barrows and sarsens all around, set in a dramatic landscape.

> 🚗 A4361 from Swindon to Beckhampton passes through the stone circle. It doesn't connect with M4 so you need to leave at J16 and take B4005 east to Wroughton and turn right onto A4361 there.

2 **PRESTON TEMPLE**, Lancashire PR6 7EQ
Another surprisingly giant place of worship has sprung up at Preston, Lancashire, where the Mormons have stuck their biggest temple outside Salt Lake City in what initially seems an oddly incongruous setting. This vast white box of a building – don't expect to be shown round the inside without an invitation – looms over nearby houses like a huge power station with a spire instead of a chimney. Still, the Mormons must like it.

> 🚗 Just west of J8 of the M61 🚆 Chorley station

3 **LEICESTER**

With its cultural cornucopia, this Midlands city offers not just great South Asian food but also, in addition to the usual churches and synagogues, the fascinating temples of its great religions, including the Muslims, Jains, Hindus and Sikhs, many of which welcome visitors. The Sikhs' **Guru Nank Sikh Gurdwara** is, perhaps aptly, in a road called Holy Bones. The **Jain Samaj Europe** temple in Oxford Street (due south of the Holiday Inn on the inner ring road), which features great carvings, is the only temple of this minority faith in Europe. Afternoons are a good time to visit, particularly Thursdays. There are two great Hindu temples, the **Shree Sanatan Mandir** in Weymouth Street, which is the oldest temple in Leicester, and the **Shree Jalaran** in Narborough Road. The best time to visit these is around 10.00, and they are likely to be closed in the early afternoon. The **Central Mosque** is on Conduit Street, next to the railway station, and the main day of prayer is, of course, Friday.

🚗 From M1 J21. Guru Nank Sikh Gurdwara: LE1 4LJ
🚂 From London St Pancras

4 **PEACE PAGODA**, Willen Park, Milton Keynes, Buckinghamshire MK15 0DL, and

5 **PEACE PAGODA**, Battersea Park, London SW114NJ

These startling apparitions in English landscapes make the point that those on the receiving end of the ultimate warfare, at Hiroshima, wish to promote global peace. The elegant constructions bring an exotic yet peaceful surprise to their waterside locations. The one in Milton Keynes has 1,000 cherry blossom trees planted behind it, so worth a visit in early spring.

MILTON KEYNES 🚗 Off M1 J14 🚂/🚗 Milton Keynes, on London Euston–Birmingham line, then bus

BATTERSEA 🚗 Between Chelsea and Albert bridges on south bank of Thames 🚂 Battersea Park station (one stop from London Victoria) then cross park to river

6 **BUDDHAPADIPA TEMPLE**, Calonne Road, Wimbledon, London SW19 5HJ 🖥 www.buddhapadipa.org

Only a good lob away from the tennis courts, this beautiful, glittering building sits serenely in a bubble of unlikely Oriental tranquillity. The exquisite murals inside are fascinating in their blend of Buddhist teaching and the Western environment.

Signed off Wimbledon Parkside, south off A3 at Tibbet's Corner, Putney Heath 🚂/🚌 Wimbledon station (District Line or main line from Waterloo) then bus 93 through Wimbledon village

7 **SAMYE LING BUDDHIST MONASTERY**, Eskdalemuir, Dumfries & Galloway DG13 0QL 🖥 www.samyeling.org
A place so windswept and cold that Tibetan monks must feel almost at home, although as the name means 'place beyond imagination' even they might find it a bit remote. It may be the place most often mentioned when weather forecasters pinpoint Britain's coldest place in the previous 24 hours, but the religion and art of oppressed Tibet are warmly alive here.

🚗 From A74 (M) J17 at Lockerbie, take B723

8 **SHAH JEHAN MOSQUE**, Oriental Road, Woking GU22 7DN
For many years this was Britain's only mosque, and was Europe's first purpose-built mosque. Its elegant dome rising through trees in leafy commuterland has long puzzled passengers on the Waterloo main line alongside. For its full story, see page 161.

🚂/🚌 Walk from Woking station, from London Waterloo
🚗 Woking from M25 J11 or A3

9 **SOUTHALL**, West London UB1 3AG 🖥 www.sgsss.org
Not so much one place of worship but a collection of temples where one can be the only chap not wearing a turban in a busy street (if one is a chap who doesn't wear turbans, that is). The authentic Indian food at authentic Indian prices plus the shops glittering with

brassware, spices, carvings, over-the-top Ali Baba shoes and endless Indian clothes make this a cultural experience for visitors.

🚗 Just south of A4020 (from Shepherd's Bush to Uxbridge). From M4 J3 take A312 north, then A4020 east (right) 🚂 Southall, from London Paddington

1○ **Swaminarayn Hindu Temple**, Neasden, London NW10 8LD
🖥 www.mandir.org
On a cathedral scale, this stone and marble edifice stands out like an exotic Oriental gem amidst the dreariest North London suburbia. Has to be seen to be believed.

🚗 Between North Circular (A406) and Brentfield Road 🚂 Neasden (Jubilee Line) or Stonebridge Park mainline station (from Euston)

Note: These sites are, of course, not tourist destinations or theme park ornaments, but places of worship. Please make sure you have permission to enter any grounds or buildings; and observe rules about removing shoes, taking photographs, etc. Turn off your mobile. I've seen enough Westerners – and other tourists in our own churches too – wandering in chewing gum, smoking, showing off bare flesh, bringing in screaming brats who fiddle with sacred ornaments, or photographing people praying, to be thoroughly ashamed.

TRAVEL INFORMATION

CLIPPING THE CHURCH, Painswick, Gloucestershire GL6 6UN
☎ 01452 813552
🚗 From M5 J13 east, or M4 J18 north, to Stroud. Painswick is 3 miles north on A46 towards Cheltenham 🚂/🚗 Stroud, on London Paddington–Gloucester line, then bus

ST DAVID'S, Pembrokeshire SA62 6PE ☎ 01437 720392 🖥 www.stdavids.co.uk. The smallest city in Britain – village size to some – with the oldest cathedral site in the country. A peninsula of pilgrimage and peace. Free map of one-hour circular walk, including St Non's Well, from tourist information.
🚗 M4 to far western end, then A40 to Haverfordwest, then A487 to St David's

TREE CATHEDRAL, Whipsnade, Bedfordshire LU6 2LL National Trust
☎ 01494 528051) ✆ 01582 471012
🚗 2 miles south of Dunstable, signed off M1 J11. There is a free car park signed off B4540.

ST IVES, Cornwall TR26 1LP ✆ 01736 796297
🚗 M5 to western end, then A38 and A30 through Cornwall. 6 miles short of Penzance, turn right on A3074 to St Ives. Parking and access can be difficult during summer weekends (use branch line to avoid this)
🚂 St Ives branch off the London Paddington–Penzance line. Change at St Erth

Taoist information
If you do not change direction, you may end up where you are going

Part Three

ECCENTRIC
PLACES

ATLANTIC
OCEAN

Orkney
Islands

Thurso

Isle of Lewis

Isle of
Skye

Inner
Hebrides

SCOTLAND

Inverness

Aberdeen

NORTH
SEA

Island of
Mull

Islay

Glasgow

EDINBURGH

Arran

ATLANTIC
OCEAN

Carlisle

Newcastle
upon Tyne

Middlesbrough

Isle of
Man

ENGLAND

IRISH
SEA

Leeds   York

Bradford

Kingston-upon-Hull

NORTH
SEA

Anglesey

Liverpool

Holyhead

Manchester

Sheffield

Grimsby

Ugly House,
Capel Curig

Cardigan
Bay

Stoke-on-
Trent

Midland Railway
Centre, Ripley

Nottingham

Derby

Norwich

Wolverhampton

Birmingham

Coventry

Cambridge

Fishguard

WALES

Ipswich

Mick Waters's Steam
Hedge, Swanbourne

Shark House,
Oxford

Swansea

CARDIFF

Friar Park, Henley

Peter Hook's
Water Tower Home,
Faversham

Reading

Bristol

Max Bowker's Garage,
Swallowfield

LONDON

Underwater Ballroom,
Witley

Dover

Bristol
Channel

Clayton Tunnel House
& Church

Southampton

Brighton

ATLANTIC
OCEAN

Exeter

Portsmouth

Railway Carriage Homes,
Selsey

Penzance

ENGLISH CHANNEL

HOME OF THE ECCENTRIC

NORTH
SEA

N

0   80 km
0   50 miles

HOME OF THE ECCENTRIC

UNLIKELY ADDITIONS

The Englishman's home is his castle, goes the cliché, but then it's all the more surprising how dull most of them are (the homes, that is). Most people live in suburban conformity, reinforced by planning restrictions that are exactingly petty in the prettier places – all part of the price of living on an overpopulated island with some of the finest heritage going.

So it is in the suburbs, not in massive stately homes, that the occasional fantastic whims really stand out. There is a massive shark sculpture plunging from the sky into the roof of a staid Oxford terrace house, for example (Travel: page 215). The slates are scattered as if the dramatically unbelievable had just happened. The 25ft glass-fibre shark is in fact supported against the gales by internal girders, and the house is otherwise quite habitable.

Despite much gnashing of teeth by the twitching net-curtain brigade, the sculpture was eventually allowed to stay by junior planning minister Tony

Baldry, who said, to his everlasting credit: 'I do not believe the purpose of planning control is to enforce a boring and mediocre conformity.'

Actually, planning control is the very reason many people feel driven to visual outbursts. South London businessman John Gladden was so incensed by Croydon Council that he erected a replica Spitfire fighter aircraft on his roof, plus a 14ft plastic marlin. Other features not normally found among the neat privet hedges of St Oswald's Road, Norbury, included a Churchill tank, a hand on a pole giving a giant V-sign towards the council offices, a 40ft replica of a Scud missile ... one could go on, and no doubt the neighbours do. One suspects Mr Gladden doesn't gladden all their hearts, but he does mine.

The original marlin – a replica of one that Mr Gladden had caught in Hawaii – was what raised the planners' ire and, had they not made an issue of it, Mr Gladden would probably have been content without all the other clobber. In the end a court ordered it all to be removed except the marlin. I was under the impression that Mr Gladden was content to keep the marlin and peace had returned to Norbury ... until I checked the situation.

'We're marching on the council with an army of sympathisers who all own tanks and military vehicles, about 50 in all. We've got our massive Churchill statue, and a huge condom mounted on a tank. When you press a button, it goes whoosh, twice as big.

'Then we're marching on Scotland Yard to give them a piece of our minds – actually a writ for a million pounds for harassment.'

I ventured: 'I bet they wish they'd never started it.' Mr Gladden agreed, and I couldn't help wishing him the best of British. Come Euro rules or high water, there is some corner of Norbury that will forever be eccentric, and a pain in the backside to nit-picking planners.

A similar case enlivened the skyline in 1995 in the North Yorkshire village of Scorton. One Geoff Harper built a 30ft Tin Man as a protest at what he called years of frustration, misery and anger at battling council planners over attempts to alter his 200-year-old Malt Kiln House. He was quoted as explaining: 'In *The Wizard Of Oz* the Tin Man had no heart, so it was appropriate that I chose him as a symbol for the council.' To underline the supposed heartlessness, he punched a hole clean through the Tin Man's chest.

ALL THINGS MUST PASS AT FRIAR PARK

Sometimes a whole house is known, colloquially rather than officially, as so-and-so's folly. Usually it's a mad millionaire's. One such was Crisp's Folly in otherwise rather respectable Henley-on-Thames in leafy South Oxfordshire. It's a tale that involves walking on water and the late Beatle George Harrison (1943–2001).

The house, properly called Friar Park, was finished in 1889 for Victorian eccentric Sir Frank Crisp, a rather successful solicitor. On the scale of an impressive railway terminus or minor museum, the ornate Gothic Revival building has 120 rooms, turrets and strange, playful features a-plenty. There were secret passageways, a maze, and underground labyrinths that you could row a boat through. The lake had stones carefully set an eighth of an inch below the surface so one could appear to walk across the water. A remarkable thing even when Jesus did it, it must have seemed indeed strange in 19th-century Henley – if you didn't know the secret. In the house there are light switches that are styled as monks' noses, for as the name suggests, Friar Park was built on an erstwhile site of a monastery.

Sir Frank obviously had an eccentric sense of humour in tune with Lord Berners (see page 219), for when he invited the people of Henley in for open days, the lawns would be marked with regular notices saying, DON'T KEEP OFF THE GRASS. That phrase, of course, could have other meanings when, the by then dilapidated pile ended up in the hands of the enigmatic 'third Beatle', George Harrison, in 1970. Harrison had a few years earlier discovered transcendental meditation and Hare Krishna – remember all that sitar music? – and so walking on water and not keeping off grass may have seemed normal to him. Harrison had even donated a mansion at Aldenham, Hertfordshire, for the Hare Krishna sect to use. And, of course, his hit of that era was *My Sweet Lord*.

He built a high-quality recording studio there and, unlike Crisp, kept the hordes of curious Henleyites beyond high gates and barbed wire. Harrison's faith, meanwhile, was devout. He once admitted to chanting 'Hare Krishna' for 23 hours non stop while driving across Europe. Pity any poor hitchhikers.

In the 1990s Harrison went on tour again, backed sometimes by Eric Clapton (born in 1945), a remarkable personal and professional link worth recalling. One of the greatest love songs and rock tracks of the 20th century, *Layla*, was written because Patti Boyd spurned Clapton to marry Harrison in 1966. The song is one of Clapton's bereft agony. Harrison wrote music about her too, including *Something*, which Frank Sinatra called 'the greatest love song of the last 50 years'. So that's two blooming amazing songs about the one woman.

When George and Patti separated in 1974 she married Clapton after all. Harrison instead married Olivia, who thus became chatelaine of Friar Park.

Harrison said he didn't believe in death, so regarded himself as a mere custodian of Friar Park for Sir Frank who, Harrison thought, was still inhabiting the Gothic property. Harrison did, in fact, die in 2001, but not before he had been attacked at Friar Park in 1999 by a deranged Beatles fan with a knife who nearly killed him. In the end it was the cancer that killed him. Perhaps he should have kept off the grass after all.

Anyway, if Harrison was right, George and Sir Frank are still there in spirit hovering over the water, free as a bird, not needing any more to step on the hidden stones ...

THE UNDERWATER BALLROOM AND A VICTORIAN MIDAS

I once heard an unlikely tale of an underwater ballroom created by some mad Midas millionaire under a lake at Wisley, Surrey. It seemed so unlikely, so eccentric, that it could only have been, well, whatever urban myths were called before they became urban. But worth checking all the same.

The bad news is that although I found a good lake beside the A3 at Wisley, where the Royal Horticultural Society has splendid gardens on the other side of the thundering Portsmouth–London road, there was no sign of a ballroom. (Of course, there wouldn't be if it were underwater, but no trace or record of its ever having existed or any old entrance, despite a website claiming that this was so.) There was, bizarrely, an ocean-going yacht on the water that, the lake being shallow and surrounded by trees, must have been for filming or testing a hull.

The good news is that I eventually heard that it was not Wisley, but Witley, a village off the A3 a few miles further south, beyond Guildford, and a stop on the London–Portsmouth railway. Here, I was thrilled to find out, there really *is* such a room – it is overstating it to call it a ballroom, more a large billiards room or smoking room. It was built very early in the 20th century and, even more surprising, it is still there and still watertight.

It comes with a suitably extraordinary story. It concerns maverick millionaire **Whitaker Wright** (1846–1904), who created what was then called Lea Park estate in the 1880s – by combining several other estates – and made his millions speculating on stocks and shares. He was called 'the Surrey Midas' and staged spectacular parties at Witley, where he had the grounds lavishly landscaped. He was a huge show-off but these events also served to boost confidence in his dodgy investment schemes, particularly as royalty and politicians were said to attend the bashes. The underwater room was not built until around 1900, but there was also a tunnel to an island in one of his lakes.

Everything was done to give an impression of solidity and wealth. Wright also had a mansion in Park Lane, London, and a large yacht.

Not long after this Wright's gambling on Australian mining shares went terribly wrong, and his shaky finances, and those of many honest investors, came crashing down, the trouble being compounded by a poor investment in a new London underground railway. He brazened it out for a while but then he and his niece fled to his wife's homeland, America, under false names. It was to no avail. When their liner *La Lorraine* docked in New York, police were waiting and arrested 'Monsieur and Mlle Andreoni'. He was sent back in chains.

Wright was put on trial for fraud, but many, including his wife, expected him to survive – indeed the villagers of Witley, who had done so well out of his largesse, prepared a torch-lit musical victory parade for the end of the trial in early 1904. It was not to take place, although he was to return somewhat differently.

He was sentenced to seven years' penal servitude. Amidst the sensation and hubbub of such a man's downfall, Wright asked court ushers if he could have a private moment. He emerged and faced the throng smiling, and took off his expensive watch and chain and gave them to a friend, saying he wouldn't be needing them any more. He asked for a cigar and took a few puffs, then fell down dead, for he had taken enough poison to kill ten men. He also had a loaded silver revolver in his pocket.

The villagers didn't get their victory parade, but only a funeral procession on 30 January 1904. The funeral service could not be held in the church, because it was a suicide, but was held in the freezing churchyard. Wright's grave can still be seen there, with his wife's alongside.

As for the underground 'ballroom' of legend, actually more like a very strong conservatory, where Wright and his guests would sit puffing on cigars and watch passing fish and swimmers in the eerie green light, it is still there. But the public are not welcome, unless they are paying a great deal, for Witley Park – rebuilt after a disastrous fire in 1952 which, naturally, didn't affect the underwater room – is one of those business conference centres where corporate bashes are staged for bonding or whatever top management do. BBC chief Greg Dyke and his top brass had a team-building session or 'thinking outside the envelope' or some such event there in 2004 – it is not for me to say whether this is a good use of licence-payers' dosh – just before Dyke became embroiled in the Gilligan affair and sank career-wise. I wonder if Dyke had a look at the 'underwater ballroom' and contemplated the downfall of another great public figure a century before?

UGLY BUT FREE

In Wales until modern times, you could keep any house you had started to build at sundown and by sunrise had the roof on and smoke coming from the chimney. Obviously it had to be on vacant land. You could also keep and fence the land around it as far as you could throw an axe. Although must of these 'Ty Un Nos' houses fell down because of being built in a hurry, or were incorporated gradually into proper houses, there is one on the A5 at Capel Curig called the **Ugly House** (Travel: page 215), built out of boulders (in fact clearly a more massive rebuild of the original). There were actually similar rules in the southwest of England, but there they had to build by *day* and the chimney smoking by sunset.

LIVING WITH THE RAILWAYS

Britain's most eccentric, not to say exclusive, country cottage could well be **Clayton Tunnel House** (Travel: page 214), a rather unlikely bungalow perched between the towers of the even more unlikely castellated north entrance to Clayton Tunnel on the Brighton line.

On one side it has the appearance of a castle. Above soar the glorious South Downs topped by the Jack and Jill windmills; before it lies the verdant sweep of the rolling Sussex Weald. And right in front, there is a suicidal drop into a gaping hole below, through which hurtle dozens of trains a day carrying holidaymakers and commuters.

Clayton Tunnel House was, until recently, the home of railway workers, and is now a family home. But its past contains a dark secret.

The house's origin and purpose are somewhat clouded, as indeed would have been its residents every few minutes in the age of steam and smoke. It hardly befits the extravagant Romanesque style of the tunnel portal created by John Rastrick (1780–1856), the genius responsible for Britain's most elegant and unsung railway viaduct across the Ouse valley, a few miles north on the same line. Being showered in smuts, having a near-cliff for a front lawn and a suicidal drop for a back garden would not be most people's idea of a nice country cottage.

It is ironic that the remarkable medieval doom paintings uncovered in Clayton church lie just a few steps to the east, depicting fearful scenes of death and the descent to the underworld. Fear of the underworld could account for the peculiar cottage's presence, and doom certainly lay in store for some early railway passengers.

When the railway, one of Britain's earliest main lines, was built in 1841, there was no way of avoiding the great ridge of the South Downs that so dramatically cuts off the Sussex Weald from the sea. Would the inexperienced passengers' fears – and at that time they were carried in open carriages behind engines belching fire, steam and smoke – prevent them from going underground in the line's longest tunnel?

The directors attempted to diminish these fears of the underworld by whitewashing the tunnel's brick lining and lighting the tunnel throughout with gas jets. The tunnel cottage's resident probably helped maintain these lights, in an attempt to convince naive people that heading into the tunnel wasn't to say farewell to daylight for ever.

But it was exactly that for the victims of the Clayton Tunnel Disaster of 25 August 1861, Britain's worst rail crash to that date. By then the Brighton line was booming as Britain's premier holiday route, but signalling technology was still based simply on dispatching trains at five-minute intervals. Rear-end collisions were thus greatly feared, particularly in tunnels.

Ironically, Clayton Tunnel was the only part of the line given more sophisticated protection, in the form of a single telegraph needle in each box at the ends of the tunnel, which dipped one way or the other to indicate 'train in tunnel' or 'line clear'.

The day disaster struck was a Sunday, which meant heavy excursion trains. It also meant that signalman Henry Killick at the south end was working a 24-hour shift so he could have his one day off later in the week. There was also a simple signal, the arm of which was supposed to be returned to 'danger' by the passing train wheels pressing a lever. This did not always work, and the Portsmouth excursion heading for London that morning failed to return it to 'danger'.

Signalman Killick telegraphed 'train in tunnel' to his colleague at the north end but failed to put the signal to 'danger' before the Brighton excursion passed some three minutes later. He *did* wave his red flag just as the heavy train steamed into the tunnel.

Now worried, he frantically telegraphed the north box and soon received the reassuring answer 'tunnel clear'. He assumed this meant that the second excursion train had left the tunnel, but, in fact, it hadn't – it was the first train the north box signalman meant. The second train's crew, having seen the red flag, had screwed down the feeble brakes of the era and the train's 17 packed carriages slowly came to a halt deep in the tunnel, then started to reverse slowly to see what was wrong.

At that moment, about four minutes after the Brighton excursion, came a third train – a regular timetabled train from Brighton to London. Killick, reassured by the telegraph's ambiguous message, waved his white flag (the equivalent of today's green). Had the earlier whitewash been kept clean and the gaslights still been lit, the driver might have seen his doom approaching. As it was, the tunnel was sooty black and filled with smoke. The resulting crash caused appalling carnage, with the third train's locomotive leaping up and crushing the earlier train's guard's van and rear carriage. Twenty-one people died and 176 were seriously injured.

More than 140 years later, Network Rail has completely restored the listed tunnel portal and cottage, and, unable to sell off the home as it sits on operational railway land, or rather over an operational hole, rents it out. The railway's Steve Tyler said: 'We believe the old railway policemen who controlled the trains by means of flags lived there. These characters wore frock coats, top hats and tails and were the reason why signalmen were known as "bobbies" well into the 20th century. We have a record of a Mr Russell who lived there with his wife and nine children.' The parents must have had their work cut out stopping them falling into the underworld.

A SIGNAL SUCCESS

Like others fortunate enough to live on the Sussex coast, Tim and Sylvia Stephens can gaze out to sea as they raise their glasses at dinner. More unusually, they can listen to telegraph bells tinkle, cast an eye over a railway section map, pull any one of a set of signal levers or wind the wheel of an old-fashioned level crossing.

Their dining room is high in a Victorian signalbox, far from any railway but not entirely incongruous in that their home, a few yards up the garden, is composed of two remarkable Victorian railway carriages, joined by a kitchen and a glassed-in conservatory whose roof groans with red grapes each autumn. Even the conservatory doors are recycled railwayana – shapely numbers that British Rail discarded when it revamped Hassocks station on the Brighton line. An unwillingness to see some railway gem trashed – nor to pass up a bargain – was central when Tim learnt that Bosham signalbox, along with a whole set of others, was to be smashed into skips when BR modernised the Portsmouth–Chichester line in the early 1990s.

'I just found out from people living nearby who knew we lived in railway carriages and thought we might be interested. I took a look and then went to BR and got them to agree to give it to me,' says Tim, a photographer and college lecturer.

'Of course it wasn't that simple. There was heaps of paperwork. We had to build a steel cradle under the box, close the road at Bosham and lift it out onto a low loader with a massive crane. Unloading was simpler. The lowloader backed in through an understanding neighbour's garden, after we took the fence down, then we jacked it up and took the lorry out from underneath.'

But there were more problems to come. First there was the urgent task of buying back all the signal fittings, which had been sent to BR's Collector's Corner near Euston, where such things are sold to enthusiasts and antique dealers. Then there was the small matter of planning permission – luckily forthcoming – and rebuilding the brick ground-floor section, which had earlier been taken to pieces at Bosham. Then followed months of refitting the box and its balcony, ideal as a sun-soaked verandah with sea views.

In fact, living in grounded railway carriages (minus the wheels, that is) made into a bungalow isn't that unusual – but is becoming more so, as railway preservation fans rediscover more and more Victorian and Edwardian gems and put them back on wheels. It dates back to the time after World War I when seaside land was being divided up cheaply, with no planning controls, and communities were allowed to sprawl. The Portakabins of the day – that is cheap, instant accommodation – were the thousands of railway carriage bodies becoming surplus as the hundreds of small railway companies were grouped into the big four great railways. Just as thousands of dismounted goods vans can still be seen up and down the country as farmers' chicken coops or toolsheds, so the carriages tended to be absorbed into houses and were often soon unrecognisable within later alterations. The Stephens's two carriages have a regular pitched roof with an upstairs between them. Yet these two were far from the average commuter sardine cans. Both have an illustrious history. The one that greets your eye as you push open the front gate was built in 1874.

'It was almost royal train standard. Just a few were made,' says Tim. At some point it became an inspection saloon used by railway top brass, hence the unusually generous end windows through which directors would have viewed the line while being propelled by steam engine and served from the kitchen compartment, still complete with mahogany cupboards behind the saloon.

The story of the second carriage came to light only in 1994. It was built by the London and North Western Railway in 1878 as a picnic saloon. The gentry would have hired it by the day and enjoyed its then long, leather, longitudinal benches and dining table. In World War I it became part of Earl Haig's unique command train of 14 carriages complete with power generators, dining car, map room, central heating and staff sleeping quarters.

The Stephens were delighted when an expert turned up a picture of their then six-year-old son Etienne's bedroom as a not very different compartment where two of Haig's clerks slept during the war. This was a little more spartan than its previous use, but was much more comfortable than the trenches, from which men would attack on orders from this very train.

The official photograph shows the partitions and the doors in the same positions as today, even down to the roller over which a leather belt ran to raise the windows. Now, after having seen all those miles of service in different eras and different places, the coach slumbers in a long retirement, the door opening on to a flower-lined garden path leading to the Stephens's splendidly eccentric signalbox dining room.

This habit of plonking disused railway carriages near a beach wasn't that uncommon, and the best place for spotting them is along East Beach, Selsey, West Sussex. **Selsey** is reached south from Chichester and the main A27 coastal highway by the winding B2145. Sailors know the place as Selsey Bill, a promontory into the English Channel so it has beaches on both sides of its point-of-a-triangle shape. Aliens know it, possibly, as home of Sir Patrick Moore, the hugely eccentric wild-haired astronomer who at the time of writing was still presenting the world's longest-running TV show, *The Sky at Night*, which has enthused amateurs since 1957.

You want the East Beach, on the left as you head into town. Park thereabouts and walk along this unmade coast road northeast (towards Bognor, although you won't get there, which may be a good thing). Look closely at the bungalows that line this track on the landward side. Many seem to be normal houses to start with, but then you see details such as brass handles, curved roofs, even frosted windows saying LADIES ONLY or THIRD CLASS from another era.

Local farmer David Rusbridge tells me his dad recalled tractors, or possibly steam traction engines, dragging old railway carriage bodies down to the beach here between the wars. 'You got the carriages, the delivery, enough timber to make it into a bungalow and the land for £60.' And what is one of the wonderfully sited homes worth now? Maybe £300,000–400,000.

Thatching a train

A truly glorious and possibly unique thatched carriage is that at a village not far from Portsmouth. It is a beauty and its owner begged for its precise location not to be publicised as he intended to leave it to the National

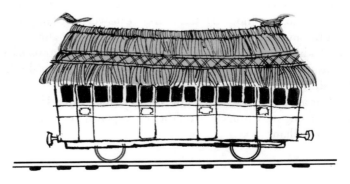

Trust, but it looks as though it might have been a London, Brighton and South Coast Railway brake-third, with the guard's special window for looking along the train for signals, stray passengers, zeppelin attacks or whatever. When I saw it, the paintwork was in first-class condition.

Hey, that's my home on Platform 3

Sometimes the carriages that were converted into homes are so old and rare (and so much better preserved than if they had spent a century thrashing up and down railways in all weathers) that enthusiasts actually reconvert them back into rail-going carriages. A case in point was a third-class coach that ran from 1865 until 1890 and was then converted into a bungalow at East Bridgford, near Nottingham. Three generations of the Curtis family were raised in the somewhat draughty but much-loved home. When the bungalow was demolished in 1983 the carriage was saved again, this time by railway enthusiasts who painstakingly restored it, mounted it on wheels again, and coupled it up at the **Midland Railway Centre**, Ripley, Derbyshire (Travel: page 215), in 1996, an amazing 131 years after it first entered service. Not until 2102 will it have run on rails as long as it rested off them.

Max impact

Car drivers in sleepy rural Berkshire can get a shock when they round a corner to see a 'Battle of Britain' class steam locomotive thundering out from under a bridge ahead of them. The train is a fabulous mural created on Max Bowker's garage door in **Swallowfield** by local artist Brian Matravers (Travel: page 215).

Quantity surveyor Max, who was never a trainspotter in the sense of writing down all the numbers, nevertheless had a good reason for choosing this subject when he decided to cover up some ugly doors.

'I used to go to school by train from Emsworth, Hampshire, to Portsmouth, and the express engines on that line were almost always these Bulleids, known as Spam Cans because of their unusual boxy shape. I've always had an affection for them, so there was no alternative for the painting.

'I told Brian, a friend who lives in the next village, that if he got one detail of the engine wrong he wouldn't get a penny for his work! But he's done a brilliant job.'

Max gave Brian a set of photos to help, but didn't specify which one. 'As it happens he chose 257 Squadron, which still runs on the Swanage line, so it's not just memories. I can pop down and see the real thing.'

A STEP UP THE HOUSING LADDER

All kinds of people have moved into former railway stations, as the once-vast network has shrunk under competition from lorries and subsidised company cars, and very good homes they can make too. Even goods sheds have become showrooms and offices, and a few signalboxes have found other uses, but water towers would not seem at all welcoming, as they usually consist of a whopping great iron tank on an unpretty brick or iron tower.

Peter Hook, luckily, didn't take that view and, as a consequence, he enjoys a splendid view – from the top of a redundant water tower at **Faversham**, Kent, where he's made a unique home (Travel: page 215).

The railway reached Faversham from Chatham in January 1858, but plans to make the line divide there and run – as indeed it now does – to either Dover or Margate had to be shelved for a couple of years because the promoters ran out of money. For those two years trains had to turn back to London from Faversham. This meant using all the town's water supply for topping up thirsty steam engines, much to the fury of the townspeople. Hence the tower. It might seem odd that it is across a road from the railway, isolated from its fire-breathing customers, but that is because the railway moved, not the tower.

Peter isn't a rail nut, still less could he tell you the classes and numbers of the trains passing through, but he likes the distant bustle of the station. 'The only problem with the railway is that when it shuts for engineering work, or at Christmas, it seems too quiet and that's when I notice it,' he says, a sentiment I have heard from others living with a usually constant background noise.

'I first went up the old iron ladder on the outside in 1984', said Mr Hook, 'and saw the possibilities of the place. I thought the climb pretty hairy, but later I spoke to a railwayman who climbed it during a wartime blackout and air raid on a winter's night with no torch, to deal with frozen valves, so my climb must have been relatively easy.'

Inside the brick tower was a vast cavity, the main features being half a dozen cast-iron pipes descending from the tank. To make the tower into a comfortable and different home with a splendid roof garden, internal stairs and floors were put in. An entrance hall, bedroom and bathroom

are on the ground floor, and stairs lead up to an office or eating area, kitchen, then up to a double-height formal dining room; from there a spiral staircase leads to a gallery sitting room. Finally a steep stair like a ship's ladder, rising through a 4ft by 8ft hole cut in the floor of the cast-iron tank, reveals a suntrap roof garden and terrace way above the other rooftops with sweeping views over picturesque Faversham and the Swale estuary.

For a rooftop party, or if someone's visiting, Peter runs a flag up the pole so the tower stands out even more than usual. A schoolteacher turned local potter, Peter is happy with his unusual home. 'It's nice being part of the town, down on the ground, and then I can go up there and be completely away from it.'

A RAILWAY ROMANCE

There's a certain romance about railway stations, as in the classic film *Brief Encounter*. Lewis and Patricia Yates certainly haven't missed the connection. But then Patricia clearly wasn't as immune as many girls (from trains, that is).

As a teenager she used to go to Oxford station just to watch the trains, but the couple (both middle-aged divorcees) got to know each other at the steam railway at Quainton Road station, Buckinghamshire, many years later. They spent some of their courting sitting at a favourite spot beside the tracks of the Oxford–Birmingham line next to the abandoned Aynho station, watching the many trains go by and others joining from the Marylebone route on a viaduct in the background. 'We used to bring some sandwiches and a Thermos of tea and sit by the derelict

Brunel-designed station building which dates from 1850. We thought it was a shame it was going to rack and ruin,' says Pat. 'Later on, when we heard the building was up for auction, we had to go for it.'

Some people thought they were crazy, and indeed some may still doubt their sanity. For one thing, the place was derelict and crumbling fast. The windows were all smashed, and the floors were rotten because water from the roof was directed to huge Victorian lead tanks which had been stolen. The lintels above the windows were rotten and in another year or two they would have brought the stonework down. There was even a tree growing out of the roof.

When they viewed the property they had to pick their way over rubbish in the dim interior. All the movable Great Western Railway fittings and notices had long been sold or stolen. 'The girl from the estate agents couldn't get out fast enough. I've been given longer to buy a pair of trousers!' recalls Lewis. But didn't Pat at that moment see the whole project as a nightmare?

'Not at all. I knew Lewis, as a carpenter, could do it. I had faith in the outcome. There was nothing the pair of us couldn't cope with, as long as we had our health.' Lewis says: 'That day it was chucking it down with rain. We nicknamed one room Niagara Falls for obvious reasons. You could hardly get through the rubbish. It was in a right old state but being in the building trade I could see it could be saved.'

The couple moved into a caravan in the station yard in September 1994 but it was two years before the station was habitable. The roof timbers were solid and only a few slates needed replacing. Remarkably, although the interior doors had been ripped out, they were found nearby and rehung in frames painstakingly built in most cases by carpenter Lewis using the undamaged ones as models. The cast-iron roof brackets are Brunel's originals, as are the Bath stone walls and unusual dark raised pointing made with locomotive ashes.

Sadly, the longer brackets over the platforms were cut short with oxy-acetylene torches when the railways abandoned the station and let it out as a coal office, but one unique feature could be restored.

'There were just three original stations between Oxford and Banbury and this is the only one that survives. Although the design was something of a GWR standard, our collection of steam-age photos shows only these three stations had unusual cast-iron lion shields on the ends of the roof brackets. Which would be great if they hadn't been stolen or sold too.

'We have tracked one of these down in a local museum and have got permission to have replicas cast so the station will look perfect as the only example.'

The second reason that people may have thought the couple a little odd in their choice of home is that their proposed home is a few feet from a busy main line. This is not one of Britain's hundreds of pretty former stations on an abandoned trackbed, or some rural mountain branch with two trains a day. Expresses from Virgin Trains hurtle through a few feet from the couple's bedroom. Local trains speed through more quietly, while massive freights rumble and thunder past, carrying coal for Didcot power station, containers for Southampton, or freight for the Channel Tunnel.

When I visited the Yateses, I soon saw that the 'up' track on the far side had what railwaymen call a dipped joint right opposite their home. While I was there a half-mile-long monster of a train from Solihull carrying hundreds of export Range Rovers and Land Rovers came through, every axle bending the rail down slightly at the joint – quite safely – and thumping over on to the next rail. Isn't this an endurance test, particularly as much freight travels at night?

'We sleep soundly. We like the trains, and the noise is occasional, unlike the non-stop roar of a motorway,' says Lewis. 'It probably adds up to just half-an-hour of noise a day.' A visitor from Canada carried back the story and Canadian Broadcasting called to arrange a live radio show, asking to fix a time when a train would be thundering past.

'I just told him to interview us there and then, and sure enough our talk was livened up by the sound of several trains going past. I suppose the Canadian listeners may have thought we were a little eccentric. I don't mind. I'm just glad we saved this place. The noise isn't a problem at all. Really, for us the biggest bonus is some 300 trains a day thundering past. The rush of sound is music to our ears.'

They mean it. They actually look at each train, call out to the other if something interesting is coming and discuss recent oddities. Pat says, 'It's wonderful when I'm hanging up my washing or in my greenhouse next to the platform and see one of these old steam engines thunder by. We saw *Britannia* come through the other day, running light on the way to do some work somewhere. That was a treat.

'We see new Tube trains being hauled to London or back for repair. There's plenty of interest.

'This station has been described as a token of our love because trains are part of us and that's fair enough. I'd far rather have this little station than the Taj Mahal.'

ONE-MAN RAIL 'PRIVETISATION'

Mick Waters of **Swanbourne**, Buckinghamshire, also lives in a station beside a track (Travel: page 215). His is still owned by Network Rail, the company that took over from nationalised British Rail. But he saw the last train rattle through on the Bletchley–Winslow section of the former Oxford–Cambridge route more than ten years ago and the mothballed, rusted track sees only rabbits and pheasants passing.

The station – sitting prettily on a curve above a stream – is hopefully named Swanbourne, but is really nowhere near that village and is only reached by a long lane up hill and down dale. Now it is left in what most people would surely judge idyllic rural peace. What Mick wants more than anything, however, is for the train service to be restored along his line. He was brought up in the railway-owned house, his late father Reg being a permanent way man. As with many thousands of railwaymen, Reg found the 'permanent' way (so called to differentiate it from temporary construction tracks) was not so permanent after all.

The route through to Cambridge was severed – insanely, most planners would now agree – at Bedford, making any connection eastwards to the King's Cross–Edinburgh line impossible for want of half a dozen miles of track. That was done, typically, immediately after millions of pounds had been spent on new signalling and a flashy concrete flyover at Bletchley; equally typically the following and partly resulting boom in road traffic has meant many millions more being spent on bypass after bypass.

Mick's father Reg, who dressed the station in mourning flags for the last stopping passenger train, started cutting the privet hedge next to the platform in the shape of one of the tough freight locomotives that frequented the line, the 'Super D' 0–8–0 type, and Mick maintains this topiary ghost train to this day. 'I can remember them coming through as a child. We also had push-and-pull little 2–6–2 tank engines on local services with just one carriage. Many's the time as a lad I got a free ride down to Winslow on the footplate!'

Mick, a jolly man, is surprisingly optimistic about the line reopening. He's pinned up press clippings that show how planners, faced with the new rail freight boom clogging up the system with trains, have realised that the route is part of a rail M25 which, for a few miles of cheap restoration, would link Cambridge to Oxford, then round to Reading, Guildford, Tonbridge and the Channel Tunnel, joining the lines in between. 'I think it's got a future for passengers too. They might not

reopen this station but Winslow down the line a couple of miles is growing fast and needs a station. The part from Oxford to Bicester has been reopened for commuters in recent years and the bit from Bletchley to Bedford has never lost its trains.' Meanwhile Mick, who works, ironically, on the roads ('We could do with getting rid of some of this heavy traffic back on to the railway') looks after not only the old station but weedkills the one remaining track for half a mile or so before it disappears into knee-high foliage round the corner.

'I really don't know what my dad would think of the state of some of the track, but I'm very hopeful the trains will come back. Everyone is in favour. I'll still be here to see them through.' And with that, the cherry blossom from the station garden blowing around like snow in the sunshine, he takes his dog for a walk up the line his family has watched over for so many decades.

TRAVEL INFORMATION

The eccentric railway homes described in this chapter are all private properties, except for the one restored to the Midland Railway Centre, and not open for general public visits. By all means have a discreet look from public rights-of-way, but please respect the owners' privacy.

CLAYTON TUNNEL HOUSE, Sussex BN6 9PG ☎ 01444 238202

This is a private home and is best viewed from the road bridge to the north. It is difficult and, indeed, dangerous to see from trains. Clayton church and doom paintings are across the road, Jack and Jill windmills up the hill.

🚗 From London/M25, take M23 and A23 then turn left 🚂 Nearest station: Hassocks, from London Victoria. Walk back alongside tracks.

MAX BOWKER'S GARAGE, Swallowfield, south of Reading, Berkshire RG7 1QX

🚗 Off M4 at J11, south on A33, and left to Swallowfield. Take care if you do have a look, as this is a narrow, dangerous road.

MICK WATERS'S STEAM HEDGE, Swanbourne, Buckinghamshire MK17 0ST

🚗 Off M1 at J13, through Bletchley on A421 to Buckingham, south on A413 Aylesbury–Winslow, left (east) on B4032 to Swanbourne then look for lane to left (north) 🚂 One day soon, we hope

MIDLAND RAILWAY CENTRE, Derbyshire DE5 3QZ ☎ 01773 747674

🚗 Signed off M1 J28, then A38 at Ripley 🚂/🚌 Alfreton Parkway station, then bus 91, 92, 93 (4 miles)

OXFORD SHARK HOUSE, New High Street, Headington OX3 7BA ☏ 01865 252200

🚗 Headington is signed on a turning to the city centre from the northern ring road on the London side 🚂/🚌 Oxford, then bus to Headington

PETER HOOK'S WATER TOWER, Faversham, Kent ME13 8EB ☏ 01795 534542

🚗 Off M2 J6, look for station 🚂 Next to Faversham station, on London Victoria–East Kent line

UGLY HOUSE, Capel Curig, Conwy LL24 0DS

🚗 About three miles west of Betws-y-Coed on the A5

ECCENTRIC GARDENS

ATLANTIC OCEAN

Orkney Islands

Thurso

Isle of Lewis

Isle of Skye

Inner Hebrides

Island of Mull

Islay

Inverness

Aberdeen

SCOTLAND

Meikleour Hedge, Perthshire

NORTH SEA

Glasgow

EDINBURGH

Arran

ATLANTIC OCEAN

N

0 — 80 km
0 — 50 miles

Newcastle upon Tyne

Carlisle

Middlesbrough

Isle of Man

Tipsy Topiary, Levens Hall

Druids' Temple, Ilton Moor

ENGLAND

York

Leeds

Kingston-upon-Hull

Bradford

NORTH SEA

Manchester

Grimsby

Anglesey

Liverpool

Sheffield

Holyhead

Stoke-on-Trent

Nottingham

Norwich

Derby

Cardigan Bay

Wolverhampton

Birmingham

Oldest Gnome, Lamport Hall

Coventry

Cambridge

Ipswich

WALES

Fishguard

Oxford

Faringdon House

Swansea

CARDIFF

Reading

LONDON

Dover

Bristol Channel

Bristol

Enchanted Forest, Groombridge Place

Gnome Reserve, West Putford

West Dean Gardens

Southampton

Portsmouth

Brighton

ATLANTIC OCEAN

Exeter

Penzance

ENGLISH CHANNEL

ECCENTRIC GARDENS

GARDEN WIT, WISDOM AND MASS WISTERIA

The British garden at its worst exhibits all the prim paranoia of the ghastly architecture that it suits so well. Outside the endless rows of characterless suburban semis, with not a neurotically twitching lace curtain out of place, stand manicured square lawns, sprayed with this or that poison to prevent a wildflower or even a daisy spoiling their plastic perfection, and surrounded by municipal-style beds of totally predictable flowers, evenly spaced with all the flair and imagination of an amoeba on Valium. The odd gnome hardly makes up for this.

Yet surprisingly, for those not constrained by the regimented suburban approach, the garden offers a haven for oddball whimsy, fantastical flair or tawdry trivia that would never be allowed in the home. Around the country can be seen whimsical gardens with a dozen or more gnomes, complete with fake ponds, windmills, waterfalls, helter-skelters or whatever.

These small-time rebels against conformity are nothing compared to the exhibition – the Ideal Gnome Show, as it were – put on by the zealous Ann Atkin at West Putford, near Bideford, Devon. The four-acre **Gnome Reserve** (Travel: page 224) features more than a thousand of the red-capped characters, as well as various frogs, toadstools, kittens, ducks, etc (all unreal) and a beech wood and wildflower plot (real). It attracts thousands of visitors every year, all of whom have to don the red cap, says Mrs Atkin, 'so as not to embarrass the gnomes'. Well, as long as *they* don't feel silly.

Gnome-add: Britain's oldest garden gnome is at **Lamport Hall**, Northampton (Travel: page 225). Victorian baronet Sir Charles Edmund Isham brought several porcelain gnomes over from Nuremberg, Germany, in the late 19th century and this chap is the only survivor. The German phrase *gnomen figuren*, meaning 'folklore figures' was mistranslated by Sir Charles to give us our phrase 'garden gnomes'.

The hedge with an edge

IF YOU FIND TRIMMING the hedge a bit of a bore, consider the world's tallest, which looms cliff-like, an average 100ft high and 580yds long at **Meikleour** in Perthshire (Travel: page 225). Planted by Jean Mercer of Meikleour in approximately 1746, it is definitely still a beech hedge, not a grown-out line of trees, for the dense foliage reaches down to ground level. It takes four men with hydraulic cranes six weeks to trim, but this is only undertaken every ten years. Here we are near Birnam, and the trimmings would indeed be enough to camouflage an army, as in Shakespeare's *Macbeth*.

Xanadu, near Andover

Well beyond the gnome stage is the garden created by the late Stanley Norbury near Andover, Hampshire. In a fairly ordinary bungalow garden, squashed between the noisy A342 and a little-used military railway, he engineered the most escapist fantasy garden possible on an heroic scale. It is the Alhambra come to Andover, a surreal Xanadu off Salisbury Plain. Better than a theme park because it is not plastic, nor for paying visitors, it is a quiet, very personal garden and, remarkably, it's all been constructed in solid concrete and Portland stone by one man working all hours on top of a full-time job. The planting was wisely restricted to species that thrive in the setting: chalky soil drained by giant beech trees lining the main road. The railway embankment, by the way, in springtime offers the most solid block of primroses I have ever seen.

Mr Norbury, who died in 1996, had started the sunken garden in 1975 by converting a kidney-shaped swimming pool he had excavated in the 1960s. He had lived on the site when a boy. Then the bungalow was a corrugated-iron former 'tin tabernacle' moved from elsewhere. After serving as a World War II pilot, he bought the much-loved property with his £150 gratuity and spent 12 years rebuilding it.

When it came to the stone and concrete garden, his realisation of a childhood dream became a little obsessive. He would get up at 05.00 to put in a few hours before work as a civil servant at the Ministry of Defence nearby, then work into the darkness in the summer evenings.

'It was hard physical work – I must have shifted tons and tons of cement and stone. I had to use levers and wedges to shift the very heavy pieces because I was on my own. One time a big pierced arch, which I had pre-formed on the flat, collapsed as I was trying to erect it. It nearly killed me.

'A lot of the detail was carved with a knife while the cement was still wet. I made some of the pieces, such as the balustrading for the bridge, in boxes, then finished with a knife.'

Someone ought to preserve this garden – they would have a hard time of a job shifting it, after all – because it is remarkable what can be achieved on a modest site with modest means. If the same thing had been built 200 years ago the great and the good of the heritage industry would be frantically raising cash to keep such a thing; if it was built five years ago the planners would probably be demanding its demolition.

DYED DOVES AND WORRISOME WYVERNS

When it comes to the aristocracy or the gentry, on the other hand, garden eccentricity has naturally been given that much more scope, although many of the wittiest gestures could be inexpensive, as in the garden of the 1930s composer-diplomat, the eccentric Gerald Tyrwhitt-Wilson, 14th Baron Berners (1883–1950) at Faringdon, Oxfordshire.

The first hint of his rather gentle eccentricity lay at the boundaries of the estate, where regularly spaced notices stated: 'Anyone throwing stones at this notice will be prosecuted.' At the entrance of **Faringdon House** itself, one of Lord Berners's rather odd notices survives – one about removing hats – and then, of course, there was the peculiar warning in his marvellous tower (see page 282).

At the house, one of the wittiest ideas of the late baron may still be seen, kept up by the present owners: a small flock of doves dipped in food dye making an extraordinary sight as they flutter around. These and many other of his foibles, such as dogs running around with jewelled necklaces, are also re-created in the Lord Merlin character, based on Berners, in Nancy Mitford's 1954 novel *The Pursuit of Love*. Berners, who had mechanical goldfish swimming round in coloured water bowls, kept a small piano in the back of his Rolls-Royce.

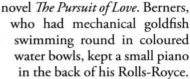

One visitor, Salvador Dalí, had a grand piano put in a shallow pond, placed chocolate eclairs on all the ebony keys and asked Berners to play for some surreal entertainment and, on another occasion, Penelope Betjeman brought her horse into the drawing room for tea and cake. Berners's companion, Robert 'Mad Boy' Heber-Percy, lived at Faringdon after Berners died in 1950.

The gardens – not now open to the public – also hold diverse, more durable testaments to his ideas. What appears to be a castle turns out to be Oxfordshire's only crenellated swimming pool. The changing room has a floor made of pennies set in cement and stained-glass windows; two fearsome, fantastical creatures, dragon-headed wyverns, sit at the shallow end. (Wyvern trivia: there was a Vauxhall Wyvern car in the 1950s and every Vauxhall car badge still includes one – have a look).

Nearby, outside the orangery, sits a bizarre half-submerged statue of General Havelock (1795–1857). It suits the spot perfectly. He looks as though he might be relieving himself, apt for the hero who relieved Lucknow during the Indian Mutiny.

THE PROBLEMS WITH SURREAL GARDENING

One very modern gardener whom Baron Berners would surely have understood is surreal gardener Ivan Hicks. Mr Hicks's surreal credentials are almost unreal. His previous employer at **West Dean Gardens**, West Sussex (Travel: page 225), was the late millionaire eccentric Edward James (1907–84), who was also a good chum of Salvador Dalí and who appears in Magritte paintings. Do you know the one showing the back of a man sitting looking into a dressing-table mirror, yet in the mirror we see his back again? That's Edward James, and an oblique commentary on this strange man who built a fantasy in the Mexican jungle, and then deliberately let the jungle regrow over the gaudy Gaudiesque creations. James often took Hicks to Mexico for advice on plants and in particular trees, his speciality. At West Dean, note the marvellous 300ft Edwardian pergola, great walled kitchen gardens and extensive vine houses.

James shared a penchant for absurd notices with Baron Berners. When someone put up signs saying 'Beware of the adders' at his Monkton House gardens, James thought the dangers trivial compared to those of gardeners working on the trees and had Ls added to all the 'adders'.

Ivan Hicks's ideas have been adopted on a grand scale at **Groombridge Place** (Travel: page 225), a perfectly preserved moated house on the Kent–Sussex border at Groombridge near Tunbridge Wells. But the Enchanted Forest, which recent owner Andrew de Candole encouraged Hicks to create, is not just another theme park.

Near the house there is a maze growing in golden and green yew, which when head height will better conceal a peculiar secret about its layout that I sense is part of some pattern or puzzle the devious Hicks is setting up. In the Enchanted Forest itself there are the things families seem to love – adventure walkways in a double spiral, with pigs and deer running free round about – but Hicks is in the detail even here, with a face carved in a tree suddenly jumping out at you, for example.

Further into the forest are things that are pure Hicks – a Serpents' Lair and a Mystic Pool, whimsical construction of *objets trouvés* around the original woodland landscape that have fairytale layers of detail repaying a close and then closer look. There are Hicksian favourites that recall his Sussex base, such as a ring of trembling aspens on an island in a small lake which will soon be bent over to make a classical temple.

As Groombridge Place's gardening curator Clifford James said: 'These are living places that Ivan has to maintain. It is not something gardening staff could fix because his vision is what drives it all. There is a subtlety that avoids being theme parky. Where we do a little of that for the children, it is very much tongue-in-cheek.'

Strolling through the Enchanted Forest, which is carpeted with wild garlic and bluebells in early spring, you could come across a Peruvian pipe player sitting in a natural amphitheatre with log seats all around, or a Romany caravan with a Gipsy woman all ready to chat or tell your fortune, with chickens and pigs running around the fire. It is not a

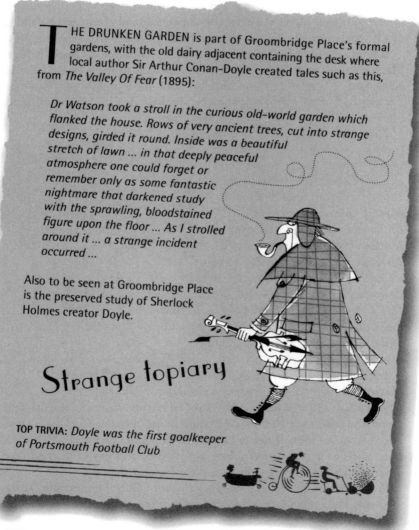

THE DRUNKEN GARDEN is part of Groombridge Place's formal gardens, with the old dairy adjacent containing the desk where local author Sir Arthur Conan-Doyle created tales such as this, from *The Valley Of Fear* (1895):

Dr Watson took a stroll in the curious old-world garden which flanked the house. Rows of very ancient trees, cut into strange designs, girded it round. Inside was a beautiful stretch of lawn ... in that deeply peaceful atmosphere one could forget or remember only as some fantastic nightmare that darkened study with the sprawling, bloodstained figure upon the floor ... As I strolled around it ... a strange incident occurred ...

Also to be seen at Groombridge Place is the preserved study of Sherlock Holmes creator Doyle.

Strange topiary

TOP TRIVIA: *Doyle was the first goalkeeper of Portsmouth Football Club* garden, nor a theatre, nor a fairground pleasure park, nor a natural environment, but a curious blend of all of them.

In terms of formal gardens, Groombridge Place is also deservedly well known. The ancient topiary and various views of the house were made famous in Peter Greenaway's 1983 film *The Draughtsman's Contract*, where each of the drawings of the house was exchanged for certain favours from the lady of the manor. Mr Hicks settled for more usual terms of employment.

For perhaps the most stunning topiary in the country, try **Levens Hall** in Cumbria, described as 'a miracle of English gardening' (Travel: page 225). It was once a medieval deer park, but by 1700 had been laid out as a stately home's park and gardens with the most remarkable yew 'tipsy topiary' – plus beautiful specimen trees and great views of the sweeping River Kent.

NEITHER UNHINGED NOR UNHENGED

Henge-building stuff did not come to an end with the druids and the Stone Age. Some of the modern henges are whimsical constructions made of lift doors, or to mark a Casanova's conquests, but others are of regular stone erected for less controversial reasons. Take professional gardener Len Ede of **Petersfield**, Hampshire. Perfectly normal, he lives in a quiet suburban bungalow in a typical cul-de-sac. He and his wife Joyce love Stonehenge, to which they regularly make the 80-mile trip. And so, when he wanted to pay tribute to his wife, to whom he'd been married for getting on 40 years, there was only one thing he could do: he built her a one-twelfth-sized Stonehenge right in the front garden, which it dominates.

'There's just something special about Stonehenge,' says Mr Ede. 'I built it for my god, and that's my wife. Other families have got gnomes and such things in their gardens but I thought she deserved something different.'

The Edes are not alone in imitating the prehistoric puzzle. On the edge of **Ilton Moor**, there stands, amid forestry, the little-known Yorkshire Stonehenge, the **Druids' Temple** (Travel: page 225). This imitation Stonehenge was put up by eccentric early 19th-century author William Danby (1752–1833), probably to alleviate local unemployment. The ever-eccentric Marquess of Bath has put up a

granite version of Stonehenge at his Wiltshire stately home, **Longleat** (Travel: page 149). In **Westleton**, Suffolk, a private garden had redundant Art Deco lift doors arranged in a Stonehenge and in **Padstow**, Cornish eccentric and arch druid Ed Prynne has arranged a circle of massive megaliths near his bungalow. He told a reporter that there was one for each woman in his life. So that's what the druids were up to … (See also *Britain's Most Magical Standing Stones*, page 265).

TRAVEL INFORMATION

DRUIDS' TEMPLE, Yorkshire HG4 4LT 🐾 01748 828747
🚗 On the edge of Ilton Moor, about 1¹/₂ miles southwest of the village of Healey and east of Leighton Reservoir. Healey is southwest of A6108 midway between Leyburn and Ripon, which is just off the A1

GNOME RESERVE, West Putford, near Bideford, Devon EX22 7XE
☎ 01409 241435 🖥 www.gnomereserve.co.uk 🐾 01237 477676
🚗 From M5 end at Exeter, A30 and A377 to Barnstaple, A39 to Bideford,

then A386, A388 towards Holsworthy south. West Putford is about 3 miles to right (north) from Venngreen

GROOMBRIDGE PLACE, Kent TN3 9QG ☎ 01892 861444
🖳 www.groombridge.co.uk ✆ 01892 515675
🚗 4 miles southwest of Tunbridge Wells on B2110. From London and M25 use A21 Hastings–Tunbridge Wells (not Tonbridge)

LAMPORT HALL, Lamport, Northampton NN6 9HD ☎ 01604 686 272
🖳 www.lamporthall.co.uk; opening limited
🚗 On the A508 between Northampton and Market Harborough

LEVENS HALL TOPIARY, Kendal, Cumbria LA8 0PD ☎ 015395 60321
🖳 www.levenshall.co.uk ✆ 01539 797516
🚗 M6 J36 🚂 Oxenholme (London Euston-Glasgow line), then taxi 5 miles

MEIKLEOUR HEDGE, Perthshire PH2 6EB (postcode of nearby hotel)
✆ 01738 627958
🚗 On A93 about 10 miles north of Perth towards Blairgowrie

WEST DEAN GARDENS, near Chichester, West Sussex PO18 0RX
☎ 01243 818210 🖳 www.westdean.org.uk
🚗 On A286 Chichester-Midhurst road 🚂/🚌 Chichester from London Victoria, then bus 60

The other gardens mentioned are private.

ATLANTIC OCEAN

Orkney Islands

Thurso

Eight-sided House, John o'Groats

Isle of Lewis

Isle of Skye

Inverness

SCOTLAND

Aberdeen

Inner Hebrides

Glenfinnan Viaduct

Neptune's Staircase, Fort William

Island of Mull

Tealing Dovecote, Angus

North Lodge, Arbroath

NORTH SEA

Rest and be Thankful

Dull

Castle, Military Dog Cemetery & Dovecote, Deacon Brodie's Tavern, Edinburgh

Islay

Falkirk Wheel

Glasgow

Phantassie Doocot, Lothian

Arran

ATLANTIC OCEAN

N

0 — 80 km
0 — 50 miles

Carlisle

Newcastle upon Tyne

Isle of Man

Crackpot

Standedge Tunnel

Transporter Bridge, Middlesbrough

ENGLAND

IRISH SEA

Temple Newsam Dovecote, Leeds

York

Kingston-upon-Hull

NORTH SEA

Bradford

Anglesey

Holyhead

Liverpool

Manchester

Sheffield

Grimsby

Anderton Boat Lift

Ashbourne Pub

Fantasy Village, Portmeirion

Pontcysyllte Aquaduct

Stoke-on-Trent

Nottingham

Cardigan Bay

Wolverhampton

Derby

Norwich

Fantasy Village, Thorpeness

Birmingham

Coventry

Rendlesham Hall Lodges, Suffolk

Tardebigge Locks

Fishguard

WALES

Wonderful Dovecotes

Willington Dovecote

Cambridge

Ipswich

Monnow Bridge Lock-up, Monmouth

Wheatley Lock-up

Hammersmith Bridge & Monument

Shenley Lock-up

Transporter Bridge, Newport

Oxford

CARDIFF

Bristol Channel

Clifton Suspension Bridge, Bristol

Pangbourne Lock-up

Victoria Gate Lodge, Hyde Park

Stag Lodge, Wimbledon

Westward Ho!

Superb Dovecote, Bruton

Lingfield Lock-up

Balcombe Viaduct

Dover

Southampton

Brighton

Transportation Bridge, Wool

Swanage Lock-up

Exeter

Portsmouth

ATLANTIC OCEAN

Lanhydrock Lodge, Bodmin

Atmospheric Railway, Starcross

Penzance

Dovecote, Cotehele House, Calstock

ENGLISH CHANNEL

A PLACE FOR ECCENTRICS

SIGNS OF SERIOUS ECCENTRICITY

Villagers of tiny Bedlam, North Yorkshire, are not exactly delighted with the name signs that have been erected there, causing one wag to add 'Twinned with L'Unacy'. No doubt they fear too many sightseers will cause, well, Bedlam.

But the novelty will wear off. Inhabitants of Nasty and Ugley, near neighbours across the Hertfordshire–Essex border, have long since got over jokes about the Nasty Boys' Choir or the Ugley Women's Institute, and if people can live in Pratts Bottom, Kent, or on Muck, Hebrides, or take jokes about what goes on at Cuckold's Cross, Hertfordshire; Over Wallop, Hampshire; Crackpot, Yorkshire; Dirt Pot, Northumberland; Hogspit Bottom, Hertfordshire or Hell Corner, Berkshire, then mere Bedlam can take it on the chin.

In fact, as with the Bedlam mental asylum once sited where the Imperial War Museum now stands, its name probably comes from Bethlehem. Like the hospital, they could always compromise with Bethlem. Or just feel like Pity Me, Durham.

Geographical confusion in some parts of Britain is more common than in Paris, Texas. We have five Californias, near Falkirk in Scotland, in Derbyshire, Norfolk, Suffolk and near Baldock in Hertfordshire; three Gibraltars, near Bedford, part of Mablethorpe, Lincolnshire, or near

Woodbridge, Suffolk; two New Yorks in Lincolnshire and Tyne & Wear; a New Zealand in Derbyshire, a Quebec in County Durham, a Rhodesia in Nottinghamshire and a Palestine near Andover, Hampshire (in the latter one travels down Mount Carmel to Zion). The former Australian penal colony of Botany Bay seems oddly popular, with at least three villages, in Avon, Kent and Middlesex, and there are countless farms named after it. Little France in Lothian, Normandy in Surrey, America in Cambridgeshire … the list of places that aren't what they say is almost endless. If you find these puzzling, there's Conundrum in Lothian.

And don't get started on international versions of British names: there are 35 Brightons around the world, plus 16 New Brightons.

Back in Blighty, **seasonal offerings** may be found at Good Easter in Essex; Easter Bush in Lothian; Cold Christmas in Essex; Christmas Common in Oxfordshire; and Christmaspie in Surrey. The only place with punctuation is Westward Ho! in Devon; the only one composed of initials is the hamlet of CB in Yorkshire; and the only one, well, of its kind, is Rest And Be Thankful, on the A83 between Arrochar and Inveraray in Argyll. No doubt Dull, Perthshire, has lists of Dull events one can enjoy.

Lower and Upper Slaughter, Gloucestershire, sound as if something terrible happened there. It didn't – it comes from *slohtre*, a muddy place. Ironically, given the name, this is one of the tiny handful of 'thankful villages', where all the men sent to World War I came safely back.

West Country places have a pleasing insanity which even P G Wodehouse couldn't have made up. Why is Toller Fratrum next to Toller Porcorum in Dorset? What goes on at nearby Ryme Intrinsica? Or at Ab Lench in Worcestershire, Praze-an-Beeble in Cornwall or Zeal Monachorum in Devon?

The Welsh have a happy habit of **running words together** in a way that even the Germans might find strange. Taken to an extreme, this gives Britain's longest railway station name sign at Llanfairpwllgwngyllgogerychwyrndrobwllllantysiliogogogoch, on the line on Anglesey to Holyhead. It may usually be seen with tourists being photographed alongside, and is often shortened to Llanfair PG. But it has a real meaning: 'St Mary's Church in the hollow of the white hazel near a rapid whirlpool and the church of St Tysilio near the red cave'. Welsh readers would already know that.

If you like the schoolboyish giggling at **silly names** – and even if you are above all that, you are now going to read this paragraph to see, aren't you? – there's Feltwell, Norfolk; Sandy Balls, Hants; Scratchy Bottom, Dorset; Crapstone, Devon; Three Cocks, Powys; Twatt, Orkney; and when it comes to roads, Booty Lane, Heck; Sluts Hole Lane, Cambs; The Knob, Kings Sutton; Back Passage, EC1; Bladda, Paisley; Hooker Road, Norwich; Slag Lane, Haydock; Spanker Lane, Nether Heage; Juggs Close, Lewes; Fanny Hands Lane, Ludford Parva. Of course they are not remotely funny, no, no, no … and well done locals for not changing it to something bladder – sorry, blander! Still, bet you're glad you don't have to put that on your headed notepaper.

Other places are staggeringly unusual because of their sheer commonness, if that makes any sense. If you include double-barrelled names or those prefixed or suffixed by South or Common or whatever, Newtown has 75; Middleton, 35; Milton, 46; Norton, 40; Upton, 33; Broughton, 23; Sutton, 52; Weston, 41; and Preston, 28.

Places that shouldn't be there at all include Nowhere in Kent; five Nomanslands in Cornwall, Devon, Hampshire, Hertfordshire and Wiltshire; Noplace in County Durham; two No Man's Heaths in Cheshire and Warwickshire; an Innominate Tarn, Cumbria; and an Inaccessible Pinnacle in Skye. Nonsuch in Ewell, Surrey, really *isn't* there; it was the site of the great Tudor palace that is, sadly, gone.

EIGHT ECCENTRIC SIDES TO JOHN O'GROATS

People who want to travel the full length of Britain – pushing a hospital bed for charity, for example – always go from Land's End, which is self-explanatory, to John o'Groats in Scotland, which isn't.

The origins of its name lie with an eccentric Scot. Or rather Dutchman. In the 16th century, Scotland's King James IV wanted to start up a ferry from the north of Scotland to Orkney, because those islands had, until recently, been part of Norway and the Scots king wanted to tie them in to his kingdom.

He persuaded a band of Dutch sailors led by Jan De Groot to set up the ferry from a place that soon took his name. The family would

celebrate their arrival in this remote place every year with a clan-like gathering. One year a dispute grew up as to which of the seven descendants of the De Groots would become head of the family after him, and Jan told them it would be settled at the annual gathering. He put up an octagonal house with eight doors and an octagonal table to make the point that they could all equally be head of the family. An eight-sided house, a successor to the original, may still be seen at the town, and a mound where the original was. This Scottish–Dutch version of King Arthur's Round Table clearly did the trick, for the De Groots' ferry service prospered for another few centuries.

THE WORLD'S ODDEST PUBS

The attempt not so long ago of a Derbyshire County Council 'equality officer' to ban the ancient if rather long pub sign **The Green Man and Black's Head Royal Hotel** in Ashbourne, in the Peak District, because it was 'racist', is by no means unique. It was evident that the humourless Martian embassy had not complained about the Green Man part from the inclusion of a crass, unsubtle leaflet about 'gollies'.

More understandably, schoolgirls had the sign of the **Labour In Vain** pub in Yarnfield, Staffordshire, repainted because it showed women scrubbing a small black boy. But many other signs have fallen victim to the easily offended. The **Silent Woman** in Oxfordshire has gone, although there are at least two Silent Womans in Slaithwaite, Huddersfield and Cold Harbour, Dorset, and in the same county there is a **Quiet Woman** at Halstock (while the **Wicked Lady** at Nomansland near St Albans, Hertfordshire, is, of course, politically correct enough). Certain Yorkshire pubs such as the **Blue Pig** have offended Muslims. Harry Walshaw, chairman of the Inn Signs Society, said at the time: 'I think **Live and Let Live** is a good sign to follow – there are a few of those in the Home Counties, and I am delighted to say there are several more **Labour in Vains**.' For downright political incorrectness, at least one **Nag's Head** has had the equine pub sign replaced by a scolding woman.

Pubs were required to have a sign from 1751, although many are much older. Some are not what they seem. The Flying Machine near Cheltenham has a picture of the Gloster Gladiator aircraft on one sign, but on another the real source – a famous stagecoach of an earlier era.

Another two-sided sign is **Deacon Brodie's Tavern** on the Royal Mile in Edinburgh (Travel: page 249), which commemorates the man who was the inspiration for Dr Jekyll and Mr Hyde: one side shows the respectable daytime businessman and the other the night villain. He was hanged, appropriately, on a gallows of his own design.

The latter instrument was that referred to by most pubs named **The Last Drop**, which lay near execution sites, rather than the name referring to beer, as people today assume. The origin of other names is much harder to guess at: there are several pubs called **The Case is Altered** in Middlesex, for instance. Despite attempts to link these to court cases, the most likely source is that the local regiment was quartered in the Casa Alta in the Peninsular War early in the 19th century.

Some names tell a sad story. The **Never Turn Back** at Caister, Norfolk, recalls lifeboat coxswain James Haylett, who was asked at an inquest why his men went bravely on into a storm and were lost. 'Caister men never turn back,' he declared.

Even a pleasant-sounding pub name can tell a story of disaster and tragedy – such as the **Snowdrop** pub, Lewes, East Sussex. It is not named after the waxy white flower. This lovely town is in a cleft in the South Downs where a river cuts through. At Christmas 1836, a huge shelf of snow built up on the 190ft cliff over Boulder Row, where the poor people lived. The cottagers had been warned of the danger, but wouldn't leave for they had nowhere to go in the cruel weather. The morning after Boxing Day, the snow wall suddenly broke away, burying seven cottages and leaving eight dead. Seven were dug out alive, including a two-year-old whose mother was among those killed.

Lastly there are plenty of pubs that locals refuse to call by their official names. Printers in Fleet Street were notorious for renaming pubs and wouldn't have had a clue where The White Swan was. But if you asked for The Mucky Duck …

THE LONG AND THE SHORT OF PUB NAMES

Whoever selected the truly bizarre name **I Am the Only Running Footman** as the name for a pub in London, W1, was giving Ashbourne's

The Green Man and Black's Head Royal Hotel a run for their money in terms of length. Running footmen used to precede the grand carriages of the great, to harry people out of the way, proclaim their masters and open gates. By the early 19th century, the fourth Marquess of Queensberry was the only noble still employing one, commemorated on the pub sign.

Much longer yet – but not quite qualifying as a pub name – is the title of a bar in the Gainsborough House Hotel, Kidderminster, Worcestershire. When locals were told it was to be renamed after one of the eponymous painter's pictures, the Blue Boy Bar might have been a reasonable guess. In fact, it is called **The Rocky Valley with Two Women and a Child, a Shepherd and Sheep with a Distant Village and Mountains Bar**.

Shortest is **Q**, Stalybridge, Greater Manchester. Deeply odd include **The Donkey On Fire**, Ramsgate, Kent, and the **Bucket of Blood**, Hayle, Cornwall.

Folksy sayings give rise to peculiar pub names, such as the **Help Me Through the World** at Bury, Lancashire. Charles Hindley in his book *Tavern Anecdotes and Sayings* suggests that this was once a common name and that the sign would have shown a man struggling through a globe, the idea being that life was tough but the pub would help you get through it.

Similar phrases include the **Live and Let Live** at Hexton, near Hitchin, Hertfordshire, and elsewhere – the sign usually shows a dog watching a plump duck waddling past. The **Who'd Have Thought It?** at Milton Combe, Plymouth; Egerton or Rochester, Kent; and Wokingham, Berkshire, sometimes refers to the landlord's surprise at being granted a licence for the pub by the court, as shown on some of the pub signs. There is a **Hit or Miss** at Stamford, Lincolnshire, and **The Same Yet** in Prestwich, near Manchester – the latter presumably a misunderstanding of the landlord's instructions on how to paint the pub sign.

Another licensing mix-up is to blame for the **Letter B** at Whittlesey near Peterborough, Cambridgeshire. The justices had a list – A, B, C, D – to choose from at as yet unnamed houses, and the Letter B stuck. The punning sign shows a lad with his arm around a reluctant lass, the image being 'Let her be'.

Some pubs fall naturally into pairs. The story of the naked noblewoman who rode through Coventry is recalled by the **Lady Godiva** in that city, as is the boy who broke the ban on looking upon her fair body, with the **Peeping Tom** in Coventry and at Burton Green, Warwickshire.

Some themes lend themselves to sets of pubs. The new town at Harlow, Essex, presented a great opportunity: all the pubs are named after moths or butterflies but the signs show punning pictures of other meanings: the **Red Admiral**, the **Purple Emperor**, the **Shark**, the **Small Copper** and the **Painted Lady** give plenty of scope for fun. The last, however, was renamed the boring Jean Harlow in an unimaginative move which spoilt the set.

Smuggling is featured in a surprising number of pub names and signs. **The Revenue**, at Devonport, Plymouth, shows customs men on a cliff watching for smugglers, and other coastal pubs include the **Smugglers' Den**, Morecambe, the **Smugglers' Barn**, Newport, Isle of Wight, the **Moonlighters**, Pegwell, Kent, or the **Rum Runners**, Southampton. The **Slippery Sam** at Petham, near Canterbury, was named after a smuggler. The **Moonraker**, at Swindon and elsewhere, could refer obliquely to smuggling. The original Moonrakers, as opposed to any Moonraker pubs named after the James Bond film, were said to be village idiots who thought the full moon reflected in the village pond was a big cheese and tried to rake it out. The better explanation is that some smugglers were caught in the act of retrieving contraband from the bottom of the village pond. They only pretended to be village idiots, the real simpletons being the revenue men who swallowed the story.

More unlikely still is the name of a pub at Copnor, Portsmouth, following in the Jolly Sailor, Jolly Farmer, Jolly Fisherman tradition. This one is the barely credible **Jolly Taxpayer**, a name probably not uninfluenced by the sizeable tax office nearby, housing many thirsty Inland Revenue staff.

THE PUB WITH NO NAME

'You want the pub with no name,' we were told, and given directions from Selborne, Hampshire, to the next-but-one village.

But the pub wasn't in the centre of that tiny hamlet, Colemore, nor was there any sign of it or to it. Over the years we travelled the various lanes leading to and from the hamlet until we had covered every possible approach, but of the Pub With No Name there was no sign. Once, on a foggy winter's night after visiting several other pubs, we were driven there, and an excellent pub it was too. But in daylight it had vanished again.

Intriguingly, on the nearby main road there is a sign, or rather a post set in an empty field with an empty oblong metal frame where a sign once swung. Its absence is no temporary affair – 90 years ago, Edward Thomas – the poet who lived at nearby Steep and was killed at the Battle of Arras – wrote about the Pub With No Name:

> *The post and empty frame I knew.*
> *Without them I could not have guessed*
> *The low grey house and its one stack under trees*
> *Was not a hermitage but a public house.*

As in 1914, the Pub With No Name still lurks under a copse of beech, well hidden from both the main road and the side road, not very near its empty sign.

When we did find it, we were served No Name bitter and found the pub does have a name, as mentioned in Thomas's poem *Up in the Wind*. But the proper moniker is the Pub With No Name, or No-No's to local youth. Let the signboard stay at the bottom of the pond where it had been thrown, long before 1914.

Curiously, the long aversion to having a proper pub name isn't at all unusual. There is the **House Without a Name** at Colchester and another at Bolton. There is a **Nobody Inn**, London N1, and another at Doddiscombsleigh, near Exeter, Devon, continuing a long line of corny inn jokes, the **No Place** at Plymouth and Gosport, and **Nowhere**, also at Plymouth. Dunkling and Wright in their excellent book *A Dictionary of Pub Names* say that the brewery explained this last by saying that a man, asked where he had been all day, could truthfully say Nowhere … If that didn't work he could be in the **Doghouse**, Kennington, London. Or drinking in **Moderation**, Reading, or with **Temperance**, Fulham.

ECCENTRIC ENGINEERING

Floating a boatload of goods down a river to save carrying them must have made sense from early times, but in the past few centuries engineers have carried the concept to absurd heights.

Fancy, for example, cruising 120ft *above* the River Dee near Llangollen, your hand trailing off the edge of the boat over the sheer drop as you cruise along for more than 1,000ft. That this is possible on the superb **Pontcysyllte Aqueduct** (Travel: page 250) is due to the brilliant engineer Thomas Telford (1757–1834), who completed the iron trough-on-stone arches marvel as early as 1805. It has a towpath and railing on one side, but on the other just plunges away.

Further along the same Shropshire Union Canal can be found another great aqueduct at **Chirk**, 710ft long, over the River Ceiriog. A railway viaduct runs parallel to this one.

What about a section of canal, 234ft long, up in the air, that can swing sideways through 90° complete with water, a boat floating on it, and, if you will, a bargee sitting on the roof smoking his pipe? This sounds like an idea that wouldn't hold water, but can be seen at the **Barton Swing Aqueduct** at Barton-on-Irwell, west of Manchester. Opened in 1894, it replaced an earlier stone aqueduct on the aptly named Bridgewater Canal to allow ships to pass beneath on the then new Manchester Ship Canal. The swing section moves slowly, as it weighs 1,500 tons when full of water.

Swinging a canal sideways is impressive enough, but upwards would be a fine trick. This can be seen in another ingenious contraption which has been restored to full working order – the **Anderton Boat Lift** (Travel: page 248), 2½ miles northwest of Northwich, Cheshire. The extraordinary-looking device can lift two canal boats at a time, in a pair of enormous caissons full of water, from the River Weaver up to the Trent and Mersey Canal. It looks as though it shouldn't work – but it has, since 1875, and has been fully restored, as befits the first one in the world. Even more eccentric is the enormous **Falkirk Wheel** near the Scots town, which raises up to six boats at a time from a canal to an aqueduct.

Raising canal boats the traditional way is taken to extremes on the Worcester and Birmingham Canal, which lifts boats 425ft from the River Severn to Birmingham. The 58 locks include 30 non stop at **Tardebigge**, the world's greatest narrowboat flight of locks (Travel: page 251). The not-so-long-ago derelict Kennet and Avon Canal has a splendid flight of 29 locks at Caen Hill near **Devizes**, Wiltshire, and the Caledonian Canal near **Fort William**, in the Scottish Highlands, has another set known as Neptune's Staircase which will get you from the sea towards Loch Ness.

Canal builders sometimes plunged their watery tunnels as deep as coal mines. 'Legging' boats – using your feet on the tunnel roof and sides while lying on your back on the

boat – was commonplace on the canal system, even on Britain's longest **Standedge Tunnel** on the Huddersfield Narrow Canal between Oldham and Huddersfield in Yorkshire. At 5,415yd long, it is also the highest canal tunnel, at around 640ft above sea level, and besides being worked mostly by narrowboat people's sturdy legs, had certain odd features. It opens out into large natural caverns at points – little suspected by walkers on the Pennine Way long-distance footpath above – and the Leeds–Manchester railway tunnel was built just above it, linked by sloping ventilation shafts. So in the days of steam the already eerie interior would suddenly be filled with smoke, steam, the distant thunder of wheels and ghostly whistles.

BRUNEL'S SCHEME FOR
SUCKERS AND A BIT OF A BLOW

One of the great Victorian engineer Isambard Kingdom Brunel's more crackpot schemes – and he had plenty – was the idea of sucking trains down tubes by pumping out the air ahead of them

To do this full scale might have been expensive but Brunel (1806–59) hit upon the idea of a piston being sucked along a pipe between the railway lines, and this pulling the train. To the rather obvious difficulty that air would leak in along the slot where the piston was connected to the train, Brunel countered with the idea of a greased leather flap. Pumping stations would be spaced along the track, and the carriages, with no need for a locomotive, would be sucked along.

Amazingly, Brunel persuaded the South Devon Railway to adopt this **'Atmospheric Railway'** for the steeply graded route between Newton Abbot and Plymouth, thought to be too much for the steam engines of the 1840s. Even more astonishingly, it occasionally worked, and in 1847 a train of 28 tons reached 68mph, a very high speed for the day. More often, though, the system failed to work at all.

Several of the pumping stations survive to bear witness to this weird venture, including one at Starcross where there's an Atmospheric Railway pub with a picture of a grumpy Brunel. A century and a half down the line, the verdict is: the whole idea sucks.

Another crackpot scheme that was built against all common sense involved blowing rather than sucking trains: George Bennie's 1930s **railplane**, a cigar-shaped carriage with aircraft propellers fore and aft, was supposed to run suspended from an impossibly complicated gantry above existing railway lines. The existing track was supposed to carry

236

heavy goods, while railplanes sped passengers and mail at 300mph. Bennie (1892–1957) paid for a demonstration line at Milngavie, near Glasgow, which opened in July 1930. The machine never reached anything like the predicted speeds, despite the great noise of thrashing the air, and World War II put paid to Bennie's dreams.

THE UGLY 'PTERODACTYLS' ON TEES

That roads can swing, lift, plunge into hills and across valleys is not so surprising, but a highway bridge high across a river where the road deck is missing except for one small section? Such a contraption is the **Middlesbrough Transporter Bridge** (Travel: page 250), still in use and indeed floodlit since the Cleveland community decided that if you must have a huge steel device dominating your town, you might as well make a virtue of necessity. The road section moves back and forth with cars and people on it, using an unlikely system of wires and trolleys running on a huge gantry.

The aim of transporter bridges is to cross a river without obstructing shipping, although the intermittent nature of the road traffic makes it more like a ferry service on wires than a regular bridge. There were others – including a large one at **Newport**, south Wales – but the Middlesbrough one is still part of the road system. The Newport bridge has been restored and trips can be enjoyed across the River Usk.

Elegant the Middlesbrough bridge isn't to most eyes, being likened by one writer to 'the fossilised skeletons of a couple of long-legged prehistoric pterodactyls, heads bent aggressively across the Tees'. Yet it has survived a collision with a steamer – 'the bridge was moving, honest, Skipper' – and a German bomb on the car deck, to remain a useful commuting route across the Tees.

Transportation bridges, on the other hand, abound in Dorset. There are a number of bridges in the county, such as at Wool (Travel: page 251) or Sturminster Newton, where cast-iron signs still threaten anyone defacing or damaging them with transportation – to Australia, that is. This might seem to offer a bargain trip to Bondi Beach, but transportation was actually to a penal colony where life was short and brutish. Return tickets were not available.

GHOSTS, A DEAD HORSE, SUICIDES AND A VIRGIN VIADUCT

Britain having virtually invented inventions – there's a village called New Invention in Staffordshire – the landscape is littered with fascinating railway relics, many of them disused, as nearby traffic jams testify. The most dramatic of these are the **great viaducts**, such as at Meldon, Devon; Chappel, Suffolk (7 million bricks); Welwyn or Digswell, Hertfordshire (100ft high, 13 million bricks); Conisbrough, Yorkshire; Lockwood, Huddersfield; and Harringworth, Northamptonshire, the longest in the British countryside at 1,275yd and God knows how many million bricks.

Trackworkers insist that the seventh pier of the spooky **Cynghordy Viaduct** in Dyfed, between Llandovery and Builth Road, is haunted. One of the children of the contractor Richard Hattersley was killed there during construction. Another allegedly haunted viaduct that contains a macabre secret is the horseshoe-curved **Glenfinnan Viaduct** (Travel: page 249) on the Mallaig Extension of the beautiful West Highland Line. The viaduct was a radical experiment by 'Concrete Bob' McAlpine (1847–1934) but during construction in 1900, the story goes, a horse and cart fell through planks into one of the hollow piers. So as you round the curve at the foot of impossibly beautiful mountains, there is a dead horse, head downwards, sealed beneath you. Or so the legend goes, unlike the clearly fictional flying Ford Anglia car that pursues a train round this viaduct in the film *Harry Potter and the Chamber of Secrets*.

The 'Virgin Viaduct' at Tadcaster was built for trains that really never came. Britain's most elegant viaduct, however, is surely that crossing the Ouse at **Balcombe** in West Sussex (Travel: page 249). Built in 1840 for the London and Brighton Railway, the 92ft-high brick arches are crowned by a stone balustrade and – a touch of genius – each end is flanked by a pair of Italianate pavilions. The Ouse viaduct has a secret splendour invisible from trains – its pierced brick arches give an extraordinary cathedral-like vista to the walker in the valley beneath.

Mention elegance and bridge in the same breath and many will recall that the great Isambard Kingdom Brunel (1806–59) threw the truly dramatic 720ft-span **Clifton Suspension Bridge** across the Avon Gorge in Bristol (Travel: page 249). Actually, it was not quite that straightforward. Brunel *did* win a competition to design it at the age of only 24, the young upstart competing against the great Thomas Telford among others. Work began in 1836 but was dogged by financial problems. Others had to finish it in 1864, five years after Brunel's death.

Notorious for suicides, the bridge bears notices from the Samaritans begging people to desist. A macabre detail is that, as the bridge stands at

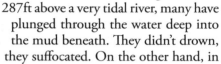

287ft above a very tidal river, many have plunged through the water deep into the mud beneath. They didn't drown, they suffocated. On the other hand, in 1885 one despairing lovelorn lady, Sarah Henley, wearing a hooped crinoline, was saved by the parachute-like billowing of her undergarments and picked up by a rowing boat. There is a good case for making all depressed people wear crinoline dresses.

If, after this, you can still bear to contemplate crossing the Clifton Bridge, you might like to consider halfway across that the chains holding it up were not new but were secondhand from Brunel's old Hungerford Bridge across the Thames in London, demolished in 1861 to make way for a railway bridge into Charing Cross.

One bridge Brunel did live to see – but only just – is the remarkable **Royal Albert Bridge** at Saltash (Travel: page 250). The quixotic engineer faced two contradictory demands in leaping the Tamar estuary between Devon and Cornwall. First there was a probably excessive requirement from the Admiralty for a 100ft clearance above high water for warships, and secondly the Cornwall Railway demanded that he make it as cheap as possible. The result, for only £225,000 and as daringly unorthodox as ever, was two enormous wrought-iron tubes with the world's only railway suspension bridge hung beneath. Somehow the whole 733ft-long bridge was erected at this great height by floating it out at high tide then building enormous stone piers beneath, as it was jacked up in time for Prince Albert to open it in 1859.

By then, Brunel was dying, and had to be drawn over the bridge on a special flat truck with a bed on it – gaining much the best view. In the end, it was his memorial, not Albert's, for Brunel's name is proudly borne in huge letters on the Devon side. His bridge totally dominates the small town of Saltash and has not been diminished one jot by the modern road bridge alongside. Could it be, then, that bridge builders are given a kind of immortality denied those who must just pay the ferryman across the River Styx of the underworld?

The answer can be found in **Hammersmith parish church**, beneath the thundering A4 flyover in west London (Travel: page 249). A memorial tablet on the wall to W Tierney Clark, who died in 1852, bears a detailed picture of Hammersmith Suspension Bridge and the fine words: 'The great suspension bridge at Pesth in Hungary, those at Hammersmith and Shoreham, and many other works attest to his talent, perseverance and skill and are lasting monuments to his fame.' Yet a close look at the bridge on his tomb shows that it is *not* the current elegant **Hammersmith suspension bridge**, clearly dated in its arches 1887, but an earlier one which Bazalgette's version replaced. As far as the throng crossing on that road every morning and night is concerned, W Tierney Clark's fame is all but extinguished – so much water under the bridge.

In fact I'd recommend a good walk about this part of Hammersmith and across the bridge, with full details in *Eccentric London*. Let me briefly say here that the church offers not only the tomb of the man who built the first bridge and joined Buda and Pest, as mentioned above, but also a **heart burial** (see page 168), and the grave of two workmen killed at the funeral of a wronged Princess of Wales, Caroline of Brunswick (1768–1821), on the northeast corner beside the main road.

It is odd after all that to find that a little-known bridge-like structure built by W Tierney Clark (1783–1852) does exist this side of Budapest – in fact at the other end of the Thames – and a suitably bizarre story is attached to its opening. It is the **Gravesend Town Pier**, which has somehow stood since its opening in 1834 and is thus the world's oldest cast-iron pier. It was built as a terminal for day-trippers coming by boat from London to what was then a resort that hoped to become a kind of Brighton-on-Thames.

However, this cut out the lucrative trade of the watermen, the taxi drivers of their day, who used to row out and meet the ships to take people in at 4*d* a go. They were angry that the pier would let people land or embark for just 1*d*. They rowed out and attacked the decking, seats and tollbooth on the pier with saws, sledgehammers, axes and crowbars. The authorities were powerless to do anything about it. Only when a rifle regiment from Chatham was called in was the riot put down. Then police could find not one witness to the event, so there was no prosecution.

However, only 15 years later the pier was as redundant as the watermen when the railway arrived in the town, and no-one bothered taking the long river trip any more. After being ignored for a mere 150 years, the rusting pier was rightly recognised as a gem by Gravesham Council in 2000 and has now been fully restored.

ODDLY, FOR ALL ITS FRILLY ornaments, the elegant Hammersmith Suspension Bridge in west London has three times come within an ace of being blown up. In the 1930s an IRA bomb was fizzing and spluttering when a passer-by threw it in the river; a wartime Nazi bomb fell in the river near the bridge; and then enough IRA Semtex explosive – the largest such bomb yet planted in Britain – intended to blow shreds of the bridge all over west London failed to detonate properly in 1996. A few months later an IRA man was shot dead in a hideout a few hundred yards away. It's well worth a visit, if it's still in one piece. There are some wonderful pubs along the north side.

Hammersmith Bridge

BRITAIN'S MOST UNLIKELY ROAD BUILDER

The greatest roadbuilder of Yorkshire, and a pioneer before Telford and McAdam improved our sorry highways, was not a likely engineer – he couldn't see a thing. **Blind Jack Metcalf** (1717–1810) of Knaresborough had not been able to see since contracting smallpox aged six. But he learned to find his way along roads around Harrogate and

York so well that he became a local guide, both day and night – it made no difference to him, of course. An accomplished horseman, during the 1745 Jacobite rebellion he recruited local men to fight Bonnie Prince Charlie, and went to Scotland to help the fight, being captured by the rebels at one point.

Twenty years later he started building new turnpike roads to high standards, realising that a convex surface and good drainage would avoid most problems. He found a way to build highways across deep bogs by laying them on top of mats and bundles of rushes and heather – a technique later adopted by great railway builders. He ended up building 180 miles of turnpike roads – all while unable to see a thing – and stopped only when canals started taking his trade away. He invented a 'viameter', which allowed him to measure distances along roads and read the result by touch. He'd long since eloped with the daughter of the landlord of the Granby Inn, whom he married, and ended up living until the age of 93 with his granddaughter at nearby Spofforth, where his grave can still be seen.

GATEWAY TO ECCENTRICITY

There has always been an unwritten law, when it comes to British country houses, that no matter how grand, dull, conformist or pretentious the big house of the village was, the lodges could be a tad more wacky. Hundreds of houses had – or 'boasted' as oily estate agents would now say – octagonal, hexagonal or round lodges, with a central finial on the roof like the handle of the lid of a giant butter dish or sugar bowl. Sometimes the chimney pokes out of the middle. The reason for this odd shape was the same as in many similar tollhouses: to give a better view of all comers from all directions.

Lodges often make a point of being over-the-top. **Lanhydrock**, overlooking the River Fowey near Bodmin, Cornwall (Travel: page 249), has one dotted with obelisks and, as the travel writer Eric Newby said, it could well have been the abode of the Red Queen in *Alice in Wonderland*.

Many a peculiar lodge has long lost the house to which it was the entrance. **Rendlesham Hall**, northeast of Woodbridge, Suffolk, has been demolished, but its somewhat eccentric lodges, built in 1790, remain. One, Ivy Lodge, is a sham ruin, a Gothic arch linking what appear to be the ruined bases of massive towers that, in fact, never existed, clad in suitable greenery; while the other, Woodbridge Lodge, a mile or so to the southwest, is an appealing Gothic octagon where the flying buttresses unite to form a central chimney.

One of the most gorgeous gatehouses in the kingdom, **Tixall Gatehouse** near Stafford, is Elizabethan confection at its most charming. The arch through this three-storey pile, which looks more like a sizeable railway station than a mere lodge to another disappeared house, is decorated with armed warriors on the outside and voluptuous ladies on the inside. The gatehouse clock in one of the turrets vaguely strikes the hour, but has no face or hands. As the Landmark Trust which owns the gatehouse, says 'Precise time here seems unimportant, even vulgar.' The Trust bought the Elizabethan ruin without roof, floors or windows, when it was being used as a cattle shelter, for £300 in 1968 and restored it splendidly so people can stay there (see box, page 296).

Another Landmark-owned lodge you can use as a holiday home, **Lynch Lodge** at Alwalton near Peterborough, Cambridgeshire, not only lost its original house but was dismantled and moved to another one, then proceeded to lose the 10-mile driveway it had acquired, so it is now definitely a gateway to nothing. But Lynch Lodge, with its stylish gable, is an elegant thing as befits its previous owners, the poet Dryden's family, whose home at Chesterton was demolished in 1807. The lodge was then taken to pieces and reassembled here by the Fitzwilliam family.

London has a smattering of loopy lodges, many isolated as the sea of banal building has swamped the rural estates they once served. The over-the-top **Stag Lodge**, Wimbledon, was built in 1801 complete with giant lead stag on the roof as a gateway for nearby Spencer House. Scrap-metal thieves take note: the valuable lead stag was replaced in 1987 with a plastic replica.

The Royal Parks of central London feature many a charming example (such as **Duck Island Cottage**, St James's Park, built for birdkeeping in 1840) or a massively ugly one (Hyde Park Corner Lodge, built in 1827 by the 'Iron Duke' as a lodge for Apsley House). However, there is something most odd about the neatly tucked away **Victoria Gate Lodge** in Hyde Park (Travel: page 251). The garden is filled with row upon row of neat little gravestones – they are the graves of 300 pets, a habit started with the Duchess of Cambridge's dog in 1880 until the mini cemetery was full in 1903. The lodge could be described as a gateway to a doggy underworld.

A Scottish lodge with a doggy secret is the private home of **North Lodge**, at Arbirlot Road West, Arbroath (Travel: page 175). This is another isolated survivor set amidst modern buildings, and was formerly a gateway to Hospital Field, a richly carved house now completely separated from it by the main Westway road. North Lodge has a dog carved on the reverse side, but just why is a puzzle. The lodge's owners, Kevin and Sally Milne, say: 'It is believed the dog is Maddie, a hero of a Walter Scott novel, but we want to investigate further.' Here the archway has been imaginatively filled in to make a generous living space. (For a splendid full-blown Scottish canine cemetery, complete with named gravestones, look over the battlements of **Edinburgh Castle** near St Margaret's Chapel.)

DOVECOTES, ROYAL DUNG AND GUNPOWDER

Dovecotes, like lodges, give the eccentric landowner a chance for a little architectural whimsy, without being as useless as a folly. The fact that there are societies devoted to their preservation is not all that surprising, but how many dovecotes there are surely is.

The Yorkshire Dovecote Society lists more than 200 in that county alone, and it is likely the country once boasted 25,000 when birds were a vital source of fresh meat in the winter. Alan Whitworth, a historian of Sleights, near Whitby, North Yorkshire, and an enthusiastic founder member of the society, says, 'The dovecote is the Cinderella of vernacular architecture. They are functional yet so diverse, they can be weird and wonderful, even grandiose. There would be 80–90 good dovecotes in Yorkshire.'

Some are huge dove cities, such as one at **Temple Newsam** near Leeds (Travel: page 251), which housed 1,200 pairs of birds in a five-storey structure. The hundreds of nesting holes – one for each pair – in the 18th-century dovecote were rediscovered when partitions put up to make the dovecote into a cottage in the 1920s were stripped away. Now it is run by Leeds Council and can be seen by visitors to the adjacent rare breeds centre. A more modern and more modest dovecote, fully occupied, stands nearby.

Alan Whitworth adds: 'They were a vital source of fresh meat in the days when all livestock except breeding pairs had to be slaughtered for the winter. It wasn't until the root vegetables arrived in the Agricultural Revolution that this became unnecessary. But the dovecotes were a valued source of fertiliser and of guano – pigeon droppings – which was a vital ingredient of gunpowder, and which was therefore the property of the king. Some villages had one dovecote for every two houses.'

In Scotland the importance of dovecotes can hardly be overestimated. Fife alone had 360 housing 36,000 birds as late as the 18th century. The birds were a severe nuisance to nearby farmers and King James VI of Scotland passed a law which said: 'No person should build a pigeon house who had not land around it or within two miles which yielded ten chalders of victuals.'

Historic Scotland has the care of two splendid isolated dovecotes besides the many attached to castles and great houses. One circular 'beehive'-style dovecote is, helpfully, in Dovecot Road, Corstorphine in **Edinburgh** (Travel: page 249), and the other, the elegant gabled 16th-century **Tealing Dovecot**, is near Dundee in Angus (Travel: page 251). For its admission price (nothing), it includes an Iron Age earth house. National Trust for Scotland also has several dovecotes in its care, including the curious-sounding **Phantassie Doocot** at Preston Mill in Lothian (Travel: page 250). It's a 16th-century lodging for 500 discerning doves and an extremely strange beehive-shaped building.

Dovecotes were not solely a northern phenomenon – they were once even more common further south. Residents of Worcester have two splendid dovecotes on their doorstep, one at **Hawford** (Travel: page 249), three miles north of the city, east of A449, and at **Wichenford** (Travel: page 251), five miles northwest, north of B4204. Both are, appropriately for the area, timber-framed in black-and-white style, and both are opened by the National Trust from Easter to October. In the same county at **Hill Croome**, three miles east of Upton on Severn, a possibly unique cruck-framed 15th-century dovecote stands next to the church.

There is a truly splendid round, tiered dovecote with cruciform arrow slits at Bemerton Farm in Wiltshire, solidly built to the instructions of a homesick Russian countess. Another vast dovecote at tiny **Willington**, near Bedford (Travel: page 251), is lined with boxes for 1,500 birds. A Cornish dovecote in National Trust hands is the medieval one at the remarkable **Cotehele House** (Travel: page 249) at St Dominick near Saltash, Cornwall. And not so far west, a superbly sited ruined dovecote stands above the prosperous little town of **Bruton**, near Shepton Mallet, Somerset.

What looks like Britain's daftest dovecote is in fact an extraordinary henhouse at **Vauxhall Farm** on the Tong estate on the Shropshire/

Staffordshire border. The pyramid dubbed the Egyptian Aviary stands about 20ft high and was inscribed with decidedly odd exhortations to the chickens, most now eroded past legibility, such as 'Scratch before you eat', 'Better come out of the way love', 'Live and let live' and 'Teach your granny'. It is part of a collection of peculiar buildings erected by Victorian eccentric George Durant in the 1840s, including another pyramid for pigs and a pulpit from which he could harangue passers-by.

THESE PEOPLE SHOULD BE LOCKED UP

Town drunks, loose women, village idiots and petty criminals used to be thrown into village lock-ups. Today, more respectable types are drawn to the remaining miniature prisons, and they have set up the Village Lock-up Association to preserve those containers of erstwhile unhappiness which have happily survived.

There's a prettily located one beside the pond at **Shenley**, near St Albans, Hertfordshire (Travel: page 250), inscribed (as many were) with an admonishing message: in this case 'Be sober, be vigilant'.

At **Wheatley**, near Oxford, a rare pyramid lock-up survives (Travel: page 177). In picturesque Pangbourne, Berkshire, on the Thames near Reading, there's a pleasing pointed-roof red-brick one that looks as though it has been lopped off a French chateau (Travel: page 250). The word 'Vigilante' is carried on the weather vane, and its massive oak door has heavy bolts. On the outside – of course. Though visible over a garden fence, the lock-up is not accessible because it's now just a garden tool shed for the house once owned by Kenneth Grahame, author of *The Wind In The Willows*. Perhaps Mr Toad could have been locked up in such a place after his motoring misbehaviour.

Not far away from Pangbourne, at **Aldermaston**, another lock-up survives behind the Hind's Head pub. It has been padlocked since its last drunken occupant burnt himself to death, his cries unheard, in the 1860s.

Swanage, in Dorset (Travel: page 251), has a splendid, suitably inscribed survivor near the town hall ('erected for the prevention of vice and immorality'), and a pepperpot-shaped solid stone one still stands at **Kingsbury Episcopi** (worth a visit for the name, surely), north of Yeovil, Somerset. Bisley, near Stroud, Gloucestershire, has an excellent example too. At **Stratton**, Cornwall, the lock-up seems to have gone – but its heavy door studded with hundreds of nails, including those spelling out the word CLINK, is on display in the church. By far the best view, for the inmates, was from the **Monnow Bridge lock-up** at Monmouth, Gwent (Travel: page 250). This 13th-century archway rising from one of the river bridge piers was a fortified gate, look-out and lock-up, and if it hasn't yet starred in a Robin Hood type of film, it should do. (By the way, when the Monnow divides in two at the bridge does it briefly become the Stereow?).

Perhaps the prettiest mini-jail is that smack in the centre of **Lingfield** (Travel: page 250), close to where Surrey, Kent and Sussex meet. It appears to have its own spire, although this was probably an old town cross to which the lock-up was added. The gnarled old tree wrapped around the Peter Pan-ish structure just adds to the charm, and one feels, contemplating the pleasant surroundings, that the last occupants – poachers thrown in there in 1882 – wouldn't have been entitled to a grouse.

To stay in a holiday lock-up, see page 294.

ECCENTRIC VILLAGES

Britain's most famous fantasy village must be the somewhat surreal **Portmeirion** in Gwynedd, Wales (Travel: page 250), not far from Porthmadog, if only because it starred in the 1960s cult television series *The Prisoner*. It offers a range of Italianate buildings, domes, pillars, arches and statuary which would not have been so odd in Tuscany but which stand out like an orange in a coal heap against the relatively grim slate-and-chapel, teetotal, no-nonsense heritage of Welsh Wales. As Gwyn Thomas said, 'There are still parts of Wales where the only concession to gaiety is a striped shroud.'

In 1926 the brilliant young Welsh architect Bertram Clough Williams-Ellis (1883–1978) bought a rambling house in this delightful spot at

the top of Cardigan Bay. He spent the next half century building this Welsh nirvana, importing unwanted bits of architecture from around the world to create surprising vistas of a stately pleasure dome amidst the rhododendron-clad grounds.

Portmeirion offers world-class pottery, while the immediate area is riddled with great little steam trains (particularly the unforgettable Ffestiniog), somehow saved from the heyday of slate mining, and it is also near the majestic ruined Harlech Castle.

Less well known but also worth examining is **Thorpeness**, Suffolk (Travel: page 251), which was started a little earlier, in 1908, when Glencairn Stuart Ogilvie inherited an estate there and started to build an upmarket holiday village. A lake called the Meare was created with dozens of little follies on islands and inviting creeks to explore, plus whimsical notices such as 'Beware of the Crocodiles' and 'Peter Pan's Property', but then Ogilvie was a friend of Pan's creator Sir J M Barrie.

You can still hire rowing boats on the Meare. Architecturally, Ogilvie let his penchant for pseudo-Tudor run wild in black-and-white beams, with strange towers and dovecotes here and there. His wittiest gesture must be the **House in the Clouds**, a glorious sham, really a water tower. Some will say today it's like Disneyland, but of course it's the other way round. Disney is a huge, clever corporation which to some extent vacuums up, blandifies and brilliantly repackages the genius and whims of original eccentrics, with its own creative spin in a simplified, synthetic form to make billions of dollars. Either you like the product or you don't but here and there in the backwaters lurk the fascinating originals, warts and all.

TRAVEL INFORMATION

ANDERTON BOAT LIFT, 2½ miles northwest of Northwich, Cheshire CW9 6FW ☎ 01606 786777 ✆ 01606 353534
🚗 From M6 J20, M56 west for one junction, south and then west on A559, Anderton is signed on left. Look out for Lift Lane 🚂 Nearest station: Northwich

BALCOMBE VIADUCT, Sussex RH16 1XP 🦶 01273 292599

🚗 From London M25, M23 to J10 then west on A264 and immediately take B2036 south (left) to Balcombe. Viaduct is on right (west) of lane to Haywards Heath before (north of) Borde Hill Gardens (signposted) 🚂 Balcombe, from London Victoria

CLIFTON SUSPENSION BRIDGE, Bristol BS8 3PA 🖥 www.cliftonbridge.org.uk 🦶 0333 321 0101

🚗 From M4 J19 or M5 J17 follow signs for city centre then Clifton 🚂 Bristol Temple Meads from London Paddington

COTEHELE HOUSE, St Dominick, near Saltash, Cornwall PL12 6TA ☎ 01579 351346

🚗 On west bank of the Tamar, 14 miles from Plymouth via Saltash Bridge; 2 miles east of St Dominick, 4 miles from Gunnislake (turn at St Ann's Chapel) 🚂/🚗 Calstock, 1½ miles (signposted from station); bus First 190 from Plymouth summer Sundays

DEACON BRODIE'S TAVERN, Royal Mile, Edinburgh EH1 2NT ☎ 0131 225 6531 🦶 0131 473 3800

🚗 The Royal Mile is best tackled on foot, and leads from Holyroodhouse near Waverley station to the unmissable Edinburgh Castle at the top of the hill 🚂 Edinburgh Waverley

EDINBURGH CORSTOPHINE DOVECOT, EH12 7LE 🦶 0131 225 3858

🚗 Off A8 between city centre and bypass 🚂 South Gyle station, two stops from Edinburgh Waverley

GLENFINNAN VIADUCT, near Mallaig, West Highland Line PH37 4LT 🦶 01687 462170

🚗 On A830 to Mallaig from Fort William, reached by A82 from Glasgow 🚂 Glenfinnan, on Glasgow–Mallaig line

HAMMERSMITH BRIDGE AND MONUMENT, London W6 9DL

🚗 On A306 just south of A4 flyover, (a continuation of M4) Ⓔ/🚗 District, Piccadilly and Metropolitan lines, or Hammersmith bus station

HAWFORD DOVECOTE, Hawford, Worcestershire WR3 7SG ☎ 01527 821214

🚗 3 miles north of Worcester, ½ mile east of A449 🚂/🚗 Worcester Foregate Street 3 miles; then bus First 303 to Hawford Lodge, ¼ mile walk

LANHYDROCK LODGE, Bodmin, Cornwall PL30 5AD ☎ 01208 265950 🦶 01208 76616

🚗 Signed off A38 Exeter (M5)–Bodmin road near Bodmin 🚂/🚗 Bodmin Parkway on main London Paddington–Penzance line

LINGFIELD LOCK-UP, Surrey RH7 6HA 🕻 01342 410121
🚗 Just north of East Grinstead, reached from London and M25 J6 via A22
🚂/🚗 Lingfield station, London Victoria–East Grinstead line

MIDDLESBROUGH TRANSPORTER BRIDGE, TS2 1PL 🕻 01642 245432
🚗 From A1(M) near Darlington, A66(M) and A66 round Darlington
🚂 Middlesbrough (from London King's Cross, change at Darlington)

MONNOW BRIDGE LOCK-UP AND WATCHTOWER, Monmouth, Gwent
NP25 3XA 🕻 01600 713899
🚗 From M5 J8, west on M50, then A40

NORTH LODGE, Arbroath, Angus
See Fraser Mausoleum, page 175

PANGBOURNE LOCK-UP, Berkshire RG8 7BB 🕻 0118 956 6226
🚗 From M4 J12, go southwest a mile to Theale, then left (north)
to Pangbourne on A340. The lock-up is up the hill to the left as you
enter village, but remember it is a private house (in garden on right)
🚂 From London Paddington to Pangbourne

PHANTASSIE DOOCOT, Preston Mill, East Linton, Lothian EH40 3DS
☎ 01620 860426 🕻 0131 473 3800
🚗 Off A1 at East Linton, 23 miles east of Edinburgh

PONTCYSYLLTE AQUEDUCT, Llangollen LL20 7TG 🕻 01978 860828
🚂 Nearest stations: Ruabon or Chirk 🚗 From M6 J10A, M54 then A5

PORTMEIRION, Gwynedd LL48 6ER ☎ 01766 512981
▨ www.portmeirion-village.com
🚗 From M6 J20, use M56 and M53 to Chester, A55 along north Wales
coast to Bangor then A487 to Porthmadog 🚂 Porthmadog, reached by
superb scenic coastal branch line from Machynlleth, and thence from
England. Or from North Wates Coast line via branch to Blaenau Ffestiniog
and then narrow-gauge steam railway through hills

ROYAL ALBERT BRIDGE, Saltash, Cornwall PL12 5LU 🕻 01752 266030
🚗 Next to A38 bridge into Cornwall, from Plymouth. Parking nearby
🚂 Saltash from London Paddington

SHENLEY LOCK-UP, Hertfordshire WD7 9DX 🕻 01727 864511
🚗 Shenley is 3 miles from M25 J22 via B556 and B5376

SWANAGE LOCK-UP, Dorset BH19 2LY ☎ 01929 422885
🖳 www.swanage.com
🚗 From London/M25, take M3 to end, M27 and A31 west to
Winterbourne Zelston, go south on B3075 through Wareham
🚂/🚌 Nearest station: Wareham on London Waterloo–Weymouth
line, then bus 142, 143, 144. Through trains coming soon

TARDEBIGGE FLIGHT OF LOCKS, Worcestershire B97 7QL ☎ 01527 831809
🚗 From M5 J5, take A38 northwards to Bromsgrove, then A448 right
(east) towards Redditch and canal crosses under road after about 2 miles.
Locks to southwest. Best seen from minor roads or from towpath
🚂 Bromsgrove, from Birmingham New Street

TEALING DOVECOT, Angus DD4 0RD ☎ 01382 527527
🚗 Off the Forfar A90 road, about 2 miles out of Dundee

TEMPLE NEWSAM DOVECOTE AND RARE BREEDS CENTRE, Leeds,
West Yorkshire LS15 0AD ☎ 0113 264 5535 ☎ 0113 242 5242
🚗 From M1 J46 take A63 towards Leeds

THORPENESS, near Aldeburgh, Suffolk IP16 4NH ☎ 01728 453637
🚗 From London/M25, A12 to Friday Street beyond Woodbridge,
right on A1094 to Aldeburgh, then coast road north 1$\frac{1}{2}$ miles

TRANSPORTATION BRIDGES, Dorset. Several locations including Wool B
H20 6BL ☎ 01929 552740
🚂 Wool, from London Waterloo

VICTORIA GATE LODGE, Hyde Park, Bayswater Road, London W1 3JH
🚗 Off Bayswater Road 🚂/🚌 Nearest tube Lancaster Gate (Central Line)
and many buses

WICHENFORD DOVECOTE, Wichenford, Worcestershire WR6 6XY
☎ 01527 821214
🚗 5$\frac{1}{2}$ miles north west of Worcester, north of B4204

WILLINGTON DOVECOTE, near Bedford ☎ 01234 838278 ☎ 01234 215226
🚗 Off A603 Bedford–Sandy (for A1) road

MONUMENTALLY ECCENTRIC

ATLANTIC OCEAN

Orkney Islands

Ring of Brogar Stone Circle

Thurso

Callanish Standing Stones

Isle of Lewis

Wolf Monument, Sutherland

Isle of Skye

Inner Hebrides

Sueno's Stone

Inverness

Stones of Clava

Aberdeen

SCOTLAND

Island of Mull

Islay

NORTH SEA

N

0 — 80 km
0 — 50 miles

Arran

Glasgow

EDINBURGH

The Twelve Apostles

Dumfries Milestone

Newcastle upon Tyne

ATLANTIC OCEAN

Laggangairn Standing Stones

Carlisle

Long Meg & Her Daughters

Wren's Egg

Nine Standards

Castlerigg

Middlesbrough

Isle of Man

'Iron Mad' Wilkinson's Monument

ENGLAND

York

IRISH SEA

Leeds

Bradford

Airship Disaster, Elloughton

Hull

NORTH SEA

Anglesey

Liverpool

Manchester

Sheffield

Grimsby

Captain Skinner's Obelisk, Holyhead

Alleluia Monument, Mold

Gelert's Tomb, Beddgelert

Arbor Low Stone Circle

Nottingham

Derby

Norwich

Cardigan Bay

Wolverhampton

Birmingham

Coventry

Thomas Clarkson Obelisk, Wisbech

Fishguard

WALES

Rollright Stones

Eleanor Crosses Northamptonshire

Cambridge

Ipswich

Plane Crash, Wolvercotes

Swansea

CARDIFF

White Horse, Uffington

Oxford

Whipsnade Lion

Slavery, Balloon & Zeppelin Monuments

Cleopatra's Needle, Embankment

LONDON

Bristol Channel

Bristol

Death Railway, Woking

White Lady Milestone, Esher

Fireplates Obelisk, Putney

Mark Bolan's Tree, Barnes

Wellington's Obelisk

Red Signpost, Winterbourne Zelston

Rebus Milestone, Maresfield

ATLANTIC OCEAN

Cerne Abbas Giant

Exeter

Southampton

Portsmouth

White Horse, Folkstone

Nine Maidens

Lymington Obelisk

Yarborough Obelisk, Isle of Wight

Brighton

Long Man of Wilmington

The Hurlers

Tolpuddle Monument

Carn Brea

Merry Maidens

Penzance

ENGLISH CHANNEL

MONUMENTALLY ECCENTRIC

OBSCURE OBSOLETE OBELISKS

Obelisks are wonderfully useless things. Typically tall, tapering four-sided pillars finished with a pyramid on top, they were set up to make a point, mark something, or recall an event or an individual. As these have been totally forgotten in the case of thousands of obelisks tucked away here and there around Britain, it follows that the pillars are mostly useless – except to be hunted down by the incurably curious.

FORGOTTEN STONES AND TALES OF HEROES

However, not all wayside monuments deserve their obscurity. Many dusty, worn-down memorials are worth a second look because they mark something that changed the world.

'Iron Mad' John Wilkinson (1728–1808) was one of the 18th century's great ironfounders and an outspoken enthusiast for the metal that he knew had a far greater future than his contemporaries could comprehend. He was scoffed at for claiming that iron would make a fine boat and defied derision to launch the first one on the River Winster, watched by crowds who expected it to sink like a stone. Of course it didn't, and all the world's ships are descended from that heroic vision. At Lindale, near Grange-over-Sands, Cumbria, can be seen **Wilkinson's obelisk** (Travel: page 270). It is made of iron, of course, as was his coffin.

At Wadesmill in Hertfordshire, forgotten beside a thundering road, there is a monument to an inspiration that led to a worldwide crusade, several wars, including to a large extent the American Civil War (1861–65), and to freedom for millions of oppressed people. It was here, as a small obelisk states, that **Thomas Clarkson** (1760–1846) decided to devote the remainder of his life to abolishing slavery. William Wilberforce, often said to be the driving force behind the abolition of slavery, was, in fact, a latecomer. There's another more elaborate monument at Clarkson's birthplace, at **Wisbech**, Cambridgeshire.

The **Alleluia Monument** near Mold, near Flint, commemorates the defeat of the heathen Picts by early Christians shouting 'Alleluia'. It is an 18th-century obelisk set in a field a mile to the west of the village.

Miles away in Sutherland, the **Wolf Monument** marks another violent turn in history. On the side of the road from Golspie to Helmsdale, south of the bottom of Glen Loth, the stone placed by the Duke of Portland in 1924 records that at this spot the last wolf in the county was slain in 1700. The last wolf on the British mainland was killed in 1743.

For a poignant Welsh wolf story, go to **Beddgelert** in Snowdonia, walk a short way along the banks of the Afon (River) Glaslyn, and look for a mound of stones. This is the grave of Prince Llywelyn's faithful dog Gelert. Llywelyn returned from hunting one day, having left his faithful hound Gelert to guard his infant son in his cradle. He found the cradle upturned, the boy gone and the dog's mouth covered with gore. In his fury, he cut off Gelert's head with one huge blow. Then he discovered a dead wolf nearby, which Gelert had fought to the death to protect the child, who was asleep unharmed under the cradle.

London's simply capital obelisks and their stories

London has its fair share of redundant yet curious obelisks. For example, in 1851 it was ringed by hundreds of Coal Dues obelisks and markers of four different designs to mark a point – you can't avoid the word – on every road, railway or canal 20 miles from St Martin's-le-Grand. It's all the fault of the Great Fire of London in 1666, after which the City of London Corporation was empowered to levy tax on coal or wine brought within a certain distance of London to pay for rebuilding.

In 1851, because of the sprawl of London, an act laid down the 20-mile radius still marked with four types of pillar, post or obelisk, all bearing the City arms or, at least, the crusader shield, red cross on white with a dagger. To complicate matters, some were moved in 1861 to coincide with the boundary of the new Metropolitan Police area, so posts such as that on Watling Street, Radlett, Hertfordshire, still have a function. It marks where the shire Mr Plods take over from the Old Bill of the Met, often, as here, nowhere near the actual county boundary.

More impressive are the 14ft stone **Coal Dues obelisks** such as the one alongside the London–Norwich main line at Chadwell Heath on the boundary of Barking and Havering boroughs; or that beside the main line at Watford, which refers on its inscription to the Coal and Wine Duties Act of 1861 (which must have updated earlier laws) and which demanded 11d (4½ pence in today's coin, but then a week's pay for some) for every ton of coal that rolled past southwards.

Like most taxes dreamt up for a specific purpose, the Coal Dues carried on long after the original point of the obelisks was forgotten, and were finally abolished in 1889, although we have the heritage of splendid Wren churches such as St Paul's to thank them for.

Even the dullest London suburbs are riddled with obelisks, if you know where to look, to testify to the great dramas that once happened there. A misty Sunday morning in Barnet doesn't sound too dramatic, but an obelisk at nearby **Monken Hadley** tells of the desperate struggle of 14 April 1471, when the Earl of Warwick's army during the Wars of the Roses attacked under the cover of mist and drove Edward IV's men right back into Barnet town centre. A swift cavalry counterattack had the Lancastrians retreating, with Warwick caught on foot and slain close to where the obelisk stands. Some 1,500 men died. (The next Tube station to Barnet, Totteridge & Whetstone, being named after the implements discarded there by soldiers sharpening their swords.)

More than 200 years later a hopeless Jacobite rebellion was crushed in 1715 and the Earl of Derwentwater was executed – an obelisk to him stands incongruously in the suburbia of Churchfield Road East, **Acton**.

Nearby quiet Brentford seems just as anxious to stress its blood-soaked history. In **Ferry Lane** by the Thames there's a pillar recalling how Cassivellaunus and his men repelled Julius Caesar and his centurions who were trying to ford the river here in 54BC; *plus* another battle fought by King Edmund 'Ironsides' against the raping and pillaging Danes in 1016; *and* commemorating the Civil War Battle of Brentford in 1642. At the time of writing Ferry Lane is being redeveloped, so the monument has been moved across the main road (Travel: page 270).

Two London obelisks have odd royal connotations. **Cleopatra's Needle** (Travel: page 270), on the Thames Embankment near to Embankment tube, has nothing to do with Queen Cleopatra, but is a fascinating 15th-century BC relic that survived being moved by the Romans in 14BC – just after that first Battle of Brentford. It was brought to England in 1878 in a sort of submarine and was nearly sunk in a storm, only to be covered in pollution and damaged by German bombs after it arrived. Its twin was erected in Central Park, New York, in 1881.

Much more obscure is an obelisk lurking in the woods near **Tibbet's Corner** on the A3 near Putney (Travel: page 270). It tells how David Hartley invited the king and queen to breakfast in 1774 and while they were eating upstairs tried to burn the house down – for which he was richly rewarded. He was voted the then fortune of £2,500 in cash by a grateful parliament and awarded the freedom of the City of London by the Corporation.

The royals, George III and Queen Charlotte, had agreed to Hartley's experiment because he wanted to demonstrate his fireplates which, he claimed, made a fireproof floor. To the great relief of courtiers, he was proved right. George III was yet to become completely mad, but if the fireplates had failed, Britain might have been even more grateful.

When MPs were heroes

Travellers from the Isle of Wight (itself home to an insanely large and superbly sited obelisk to the not very interesting **Earl of Yarborough** on beautiful Bembridge Down; Travel: page 271) are greeted by another well-sited obelisk across the harbour from **Lymington**, Hampshire (Travel: page 271) – a remarkably fine one, looking as if it were built in 1980, not in 1840. It is up a road near the ferry terminal called, helpfully, Monument Lane.

It was built in memory of Admiral Sir Harry Burrard Neale (1765–1840) and details his achievements at sinking or capturing 20 enemy men o' war and also keeping the crew of HMS *San Fiorenzo* loyal during what is euphemistically described on the monument as 'the critical position of the Fleet at the Nore in 1797'. I suspect they meant the worst mutiny the Royal Navy has ever seen. Sir Harry was Lymington's MP for 40 years, and the monument details the war hero's charity at great length:

'He delivered the poor and fatherless and him who had none to help him and caused the widow's heart to sing for joy … His daily walk with God

exemplifying the grace of his Christian charity, above all in the largeness of his charity and the beauty of his humility.'

Not much like most of todays MPs then.

A RAVEN-MAD, WILD-WEST WELSH ECCENTRIC

On a hill above Holyhead harbour on Anglesey (well, on **Holy Island** at the end of Anglesey) stands a rather splendid obelisk, which stands as a memorial to a rather splendid man. **Captain McGregor Skinner** (1760–1832) was the one-eyed, one-armed former naval captain who, in 1793, was captain of the posts on the Holyhead–Dublin mail route.

Very popular as he gave most of his generous pay to the poor, Skinner had but one valuable possession – his wonderfully wise raven. The raven would fly out to sea only when Captain Skinner's boat was coming and land on the deck to greet him. Once, the local story goes, as the boat from Ireland was overdue in murky weather and relatives of those aboard paced the harbour-side worriedly, the raven was seen to leap off its perch and flap out into the mist. One of those waiting was told: 'Don't fret. The Captain will be coming in within the hour. That bird is never wrong.'

Like a lot of the crow family, this raven was more intelligent and more mischievous than he should have been. The raven could say a few words. His favourite trick in Holyhead was to call out local dogs by name, each correctly. When the first dog ran at him, he would take off and repeat this with another dog. Eventually it would hop along the ground, sometimes pretending to have a broken wing, with half the town's dogs trailing, barking furiously behind him. Then he would perch on the edge of the quay and fix them with his beady black eye. The dogs would charge him angrily, and he would flap off into the harbour as they all fell into the water. Then he'd go home for a rest, picking bits of abandoned dogs' food on the way as the stupid animals floundered in the harbour. And a week or two later he would repeat it and the same dumb mutts would end up in the drink again.

257

One of his party pieces, sadly, was the end of him. If he, the raven, was holding forth and someone ignored him, he would land on the man's trouser legs and be dragged along the ground as the man tried to get away. It was supposed to be endearing, but he once tried it on a stranger. The man panicked, drew a gun and shot the raven dead – and nearly shot himself in the foot.

Captain Skinner was heartbroken. His own end was sadly ironic. He campaigned for years for the improvement of the mail packet boats that took the post and passengers across the Irish Sea. Just after he got a petition up about the dangerously rotten woodwork of these vessels, he was returning to Holyhead in 1832 when a large wave washed him and a companion across the deck. They should have been saved by clinging to the ship's rail, but being rotten, it broke and they were drowned.

The grief in Holyhead at the death of the big-hearted skipper was huge. The then enormous sum of £130 was raised, which paid for a marble tablet in the church and the obelisk on the hill – which turned out to be a superb aid to mariners, something Captain Skinner would have approved of.

The Captain had become a great British eccentric, but he was born in what became the United States during his lifetime. Not that he was on the revolutionaries' side. In fact he got his wounds serving in the Royal Navy *against* the rebels, as he saw them, and took part in the storming of forts Lee and Washington, fighting on despite his injuries.

After Skinner's death, the Post Office which had proved incompetent and careless in running the shipping service had its authority taken away as a result of the investigations Skinner had started into the Holyhead mail service, and the Admiralty was put in charge. And the odd thing is that Anglesey is still a good place for ravens. Not so far away, at Newborough, is still the best roost for miles.

One of the best-sited obelisks in Britain must be that on the **Blackdown Hills** in Somerset, devoted to the Duke of Wellington (Travel: page 271). It is 175ft tall and the base is 80ft wide, and if you want to climb it up the internal staircase to a viewing platform – and you can see Wales over the Bristol Channel on a good day – you must ask for the key at nearby Monument Farm. It is a few miles south from Wellington, the town from which the Iron Duke took his title. It is owned by the National Trust and there is free parking and a rather good walk from the car park. Two points (that word again): the stairs might not be repaired by the time you visit, so you may not be allowed to climb to the top; and the rather strange cross section shouldn't be explained to French visitors. It is that of the bayonet used at Waterloo.

MILESTONES IN ECCENTRICITY

Milestones may be apparently less eccentric than obelisks – at least they have a purpose. But those that don't tell you where they are measuring to – or give completely wrong or irrelevant distances – must be considered a little odd.

Many a traveller on the A22 between London and Eastbourne has been puzzled by milestones, such as that beside a pub in **Maresfield**, that show a mileage plus a ribbon tied in a bow and some bells hanging from it. The design is a rebus – a visual pun – spelling out the Bow Bells, the spot in the City of London to which mileages were traditionally measured (see page 255).

The **Brass Crosby Milestone** (Travel: page 270) that is neither brass nor tells accurate mileages from where it is, despite distances shown on it being detailed down to the last foot, can be found in St George's Road, London SE1 outside the Imperial War Museum.

It is named after the lord mayor of London, Brass Crosby (1725–93), who became a national hero in 1771 when he refused parliament's order to jail a printer who dared to report their proceedings in the press. Brass Crosby was thrown into the Tower but public outcry assured his release, and he eventually won his campaign for the free reporting of parliament. The milestone was set up in St George's Circus as a memorial to him, but removed during rebuilding in 1905 to its present site, making the rather precise measurements on it singularly useless.

The present spot may have been chosen because during Crosby's life, the Imperial War Museum was the original Bedlam lunatic asylum (a corruption of Bethlehem giving its name), and Crosby was appointed president of the asylum in 1772, helping the process of reform.

To complicate matters further, the parishioners around St George's Circus built a replica of the Crosby milestone, not near the original site, but at **Brookwood Cemetery** (see Shah Jehan Mosque, page 192) in Surrey where in the 19th century parishioners started to be buried. Now that one has fallen down, but at least it doesn't bear wrong distances to anywhere.

The **White Lady of Esher** in Surrey is one of the most ridiculously over-the-top large milestones in the country and can be found outside Café Rouge at the junction of Portsmouth road and Station Road. It was set up by the Duke of Newcastle, not so much to help travellers on the

Portsmouth Road but to mark his estate. He was fed up with travellers from London missing the turning and ending up in Guildford.

Some milestones dating from the horse-and-carriage age are odd because they give odd distances. One at **Dumfries**, fixed to the side of the Midsteeple in the pedestrianised town centre, from where one might contemplate a day's ride to Castle Douglas or Carlisle, in fact gives the distance to Huntingdon, a town of little global import in Cambridgeshire, hundreds of miles away. (Reader Keith Crowther kindly points out that Malcolm IV of Scotland was also Earl of Huntingdon, so that may be why). Another at **Craven Arms**, Shropshire, shows off somewhat esoteric mileages to 36 places, such as 233 to Newcastle.

CONVICTS AND MARTYRS – AUSSIE LANDMARKS

Australian tourists might pause, ponder and perhaps shudder if they knew the meaning of a couple of wayside monuments, one in pretty Dorset countryside and one near a London tourist honeypot.

On the A31 Dorchester–Wimborne road, at Winterbourne Zelston, is a **red signpost** (Travel: page 271), and many passers-by have little idea why authorities paint this one fingerpost in the county red year after year. The answer lies down the lane to Bloxworth, where, some 100 yards from the signpost, Botany Bay Farm lies on the right. A now-ruined prison-like barn with narrow window slits was used to house prisoners condemned at Dorchester Assizes to transportation to the Botany Bay penal colony in Australia. The ragged prisoners were force-marched the 70-odd miles from Dorchester to the prison fleet at Portsmouth, and this barn, 14 miles from Dorchester, was the first stop. Prisoners were shackled for the night to the massive central post. It was the first night of suffering of many to come, but life was short for many transportees. The sign was red, by the way, so that the illiterate guards could recognise it.

Nearby at **Tolpuddle** (Travel: page 271) can be seen the memorials to the most famous six ever sentenced to transportation – the Tolpuddle martyrs. These six were transported for seven years in 1834 for the crime of forming a prototype trade union to combat poverty and a cut in wages after a bad harvest. This was at a time when children in rural Britain could still die of hunger during famines. The six, led by George Loveless, met under the Martyrs' Oak, as it is now known, outside the church, and the memorial cottages at the west end of Tolpuddle also mark their sacrifice. At the other end of the village a small Methodist chapel dedicated to their memory bears their names carved on its entrance, plus a moving passage from George Loveless's defence:

> 'We have injured no man's reputation, character, person or property. We were uniting together to preserve ourselves, our wives and our children from utter degradation and starvation.'

An annual march and street fair in July recalls their martyrdom.

The other place to recall those bleak days is right outside the Tate Britain Gallery on **Millbank**, on the Thames in London (Travel: page 271). A squat bollard marks the spot where thousands of prisoners clanking their chains passed 'Down Under' in a special tunnel under the road from Millbank Prison – where the gallery now stands – to barges that carried them downriver to ships waiting to take them to the other side of the world. This sad traffic ended in 1867.

Dorset, famed more for bloody, ruthless 'justice' down the centuries than for today's cream teas, also has excellent statues in Dorchester by Dame Elisabeth Frink of the Dorset Martyrs. But these martyrs are Catholics, who were burnt and hanged for their faith during the post-Reformation years. Enjoy your scone…

SHRINES BY THE WAYSIDE

When the funeral of Diana, Princess of Wales, in 1997 followed a route through north London up the M1 to Northampton, many were surprised by the crowds and flowers that lined every available bridge. But these were soon all gone, with surprisingly few permanent monuments, unlike the tributes to a dead queen who passed this way, in the opposite direction, 600 years previously.

The grieving Edward I, whose beloved queen Eleanor (1241–90) died at Harby in Nottinghamshire, didn't just order one monument but a whole set of **Eleanor Crosses**, intricate Gothic freestanding spires to be erected at every spot where the funeral cortège stopped for a night. Only three of the original dozen elegant and richly carved spires survive – at Geddington and Hardingstone, near Northampton, and at Waltham Cross, Hertfordshire. The latter place is named after its Eleanor Cross, as is London's Charing Cross. But the soaring spire outside the station of that name is in fact a 19th-century reproduction.

One of London's oddest other memorials is a tree in Barnes. It is the one pop star **Marc Bolan** (1947–77) hit in his Mini, causing his early death aged 29. The flowers, photographs and loving messages tied *daily* to his tree make this London's most enduring unofficial memorial. The effect is a little spoilt by the crash barrier in front of the tree, but given its history, I suppose that's understandable (Travel: page 271).

There is no footpath on that side of this fast and narrow road, so view from the opposite side. Locals once vandalised the T-Rex star's memorial, leading to the brilliant if verging on bad taste headline 'Tree wrecks' on Nigel Dempster's diary page.

CRANKS, PIONEERS AND HEROES OF THE SKIES

The adventures, tragedies and insanities of Britain's early aeronautical eccentrics and adventurers can be traced through the landscape even today, thanks to various monuments. Many of these, including the earliest, are in Hertfordshire.

The first balloon flight in Britain ended in 1784 at **Standon Green End**, in a field west of the main road about three miles north of Ware, Hertfordshire. A marker stone surrounded by railings carries a brass plaque engraved with a picture of a balloon and declaring:

'Let Posterity Know and Knowing Be Astonished That on the 15th Day of September 1784, Vincent Lunardi of Lucca in Tuscany, the First Aerial Traveller In Britain Mounting From The Artillery Ground in London and Traversing the Regions of the Air for 2 hours and 15 minutes In this Spot Revisited the Earth …'

Lunardi's cat accompanied him on this flight. The monument is on private land.

Not far from this spot of ballooning pilgrimage is another monument, to what happened when the Germans developed the idea more than a century later. During World War I, zeppelins attacked the area – Hertford was blitzed in October 1915 with great loss of life and property. Men, women and children died, seemingly defenceless against the merciless monster in the skies. German magazines gleefully published illustrations of British towns burning beneath the great airships, which hovered out of range of gunners, so later claims about Germany being 'forced' to bomb civilians are somewhat hollow.

But airships filled with explosive hydrogen proved spectacularly vulnerable to newfangled aircraft firing incendiary bullets, and in September 1916 the first zeppelin to be shot down over England fell in flames at Cuffley near Hertford, after being attacked by Lt William Leefe Robinson of the Royal Flying Corps. A month later another was shot down nearby at Potters Bar. Leefe Robinson became an instant national hero. He was awarded the Victoria Cross and a fine monument to him was built at **Cuffley** (Travel: page 271), while a pub called the Leefe Robinson at Harrow Weald, Middlesex also recalls the feat. But the aviator himself, captured on the Western Front, died soon after returning from prison camp at the end of the war.

Fixed-wing aviation was growing up fast but Leefe Robinson's courage was remarkable because Britain's first, faltering, powered flight took place less than ten years before, on 16 October 1908, at Cove Common in Hampshire. The aircraft was British Army No 1 and the pilot the American **'Colonel' Sam Cody** (1867–1913), whose flamboyant aviator's garb of white coat and stetson made him the darling of the British public. Cody was attached to the Army's Balloon School at Aldershot and trying unsuccessfully to demonstrate to British brass hats that aircraft could be used in war.

The secretary of war decided Cody was a crank and would have to continue on his own while the Army attended to serious business such as mounted cavalry. Cody, a popular former cowboy, soldiered on.

Cody was killed in an air crash at **Farnborough**. His official memorial is a tree to which he had tethered his machine for tests in May 1908 before that first powered flight. It is, in fact, a replica of the tree in, appropriately for the industry, aluminium. His real memorial is the vast Royal Aircraft Establishment that sprang up at the common at Farnborough, and the biennial airshows at which all the world's latest aircraft soar over Cody's grave, proving that he was right all along.

A few months later the first all-British powered flight took place on 23 July 1909, when a wooden-frame, paper-wrapped triplane contraption powered by a JAP 9hp motorbike engine took to the air at **Walthamstow Marshes** in East London. Its pilot, **Alliott Verdon Roe** (1877–1958), was also regarded as a dangerous crank and was dissuaded from using various other sites around the country, but on that day he flew 850ft at an altitude of 10ft and a speed of 25mph, despite Leyton Borough Council's attempts to ban him. A blue plaque marking the spot is fixed on a railway arch where the line crosses the River Lea off Lea Bridge Road, Walthamstow, London E10.

More accessible is the aircraft itself, hanging in the **Science Museum**, South Kensington (Travel: page 271), like an impossibly fragile kite, with a Cody 1912 biplane and many other pioneering aircraft. A V Roe went on to found the Avro aircraft factory at Wembley, which made winning aircraft for both world wars, including the dambusting Avro Lancaster bombers. Incidentally, he started painting his name on a shed he rented at Brooklands, Surrey, before moving to Wembley, but failed to leave enough room for the final E – hence Avro.

A year later, on 13 July 1910, the Honourable **Charles Stewart Rolls** (1877–1910), aged 32, co-founder of Rolls-Royce, was the first Briton to be killed flying a plane, not long after making the first return crossing of the English Channel. The crash happened in front of a horrified crowd at a Bournemouth competition for the 'alighting prize' by which early aviators attempted to follow a course and land within a 100ft bullseye. The lettering on Rolls-Royce cars was that day changed to black. Rolls was a little eccentric, and dubbed by his fellow aviator Tommy Sopwith 'the meanest man I know' for his habit of sleeping under his car to avoid having to pay hotel bills.

Back in Hertfordshire, some brave military flyers are commemorated by a pillar at the spot where they crashed in 1912, between Willian and **Great Wymondley** (Great Wymondley being the *little* hamlet near the much greater one of Little Wymondley, of course). A similar monument from the same year may be seen in **Wolvercote**, Oxford. Look on the wall on the right hand side as you drive through the village.

Parachuting, surprisingly perhaps, is about a century older than powered flight, so the courage of its pioneers was all the greater, but there are few monuments to their heroic balloon-based experiments. In 1802, **André-Jacques Garnerin** (1769–1823) made the first parachute descent in Britain, having started the new sport in Paris in 1797. He ascended beneath his balloon from Grosvenor Square, jumped out and landed near the site of today's Marylebone station, to the amazement of onlookers.

Thirty-five years later, **Robert Cocking** (1776–1837), the first Briton to make a successful parachute jump, failed to make the first successful landing. His inverted cone chute collapsed and trailed him to his death in a Kentish field. The first totally successful British parachutist was **John Hampton**, a year after Cocking's death, but it was nearly a century later before the air force fell for the idea.

An almost completely forgotten **airship disaster** is commemorated in a memorial in Elloughton Church, near Hull, Yorkshire (Travel: page 265). On 24 August, 1921, a giant British airship of novel design called the R38 was being tested by the American Navy, to whom it had been sold. When it made some high-speed turns above the River Humber, it split in half and crashed in flames, killing 44 of the 49 crew aboard. According to American reports, the British had equipped the airship's mascot, a kitten called Goldflake, with its own parachute, but not the crew.

BRITAIN'S TEN MOST MAGICAL STANDING STONES

Every tourist comes to Britain having heard of Stonehenge, and quickly finds out that **Avebury** (see page 190) not so far away offers another great circle of stones. But both of these, impressive though they are, have had their once mystical setting spoilt by cars, roads, gift shops and, yes, tourists. Luckily Britain is host to many, many more standing stones and stone circles where the only other visitor apart from you may well be a curly-horned sheep.

1   **NINE MAIDENS** and **MERRY MAIDENS**, Cornwall
☎ 01736 362207 *(Penzance)*
There seems to be confusion about the legend for the **Nine Maidens**, which are one of several rings of stones thus named in Cornwall even when the number clearly isn't nine, but the **Merry Maidens** legend is secure and long-lived and represent a perfect circle of maidens turned to stone for dancing on Sunday. There are two more stones nearby, granite pillars called **the Pipers**, which

were devils who played a tune on a summer Sabbath evening to trick the maidens into dancing. A bolt of lightning came down and petrified the lot. Aubrey Burl, the learned scholar of such stones, records that locals said that two stones dislodged in the mid 19th century returned of their own volition, and that when an attempt was made to plough the field in World War I, the horse dropped dead as the first furrow was started. These are typical of the legends of Celtic stones.

> **NINE MAIDENS**, south of A39 between Wadebridge and St Columb Major, before reaching B3274. **MERRY MAIDENS**, south of B3315, 4 miles southeast of Penzance

2 THE HURLERS, Cornwall ☎ 01208 76616 *(Bodmin)*
This supposedly represents a group of men throwing a ball on the Sabbath who were petrified for their sacrilege.

> On the east edge of Bodmin Moor, near Minions, off B3254

3 THE TWELVE APOSTLES, Dumfries ☎ 01387 253862
A rather special spot, but that name: someone couldn't count to 12, or has someone nicked a stone, and how did the Bronze Age people know the 12 Apostles were going to exist thousands of years later? So what were these stones, put here with such huge effort, really for?

> A couple of miles north of Dumfries on A76, turn left at Holywood following B729 towards Dunscore for 400 yards. Roadside car parking, waymark and a stile over the dyke

4 STONES OF CLAVA, Inverness-shire ☎ 01309 672938
These strange domed cairns surrounded by circles of standing stones are late neolithic. Nearby, **Sueno's Stone**, at Forres near A96, off the road to Findhorn, is judged the most remarkable sculptured stone in Britain and dates from about AD1000. It is a shaft of sandstone carved with battle scenes and has been covered by glass to protect it.

> Near Culloden Battlefield, off B851 which turns northeast from A9 a couple of miles south of Inverness

5 CALLANISH STANDING STONES, Lewis, Western Isles
☎ 01851 703088
In a wild moorland setting, 13 stones stand huddled in groups around what was probably a burial cairn, with rows of stones extending to north, south and in other directions. Atmospheric in

the extreme. There is another stone circle nearby at Siadar on the north coast of Lewis, off A857.

🚗 Beside A858, reached via ferry from Ullapool

6 **NINE STANDARDS**, Cumbria ☏ 017683 71199
There is nothing more spooky than plodding across the boggy mountaintop in the mist and seeing these nine shapes taller than a man, created by God knows whom, loom up suddenly and menacingly and then disappear again in a swirl of cloud.

🚗 On the Pennine watershed to north of B6270 between Kirkby Stephen and Keld

7 **LONG MEG AND HER DAUGHTERS**, Cumbria ☏ 01768 867466
Long Meg was a witch and the other stones her coven. For an absolutely lovely setting nearby, visit **Castlerigg Stone Circle** about 16 miles on the other side of Penrith, going west on A66 just before Keswick. To south of road near Briery.

🚗 North of the road between Little Salkeld and Gamblesby, about seven miles northeast of Penrith

8 **ROLLRIGHT STONES**, Oxfordshire ☏ 01789 868191
Unexpected, somehow, these stones lie in a less bleak setting than usual, and are full of legend. For a start there are said to be 77 stones, but they have never been counted to the same number twice. You try it. The King's Men are a ring of standing stones about 30 yards across, and were supposedly the army of the king, who is now the bent and lonely King Stone some 300 yards away. He was promised a new kingdom by a witch if he could see Long Compton from where he was. Having strained and strained, the king moved up the hill a little and was petrified, as was his army. On a hot summer's night, the stones are said to rush down to a nearby brook to drink. Nearby, the whispering knights huddle in a sinister conspiracy – unless they are the remains of a massive burial barrow.

🚗 West of A3400 Oxford–Stratford-upon-Avon road, between the villages of Little Rollright and Great Rollright

9 **WREN'S EGG STANDING STONES**, Dumfries & Galloway ☏ 01776 702595
These are included if only for the charming name, but this is a good area for standing stones. About 10 miles north, **Torhouse Stone Circle** is south of B733 between Bladnoch and Clugston,

two miles west of Wigtown and on the Southern Upland Way long-distance footpath, and the **Laggangairn Standing Stones** are at Killgallioch about five miles' hike from Knowe on the way to Stranraer. These two are very early Christian stones. Access is difficult through forestry, although there are some signposts.

One mile north of the coastal village of Monreith on A747 between Stranraer and Whithorn, on private land at Blair Buy Farm

10 **Ring of Brogar Stone Circle**, Orkney Islands
01856 850716
A magnificent, well-preserved ring of upright stones in a beautiful setting. In some ways this is better than Stonehenge, with no tourists

THE CUTTING OF WHITE HORSES on hillsides – leucipottomy – may not be regarded by the British as eccentric, but it surely is, as each one takes a whole bunch of people about two weeks to carve and needs to be maintained for thousands of years to stop it grassing over.

The best, oldest (probably Bronze Age) and most famous is the one at **Uffington**, Oxfordshire (Travel: page 271), and there are 12 in the south of England. There is a herd of eight in Wiltshire, and one of these, at **Devizes**, was carved in 1999. Another new one was recently created at the Channel Tunnel entrance, **Folkestone**.

Little-known outriders are at **Kilburn**, North Yorkshire, and, I'm told, at **Strichen**, Aberdeenshire. Non-equine contenders include the particularly curious **Long Man of Wilmington**, Sussex (south of the A276 just west of Eastbourne), a lion at **Whipsnade**, Bedfordshire, and odd regimental badges around Salisbury Plain; but the best of these has to be the **Cerne Giant**, Dorset (Travel: page 270). The huge figure of prehistoric origins carries a massive club but is more memorable for his whopping great sexual organ. I'm surprised the Victorians didn't have it dug up. (By the 20th century, many of the Piddles in nearby place names had long been changed to Puddles by prim and prudish Dorset folk.)

Curiosities in chalk

and no admission charge. The Orkneys are littered with impressive stones and magnificent chambered cairns that would be packed with visitors if nearer to greater populations.

🚗 About 5 miles northeast of Stromness

NB ARBOR LOW STONE CIRCLE, Peak District, Derbyshire, is a spectacular setting at about 1,200ft high, but the stones themselves are less spectacular, indeed not standing at all, having all toppled.

🚗 East of A515 Buxton–Ashbourne road and south of a minor road from A515 to Youlgreave

For more eccentric stone circles, see page 223.

Back to the giant. The legend locally is that if a barren woman sleeps on the said organ for the night, she'll be pregnant before the year's end. If it is true, then the giant doesn't seem responsible, because the delightful countryside around Cerne Abbas doesn't feature lots of yokel offspring walking around holding huge implements. On May Day the Wessex Morris Men dance on the Cerne Giant at 7am, then dance through the village beating the ground to 'awaken the spring', ending in the square at 9am. But then May Day is a good day for West Country fertility dances generally (see page 20). The outline is best viewed after the local girl guides or whoever have whitewashed the lines, as it can get a bit grey at times. In the beautiful village, by the way, they sell delicious Dorset Knobs, which are good with butter.

The names of the nearby villages are equally eccentric: the nearest are Up Cerne, Minterne Parva, Piddletrenthide, Nether Cerne, Minterne Magna, Up Sydling. I'm just glad they didn't put the giant six miles northeast, at Droop. You really couldn't make it up.

TRAVEL INFORMATION

AIRSHIP DISASTER MEMORIAL, St Mary's Church, Elloughton, Yorkshire HU15 1SP ☎ 01482 223559

🚗 From the A1 take the M62 and A63 towards Hull and the village is on the edge of Brough 🚂 Brough station, about a mile away

BRASS CROSBY MILESTONE, Lambeth, London SE1 6HZ

🚇 Lambeth North (Bakerloo line)

CERNE GIANT, Cerne Abbas, Dorset DT2 7JF ☎ 01305 267992

🚗 Off A352 Dorchester–Sherborne road. From London/M25, M3 then A303, south on A359 near Yeovil, B3148 to Sherborne

CLARKSON MONUMENT, Hertfordshire ☎ 01992 584322

🚗 On west side of A10, old London–Cambridge road near Wadesmill

CLEOPATRA'S NEEDLE, Thames Embankment, London WC2N 6ND

🚇 Embankment, Northern, Bakerloo, Circle and District lines

FERRY LANE MONUMENT, Brentford, Middlesex TW8 0AT

🚗 Brentford is near M4 J2 🚂 Brentford, from London Waterloo

FIREPLATES OBELISK, Tibbet's Corner, near Putney, London SW19 6AN

🚗 In woodland beside northbound slip road off A3 signed Putney. From Tibbet's Corner roundabout (don't go through A3 underpass) take third exit (signed Wimbledon), then immediately left into Withycombe Rd. Park and walk back under roundabout on footpaths to woodland on the far side, keeping sharp left alongside the A3. If you want a good pub, retrace your steps from obelisk until track and fence, turn left (away from the A3) to the Telegraph 🚂/🚌 Putney from London Waterloo, turn left and walk up to top of Putney Hill 🚌 14 to southern terminus

'IRON MAD' WILKINSON'S MONUMENT, Lindale, Cumbria LA11 6LE
☎ 01229 587120

🚗 Off A590, west from M6 J36 🚂 Grange-over-Sands, from London Euston

LYMINGTON OBELISK, Hampshire (near Sway and Luttrell's towers)
SO41 5SE ☎ 01590 689000

🚗 From London or M25, take M3 to J14 near end, M27 west to J1, then A337 to Lymington 🚂 Lymington branch from Brockenhurst on London Waterloo–Weymouth line

MARC BOLAN'S TREE, Queen's Ride, Barnes, London SW13 0HZ

🚗 On A205 South Circular, going east from Putney, turn right (north) on Gipsy Lane to end, turn left 🚆 Barnes station, from London Waterloo, then walk over road bridge at station and turn left back to previous bridge over the tracks 🚌 22 from Piccadilly ends on Putney Common at other end of Queen's Ride. Continue across common and fork left

MILLBANK TRANSPORTATION BOLLARD, London SW1P 4RG

🚗 On Millbank, outside Tate Gallery 🚆/🚇 Vauxhall (from Waterloo mainline or Victoria Line) , cross bridge to north side of Thames, turn right

REBUS MILESTONES, Sussex TN22 2HQ ☎ 01273 483448

🚗 A22 from London and M25 to Eastbourne, although some villages with old milestones have been bypassed (eg: Maresfield)

RED SIGNPOST, Dorset ☎ 01305 267992

🚗 On south side of A31 Southampton–Dorchester road near Winterbourne Zelston DT11 9ET

SCIENCE MUSEUM, South Kensington, London SW7 ☎ 020 7942 4000

🖳 www.nmsi.ac.uk

🚇 South Kensington tube (Circle, District and Piccadilly lines)

TOLPUDDLE MARTYRS' MUSEUM, Tolpuddle, Dorchester, Dorset DT2 7EH ☎ 01305 848237 🖋 01305 267992

🚗 Off the A35 Bournemouth to Dorchester road, reached via M3 and A31

WELLINGTON MONUMENT, Somerset TA21 9RE ☎ 01823 663379

🚗 M5 J26, A38 towards Exeter, third left is Monument Road

WHITE HORSE, on edge of Vale of White Horse, Uffington, Oxfordshire SN7 7RP ☎ 01367 242191

🚗 From M4 J14 north on A338 to Wantage, east on B4057

YARBOROUGH OBELISK, Isle of Wight (near Bembridge Fort) PO36 8QT ☎ 01983 813818

🚗 From London or M25 take A3 to Portsmouth, ferry to Fishbourne, then A3054 east to Ryde, A3055 south past Brading, then left on B3395. Look for second lane on right 🚆 Sandown station (from London Waterloo). Trains go on to piers either side of Solent for foot ferry (included in ticket). Then walk from Sandown along coast northwards (1 hour, steep)

ZEPPELIN MONUMENT, Cuffley, Hertfordshire EN6 4DW ☎ 01992 584322

🚗 From M25 J24, north on A1000 then right on B157 to Cuffley

🚆 Cuffley is on London King's Cross–Hertford North line

TOWERING ECCENTRICS

ATLANTIC OCEAN

Orkney Islands

Thurso

Isle of Lewis

Isle of Skye

Inner Hebrides

Island of Mull

Islay

Arran

ATLANTIC OCEAN

Inverness

SCOTLAND

Aberdeen

NORTH SEA

Wallace Monument, Stirling

Glasgow

The Pineapple, Dunmore

EDINBURGH

Rosslyn Chapel

Melrose Abbey

N

0   80 km
0   50 miles

Carlisle

Newcastle upon Tyne

Middlesbrough

Culloden Tower, Richmond

ENGLAND

IRISH SEA

Isle of Man

Wainhouse Tower, Halifax

Leeds

Bradford

Red Devil, York

Swag Rabbit, Beverley

Kingston-upon-Hull

NORTH SEA

Anglesey

Holyhead

Liverpool

Manchester

Sheffield

Grimsby

Wentworth Woodhouse Follies

Lincoln Imp & Sexual Carvings

Cardigan Bay

Mow Cop, Mock Ruin

Derby

Nottingham

Norwich

Wolverhampton

Birmingham

Coventry

Triangular Lodge, Rushton

Cambridge Gargoyles

Ipswich

Fishguard

WALES

Broadway Tower

Winchcombe Worthies

Oxford Gargoyles

Gothic Temple, Stowe

Palladian Church & Ruin, Ayot St Lawrence

Tattingstone Wonder

Nelson's Tower, Llanarthney

Baron Berners's Folly, Faringdon

West Wycombe Cottages

Swansea

Cardiff Castle

Bristol

Beckford's Tower, Bath

Reading

LONDON

Severndroog Castle, Greenwich

Bristol Channel

Leith Hill Tower

May's Folly, Hadlow

Dover

Massey's Folly, Farringdon

Mad Jack Fuller's Follies, Brightling

ATLANTIC OCEAN

Crewkerne Minster Gargoyles

Haldon Belvedere, Exeter

Peter's Tower, Lympstone

Barwick Park Follies

Southampton

Sway Tower

Luttrell's Tower, Eaglehurst

Royal Pavilion, Brighton

Cothele House, Calstock

I of Wight

Penzance

ENGLISH CHANNEL

TOWERING ECCENTRICS

UTTER FOLLIES

Few follies are as absolutely useless as their strict definition requires. Even those wonderfully peculiar buildings leased to well-to-do holidaymakers by the Landmark Trust (see page 294) have a present use, as accommodation, and often a past one, however unusual the former prisons, forts, pigsties or lighthouses might be.

Occasionally, however, a delightfully dotty eccentric, with more money than sense, some would say, dots his bit of Britain with a collection of totally useless and inexplicable structures.

Such a group are **Mad Jack Fuller's Follies** (Travel: page 295) around Brightling, East Sussex, near Kipling's house, Bateman's. One of these, the conical steeple shape of the Sugar Loaf, rises on a hill near Wood's Corner crossroads. (You'd have to be pretty long in your sweet tooth to remember sugar loaves, although there are suitably shaped mountains named after them all over the world, but they were conical blocks of sugar sold by grocers that would keep a sweet-toothed family happy for months.) From here you can see the Observatory, a domed building amidst trees, and the Brightling Needle, a very fine obelisk that Cleopatra would have appreciated. The other side of the village offers the

Brightling Tower, which looks like a windmill sliced off at an angle, and the Rotunda Temple, a circular affair with pillars. In the village churchyard is Fuller's quite splendid Pyramid (see page 154).

Mad, Honest or Jolly Jack Fuller (1757–1834), the wealthy sponsor of a certain chemist and physicist, Michael Faraday, was from a family that had made its fortune landowning in the High Weald, iron founding when Sussex made the best guns for the Navy, and from slaves in Jamaica. He wasn't entirely mad, with various local philanthropic efforts – in marked contrast to his endorsement of slavery overseas – such as buying a lifeboat for Eastbourne or building a wall round the estate at Brightling to relieve unemployment. Indeed this, rather than just livening up the view, might have been his motive for building the follies.

But the Sugar Loaf is said to have arisen from a drinking session between friends of this rich young man (who was later to decline a peerage). He wagered that a certain number of church steeples could be seen from his home, Brightling Place. Sobering up in the morning, he found he was wrong by one – Dallington spire was not in sight. So he had an imitation one immediately raised on the horizon instead.

A wager led to the building of another fine folly in a patch of Yorkshire littered with magnificent and eccentric buildings – the Wentworth Woodhouse estate, around the quite astonishingly enormous great house, or rather pair of houses, one with a 600ft Palladian façade – that better deserve the name palaces.

In 1780 the second Marquess of Rockingham (twice prime minister) bet that he could drive a coach and horses through the eye of a needle. The needle-like pyramid called the Needle's Eye has a suitably shaped opening in it through which he was able, just, to drive his carriage.

The estate also offers a domed and vaulted bear pit, a large mock castle, a rotunda, another obelisk, the second marquess's seriously over-the-top three-storey mausoleum at Nether Haugh, a fine obelisk to Lady Montagu who, an inscription says, introduced smallpox inoculation in 1720, and the extraordinary Hoober Strand tower (see page 288).

A cluster of totally pointless follies, if not without points, can be found at **Barwick Park**, Somerset, just south of Yeovil on A37 road to Dorchester (Travel: page 295). Landowner George Messiter is said to have had them put up in the early 19th century to create employment during a slump in trade.

They include a needle-sharp obelisk (on the left just before A37 crosses the railway); a thing that looks like an extended dovecote on top of arches with a ball on top; and the oddest, Jack the Treacle Eater. This is a rough stone arch, built in the fashion of pretending to be a ruin, incongruously holding aloft the much finer masonry of a round tower, a conical roof and a statue of said Jack, a messenger who worked for Messiter and was, it is said, fuelled by treacle.

Like all these stories attached to follies, it is hard to know if the legend was created to explain the folly or the other way round. All the Barwick follies could have been simply eye-catchers, to improve the long views from the house. But then if they are true follies, it would be folly indeed to try to find much of a purpose for them.

Even royalty are not immune from creating follies – in fact they can make them bigger and better than most.

One is the splendid **pagoda** at Kew Gardens (Travel: page 296), which soars storey after storey like a backdrop for *The Mikado*, commissioned by a princess, Augusta, mother of George III.

The other is the astounding Oriental-styled **Royal Pavilion** in Brighton (Travel: page 296), created by the Prince Regent who became George IV in 1820. As Prince of Wales, he carried on an affair with a divorcee here, and the ensuing fuss made the recent sad tale of the 1990s Princess of Wales seem a re-run of history. (In fact the whole story was even sorrier, as you can find by checking the tomb of two tradesmen killed at the spurned Queen Caroline's funeral, see page 240. For the full amazingly similar story, see *Eccentric London*.)

Be that as it may, the prince's love life in Brighton set the racy reputation which the former quiet fishing port of Brighthelmstone has enjoyed ever since as the dirty weekend capital of Britain. Whether the countless Mr and Mrs Smiths checking into the resort's hotels in the mid-20th century took any notice, John Nash's extravagant Royal Pavilion is thoroughly and incurably eccentric, and much more enduring than any outrage at whatever that particular Prince of Wales got up to.

BRITAIN'S TOP TOWERS (MOSTLY WITH TALL STORIES)

1   **WALLACE MONUMENT**, Causewayhead, Stirling FK9 5LF
🖼 www.nationalwallacemonument.com ☏ 01786 472140
Spectacularly sited atop Abbey Craig, this 220ft tower bursts from the trees like a romantic rocket blasting into science fiction orbit.

Hollywood couldn't do it better, although the film *Braveheart* lit the boosters under interest in Wallace, numbers of visitors to the tower trebled, and a tacky – to some tastes – sculpture of Mel Gibson (well, it looks like him) was installed at the shop. Ignore it if you don't like it, but the views from the superb tower are exceptional. Don't rush through Stirling itself, it's worth a closer look.

M9 from Edinburgh to J10 Stirling, from Glasgow or Edinburgh

2 **SWAY TOWER**, Hampshire SO41 6BA ☎ 01590 689000
Near the New Forest village of Sway, Sway Tower is aptly named, for it was built to prove it wouldn't, but nearly did. Judge A T T Peterson, retired from the Calcutta High Court, wanted to prove the efficacy of Portland cement concrete blocks without reinforcement. He persuaded local workmen to assemble the blocks like a giant Lego kit into the slim 218ft-high tower entirely without scaffolding, so they had to be well paid.

Built in Indian-Gothic style (1876–79), and accompanied by another smaller tower nearby, the main tower has a hexagonal turret taking a spiral staircase up 330 steps, and 11 rooms. On top is a Mogul-style lantern, but the judge was refused permission for a light, the Admiralty decreeing that it would confuse shipping looking for the Needles lighthouse, only six miles away.

In fact, building such a slender tower of unreinforced concrete was stretching a point, and it has since been reinforced. Nearby are various concrete lodges and walls, none of them now remarkable, as is always the case with truly pioneering endeavours. In other words, the judge was right about the coming age of concrete.

From south end of M3 from London/M25, continue to west end of M27, take A337 south to Brockenhurst, then B3055 to Sway
Sway, from London Waterloo

3 **FARINGDON**, Oxfordshire
This Faringdon has the fascinating folly of Lord Berners (see page 282), the last true folly built by, perhaps, one of the last eccentrics. But why does Farringdon, Hampshire, also have one, not to mention a mystery one in Farringdon, London? See page 284.

4 **MAY'S FOLLY**, Hadlow, Kent TN11 0AL ☎ 01732 770929
An extraordinary flight of fancy soaring heavenwards like a French cathedral or Bruges Town Hall from open countryside in storey

after neo-Gothic storey, it is improbable that May's Folly has survived nearly two centuries.

The story goes locally that Squire May built the thing either to see the sea, in which case he would have been disappointed, or that he had an unfaithful wife, and that the 170ft tower was to give her the feeling that wherever she went in Kent, he was watching her. The truth isn't known, but Walter Barton May (1783–1853) inherited not only stacks of money (twice) but also his father's love of grandiose building – his father had built Hadlow Castle, a fabulous neo-Gothic pile. To save on running costs and sell the scrap building materials, the castle was demolished in that widespread fashion of the 1930–1950s, completely incomprehensible only 20 years later, of pulling down entire, beautiful stately homes. Today it would have been converted into bijou apartments or been sold for millions – with its sumptuous interiors it would have rivalled Knebworth House, Hertfordshire, for frequent use as a neo-Gothic filmset.

The tower, some stables and outbuildings and lodges are today still private homes and other houses have filled gaps in the grounds.

Suspicious Squire May's 1838 effort has just about survived near on two centuries; it is true that his wife left him at about the time the tower was started. Whether the obsession with piling stone upon stone caused the marriage break-up or was caused by it will never be clear, but Squire May left his mark on Kent. In 1994 emergency repairs to the crumbling tower included dismantling the lantern and certain gables and parapets to lessen the weight. The search was on in 1998 for a million pounds to repair the structure. You may think if the National Lottery can fund endless ugly follies elsewhere, why not repair this splendidly barmy one?

Little Berkhamsted, not far from Hertford, has a tower called **Streatton's Folly** with a story that is in some ways similar. This, too, is actually someone's home rather than being part of the heritage industry, so must be viewed from the road. The story is that a rich and canny merchant built it so high that he could see the Thames near Tilbury. Through his telescope he could identify which ships had come from where and, armed with this intelligence, would saddle a fast horse and ride into London to take advantage of merchants not quite so up-to-date.

🚗 From London/M25, A21 to Tonbridge (not Tunbridge Wells), then A26 northeast about 4 miles 🚋/🚌 London Charing Cross or Victoria to Tonbridge, then bus 7

5 **BECKFORD'S TOWER**, Lansdown Road, Bath BA1 9BH
☎ 01225 460 705 ✇ 0906 711 2000 (premium rate).
There was a fad in the early 19th century to build towers apeing a recently described and pictured octagonal tower in Portugal; at Fonthill Abbey in Wiltshire the eccentric bisexual playboy and mad party-giver William Beckford (1760–1844) built a 300ft similar tower in 1812; he was aiming for 450ft, but it collapsed in 1825, an earlier one having collapsed too. His habit of plying his workmen with alcohol and making them work round the clock probably didn't help. Their habit of not using foundations definitely didn't. Beckford had earlier built a seven-mile, 12ft-high wall round his estate. In 1825 – he had sold Fonthill for a fortune three years before it collapsed – he also built an eerie, octagonal 154ft-high lookout tower at Lansdown Hill, Bath, near his new home. Beckford and his attendant, the exceedingly smelly dwarf Porro, are buried here. Worth a visit for great internal spiral staircase and cosmic views.

🚗 From M4 J18, Bath is 10 miles south on A46. Beckford's Tower is on the northern fringes of Bath, up a steep hill west of Charlcombe
🚂 From London Paddington to Bath

6 **PETERS TOWER**, Lympstone, Devon EX8 5EY ✇ 01392 265700
🖳 www.lympstone.org
This tower, vaguely based on St Mark's in Venice, appropriately stands right on the water's edge in the wide Exe estuary south of Exeter. The clocktower is a memorial to Mary Jane Peters, built by her grieving husband William Peters in 1885, and has been carefully restored after being given to the Landmark Trust (see page 294), so you can holiday in it, at a price, but not visit.

🚗 From M5 J30 near Exeter, a few miles south on A376 🚂 On Exmouth branch line from Exeter

7 **CARDIFF CASTLE**, Cardiff CF10 3RB
☎ 029 2087 8100 🖳 www.cardiffcastle.com
✇ 0845 010 3300
For a completely over-the-top clocktower, with ingenious and extraordinary decorations, don't miss the one at Cardiff Castle. You may not be able to stay the night there, but the whole castle offers romantic eccentricity and

flamboyant architectural detail on a grand and sometimes amazing scale, thanks to the flamboyantly rich third Marquess of Bute and his eccentric architect William Burges.

🚗 M4 to Cardiff. Look for Castle Street in the city centre 🚂 London Paddington and other centres to Cardiff; walk about 500 yards down Westgate Street to castle

8 BROADWAY TOWER, Broadway, Worcestershire WR12 7LB
☎ 01386 852390 📠 01386 852937

A classic folly well known because of its superb situation beside the A44 Oxford–Worcester road as it plunges over the escarpment down into the Cotswolds. The tower at the top of Fish Hill is alleged to offer a view of 12 counties and was built by the sixth Earl of Coventry in 1789. It includes on its three floors exhibitions on the surrounding country park and the Pre-Raphaelite Brotherhood. This is relevant because William Morris (1834–96) used it as a holiday home and in 1876 wrote a letter calling for the formation of the Society for the Protection of Ancient Buildings. So the now overblown and top-heavy heritage industry, then of course much needed, started here. Ironically, Broadway Tower isn't in the grip of one of those great bureaucracies, but is privately owned yet open to the public. A little-known relative of Broadway Tower is the Dunstall Castle Folly off the A4104 near Upton upon Severn. This was another eye-catcher for the once-vast Croome estate and is a mock-Norman castle ruin, built as a ruined arch with towers.

🚗 On Oxford–Worcester A44 (connecting there with M5 J7) 🚂/taxi Moreton-in-Marsh (London Paddington–Worcester line) then taxi

9 CULLODEN TOWER, Richmond, Yorkshire DL10 4HS
📠 01748 850252 🖳 www.richmond.org

It is odd to see something so handsome commemorating something so bloody as the battle of 1746, but the tower was started in that year by the MP for Richmond, John Yorke, to mark the defeat of the last serious challenge to Hanoverian rule, when Bonnie Prince Charlie's rebel army had reached much further south than this.

The octagonal shaft rises like a pillar from parkland in this gem of a town. Perched above the tumbling waters of the River Swale, the tower offers the highest standards of Gothic and classical carving on different levels, and as a Landmark Trust property, is available for holiday lets (see page 294) but not tourist visits inside. The dramatic Hoober Strand (see page 288) was built to commemorate the same battle.

🚗 Off A1 south of Darlington 🚂/🚌 Darlington, from London King's Cross then bus

10 **LEITH HILL TOWER**, near Coldharbour, Surrey
☎ 01306 712711 ✆ 01483 444333

The views from here are quite extraordinary, but as this 18th-century tower is atop the highest point in the southeast, with its top 1,029ft above sea level, this is logical. Even so, when I realised on a crystal clear day that *everywhere* I had previously visited that week – the Docklands of London, Crowborough, Sussex, the sea at Shoreham, and the South Downs near Petersfield, Hampshire, were all visible – I gripped the battlements in astonishment. The height lets you see through the gap in the South Downs to Shoreham, and you look down on Gatwick as if from a plane.

There is a steep but pleasant half-mile walk to the tower from the car park through woods. You wouldn't imagine that a desperate battle here in AD851, involving perhaps 30,000 men, saw the heathen Danes who had burnt London wiped out by the Christian army of Ethelwulf, Alfred the Great's father. Blood flowed and severed heads and limbs fell thick on the hillside, say the chronicles, but don't let it spoil your picnic.

The tower was built by local eccentric Richard Hull in 1766 as a 'Prospect House' and he was buried at the foot of the tower at his request in 1772. It has since been restored. It is National Trust-owned (the Trust also owns Hull's nearby home at Leith Hill Place), with a tea and cake bar in the base of the tower, smack over Hull's bones. (As for Alfred the Great, another great tower for views is the National-Trust-managed 160ft **King Alfred's Tower** on the Stourhead estate, Warminster, Wiltshire; ☎ 01747 841152.)

🚗 Difficult to find. You need the east–west A25, an old route parallel and south of the M25 and connecting with radial routes from London/M25 such as A24 at Dorking or A23 at Redhill; or approach via A247 from A3 north of Guildford. At Abinger Hammer on A25, turn south on B2126, then left (east) to Abinger and right (south) from that village, and look for signs. Postcode RH5 6HD is for the pub in Coldharbour, you need to be a mile west
🚂 Only two (steep) miles from Ockley on the London Waterloo–Horsham (via Dorking) line, for energetic walkers or mountain bikers

11 **THE PINEAPPLE**, Dunmore, Stirlingshire FK2 8LU
☏ 08707 200620 💻 www.visitstirling.org
Absolutely extraordinary, eccentric, witty and a brilliant creation,
The Pineapple is a two-storey summerhouse built for the fourth Earl
of Dunmore. The seamless stone blend from classical architecture to
rampant fruit is magic, on a par with the fur coats turning to fir trees
in *The Lion, the Witch and the Wardrobe*. It is also an elaborate joke.

The fourth Earl of Dunmore was governor of Virginia where
sailors used to stick a pineapple on a gatepost to announce their
return home. Lord Dunmore's attitude, on being forced home in
1777, was that as governor he would have the biggest pineapple
of the lot to mark his own reluctant return.
Dunmore done more, as it were. It is now
owned by the National Trust for Scotland,
and leased to the Landmark Trust (see page
294). At the time it was built, pineapples
were practically unknown in Britain.
The first one was grown at Dorney,
Buckinghamshire, in 1665, which is why
there is a Pineapple pub there.

🚗 Dunmore is off A905 east of Stirling.
From M9 J7, use M876 spur to north,
then A905 northwest towards Stirling
🚍/🚗 Stirling, then bus 75 and ask to
be dropped off at turning

12 **LUTTRELL'S TOWER**, Eaglehurst, near Southampton SO45 1BR
☏ 023 8083 3333
A well-situated and pretty – you could say refined if you did not
know what was round the corner – Georgian folly, right on the
edge of the Solent near the corner of Southampton Water, with
views down both approaches and across to Newport on the Isle of
Wight. There are particularly good views of the container ships,
ferries and cruise liners coming out of bustling Southampton, plus
the giant tankers turning in front of the tower heading for the huge
Fawley refinery and power station just around the corner, but out
of view. If you love Georgian architecture *and* modern shipping,
this is nirvana, with a grand oriel window (a bay window projecting
upstairs) overlooking the maritime view.

The tower was built for Temple Luttrell, who died in 1803. He
was an MP and a smuggler, which probably explains why a tunnel

leads from the basement directly to the beach. It's now run by the Landmark Trust, so available as a holiday home (see page 294). But everyone may see it by driving to Calshot, where to the left there's a good castle, one of many guarding the Solent. Walk instead half a mile to the right along the pebbly beach and you'll see the folly at the top of a ridiculously over-the-top staircase and its ruined boathouse on the beach.

A326 from M27 J2, and then B3053 (in fact straight on) down the west side of Southampton Water, along the edge of the New Forest, as far as one can go to Calshot / Southampton from London Waterloo and other centres, then bus X9 to Calshot beach

13 **WAINHOUSE TOWER**, Halifax, West Yorkshire HX3 0HB
01422 368725
At 275ft, this is the highest folly in the world. In fact, it was intended to have a use, as a chimney for a dye works, but a dispute by truculent troublemaker John Wainhouse left it with no purpose, so it was finished with 403 steps inside and an elaborate viewing platform. And when I say elaborate, don't think this is a mere factory chimney – it's an orgy of stonework. That great author on all things folly, Gwyn Headley, wrote: 'The result of the four years' work is a belvedere tower by a medieval watch tower out of Chateau Chambord.' *Exactement – superbe!*

The Leeds-Manchester A58 goes right past Sowerby Bridge, less than a mile away

TRUE FOLLIES COME IN THREES

The last great private folly – that is, a totally pointless building – built in Britain, before the commercial fibreglass fakery of theme parks took over , was the **Faringdon folly** in Oxfordshire (Travel: page 295). Built by the truly eccentric composer-diplomat, the 14th Baron Berners (1883–1950, see page 282), the tower sits atop a hill crowned with pines and beeches just outside the town, and is a fine sight from Berkshire or the Wiltshire Downs. The 100ft-square brick tower's bulk is concealed by trees, leaving the octagonal neo-Gothic top poking out with its eight pinnacles and flagstaff.

The folly has generated much controversy and legend in its short life. Plans to build it received much publicity and the local council refused it, without the benefit of details, purely on hearsay about Lord Berners's supposed plans to use the folly as a lighthouse, probing the rural darkness with a great beam, and to install a powerful siren on top. A public inquiry ensued, which gave Fleet Street diary writers the chance to record this exchange between the architect and crusty old Admiral Clifton Brown, who objected that the tower would spoil his views:

> Architect: *'But you could not see the tower from your garden without a telescope!'*
> Admiral: *'Sir, it is always my custom to look at the view through a telescope.'*

As for legend, if there are some inaccuracies they were not exactly weeded out by the late Robert Heber-Percy, who died in 1987 having donated the folly to the community in 1983. He told how Lord Berners had given him the tower as a 21st birthday present and how annoying this was, as he had requested a horse. He also recounted how Lord Berners wanted, once dead, to be stuffed and mounted in the belvedere room at the top of the tower, eternally playing cheerful tunes on an automatic grand piano. Heber-Percy said that he 'funked it' because of the impossibility of getting a grand piano up the narrow wooden stairs that cling to the tower's plunging and otherwise blank interior.

The trust which now opens the tower to the public tries to bring down to earth some of the tall stories attached to the tower. It corrects books that claim a 140ft height and insists on a mere 100ft. It denies that you can see six counties from the top and lists a mere five. It denies the claim – made about many a folly from Dorset to Sussex – that it was built to alleviate dire unemployment at the time. Only one extra man was taken on the estate staff. It even points out that Mr Heber-Percy was born in 1911, so it would have been a late 21st birthday present.

However, some elements of the story remain unchallenged. First, the hill was called Folly Hill long before the tower was built. Secondly, the fine trees were planted by Poet Laureate Henry James Pye in the late 18th century. (He built Faringdon House and wrote a poem at Eaglehurst, which also boasts a fine tower. He was such a lousy poet that the full version of the rhyme *Sing a Song of Sixpence* originated as a lampoon of his corny style.) Thirdly, the bones of Cromwellian soldiers *were* unearthed while the tower was being built – Parliamentary forces laid siege to an earlier Faringdon House. Fourthly, the eccentric notices plastered by Lord Berners about his estate did include one at the top of the tower stating: 'Members of the public committing suicide from this tower do so at their own risk.' And finally, in another war – World War II – the tower was employed as an observation post, soon thankfully returning to the uselessness which qualifies it as a true folly.

Even if you know the other **Farringdon** – near Alton, Hampshire – you may not know there's a jolly good folly there too, as it's tucked away in the village centre off the main roads. A tiny, sleepy village with thatched cottages, Farringdon had an eccentric vicar in the Revd T H Massey from 1857 to 1919 (his grave may be seen outside the church door). He decided Farringdon needed a town hall on a scale that would have suited a city like Winchester or made a substantial part of a small university or a railway station for a grand spa town (when the railway did arrive at the other end of the village, Farringdon Halt was a few measly planks beside a single line and has long since closed).

The resulting pile of castellated towers, red brick and decorative terracotta panels can still be seen (Travel: page 296), although the Revd Massey tore down several towers which displeased him. When he wasn't building follies, he was either alienating his flock by his offensive preaching, so that he was left with a congregation of two, or buying up houses to prevent Methodists, whom he detested, living in Farringdon.

If you now expect another piece of architectural eccentricity in Britain's third Farringdon, between Fleet Street and King's Cross in London, I won't disappoint you. Walk the full length of Farringdon Road north to King's Cross, and where Gray's Inn Road and Pentonville Road converge what is known as the **King's Cross Lighthouse** (Travel: page 295) sits atop the otherwise very plain four-storey buildings.

Some claim it was once a fairground helter-skelter but it would have to have been, impossibly and improbably, moved up there. Inspections of the interior, say Camden Council, show that it can't have been a clocktower or a camera obscura. Obscurer are its origins, and maybe it was a totally useless architectural flourish, a genuine third Farringdon folly.

THE TRIANGULAR ANGLE

Not long ago, one of Britain's most astonishing yet little-known buildings reached the 400th anniversary of its completion. Far more than an intriguing folly, Sir Thomas Tresham's **Triangular Lodge** (Travel: page 297) tells a story of religious oppression, torture and courage through its mathematical puzzles and secret codes in stonework. Surprisingly, it is neither unique in Britain in being triangular, nor in putting a passionate story into our architectural heritage.

There is something mystical or magical about the figure three, trefoils, or tridents – the image crops up in theology from the ancient Greeks to Shiva, star of the Hindu pantheon, as well as the more obvious Holy Trinity of Christian worship.

Few can have taken this latter more seriously than the late 16th-century English Catholics who defied persecution by the Protestant authorities. Of these Sir Thomas Tresham (d 1605), whose coat of arms included the trefoil, immortalised his passionate faith in stone.

Sir Thomas's Triangular Lodge at Rushton, Northamptonshire, is a brilliant and astonishingly well-preserved folly, a mathematical essay in stone to the Trinity, and was built between 1593 and 1595.

The pleasure of this triangular building starts with looking at the apparently square elevation, then walking round to see the knife-edge 60° corners, the floor plan being an equilateral triangle, with each side exactly one-third of 100ft long. There are three three-by-three gables on each side, each crowned by three-sided pinnacles rising through stone triangles.

The mathematical conceit goes on and on: there are three floors with three windows on each, all decorated with triangles, trefoils or other emblems. On a frieze running round the 33ft-long sides is an inscription with 33 letters on each side, and there are three sets of three gargoyles. Each face is dedicated to one of the Holy Trinity and the inscription varies accordingly.

Inside, each floor has one large hexagonal room, leaving three tiny triangular ones, one of which accommodates the stairs. It is a magical construction, with the odd patches of light from triangles, diamonds and cruciform slits thrown on to the geometric walls. Any hint of humourless mathematical severity is relieved by flamboyant and crazily detailed motifs on the roof gables and pinnacles.

The iron fastening rods running through the building are finished with a large black 15 on one face and a 93 on another – both divisible by three, of course, but together giving the start date of the building – with TT for Thomas Tresham on the third.

'Some brilliant details of the mathematical puzzle have gone unsolved until this century,' said English Heritage's custodian at the time of my visit, John Froment, 'For example, what appear to be dates in the triangular gables. On the north face, the face of God, so to speak, the dates are 1641 and 1626, clearly in the future at the time of construction. Subtracting the start date, 1593, however, gives the supposed dates of the deaths of Jesus and the Virgin Mary – AD33 and AD48.'

Similarly, the numbers on another pair, 3898 and 3509, are the BC dates of the Great Flood and the call of Abraham. What about the puzzling code – 5555 – above the door? John Froment adds: 'Some have read this as 3333, which caused puzzlement. If you add Bede's calculation of the date of Creation – 3962BC – and the start date of the Lodge, 1593, you have 5555.' The sum of two creations, one vast, one small.

Other details are yet more cryptic. The waterspouts are each marked with one initial, realised centuries later to form an acronym, the first letters of a key part of the Latin mass, then banned on pain of huge fines and imprisonment, both of which Tresham endured for his faith.

Still more architectural puns, perhaps, remain unsolved. Over the door, one inscription seems clear enough – *Tres Testimonium Dant*, meaning 'these three bear witness'. English Heritage's booklet on the Lodge, pointing out that Tres was Tresham's wife's pet name for him, suggests the inscription also means 'Tresham bears witness'. This would, however, be bending Latin grammar – the equivalent of saying 'Tresham bear witness' in English – more than such a fastidious man could bear, despite his wit.

(If I told you that directions to John Froment's nearby house included *third* street on the left, then *third* door on the right, and that the street name begins *Tre-*, you might think I was taking a serious work too trivially. It must be merely coincidence. But odd!)

It has also been debated by scholars whether Tresham's obsession with numbers was purely religious or, as some sensationalists or idle theorists have suggested, a cover for black magic.

It is true that some ten miles away lies the shell of **Lyveden House**, sadly unfinished before Tresham's death in 1605. There, several other numbers are explored, chiefly the figure five. The cruciform building ends in walls with bay windows, each starting 5ft from the corner, going out 5ft, along 5ft, in 5ft, and 5ft to the next corner, making five fives. The ground plan is of four squares in the wings and a central one, making five. The top frieze has quotations from the Latin Bible carved at one letter per foot, worked out so that each side starts and finishes with the five-letter words 'Jesus' and 'Maria'; and, over the main door, each word has five letters.

Black magic? Far from it: Sir Thomas was a deeply religious man with a brilliant mind, who enjoyed a contrived conceit as much as the metaphysical poets of the era. Perhaps he knew that Cromwell's commissioners, half a century later, would smash down anything overtly Catholic, as they did with many a beautiful medieval stained-glass window or church statue.

In any case, the detail on this delightful lodge is as sturdy a survivor of bitter religious division in this country as that long-lived children's song that goes 'Do the hokey cokey…' – a satire on the Catholic Latin Mass *Hoc est enim corpus meum hoc est corpus meum*, the Latin words that the priest said over the bread in the Mass, which mean 'This is my body'. 'And you turn around' refers to the action of the priest after consecrating the bread and wine: because the altar was against the east wall of the church, he had his back to the people, so he had to turn around to show them the consecrated bread. The same ridicule gives us the phrase *hocus-pocus*. Both remnants in our culture bear witness, as does Tresham's tremendous lodge, to desperate divisions and prejudice.

Swashbuckling at Severndroog

Religious piety was not the inspiration for another triangular tower with a tale to tell which overlooks the homes of thousands of Londoners; it came about after a swashbuckling fight against pirates in the exotic east.

Severndroog Castle (Travel: page 297) in Castlewood Park off Shooters Hill, in southeast London, was built in 1784 for the widow of Sir William James as a tribute to the heroic attack he led, with four ships and thousands of men, on the original Severndroog Castle, a nest of pirates on the Malabar coast of India. That castle was taken in 1755.

With turrets at the corners rather than sharp angles, the tower is 46ft higher than St Paul's, so it is worth a visit for the splendid view. Early on the tower was used for surveying, and later, in the 19th century, ladies and gentlemen would meet there to dance quadrilles to a military band. Today the ground floor houses a tearoom, so you may have your own version of these genteel picnics.

No chicken Madras

Oddly, at least two other triangular towers sport an Indian connection. The superbly sited **Haldon Belvedere** (Travel: page 295), 800ft up on the hills near Exeter, was built in 1788 by former governor of Madras

Sir Robert Palk, then MP for Ashburton, as a memorial to his friend General Stringer Lawrence, father of the Indian Army. The romantic folly on a wooded Devon hilltop, fully restored at a cost of £450,000, was leased to the Devon Historic Buildings Trust in 1994. The tower had been bought by a Mrs Annie Dale for £650 in 1933, and her son Edward, who bequeathed it indirectly to the Trust, lived there until his death in 1994.

Equally well sited is **Nelson's Tower** (also known as Paxton's Tower) at Llanarthney (Travel: page 296), Carmarthenshire, built by the Master of Calcutta Mint, Sir William Paxton, after the Battle of Trafalgar in 1805. Again turreted on the corners, and now in the care of the National Trust, this tower has three doors. Over each is an inscription praising the 'invincible commander, Viscount Nelson, in commemoration of deeds before the walls of Copenhagen, and on the shores of Spain …' One side is in English, one in Welsh and one in Latin. You cannot stay in the tower, but you can in **Tower Hill Lodge**, which has a superb view of it, through the Landmark Trust (Travel: page 294). From the tower itself, the view is described as one of the best in Britain.

YET MORE TRIANGLES

Not all triangular towers are massive. In Cornwall there is an unusual triangular tower with dished sides at **Cotehele House**, Calstock (see page 245), standing some 60ft high complete with sham windows. This is a straightforward folly.

More massive by far is the impressive, lighthouse-like **Hoober Strand**, a truncated pyramid with rounded corners, part of Britain's most marvellous and imaginative group of follies at Wentworth Woodhouse in Yorkshire (see page 274). Hoober Strand, topped by a lantern and railing, contains an elegant spiral staircase, and was built in 1748, ostensibly as a tribute to George II subduing 'a most unnatural rebellion in Britain'.

Sadly, one of the few 20th-century triangular towers, a striking Art Deco example at **Lee-on-the-Solent**, is no more. This prospect tower, which had an excellent view across the Isle of Wight, has been demolished by a community that seems to have had all the flair and imagination of an amoeba on Valium, having also filled in its seafront lido, lost its pier and cut off its railway branch line in its seeming desperation to return to prim, suburban, and well-deserved obscurity. No doubt they will say they were victims of bigger forces, but did they fight hard enough?

Lastly, a truly exotic triangular building, the **Gothic Temple** at Stowe (Travel: page 295), Buckinghamshire, is another which fans of eccentric buildings can also enjoy as a holiday home, through the Landmark Trust (see page 294).

Stowe – the great house itself has been occupied by Stowe public school since 1923 – is where Lord Cobham had Capability Brown (1716–83) create elegant landscaping in the mid 18th century. This was adorned by dozens of follies and architectural oddities.

James Gibbs (1682–1754) designed the Temple, built in 1741, which is formed on a triangular plan with hexagonal turrets adjoining each corner. All the rooms are circular, with the main triangle housing a large circle on the ground floor and a circular gallery on the first floor, giving a spacious view of the domed and gorgeously painted heraldic ceiling.

Two of the side hexagons contain small circular rooms on each level – bedrooms, kitchen, bathroom – and the third a circular staircase which leads to a hexagonal belvedere at roof level, giving a splendid view over the landscape now managed by the National Trust.

ALL A SHAM

Towns in Western films called Vulture Gulch or Carcass Creek, where the bank, sheriff's office and saloon are merely one plank thick frontages, turn out to be heirs to a barmy British tradition: the sham. Sham castles, sham churches, sham ruins and even sham smart townhouses can all be found, although you would, naturally, miss them at first glance.

Some are frontages put up to maintain discreet appearances, some are fantasy follies to make a picturesque view, and some are infamous disguises to make the banal or scatological appear more fragrant.

West Wycombe in Buckinghamshire (see page 168), which has so many eccentric features, includes in West Wycombe Park a pair of cottages disguised as St Crispin's Chapel and set behind the lake to improve the view from the great house. That the cottages are somewhat small adds to the false perspective, although they do therefore look most odd from Chapel Lane, which they front on the High Wycombe side. Chapel Lane is on the left on the main A40 from High Wycombe before you reach West Wycombe.

Aristocrats have often been high-handed in their attempts to create views for the fashionable parks around their homes. At **Ayot St Lawrence** near Hatfield in Hertfordshire (Travel: page 297) – the same village where playwright George Bernard Shaw spent his declining years in a revolving summerhouse, still to be seen – there's an apparently large Palladian church, with a splendid white pillared front neatly facing Ayot House. Behind this somewhat two-dimensional façade, however, there's a much smaller and undecorated plain brick church holding the larger frontage up. The white rendering of the façade, it should be noted, ends just where it goes out of sight of the great house. White or not, the sham church has been persistently associated – even in the second half of the 20th century – with black magic ever since it was built.

This church, Sir Lionel Lyte's whim, also meant the demolition of the ancient parish church set more conveniently – for other people – in the village, but its destruction was not complete. An equally fashionable 'Gothic' ruin was desired – and is even repaired, as a ruin of course.

This flippant whim of an arrogant all-powerful aristo was far from unusual. Not far away at **Tring**, Sir Robert Whittingham had the thriving village of Pendley flattened in the 15th century to improve his view.

Neither is vandalising a church that rare. At **Mount Edgcumbe** (Travel (Cupid's Obelisk): page 149), near Plymouth, there's a splendidly convincing ruin stuffed with medieval stonework, gargoyles and window tracery, but it's not in the least medieval. The whole thing is a folly, put up as a purpose-built ruin in the 18th century with stones taken from churches that the Mount Edgcumbe family owned at Stonehouse, across the water.

Ruins built as such, as romantic eye-catchers, are almost as common as muck, if a little misleading. **Mow Cop** (Travel: page 296) on the Cheshire-Staffordshire border, that splendid natural outcrop, is topped by a totally fake ruin, for example. It wouldn't get planning permission nowadays, but would anything imaginative?

Such ruins were usually placed at a suitable viewing distance from the great house, as at **Uppark**, near Harting, Sussex (Travel: page 297). Uppark itself became a real ruin when it burnt down accidentally in 1990, but the National Trust simply re-created it at a cost of many ruinous millions. But the fake ruin is maintained, as a ruin, of course.

Some shams you could pass every day without noticing. If you deal with anyone who gives a London address at 23 or 24 **Leinster Gardens** (Travel: page 295) – neighbours in such a respectable street – you may be dealing with a con artist. The two houses appear there in the right sequence, but they are a thin sham without foundations or substance, even the windows being painted on. When the gracious wedding cake five-storey terrace was broken in 1865 for the South Kensington extension of the newfangled underground railway, property owners demanded that instead of a yawning gap over the railway track, a phoney frontage be erected to continue the line of the buildings. At first glance, you hardly notice the join, though from the back – it is between Bayswater and Paddington stations – the thing looks like a filmset.

Suffolk is a good county for shams, one of them being the well-known **Tattingstone Wonder** (Travel: page 297), built in 1760. A farm building masquerades as a castle with the aid of a three-sided tower grafted onto a barnlike roof, complete with buttresses and battlements, looking most imposing from one side but an obvious sham from the other. It is a quarter-mile south of Tattingstone Place, from where it was designed to be an eye-catcher.

CARTOONS OF THE SKY

Why should Britain's Christian churches and ancient halls of learning be attended by grinning demons, obscene oafs and spitting monsters? I refer not to the inhabitants but to gargoyles, the sometimes ghastly and grotesque effigies of horror or humour high on walls that the busy traveller will miss.

The true gargoyle, by the way, conveys water from the guttering and vomits it forth over the pavement well clear of the wall, thus avoiding the need for greatly overhanging eaves (it is these which create the dry band of pavement or 'eavesdrop', within which one might secretly listen to the conversation within the house). So it's no coincidence that gargoyle and gargle are alike words, linked by these literally spitting images. Carvings of faces and monsters which decorate edges or corners of roofs but don't convey water are, strictly speaking, grotesques. Let's not be that pedantic. (By the way, if I were as brilliant a writer as Terry Pratchett I'd describe how gargoyles spy for the city authorities and snack on passing pigeons.)

GARGOYLES OF ACADEME

Oxford is the best place for fantastic and fanciful gargoyles, and there it's no forgotten medieval art. Thus the 1960s restoration of **St Edmund Hall** has modern gargoyles depicting college characters of the day in somewhat cartoon fashion: the dean and his favourite Labrador dog; the bursar and his moneybags; the principal and his squash racket.

Three other colleges – Brasenose, Magdalen and New – plus the Bodleian Library, offer some of the best ribaldry in stonemasonry, often on a good and evil theme. The 15th-century Duke Humfrey Library at the Bodleian near the Sheldonian (itself ringed with giant heads) has a choir of angels facing a choir of demons.

New College has the Seven Virtues on the sunny south side of the Bell Tower and, perhaps more interestingly, the Seven Deadly Sins on the dark north side. The vulgar and bawdy is quite permissible at gargoyle level. At **Magdalen College**, which features a busty wench modelled cheekily on one of the college serving maids, a monkey squats defecating into a drainhead. This is despite a pious-looking bishop overlooking the bridge and blessing travellers. Many of the carvings serve to mock mankind, as with the grotesque pulling a face behind a serious soldier on the side of the **Bodleian Library**. To see for yourself in detail, take the excellent walking tour recommended in the inexpensive and excellent book *Oxford's Gargoyles and Grotesques* by John Blackwood.

A BELIEF IN IMP POSSIBILITIES

Gargoyles have been credited with bringing bad luck or good right into the modern era. Notorious is the **Lincoln Imp** (Travel: page 295).

Legend says the little cross-legged grinning imp was sent to earth on the wind by the Devil to work some mischief. When Lincoln Cathedral was being built in the 11th century, the imp pushed his luck in tripping up the bishop and trying to knock over the dean, the story goes. A watchful angel turned him to stone, but he has sought to exercise his harmful influence ever since. In the mid-1990s, for example, a particularly bitter dispute among the dean and chapter hit the headlines. Who was really behind this? Who, for that matter, was responsible for the bad luck of Lincoln (nickname the Imps) in home football games?

In fact if you look on Lincoln Cathedral's west front, you will see the most amazingly explicit set of sexual carvings. They show a man being punished for lust as being surrounded by buxom naked women and being bitten in the groin by dragons and serpents. Why the cathedral asked Prince Philip to unveil the new copies of the carvings (the medieval originals were wearing away and were put on display inside) I don't know. A Red Devil may be seen in Stonegate, an ancient street in central **York**, near the glorious York Minster. It is said to be bad luck to catch his eye. It would certainly be bad luck to catch one of his two sharp horns.

Gargoyles can even be used to settle 450-year-old scores. When Magdalene College, **Cambridge**, redeveloped a disused wharf in the city into the Quayside Centre in the 1980s, an unusual detail was specified – a particularly ugly gargoyle of a banker who had cheated the college of its endowment in 1542. Long memories...

A GAGGLE OF GIGGLING GARGOYLES

Not all gargoyles are malignant by any means. **Crewkerne Minster** (Travel: page 295) boasts one of the best west fronts in Somerset, but the passing visitor might miss the happy gargoyles playing musical instruments on the south side.

The 40 splendid gargoyles at St Peter's Church, Winchcombe in the Cotswolds are known as the '**Winchcombe Worthies**' (Travel: page 297), and my favourite is the worried-looking chap with the top hat and wings.

That such figures of fun go back a long way is demonstrated by a gargoyle of a pig playing the bagpipes at Scotland's romantic ruined **Melrose Abbey** (Travel: page 296). This, once the richest abbey in Scotland, has much other surviving Gothic stonework of the highest order and some interesting later graves (see page 171).

For more mute and mutant stonework of a rather curious sort, try the quite remarkable **Rosslyn Chapel** near Edinburgh (Travel: page 296). Here you will find fallen angels, a Prentice's Pillar of extraordinary detail (the apprentice who carved it in the master mason's absence was struck dead with the mason's mallet in a fit of jealousy) and inexplicable, fantastical dark carvings thought to be related to the Knights Templar. But then unnatural goings-on are still happening in the area – the nearby Roslin research institute is where Dolly the cloned sheep was created in the 1990s. And the chapel was central to the book and film *The Da Vinci Code*. You can stay in nearby Rosslyn Castle for a week or so (see page 194).

An English church with peculiar carvings not to be missed is **St Mary's**, Beverley, Yorkshire (Travel: page 297). Aside from the remarkable range of musical carvings, and more depicting 14th-century ailments, see if you can detect the bag-carrying pilgrim rabbit, said to have been an inspiration for Lewis Carroll's White Rabbit in *Alice In Wonderland*.

I F YOU'VE EVER WONDERED about spending a night in a brothel, or putting the children behind bars, now's your chance. Or, indeed, you could enjoy a stay in a lighthouse, an onion store or an old fort – all are on offer from the DISTINCTLY DIFFERENT group of B&Bs and hotels.

The properties have all been converted to hotel or B&B accommodation. There is a village lock-up at Farndon, near Chester (which retains its barred windows) or another at Wirksworth, Derbyshire that keeps its iron-studded doors with trapdoors for feeding and locks on the outside.

Then there are the possibilities of wild nights – weatherwise – at old lighthouses at West Usk lighthouse, St Brides Wentlloog, Gwent; Great Orme Head, Llandudno, or Kirkcolm, near Stranraer, which last affords views across to Northern Ireland and the Mull of Kintyre.

How to stay eccentric

The Boatmen's Brothel at Jackfield near Ironbridge, Shropshire, has had its cubicles converted to more respectable use, while the onion store is at Wellow Mead, on Florence Nightingale's old estate at Sherfield English, Romsey, Hampshire. Or, if you feel besieged by life, you can hire a massive Victorian fort accommodating up to 30 people complete with deep cannon casemates at Polhawn Fort, Rame, Torpoint, Cornwall. All are marketed through Distinctly Different.

The LANDMARK TRUST lets a truly remarkable range of whole properties for longer periods as holiday homes, be it a water tower at Sandringham, Norfolk, a bathhouse at Stratford-upon-Avon, a House of Correction near Grantham, Lincolnshire, various fantastic or grim castles or towers (many detailed in this book) and even a pigsty at Robin Hood's Bay, North Yorkshire. These properties are not cheap, particularly in high season, and the Trust's foreign purchases such as Italian villas seem to fit oddly with the whole concept, but as a major building preservation charity it has saved and restored many extraordinary gems at great expense, and as the castles, watchtowers, etc, often accommodate a large number of visitors, the cost can be divided among like-minded friends. The catalogue makes a great coffee-table browser.

And don't come home complaining that a medieval castle is a bit cold in January, as one Sunday paper hack did recently. What a prat.

DISTINCTLY DIFFERENT ☎ 01225 866648; www.distinctlydifferent.co.uk
THE LANDMARK TRUST ☎ 01628 825925; www.landmarktrust.co.uk

TRAVEL INFORMATION

BARON BERNERS'S FOLLY, Faringdon, Oxfordshire
🕿 01367 242191 🖳 www.faringdon.org
🚗 From M4 J15 at Swindon, A420 towards Oxford to Faringdon

BARWICK PARK FOLLIES, near Yeovil, Somerset BA22 9TA 🕿 01935 462991
🚗 Off A37 a couple of miles before Yeovil coming from Dorchester. Look out for needle; the rest are within a mile to east and north. From London/M25, M3 to J8, then A303 to Yeovil 🚉/🚌 Yeovil Junction, on London Waterloo–Exeter line; turn immediately right and then left into Two Towers Lane. Follies on right-hand side, village on left

CREWKERNE MINSTER, Somerset TA18 7JU 🕿 01935 462991
🚗 From M5 J25 take A358 southwest, then A30 east 🚉 On London Waterloo–Exeter line

GOTHIC TEMPLE, Stowe, Buckinghamshire MK18 5DQ ☎ 01280 822850 (National Trust) 🕿 01280 823020
🚗 From M1 J15A, A43 south, then A413 towards Buckingham. Stowe is on the right 🚉/🚌 Milton Keynes then bus

HALDON BELVEDERE, near Exeter, Devon EX6 7QY ☎ 01392 833668 (for event hire); 01386 701177 (for holiday apartment hire) 🕿 01392 265700
🚗 Signposted from A38 going towards Plymouth, look for white tower. At Dunchideock

KING'S CROSS LIGHTHOUSE, King's Cross, London N1 9AP
🚗 East end of Euston Road ring road 🚉 Opposite King's Cross main line and tube 🚌 Many routes

LEINSTER GARDENS, Bayswater, London W2 3AN
🚉 Use Bayswater tube, then follow line towards Paddington on foot

LINCOLN IMP, Lincoln Cathedral LN2 1PX 🕿 01522 873256
🚗 From A46 from A1 at Newark and also from Leicester and English Midlands 🚉 From London King's Cross

MAD JACK FULLER'S FOLLIES, East Sussex TN19 7DS 🕿 01424 773721
🚗 From London or M25, take A21 Hastings road to Hurst Green then right on A265 to Burwash. Explore roads to Brightling to left

MASSEY'S FOLLY, Farringdon, Hampshire GU34 3ED 🐝 01420 88448
🚗 Off A3 at only roundabout between London outskirts and Portsmouth, 50 miles from London. Turn north up B3006 towards Alton through Selborne (pubs, shop and museums), then Farringdon is down narrow lanes to left

MELROSE ABBEY, Borders TD6 9LG 🐝 01896 822562
🚗 From Edinburgh, or A1 near Darlington, take A68 which passes close to Melrose 🚋/🚌 Edinburgh Waverley station; then bus from St Andrew's bus station

MOUNT EDGCUMBE HOUSE AND COUNTRY PARK, Cornwall see page 149

MOW COP, near Stoke on Trent, Staffordshire ST7 4NE 🐝 01260 271095
🚗 From M6 J17 travel east on A534 to Congleton, then south on A34 for about 5 miles and it is on the left (east)

NELSON'S OR PAXTON'S TOWER, Llanarthney, Carmarthenshire SA32 8HX 🐝 01558 824226
🚗 From the end of the M4 continue towards Carmarthen. Turn right (north) on B4310 and after about 2 miles right again on B4300 going east. The tower is on the right after Llanarthney.

PAGODA, Kew Gardens, Surrey TW9 3AB ☎ 020 8332 5655 💻 www.kew.org
🚗 South of Kew Bridge on the north/south circular roads and north of A316 which links M3 to Chiswick 🚋/⊖ Kew Gardens, District Line tube and North London main line

PALLADIAN CHURCH AND RUIN, Ayot St Lawrence, Hertfordshire AL6 9BX 🐝 01727 864511
🚗 Travel north on B651 from St Albans (signed from M25 and M1) through Wheathampstead; turn right at end of village and look for signs on left.

ROSSLYN CHAPEL, Roslin, Midlothian EH25 9PU ☎ 0131 440 2159
💻 www.rosslynchapel.org.uk 🐝 0131 225 3858
🚗 Signed off A701, south from Edinburgh a couple of miles from A720 ring road 🚋/🚌 Edinburgh Waverley station; then bus from St Andrew's bus station

ROYAL PAVILION, Old Steine, Brighton BN1 1EE ☎ 03000 290900
🐝 01273 290 337
🚗 From London and M25, A23 🚋 From London Victoria and other centres

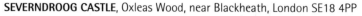
SEVERNDROOG CASTLE, Oxleas Wood, near Blackheath, London SE18 4PP
🚗 From Rochester Way A2, turn north on Well Hall Rd, then right on A207 Shooters Hill. Park is on the right 🚂 Eltham, from Charing Cross, then walk up Well Hall Road

SHAW'S CORNER, Ayot St Lawrence, near Welwyn, Hertfordshire AL6 9BX ☎ 01438 829221 (National Trust) 📞 01727 864511
🚗 Take A1(M) to Welwyn and go west about 2 miles through Ayot St Peter, or north from St Albans on B651 and turn right after Wheathampstead.

ST MARY'S CHURCH, Beverley, Yorkshire HU17 7DX
📞 01482 391677
🚗 8 miles north of Hull. From M6, M1 or A1 use M62 east to J38, then B1230 🚂 From London King's Cross, change at York or Hull

TATTINGSTONE WONDER, Suffolk IP9 2NF 📞 01473 258070
🚗 From London or M25 take A12 and look for right turn at Capel St Mary about 4 miles short of Colchester

TRIANGULAR LODGE, Rushton (not nearby Rushden), Northamptonshire NN14 1RP 📞 01536 410266
🚗 From M1 J19, A14 east to Rothwell, A6 north to Desborough then turn east (right) for Rushton

UPPARK HOUSE AND GARDEN, South Harting, Petersfield, West Sussex GU31 5QR ☎ 01730 825857
🚗 A3 from London to Petersfield, then 5 miles south east of Petersfield on B2146 to Harting. Then 1½ miles south of South Harting
🚂/🚗 Petersfield station then countryliner 54 Petersfield–Chichester (bus stop is 500 yards away via a steep hill)

WINCHCOMBE WORTHIES, Winchcombe, Gloucestershire GL54 5PS
📞 01242 602925
🚗 About five miles north-east of Cheltenham on the B4632

COUNTY INDEX

ALPHABETICAL INDEX